PLAYS BY RENAISSANCE AND RESTORATION DRAMATISTS

General Editor: Graham Storey

MIDDLETON

VOLUMES IN THIS SERIES

PUBLISHED

The plays of Cyril Tourneur, edited by George Parfitt: *The Revenger's Tragedy; The Atheist's Tragedy*

The selected plays of Philip Massinger, edited by Colin Gibson: *The Duke of Milan; The Roman Actor; A New Way to Pay Old Debts; The City Madam*

FORTHCOMING

The selected plays of John Marston, edited by Robert Cummings: *Antonio and Mellida; Antonio's Revenge; The Malcontent; The Dutch Courtezan; Sophonisba*

The selected plays of Ben Jonson, edited by Johanna Procter: *Sejanus; Epicoene,* or *The Silent Woman; Volpone; The Alchemist; Bartholomew Fair*

The plays of George Etherege, edited by Michael Cordner: *The Man of Mode; She Would if She Could; The Comical Revenge*

The selected plays of John Webster, edited by Inga-Stina Ewbank and Jonathan Dollimore: *The White Devil; The Devil's Law Case; The Duchess of Malfi*

The plays of William Wycherley, edited by Peter Holland: *Love in a Wood; The Gentleman Dancing Master; The Country Wife; The Plain Dealer*

THE SELECTED PLAYS OF THOMAS MIDDLETON

A Mad World, My Masters

A Chaste Maid in Cheapside

Women Beware Women

The Changeling
(with William Rowley)

EDITED BY
DAVID L. FROST
Professor of English, University of Newcastle, New South Wales

CAMBRIDGE UNIVERSITY PRESS
CAMBRIDGE
LONDON · NEW YORK · MELBOURNE

Published by the Syndics of the Cambridge University Press
The Pitt Building, Trumpington Street, Cambridge CB2 1RP
Bentley House, 200 Euston Road, London NW1 2DB
32 East 57th Street, New York, NY 10022, USA
296 Beaconsfield Parade, Middle Park, Melbourne 3206, Australia

First published 1978

Printed in Great Britain
at the University Press, Cambridge

Library of Congress Cataloguing in Publication Data
Middleton, Thomas, d. 1627.
The selected plays of Thomas Middleton
(Plays by Renaissance and Restoration dramatists)
CONTENTS: A mad world, my masters. – A chaste maid in Cheapside. – Women beware women. – The changeling.
I. Title. II. Series.
PR2711.5.F7   822′.3   77–23339
ISBN 0 521 21698 2 hard covers
ISBN 0 521 29236 0 paperback

PREFACE TO THE SERIES

This series provides the best plays (in some cases, the complete plays) of the major English Renaissance and Restoration dramatists, in fully-annotated, modern-spelling texts, soundly edited by scholars in the field. Although the first three volumes are devoted to Renaissance dramatists, future volumes will present the work of such Restoration playwrights as Etherege and Wycherley.

The introductory matter in each volume is factual and historical rather than critical: it includes, where appropriate, a brief biography of the playwright, a list of his works with dates of plays' first performances, the reasons for the volume editor's choice of plays, a short critical bibliography and a note on the texts used. An introductory note to each play then gives the source material, a short stage-history, and details of the individual editions of that play. Facsimiles of the original or early title-pages are given.

Annotation is of three types. Short notes at the foot of the page are designed to gloss the text or enlarge on its literary, historical or social allusions. At the end of the volume, in two separate appendices, editors have added more substantial explanatory notes and have commented on textual variants.

The volumes are intended for anyone interested in English drama in two of its richest periods, but they will prove especially useful to students at all levels who want to enjoy and explore the best work of these dramatists.

Graham Storey

CONTENTS

Preface to the series v

Introduction ix

A MAD WORLD, MY MASTERS

Introductory note 3

Text 4

A CHASTE MAID IN CHEAPSIDE

Introductory note 91

Text 93

WOMEN BEWARE WOMEN

Introductory note 187

Text 190

THE CHANGELING

Introductory note 307

Text 310

Notes

Textual notes 399

Additional notes 410

INTRODUCTION

Life

A tract which Thomas Middleton brought out in 1609, *The Marriage of the Old and New Testament*, places the prophecies of Hebrew scripture beside their fulfilment in the gospels, and demonstrates that everything was foretold that happened, and that nothing happened that was not foretold. If there is no more Calvinism in this than in most run-of-the-mill Anglican devotion of the time, nevertheless Middleton's choice of a topic is a significant one, and is consonant with the predestinarian flavour of his late tragedies. Middleton's life and art both suggest one who responded to rather than created circumstances, who was pessimistic about his ability to shape events, and painfully conscious of the limitations placed on human freedom by social and economic conditions.

Physically and intellectually, he was circumscribed by the bounds of the professional and commercial middle classes of London. He was baptised in St Lawrence Jewry on 18 April 1580, the son of William Middleton, citizen and bricklayer, and seems to have chosen to live most of his adult life in Newington Butts, about a mile south of Southwark: a lawsuit of 1609 mentions his residence there, as does a heralds' visitation in 1623, and on 4 July 1627 he was buried in the parish church of St Mary. Some time before 1604, when his son Edward was born, he married Maria or Magdalen, daughter of Edward Morbeck, a Clerk of Chancery whose son Thomas was an actor and musician, and whose father, John Merbeck, had been a noted composer and organist.

Middleton's constant equation in his plays of sexual desire with commercial acquisitiveness, and his preoccupation with the buying and selling of affections, are probably to be traced not so much to this obviously prudent match as to his family circumstances after the death of his father on 20 January 1585/6. William Middleton left a modest estate to his widow Anne, his five-year-old son and his daughter Avice, but this security was immediately jeopardised by the mother's emotional vulnerability. On 7 November 1586 Anne Middleton married Thomas Harvey, a penniless adventurer, 'poor and unable to pay his creditors', who had returned that July with Drake from Virginia; and her second marriage proved to be a succession of squabbles and lawsuits over her first husband's legacy. To protect her children's interests, Anne embarked on a series of stratagems not unworthy of Middleton's city comedies: in one crisis, she had herself arrested by the Lord Mayor's officer for failing to honour her financial obligations to her children, and thus compelled her husband (who was legally responsible) to go to her bond to the extent of £200 and to give security for his appearance at the next court day. Harvey eventually went off to the Low Countries and Portugal, but by 1590 he had returned to beg for money and to trouble the family; on one occasion his step-son had to evict him from the family home.

No doubt constant litigation made personal the hostility to lawyers common in plays of the period; most probably, it exhausted any ready money that might have been available for Middleton's education. Though he subscribed as an undergraduate at Queen's College, Oxford, on 7 April 1598, he had difficulty in supporting himself, and on 28 June 1598 sold his interest in some of his father's property to his sister's husband, Allen Waterer, in return for an allowance 'for maintenance with meat, drink and apparel' and 'for my advancement and preferment in the University of Oxford'. Even then, lawsuits compelled him at least once to leave his studies so as to defend his own and his mother's interests, and he appears never to have taken a degree. By February 1600/1 it is reported that 'now he remaineth here in London daily accompanying the players'. From the plays it appears that he carried from Oxford no great heights of Latinity, but chiefly the presumption that pedants and ninnies come from Cambridge.

Three early works, *The Wisdom of Solomon Paraphrased* (1597), *Micro-Cynicon* (1599) and a continuation of Shakespeare's *Lucrece, The Ghost of Lucrece* (1600), look like youthful fishing for patrons, but none seem to have bit, and by 1602 Middleton was engaged in hack work for the actor-manager Henslowe, collaborating with Dekker, Drayton, Munday and Webster on plays now lost. At the same time he began writing, with Dekker and alone, a series of satirical city comedies for the boys' companies of Blackfriars and Paul's, and he seems to have enjoyed some success until these companies folded around 1607.

Middleton had chosen to write in a voguish satirical genre where Jonson was the main innovator and Marston a major contributor; but Middleton himself became an important influence on its development, through his incorporation, combination and development of old materials which lay to hand in moral satire, in jest-books and coney-catching pamphlets, in moralities, interludes and in Italian intrigue comedy. Reaction to Middleton's city comedies, of which *A Mad World, My Masters* and *A Chaste Maid in Cheapside* are early and late examples, is bound to differ according to the demands one makes upon art. The 'mock actors' plot of *A Mad World* is a perfect example of Middleton's genius for constructing comic intrigue of the coney-catching variety, whilst in Allwit of *A Chaste Maid* we have an instance of the dramatist's ability to create figures who become horrific grotesques only because they consistently, and with urbane rationality, act on the premises of their total egotism. On the other hand, it must be admitted that Middleton does not in these comedies step outside conventional attitudes to analyse his society, nor does he come within human personality to explore it: the targets of his satire are as traditional as his grounds of criticism, there is little perception of the real moral cruxes of his day, whilst the creation of an Allwit is perhaps dependent on an insensitivity to what such solitary egotism would do to a personality outside the never-never land of vice.

The savage ironies of the christening at the cuckold's home in *A Chaste Maid*, where Sir Walter Whorehound stands as godfather to his own bastard, could not have been conceived by a dramatist who had no sense of moral outrage; and details of a very early play, *The Phoenix*, where a passionate widow rashly marries a sea-captain and has her body sold by him for cash, have led biographers to derive Middleton's satiric impulse from the experiences of his early life. But such experiences proved limiting for his art: the obsessive presumption that all human beings are dominated by egotism, pride and greed, that love is only lust under a fancy hat (though it may be an appealing stance to the generality of an audience), leads to disjunctions in the plays that are not to be explained merely by pointing to Middleton's disparate materials. A dramatic world in which all are crooks distorts an audience's perception of the values by which that world is satirised: for the satisfaction of its moral sense the audience is dependent on super-rogues who by their intelligence and audacity expose, exploit and punish the viciousness of lesser men. The audience comes to value witty and audacious criminality, and by devices such as irony is drawn into imaginative collusion with it. To restore a moral perspective, these eminently viable rogues have to be dispatched by unlikely peripeteia or improbable repentance, devices that disclose the authorial hand rather more than they suggest the predestining control of Providence.

After 1607 Middleton's artistic career seems to lack direction. If experience and a Calvinistic theology both inclined him to believe that mankind untouched by grace was totally depraved, that is hardly a creed to support the satirist's image of himself as reforming zealot: the persistent satirists, Jonson and Pope, are Catholics subscribing to a doctrine of works efficacious to salvation. Throughout Middleton's satire, from the early comedies to *A Chaste Maid in Cheapside* (1611–13), which gathers up many of the themes and motifs of his city plays, there is that disturbing fascination with oddities of vice which sometimes accompanies acceptance of vice's inevitability; and it leads persistently to contradictory and ambiguous artistic effects. At times in *A Chaste Maid* invention becomes liberated well-nigh entirely from moral intent: the contrasted couples of the sub-plot, the Kixes who are impoverished and disrupted by the failure to beget, and the Touchwoods who are made poor and driven apart by their extravagant success in begetting, exist less for any satiric purpose than for the black humour of their 'providential' fitness to solve each others' problems.

Turning from satire, Middleton tried his hand at a variety of dramatic forms: at melodrama and sensational journalism in *The Witch*, at Fletcherian tragi-comedy in *The Widow*, at Ancient British history in *Hengist, King of Kent*, at a study of the ethics of duelling in *A Fair Quarrel*, at a theatre-masque in *A World Tossed at Tennis*, at political allegory in *A Game at Chess*. He wrote alone and in collaboration, chiefly with William Rowley but also with others, for several different companies: for Prince Charles's Company, for Lady Elizabeth's Men, and extensively after 1615 for the King's Men. Financial pressures probably had much to do with Middleton becoming once again a jobbing dramatist. There were problems over debts in 1610–11, and from 1613 he wrote a succession of shows for dignitaries of the City of London, including the majority of yearly Lord Mayor's Pageants up until 1627; perhaps significantly, he wrote no more satires on the City after 1613. No doubt the writing of civic entertainments was honourable employment, and it led eventually to the profitable post of City Chronologer; but the production of such ephemera was perhaps as much bread-and-butter work as was the keeping of the City 'Annales' after 1620, a record of events concerning the City of London, complemented by a 'Farrago' of social, political and miscellaneous gossip. Middleton is said to have worked conscientiously at these compilations, now lost; but after his death, his widow Magdalen was obliged to petition the City for a grant to relieve her poverty.

It is likely that circumstances as much as anything are

responsible for a striking development in Middleton's work after 1615, which culminates in his two tragic masterpieces, *Women Beware Women* and *The Changeling* (a collaboration with Rowley). Middleton's first play for the King's Men, *The Witch*, was a flop, and he seems to have made some attempt to adapt his style to the expectations of a new audience. Material from *The Witch* was incorporated in a revival of Shakespeare's *Macbeth* around 1616 which Middleton may have supervised, and it is likely that in the psychological degeneration attendant on Macbeth's crimes Middleton met a concept of the operation of the moral order infinitely more subtle than his own imposed peripeteias: thereafter, first in *Hengist*, a play for the King's Men which is also built round an ambitious usurper, and then in *Women Beware Women* and *The Changeling*, Middleton takes an increasing interest in human psychology, in the interplay of personalities, in the developing and degenerating tragic character, in a world where character conditions action and deeds react upon character.

If there is a new sense of the inherent self-destructiveness of evil, and one not to be explained simply by the changeover from comedy to tragedy, Middleton's general attitudes have not altered. The Italy of *Women Beware Women* is little different to the City of London: pride, lust and greed are still the dominant motives in a society where economics determine human destiny; and there is the same preoccupation with those who trade sex for power, security and cash. Middleton remains cynical about the possibility of human love: in both tragedies, hopes of amorous bliss initiate disaster, and *The Changeling* is the only play of the period that, by its opposition of sub-plot to main plot, seems to exalt a loveless arranged marriage above a romantic match. But if Middleton is no less pessimistic about the possibilities of human nature in his satires, these tragedies are not a spectacle of general depravity but a study of human beings in transition from potential to actual damnation. The dramatist's eye upon humanity may be as cold as ever; but his characters have aspirations towards fidelity, honesty and love, they dream of restoring a lost Paradise. The whole audience is involved in the general tragedy, in their discovery that their circumstances and natures render these dreams unattainable; indeed, that the dreams themselves have been a major cause of catastrophe.

The Changeling was a highly popular play from its first production in 1622 and *Women Beware Women* is said to have been well received, though nothing is known about the circumstances of its performance. A more immediate success was Middleton's *Game at Chess*, a political allegory directed against James's alliance with Spain, which was performed for 'nine days together at the Globe on the Bankside' by the King's Men in August 1624; it was seen by thousands, and enjoyed the longest known run of any Jacobean play. At first sight, *A Game at Chess* seems uncharacteristically daring for Middleton, and he was forced to go into hiding whilst the players were imprisoned and his son Edward hauled up in his place before the Privy Council. But the Master of the Revels had licensed the play, and a policy of friendship with Spain was repugnant to the vast majority of Englishmen: probably Middleton took no great risk and had friends in high places who encouraged and supported him. William Heminges, in his *Elegy on Randolph's Finger* (1632), noted that the Puritans 'seemed much to adore' Middleton for his satire against the Spanish ambassador. The trouble soon blew over, though a late tradition has it that Middleton was himself imprisoned for a while; perhaps he felt he had burnt his fingers, for after 1624 he wrote no more plays. He continued to hold the post of City Chronologer given him in 1620, but he next appears in the records in connection with complaints about the 'ill-performance' of his Lord Mayor's Pageant, *The Triumphs of Health and Prosperity*, 29 October 1626. His own health was less than triumphant, and eight months later he was dead, leaving an impoverished widow who survived him by no more than a year.

Works

(Attribution and dating are in some cases very conjectural.)

The Wisdom of Solomon Paraphrased (poem)	1597
Micro-Cynicon: Six Snarling Satires (poems)	1599
The Ghost of Lucrece (poem)	1600
Unnamed lost play for Henslowe	1602
Caesar's Fall or Two Shapes (lost; with Dekker, Drayton, Munday and Webster)	1602
The Chester Tragedy or Randal, Earl of Chester (lost)	1602
The Family of Love (with Dekker – ? revised by Lording Barry *c.* 1607)	*c.* 1602
[*Blurt, Master Constable or The Spaniard's Night Walk* (probably Dekker alone)]	*c.* 1602

The Phoenix	*c.* 1603
The True Narration of the Entertainment of His Royal Majesty from Edinburgh till London (pamphlet)	1603
1 Honest Whore (with Dekker)	1604
The Ant and the Nightingale or Father Hubbard's Tales (pamphlet)	1604
The Black Book (pamphlet)	1604
A Mad World, My Masters	*c.* 1604–6
A Trick to Catch the Old One	*c.* 1604–6
The Puritan or The Widow of Watling Street	*c.* 1604–6
Your Five Gallants	*c.* 1604–7
The Roaring Girl or Moll Cutpurse (with Dekker)	*c.* 1604–8
Michaelmas Term	*c.* 1605
The Viper and Her Brood (lost; sometimes identified with the next)	1606
The Revenger's Tragedy (sometimes erroneously assigned to Tourneur)	1606–7
The Two Gates of Salvation, or the Marriage of the Old and New Testament (pamphlet)	1609
Sir Robert Sherley's Entertainment in Cracovia (pamphlet)	1609
The Second Maiden's Tragedy	1611
No Wit, No Help Like a Woman's	1611–12
A Chaste Maid in Cheapside	1611–13
Entertainment at the Opening of the New River (civic entertainment)	29 September 1613
Wit at Several Weapons (with Rowley and ? Fletcher)	1613
The Triumphs of Truth (civic pageant)	29 October 1613
The Masque of Cupid (lost)	4 January 1613/14
The Witch	*c.* 1615
More Dissemblers Besides Women	*c.* 1615
The Widow	*c.* 1616
The Nice Valour or The Passionate Madman (? with Fletcher)	*c.* 1616
Hengist, King of Kent or The Mayor of Queenborough	*c.* 1616–20
Civitatis Amor (civic pageant)	4 November 1616
A Fair Quarrel (with Rowley)	*c.* 1615–17
The Triumphs of Honour and Industry (civic pageant)	29 October 1617
The Old Law or a New Way to Please You (with Rowley and ? Massinger)	*c.* 1618

The Peacemaker or Great Britain's Blessing (pamphlet)	1618
The Inner Temple Masque or Masque of Heroes	1618/19
Anything for a Quiet Life (with Webster)	1619
The World Tossed at Tennis (a theatre masque; with Rowley)	Winter 1619/20
The Triumphs of Love and Antiquity (civic pageant)	29 October 1619
On the Death of Richard Burbage (elegy)	1619
Women Beware Women	*c.* 1621
Honourable Entertainments (civic entertainments)	1620–1
The Sun in Aries (civic pageant; with Munday)	29 October 1621
The Changeling (with Rowley)	1622
An Invention for the Lord Mayor (private entertainment)	1622
The Triumphs of Honour and Virtue (civic pageant)	29 October 1622
[*The Spanish Gypsy* (almost certainly by Dekker and Ford)]	1623
The Triumphs of Integrity (civic pageant)	29 October 1623
A Game at Chess	6 August 1624
The Triumphs of Health and Prosperity (civic pageant)	29 October 1626
Unnamed, unacted pageant for the entry of the King and Queen	1626
The Puritan Maid, The Modest Wife and The Wanton Widow (lost)	date unknown
The Conqueror's Custom or The Fair Prisoner (lost)	date unknown

The text of this edition

Basis of the text

In each instance, the first printing of a Middleton play has served as the foundation text. I have made extensive use of textual collation and annotation by nineteenth- and twentieth-century scholars; but persisting small inaccuracies, problems of lineation, and (especially) the difficulties attendant on the production of a modernised text have made it impossible to accept as a basis either the nineteenth-century editions of Dyce or Bullen, or the admirable work done by editors of single plays in the Fountainwell, New Mermaid, Regents Renaissance and Revels series.

Extent of modernisation

In the interest of the general reader and the actor of Middleton's plays, spelling and punctuation have been modernised to conform to current practice. In the case of spelling, however, this modernisation is less extensive than in some recent editions, for there is a growing unease among scholars at the extent to which such 'up-dating' leads to subtle changes in the nature of seventeenth-century texts. I have preserved seventeenth-century spellings where these seemed to indicate consonantal or syllabic values significantly different to the modern: for example, at II.ii.18 of *A Mad World, My Masters*, where the only modern text reads 'champaign grounds', this edition preserves the seventeenth-century variant from the quarto, 'champion grounds'. It has been less easy to be sure if old spellings represent very different vowel values to those of modern English, and vowel values are anyway subject to wide regional and social variation, both in Jacobean and in modern speech. Only occasionally, therefore, are unusual vowel spellings reproduced, and those concerned to reconstruct the precise sound of Middleton's lines should use this edition in conjunction with a work on Elizabethan pronunciation such as E.J. Dobson's *English Pronunciation, 1500–1700* (Oxford: Clarendon Press, 1957).

There are sometimes variant spellings of words such as *murderer/murtherer* in the quartos of different Middleton plays, and even within a single quarto. Such variations probably reflect only the taste (and perhaps the pronunciation) of different compositors, but I have preferred to retain these inconsistencies, except in those cases where it can be established from the holograph of *A Game at Chess* that Middleton himself had an invariable preference. Similarly, I have reproduced the contractions and expansions of the early texts, with the single exception of endings in *-ied* (e.g. *cried*, *died*, *replied*): it seemed better to follow possibly inaccurate quartos than to impose a regularity which may not be Middletonian. Again, since Middleton on occasions uses a plural noun with a singular verb, I have generally refrained from 'correcting' his grammar; and I have also avoided 'improving' his Latin.

Lineation

Middleton tended to write a prosaic blank verse and a prose which has many of the qualities of verse, whilst in a play such as *A Chaste Maid in Cheapside* he could move easily and rapidly from one medium to the other. For reasons of space, Middleton's first printers occasionally rendered his prose as verse and his verse as prose. Lineation would therefore be peculiarly difficult, did not the survival of a holograph of Middleton's *A Game at Chess* (in Trinity College, Cambridge, MS 0.2.66) give editors an unusual opportunity to establish the author's own practice. From this it appears that Middleton was altogether less 'regular' than his editors: he rarely capitalised the beginning of lines or bothered to indicate when the dialogue between speakers was technically part of a single blank verse line; he sometimes inserted additional phrases within the run of a blank verse speech and he often wrote extra-metrical phrases at the beginning and at the end of speeches; he frequently wrote lines with only four stresses.

The examination of Middleton's holograph suggests that printed quartos were often more faithful to the dramatist's practice than later editors have tended to think; in consequence, this present edition preserves quarto lineation unless there is very good reason to emend it. From his manuscript, it would appear that Middleton lineated not so much to show the metrical structure as to aid actors in phrasing their speeches: the necessarily subjective re-lineations of this edition, therefore, are undertaken with the needs of readers and actors chiefly in view. Those passages which seem to demand something more than ordinary speech rhythms have been printed as verse, and single lines of blank verse divided between speakers are indicated where they occur within this more formal utterance.

Corrections and emendations

Additions to the first printed texts are indicated by square brackets [ ], but some trivial errors have been corrected silently. All significant departures from the foundation text are given in the Textual notes at the end of the volume. These notes include also important variants from later seventeenth-century editions, together with suggested emendations or alternative readings which have not been accepted into the text, but which may be of interest to the reader or producer. An Introductory note to each play lists editions where textual problems can be pursued more fully.

Stage directions

Stage directions derived from early quartos or octavos are

printed in the text, and all necessary supplementary directions are given within square brackets [ ]. Indications of place or time appear only if these are found in the original printed text.

Annotation

I am gratefully indebted to previous editors, who have done much of the spadework of the annotation, and an Introductory note before each play lists earlier editions where supporting information and explanation may be found. Only where I felt I had something to add to previous commentary have I fully argued a point. It is not possible in an edition of this nature to indicate disagreements with other scholars, but, in general, silence may be taken to mean that I do not accept an interpretation that I have omitted. Fuller explanation of some points can be found in Additional notes at the end of the volume, and page reference is made to them in the annotation.

A single stroke / between two or more explanations of a word indicates that several meanings are being employed together: A *double* stroke // denotes an ambiguity of which the speaker is presumed to be unaware, but which is apparent to a second speaker, or to an audience.

A select bibliography

Editions

As yet there has been no complete twentieth-century edition of Middleton, and readers must still turn to Alexander Dyce's five volumes of *Middleton's Works* (London, 1840), or to the rare eight-volume edition of *Middleton's Works* by A.H. Bullen (London, 1885–6; but reprinted in New York: Ames Press, 1964) which for the most part is virtually a reprint of Dyce. Ten plays (*A Trick to Catch the Old One*, *The Changeling*, *A Chaste Maid in Cheapside*, *Women Beware Women*, *The Spanish Gypsy*, *The Roaring Girl*, *The Witch*, *A Fair Quarrel*, *The Mayor of Queenborough or Hengist, King of Kent*, and *The Widow*) are more generally accessible in a two-volume Mermaid collection, poorly edited by A.C. Swinburne (vol. I) and Havelock Ellis (vol. II) (London: Vizetelli, 1887–90).

Individual plays, edited according to modern standards and with explanatory annotation, have appeared in the Revels series (London: Methuen), in Regents Renaissance (London: Edward Arnold; Nebraska: University of Nebraska Press), New Mermaid (London: Ernest Benn) and Fountainwell Drama

Texts (Edinburgh: Oliver & Boyd), the last being old-spelling editions. Much of the most perceptive comment on Middleton's plays is to be found in the introductions to these editions, those of the Revels and the Regents Renaissance being particularly distinguished. Beside the four plays included in this volume, the following Middleton plays are currently available: *A Trick to Catch the Old One* (ed. C. Barber, Fountainwell, 1968, and ed. G.J. Watson, New Mermaid, 1968), *Michaelmas Term* (ed. R. Levin, Regents Renaissance, 1966) and *A Game at Chess* (ed. J.W. Harper, New Mermaid, 1966). The anonymous *Revenger's Tragedy*, now commonly attributed to Middleton, has been edited by R.A. Foakes (Revels, 1966), L.J. Ross (Regents Renaissance, 1966), B. Gibbons (New Mermaid, 1967) and George Parfitt (for this series). A Middleton–Rowley collaboration, *A Fair Quarrel*, has been edited by R.V. Holdsworth (New Mermaid, 1974). Rather less accessible are two scholarly monographs, *A Critical Edition of Thomas Middleton's 'The Widow'* ed. R.T. Levine (Salzburg: Institut für Englische Sprache und Literatur, Universität Salzburg, 1975) and *'Michaelmas Term' and 'A Trick to Catch the Old One': a Critical Edition* ed. George R. Price (The Hague – Paris: Mouton, 1976).

Books

The first book-length study of Middleton to appear was S. Schoenbaum's *Middleton's Tragedies* (New York: Columbia University Press, 1955), which in addition to those tragedies printed in this volume attributed to Middleton the anonymous *Second Maiden's Tragedy* and *The Revenger's Tragedy*. Though much of the book is necessarily concerned with problems of authorship, Schoenbaum offers a sound introduction to the plays. His acknowledged debt to his mentor R.H. Barker stimulated the publication of Barker's *Middleton* (New York: Columbia University Press, 1958), a broader study written some fifteen years earlier, with chapters on Middleton's biography, on the canon and dating of his works, and with a pioneer description of Middleton's comic technique. Both works display more critical acumen than the superficial general study by D.M. Holmes, *The Art of Thomas Middleton: a Critical Study* (Oxford: Clarendon, 1970). Shorter works are N.A. Brittin's *Thomas Middleton* (New York: Twayne's English Author Series, 1972) and D.M. Farr's *Thomas Middleton and the Drama of Realism* (Edinburgh: Oliver & Boyd, 1973). By far the most comprehensive consideration of

Middleton's oeuvre known to me, Ruby Chatterji's 'A Critical Study of the Work of Thomas Middleton', languishes at present as an unpublished PhD thesis in the University Library, Cambridge, where it is available on request. D.J. Lake has produced an exhaustive study of *The Canon of Middleton's Plays* (Cambridge: Cambridge University Press, 1975).

Essays

Among the major nineteenth-century critics, W. Hazlitt noticed Middleton in his *Lectures on the Dramatic Literature of the Age of Elizabeth* (London, 1818) and Swinburne contributed an introduction to the Mermaid collection. A. Symons's section on 'Middleton and Rowley' in *The Cambridge History of English Literature* ed. A.W. Ward and A.R. Waller, vol. VI (Cambridge: Cambridge University Press, 1910) is still worth reading.

Anything like a general recognition of Middleton's importance had to await the publication of T.S. Eliot's essay in *For Lancelot Andrewes* (London: Faber & Faber, 1928, later reprinted in *Selected Essays*, 1932) which offered little critical examination but impressed by its conviction that Middleton 'wrote one tragedy which more than any play except those of Shakespeare has a profound and permanent moral value and horror'. M.C. Bradbrook's chapter in *Themes and Conventions of Elizabethan Tragedy* (Cambridge: Cambridge University Press, 1935) combined sensitive criticism with scholarly understanding of the literary and dramatic convention in which Middleton wrote, and it remains essential reading. A more traditional study was U. Ellis-Fermor's essay in her *Jacobean Drama* (London: Methuen, 1936 revised 1958), which sought to illustrate Eliot's praise of Middleton as a 'great observer of human nature'. L.C. Knights, on the other hand, with a brief but important discussion of Middleton's comedies in his *Drama and Society in the Age of Jonson* (London: Chatto & Windus, 1937), severely qualified Eliot's view of the dramatist as a social realist.

Since the Second World War, studies of Middleton have proliferated but have been greatly variable in quality. On the tragedies, G.R. Hibbard has a perceptive critique of Middleton as 'a man with fresh intuitions about the nature of tragic experience' who was unable fully to liberate himself from the tradition he inherited ('The tragedies of Thomas Middleton and the decadence of the drama', *Nottingham Renaissance and*

Modern Studies, I (Nottingham: Nottingham University Press, 1957), 35–64). J.D. Jump ('Middleton's tragic comedies', in *The Pelican Guide to English Literature*, vol. 2, *The Age of Shakespeare*, ed. B. Ford (Harmondsworth: Penguin, 1955), 355–68) gives a short, sensible account of the techniques, dramatic construction and language of the two major tragedies, concluding that these are 'not naturalistic plays of the modern kind'. Chapters in general studies of Jacobean tragedy have been less happy, though most have something to offer: R. Ornstein's *The Moral Vision of Jacobean Tragedy* (Madison: University of Wisconsin Press, 1960) has some strikingly inaccurate observations, though it is not without occasional insights; I. Ribner's *Jacobean Tragedy: the Quest for Moral Order* (London: Methuen, 1962) is as moralistic and schematised as its title suggests, if a more sober study than Ornstein's. T.B. Tomlinson, writing on the 'Naturalistic comedy and tragedy' of Middleton in his *Study of Elizabethan and Jacobean Tragedy* (Cambridge: Cambridge University Press, 1964), seems by crediting the dramatist with 'accurate observation' and the 'presentation of facts' to ignore all the qualifications made of Middleton's supposed realism. Tomlinson offers an extended and sometimes over-ingenious account of language and image themes, but seems to make regrettably little use of C.B. Ricks's two brilliant studies of Middleton's poetic language, 'The moral and poetic structure of *The Changeling*', *Essays in Criticism* (1960), 290–306, and 'Word-play in *Women Beware Women*', *Review of English Studies* new series 12 (1961), 238–50. David Frost's chapter on Middleton in *The School of Shakespeare* (Cambridge: Cambridge University Press, 1968) attempts to examine the nature and extent of the dramatist's debt to Shakespeare and offers corrections to current readings of the tragedies, and an appendix summarises the scholarly debate over Middleton's supposed authorship of *The Revenger's Tragedy*.

Understanding of Middleton's comedies has advanced significantly in the last twenty years. M.C. Bradbrook's *Growth and Structure of Elizabethan Comedy* (London: Chatto & Windus, 1955, new edition 1973) attempted to relate Middleton to the developing comic tradition, but did so with less coherence and insight than in her corresponding study on tragedy. This chapter has been partly superseded by Brian Gibbons's book-length study of *Jacobean City Comedy* (London: Rupert Hart-Davies, 1968), a comprehensive survey of the genre and its contributors, including Middleton, which is particularly useful for its examination of the plays as social satire and for its sense of theatre. Besides the introductions to individual plays in modern editions, two shorter essays repay attention, S. Schoenbaum's '*A Chaste Maid in Cheapside* and Middleton's City Comedy' in *Studies in English Renaissance Drama* ed. J.W. Bennett *et al.* (London, 1959) and R.B. Parker's study of 'Middleton's experiments with comedy and judgement' in *Stratford-upon-Avon Studies I: Jacobean Theatre* ed. J.R. Brown and B. Harris (London: Arnold, 1960), 179–99; Parker explores 'the tension between the presentation of manners and the desire to denounce immorality' in the comedies and in *Women Beware Women*.

Most of what is known about Middleton's biography is contained in the first chapter of Barker's *Middleton* and in N.W. Bawcutt's introduction to his Revels edition of *The Changeling* (Revels, London: Methuen, 1958). Comprehensive bibliographies are S.A. Tannenbaum, *Middleton: a Concise Bibliography* (New York, 1940 reprinted in S.A. and D.R. Tannenbaum, *Elizabethan Bibliographies*, V, New York: Kennikat Press, 1967) and D. Donovan, *Elizabethan Bibliographies Supplements I: Middleton 1939–65* (London: Nether Press, 1967), and a more up-to-date and discriminating list is to be found in *The New Cambridge Bibliography of English Literature*, ed. G.G. Watson, vol. I, *600–1660* (Cambridge: Cambridge University Press, 1974).

References

Editions of dramatists cited in the notes of this edition are: Shakespeare, *Complete Works,* ed. P. Alexander (London: Collins, 1951); Chapman, *The Widow's Tears*, ed. A. Yamada (London: Methuen (Revels), 1975); Jonson, *Works*, ed. C.H. Herford and P. Simpson (Oxford: Clarendon, 1925–52); Marlowe, *Complete Works*, ed. F. Bowers (Cambridge: Cambridge University Press, 1973); Marston, *Plays*, ed. H. Harvey Wood (Edinburgh: Oliver & Boyd, 1934–9); Massinger, *Plays and Poems*, ed. P. Edwards and C. Gibson (Oxford: Clarendon, 1976); Middleton, *Works*, ed. A.H. Bullen (London, 1885–6).

A

MAD WORLD,

MY

MASTERS.

As it hath bin lately in Action by the Children of Paules.

Composed by T. M.

LONDON,

Printed by *H. B.* for WALTER BVRRE, and are to be sold in Paules Church-yard, at the signe of the Crane. 1608.

Title-page of the 1608 Quarto of *A Mad World, My Masters*, reproduced by permission of the Trustees of the British Museum.

INTRODUCTORY NOTE

A British Museum copy (644.f.7) of the first quarto (1608) has served as copy-text for this edition. The quarto survives in corrected and uncorrected states, but is generally well-printed; it was almost certainly set up from a Middleton holograph, and probably from foul papers that contained authorial revisions. A second quarto (1640) merely reprints Q1, correcting some obvious errors and making many more. Two modern editions of the play exist as unpublished dissertations, by G.J. Eberle (University of Wisconsin, 1944) and by M.J. Taylor (University of Birmingham, 1963). Eberle's work has been gathered up by S. Henning in his edition for Regents Renaissance (1965), which is moderately annotated but has a particularly good critical introduction. Though Henning does not make clear how much collation of the ten surviving copies of Q1 he has undertaken, his notes record variants between Q1, corrected Q1, and Q2.

Nothing is known of any sources for Middleton's play, though the materials are like many conventional episodes in coney-catching pamphlets, jest-books and ballads, in the Italian *novella* tradition, and in popular drama in England and on the Continent. It seems unlikely that Middleton would have needed to have recourse to any particular source.

The title-page of Q1 (1608) refers to recent performances by the Children of Paul's, for whom the play was almost certainly written, whilst Q2's title-page (1640) states that it 'hath been often acted at the Private House in Salisbury Court by Her Majesty's Servants' (i.e. Queen Henrietta's Men). No details are known of these performances. After the Restoration, it was performed at Oxford on Friday, 5 July 1661 'in the morning', and Sir Edward Browne's Memorandum Book notes another performance at the Red Bull Theatre in Clerkenwell around 1662. In the eighteenth century, the play suffered adaptation by Leonard Macnally as an afterpiece for Covent Garden, *The April Fool, or, The Follies of a Night*, performed on Saturday, 1 April, Friday, 28 April, and Friday, 5 May 1786. Only the name 'Harebrain' survives from the Dramatis Personae of the original. *A Mad World, My Masters* also provided themes for Kerrick's *The Spendthrift*, performed at Covent Garden in 1778.

[DRAMATIS PERSONAE]

The Actors in the Comedy

SIR BOUNTEOUS PROGRESS, *an old rich knight.*
RICHARD FOLLYWIT, *nephew to Sir Bounteous Progress.*
MASTER PENITENT BROTHEL, *a country gentleman.*
MAWWORM, a lieutenant }
HOBOY, an ancient } *comrades to Follywit.*
MASTER INESSE }
MASTER POSSIBILITY } *two [elder] brothers.*
MASTER HAREBRAIN, *a citizen.*
GUNWATER, *Sir Bounteous's man.*
JASPER, *Penitent's man.*
RAFE, *Master Harebrain's man.*
TWO KNIGHTS.
ONE CONSTABLE.
A SUCCUBUS [*as* MISTRESS HAREBRAIN].
WATCHMEN.
A FOOTMAN.
AN OLD GENTLEWOMAN, *mother to the courtesan.*
MISTRESS HAREBRAIN, *the citizen's wife.*
FRANK GULLMAN, *the courtesan.*
ATTENDANTS.

The Actors in the Comedy: This list derives from the Second Quarto (1640).

4 PENITENT BROTHEL: See Textual note, p. 399.

5 MAWWORM: an intestinal worm, a parasite; its activities lead to peevish temper.

7 HOBOY, *an ancient*: 'Oboe, an ensign'; the name is ostensibly derived from the timbre of the character's voice, necessarily high when played by a child actor.

8, 10 INESSE, POSSIBILITY: The names derive from legal terms: an estate *in esse* gave possession of land, an estate in possibility (or *in posse*), gave potential possession. In fact or expectation, the characters are rich.

11, 21 HAREBRAIN: See Textual note, p. 399. Hares exhibit in spring a proverbial madness, stimulated by sexual jealousy.

12 GUNWATER: See Textual note, p. 400.

17 SUCCUBUS: a demon in female form supposed to have intercourse with men in their sleep.

22 FRANK GULLMAN: 'Frank' is a diminutive of 'Francis', giving Middleton a characteristic oxymoron: 'Honest Cheater'.

A MAD WORLD, MY MASTERS

ACT I

SCENE I

Enter DICK FOLLYWIT, *and his consorts,* LIEUTENANT MAWWORM, ANCIENT HOBOY, *and others his comrades.*

MAWWORM. O captain, regent, principal!

HOBOY. What shall I call thee? The noble spark of bounty, the lifeblood of society!

FOLLYWIT. Call me your forecast, you whoresons. When you come drunk out of a tavern, 'tis I must cast your plots into form still; 'tis I must manage the prank, or I'll not give a louse for the proceeding; I must let fly my civil fortunes, turn wild-brain, lay my wits upo'th' tenters, you rascals, to maintain a company of villains whom I love in my very soul and conscience.

MAWWORM. Aha, our little forecast!

FOLLYWIT. Hang you, you have bewitch'd me among you. I was as well given till I fell to be wicked, my grandsire had hope of me, I went all in black, swore but a' Sundays, never came home drunk but upon fasting nights to cleanse my stomach; 'slid, now I'm quite altered, blown into light colours, let out oaths by th'

Title *A MAD WORLD, MY MASTERS*: Proverbial; see M.P. Tilley, *Dictionary of Proverbs in England in the Sixteenth and Seventeenth Centuries* (Ann Arbor, 1950), W 880.

4 *forecast*: one who considers the future and makes appropriate plans.

8 *civil fortunes*: the chance of a civilian/well-conducted career.

8–9 *wits upo' th' tenters*: faculties stretched like cloth upon a frame.

12–24 A direct imitation of Falstaff's speech in *1 Henry IV*, III.iii. 12–20, perhaps intended to allow the boy actor a parody of an adult rival in Shakespeare's company.

14–15 *swore but a' Sundays*: i.e. when uttering the names of God in public worship.

15–16 *drunk . . . to cleanse my stomach*: presumably, drinking on an empty stomach to induce vomiting.

17 *blown into light colours*: matured (like a flower) into gaudy clothes; 'blown' is probably intended to suggest the extravagantly padded costumes which were then the fashion.

minute, sit up late till it be early, drink drunk till I am sober, sink down dead in a tavern and rise in a tobacco shop. Here's a transformation. I was wont yet to pity the simple, and leave 'em some money; 'slid, now I gull 'em without conscience. I go without order, swear without number, gull without mercy, and drink without measure.

MAWWORM. I deny the last, for if you drink ne'er so much, you drink within measure.

FOLLYWIT. How prove you that, sir?

MAWWORM. Because the drawers never fill their pots.

FOLLYWIT. Mass, that was well found out; all drunkards may lawfully say they drink within measure by that trick. And, now I'm put i'th' mind of a trick, can you keep your countenance, villains? Yet I am a fool to ask that, for how can they keep their countenance that have lost their credits?

HOBOY. I warrant you for blushing, captain.

FOLLYWIT. I easily believe that, ancient, for thou lost thy colours once. Nay, faith, as for blushing, I think there's grace little enough amongst you all; 'tis Lent in your cheeks, the flag's down. Well, your blushing face I suspect not, nor indeed greatly your laughing face, unless you had more money in your purses. Then thus compendiously, now. You all know the possibilities of my hereafter fortunes, and the humour of my frolic grandsire, Sir Bounteous Progress, whose death makes all possible to me: I shall have all when he has nothing; but now he has all, I shall have nothing. I think one mind runs through a million of 'em: they love to keep us sober all the while they're alive, that when they're

---

21 *'slid*: 'by God's eyelid', a mild oath.

28 *drawers*: tapsters, barmen.

32 *keep your countenance*: 'control your expression'/'maintain your reputation'.

35 *I warrant you for blushing*: 'I guarantee I won't blush.'

37 *colours*: i.e. the flag of the regiment, entrusted to the ancient, or ensign, who would be disgraced if he survived its loss to the enemy.

38–9 *'tis Lent in your cheeks, the flag's down*: i.e. their cheeks lack colour. The flag on a theatre which was flown during performances would be taken down in Lent, when playing was prohibited.

43 *humour*: whim.

dead we may drink to their healths; they cannot abide to see us merry all the while they're above ground, and that makes so many laugh at their fathers' funerals. I know my grandsire has his will in a box, and has bequeath'd all to me when he can carry nothing away; but stood I in need of poor ten pounds now, by his will I should hang myself ere I should get it. There's no such word in his will, I warrant you, nor no such thought in his mind.

MAWWORM. You may build upon that, captain.

FOLLYWIT. Then since he has no will to do me good as long as he lives, by mine own will I'll do myself good before he dies. And now I arrive at the purpose. You are not ignorant, I'm sure, you true and necessary implements of mischief, first, that my grandsire Sir Bounteous Progress is a knight of thousands, and therefore no knight, since one thousand six hundred; next, that he keeps a house like his name, bounteous, open for all comers; thirdly and lastly, that he stands much upon the glory of his complement, variety of entertainment, together with the largeness of his kitchen, longitude of his buttery, and fecundity of his larder, and thinks himself never happier than when some stiff lord or great countess alights to make light his dishes. These being well mix'd together may give my project better encouragement, and make my purpose spring forth more fortunate. To be short, and cut off a great deal of dirty way, I'll down to my grandsire like a lord.

MAWWORM. How, captain?

FOLLYWIT. A French ruff, a thin beard, and a strong per-

---

65 *no knight, since one thousand six hundred*: i.e. only a knight since 1603, when James I insisted that landholders worth forty pounds a year assume a knighthood or pay a fine; Bounteous has cash, not birth.

75–6 *cut off a great deal of dirty way*: proverbial; cf. *The Revenger's Tragedy*, II.i.17.

79 *French ruff*: a deep ruff, which hung down from the top of a high stock which was fastened up to the chin; it was more fashionable than the English ruff, which extended at right angles to the neck.

fume will do't. I can hire blue coats for you all by Westminster clock, and that colour will be soonest believed.

MAWWORM. But prithee, captain –

FOLLYWIT. Push, I reach past your fadoms: you desire crowns.

MAWWORM. From the crown of our head to the sole of our foot, bully.

FOLLYWIT. Why, carry yourselves but probably, and carry away enough with yourselves.

Enter MASTER PENITENT BROTHEL.

HOBOY. Why, there spoke a Roman captain. Master Penitent Brothel –

PENITENT. Sweet Master Follywit –

Ex[*eunt all but* PENITENT BROTHEL].

Here's a mad-brain a'th'first, whose pranks scorn to have precedents, to be second to any, or walk beneath any madcap's inventions; h'as play'd more tricks than the cards can allow a man, and of the last stamp, too; hating imitation, a fellow whose only glory is to be prime of the company, to be sure of which he maintains all the rest.
He's the carrion, and they the kites that gorge upon him.

80–1 *blue coats for you all by Westminster clock*: Blue coats were the dress of servants and since Westminster was the site of the Court and the Law Courts, impecunious servants could no doubt be found to sell or loan their clothes. John Stow, *Survey of London* (1633 edition), p. 524, mentions the 'Tower of Stone, containing a Clocke', 'called the Clock-house', in the courtyard of Westminster Palace.

84 *I reach past your fadoms*: 'I go beyond your comprehensions'.

85 *crowns*: coins bearing the imprint of a crown, with a value of one quarter of £1.

88 *carry yourselves but probably*: 'only put on a plausible act'.

90 *a Roman captain*: Follywit is so called because he follows the custom of a Roman leader in allowing his troops to pillage what booty they can carry.

93 *a'th'first*: of the top quality.

96 *of the last stamp*: up to the minute, of the most recent minting.

But why in others do I check wild passions,
And retain deadly follies in myself?
I tax his youth of common receiv'd riot,
Time's comic flashes, and the fruits of blood;
And in myself soothe up adulterous motions,
And such an appetite that I know damns me,
Yet willingly embrace it: love to Harebrain's wife,
Over whose hours and pleasures her sick husband,
With a fantastic but deserv'd suspect,
Bestows his serious time in watch and ward.
And therefore I'm constrain'd to use the means
Of one that knows no mean, a courtesan,
One poison for another, whom her husband
Without suspicion innocently admits
Into her company, who with tried art
Corrupts and loosens her most constant powers,
Making his jealousy more than half a wittol,
Before his face plotting his own abuse,
To which himself gives aim,

Enter COURTESAN.

Whilst the broad arrow with the forked head
Misses his brow but narrowly. See, here she comes,
The close courtesan, whose mother is her bawd.

COURTESAN. Master Penitent Brothel!

PENITENT. My little pretty Lady Gullman, the news, the comfort?

---

103 *I tax his youth of common receiv'd riot*: 'I reproach him for youthful follies which are widespread and accepted.'

104 *blood*: See Additional note, p. 410.

109 *fantastic but deserv'd suspect*: brainsick but justified suspicion.

110 *watch and ward*: This is the traditional phrase for the duties of the sentinel or watchman.

112 *mean*: moderation, decent limit.

117 *wittol*: a conniving cuckold.

119 *gives aim*: directs (in archery, a man standing at the butts gives aim by reporting the accuracy of the shot).

120 *the broad arrow with the forked head*: alluding to the cuckold's horns.

122 *close*: secret.

COURTESAN. Y'are the fortunate man, Sir Knight a'th' Holland Skirt. There wants but opportunity and she's wax of your own fashioning. She had wrought herself into the form of your love before my art set finger to her.

PENITENT. Did our affections meet, our thoughts keep time?

COURTESAN. So it should seem by the music. The only jar is in the grumbling bass viol, her husband.

PENITENT. Oh, his waking suspicion!

COURTESAN. Sigh not, Master Penitent, trust the managing of the business with me; 'tis for my credit now to see't well finish'd. If I do you no good, sir, you shall give me no money, sir.

PENITENT. I am arriv'd at the court of conscience! A courtesan! O admirable times! Honesty is removed to the common place. Farewell, lady. *Exit* PENITENT.

Enter MOTHER.

MOTHER. How now, daughter?

COURTESAN. What news, mother?

MOTHER. A token from thy keeper.

COURTESAN. Oh, from Sir Bounteous Progress. He's my keeper indeed, but there's many a piece of venison stol'n that my keeper wots not on; there's no park kept so warily but loses flesh one time or other, and no woman kept so privately but may watch advantage to make the best of her pleasure. And in common

---

126–7 *Sir Knight a' th' Holland Skirt*: Jocular titles coined on the analogy of popular romances were common. 'Holland Skirt' probably means 'Dutch skirt', i.e. a whore, with an innuendo on 'hole-and-skirt' (Holland was a good-quality linen): Master Penitent is the 'Knight of Loose Ladies'. But see Textual note, p. 400.

134 *bass viol*: with a pun on 'base' (so Q) and 'vile'.

140 *the court of conscience*: the Court of Requests, a court which dealt with civil actions for litigants too poor to sue in other courts.

142 *the common place*: a pun on the Court of Common Pleas, to which civil actions between subjects might be removed from another court; the common place is land publicly owned, and becomes a metaphor for a whore (see Shakespeare, *Sonnets*, 137.10). A 'common-house' = a brothel (*Measure for Measure*, II.i.43).

148 *wots not on*: does not know of.

reason one keeper cannot be enough for so proud a park as a woman.

MOTHER. Hold thee there, girl.

COURTESAN. Fear not me, mother.

MOTHER. Every part of the world shoots up daily into more subtlety. The very spider weaves her cauls with more art and cunning to entrap the fly.
The shallow ploughman can distinguish now
'Twixt simple truth and a dissembling brow;
Your base mechanic fellow can spy out
A weakness in a lord, and learns to flout.
How do's't behoove us then that live by sleight
To have our wits wound up to their stretch'd height!
Fifteen times thou know'st I have sold thy maidenhead
To make up a dowry for thy marriage, and yet
There's maidenhead enough for old Sir Bounteous still.
He'll be all his lifetime about it yet,
And be as far to seek when he has done.
The sums that I have told upon thy pillow!
I shall once see those golden days again;
Though fifteen, all thy maidenheads are not gone.
The Italian is not serv'd yet, nor the French;
The British men come for a dozen at once,
They engross all the market. Tut, my girl,
'Tis nothing but a politic conveyance,
A sincere carriage, a religious eyebrow
That throws their charms over the worldlings' senses;
And when thou spiest a fool that truly pities
The false springs of thine eyes,
And honourably dotes upon thy love,
If he be rich, set him by for a husband.
Be wisely tempered and learn this, my wench:

---

152 *proud*: fine/arrogant/sexually aroused.
157 *cauls*: webs.
161 *mechanic*: labouring.
162 *flout*: act or speak sneeringly.
163 *sleight*: cunning, dexterity.
165–75 This alludes to the practice of gratifying the male taste for virgins by simulating a hymen by means of surgical sewing.
170 *told*: made, counted up.
174 *British*: probably Bretons.
175 *engross*: monopolise, wholly absorb.
176 *politic conveyance*: crafty managing.

Who gets th' opinion for a virtuous name
May sin at pleasure, and ne'er think of shame.

COURTESAN. Mother, I am too deep a scholar grown
To learn my first rules now.

MOTHER. 'Twill be thy own;
I say no more. Peace, hark. Remove thyself.

[*Exit* COURTESAN.]

Oh, the two elder brothers.

Enter INESSE *and* POSSIBILITY.

POSSIBILITY. A fair hour, sweet lady.

MOTHER. Good morrow, gentlemen, Master Inesse and Master Possibility.

INESSE. Where's the little sweet lady, your daughter?

MOTHER. Even at her book, sir.

POSSIBILITY. So religious?

MOTHER. 'Tis no new motion, sir; sh'as took it from an infant.

POSSIBILITY. May we deserve a sight of her, lady?

MOTHER. Upon that condition you will promise me, gentlemen, to avoid all profane talk, wanton compliments, undecent phrases, and lascivious courtings (which I know my daughter will sooner die than endure), I am contented your suits shall be granted.

POSSIBILITY. Not a bawdy syllable, I protest.

INESSE. [*aside*] 'Syllable' was [well-] plac'd there, for indeed your one syllables are your bawdiest words: prick that down.

Exeunt [MOTHER, INESSE *and* POSSIBILITY].

SCENE II

Enter MASTER HAREBRAIN.

HAREBRAIN. She may make nightwork on't; 'twas well recovered.
He-cats and courtesans stroll most i'th' night;
Her friend may be receiv'd and convey'd forth nightly.
I'll be at charge for watch and ward, for watch and ward, i'faith;

---

184 *opinion*: reputation.
196 *motion*: inclination.
207 *prick that down*: 'note that down', with a pun on 'prick' = penis, one of the offending monosyllables.
1 *recovered*: recalled to mind.

And here they come.

Enter two or three [WATCHMEN].

FIRST WATCHMAN. Give your worship good even.

HAREBRAIN. Welcome, my friends; I must deserve your diligence in an employment serious. The troth is, there is a cunning plot laid, but happily discovered, to rob my house; the night uncertain when, but fix'd within the circle of this month.
Nor does this villainy consist in numbers,
Or many partners; only someone
Shall, in the form of my familiar friend,
Be receiv'd privately into my house
By some perfidious servant of mine own,
Address'd fit for the practice.

FIRST WATCHMAN. Oh, abominable!

HAREBRAIN. If you be faithful watchmen, show your goodness, [*Gives money*.]
And with these angels shore up your eyelids.
Let me not be purloin'd [*aside*] purloin'd indeed; the merry Greeks conceive me. – There is a gem I would not lose, kept by the Italian under lock and key; we Englishmen are careless creatures. Well, I have said enough.

SECOND WATCHMAN. And we will do enough, sir.

Exeunt [WATCHMEN].

HAREBRAIN. Why, well said, watch me a good turn now; so, so, so.

10–11 *fix'd within the circle of this month*: This circumlocution alludes to the practice of raising and restricting evil spirits within the circumference of a circle; the evil is to be perpetrated within a month.

17 *Address'd fit for the practice*: prepared ready for the trick.

19 *angels*: gold coins stamped with the figure of St Michael killing a dragon.

20 *purloin'd*: robbed; but as 'pur' is the knave in the card game 'Post and Pair' and 'to loin' = 'to copulate', there is probably a pun on 'loined by a knave'.

20–1 *the merry Greeks*: a common slang phrase for roisterers, usually of loose habits.

22 *kept by the Italian*: According to Burton's *Anatomy of Melancholy*, III.iii.1.2, the Italians 'lock up their women, and will not suffer them to be near men so much as in the church, but with a partition between'.

Rise villainy with the lark, why, 'tis prevented;
Or steal't by with the leather-winged bat,
The evening cannot save it. Peace –

[*Enter* COURTESAN.]

Oh, Lady Gullman, my wife's only company, welcome! And how does the virtuous matron, that good old gentlewoman thy mother? I persuade myself, if modesty be in the world she has part on't. A woman of an excellent carriage all her lifetime, in court, city, and country.

COURTESAN. Sh'as always carried it well in those places, sir. [*Aside*] Witness three bastards apiece. – How does your sweet bedfellow, sir? You see I'm her boldest visitant.

HAREBRAIN. And welcome, sweet virgin, the only companion my soul wishes for her. I left her within at her lute; prithee give her good counsel.

COURTESAN. Alas, she needs none, sir.

HAREBRAIN. Yet, yet, yet, a little of thy instructions will not come amiss to her.

COURTESAN. I'll bestow my labour, sir.

HAREBRAIN. Do, labour her, prithee; I have convey'd away all her wanton pamphlets, as *Hero and Leander*, *Venus and Adonis*; oh, two luscious mary-bone pies for a young married wife. Here, here, prithee take the *Resolution*, and read to her a little.

COURTESAN. Sh'as set up her resolution already, sir.

HAREBRAIN. True, true, and this will confirm it the more. There's a chapter of Hell, 'tis good to read this cold weather. Terrify her, terrify her; go, read to her the horrible punishments for itching wantonness, the pains allotted for adultery; tell her her thoughts, her very dreams are answerable, say so; rip up the life of

---

36 *carried it well*: behaved well/borne her child successfully/ supported men in intercourse.

47 *labour*: work upon, endeavour to influence.

48 *Hero and Leander, Venus and Adonis*: erotic Ovidian poems by Marlowe and Shakespeare.

49 *mary-bone pies*: marrowbone pie, regarded as aphrodisiac.

51 *Resolution*: *The First Book of the Christian Exercise Appertaining to Resolution* (1582), a popular book of devotion by the Jesuit Robert Parsons, chapter IX.

a courtesan, and show how loathsome 'tis.

COURTESAN. [*aside*] The gentleman would persuade me in time to disgrace myself, and speak ill of mine own function. *Exit.*

HAREBRAIN. This is the course I take (I'll teach the married man
A new selected strain): I admit none
But this pure virgin to her company;
Puh, that's enough. I'll keep her to her stint,
I'll put her to her pension:
She gets but her allowance, that's [a] bare one;
Few women but have that beside their own.
Ha, ha, ha! Nay, I'll put her hard to't.

Enter wife [MISTRESS HAREBRAIN] *and* COURTESAN.

MISTRESS HAREBRAIN. Fain would I meet the gentleman.

COURTESAN. Push, fain would you meet him! Why, you do not take the course.

HAREBRAIN. [*aside*] How earnestly she labours her, like a good wholesome sister of the Family. She will prevail, I hope.

COURTESAN. Is that the means?

MISTRESS HAREBRAIN. What is the means? I would as gladly to enjoy his sight, embrace it as the –

COURTESAN. Shall I have hearing? Listen –

HAREBRAIN. [*aside*] She's round with her, i'faith.

COURTESAN. When husbands in their rank'st suspicions dwell,

---

64 *A new selected strain*: The metaphor is probably from the breeding of livestock and plants; Harebrain will produce a new quality in his wife and offspring by keeping base men from her, and allowing her to mix only with the purest virgins and propagate with himself alone.

66–9 *I'll keep her . . . their own*: He will restrict her to 'bare necessities', keeping her to 'rations', her husband's favours; whereas most women have those supplemented by other 'supplies'.

75 *the Family*: the Family of Love, an Anabaptist millennial sect who believed themselves to be living under the liberty of the Spirit of Love, which brought them into one family; they were suspected (with some cause) of disregarding conventional morality, and were frequently attacked in the drama for sexual licence.

Then 'tis our best art to dissemble well.
Put but these notes in use that I'll direct you,
He'll curse himself that e'er he did suspect you.
Perhaps he will solicit you, as in trial,
To visit such and such; still give denial.
Let no persuasions sway you; they are but fetches
Set to betray you, jealousies, slights, and reaches.
Seem in his sight to endure the sight of no man;
Put by all kisses, till you kiss in common;
Neglect all entertain; if he bring in
Strangers, keep you your chamber, be not seen;
If he chance steal upon you, let him find
Some book lie open 'gainst an unchaste mind,
And coted scriptures, though for your own pleasure
You read some stirring pamphlet, and convey it
Under your skirt, the fittest place to lay it.
This is the course, my wench, to enjoy thy wishes;
Here you perform best when you most neglect;
The way to daunt is to outvie suspect.
Manage these principles but with art and life,
Welcome all nations, thou'rt an honest wife.

HAREBRAIN. [*aside*] She puts it home, i'faith, ev'n to the quick.
From her elaborate action I reach that
I must requite this maid. Faith. I'm forgetful.
[*Draws back.*]

MISTRESS HAREBRAIN. Here, lady,
Convey my heart unto him in this jewel.
Against you see me next you shall perceive
I have profited. In the mean season, tell him
I am a prisoner yet, a'th' master's side:

---

88 *fetches*: decoys (and compare Massinger, *Parliament of Love*, IV.iii.34, where the sense seems to require the meaning 'pimp').

89 *reaches*: contrivances.

96 *coted scriptures*: 'quoted scriptures', perhaps a selection of relevant Bible passages, but more likely, a copy of the scriptures with annotations, such as were popular in Puritan circles.

101 *daunt*: overcome.

105 *I reach that*: I conclude that.

111 *a'th'master's side*: an allusion to the name of the most comfortable of the four 'wards' or divisions in the London Counters, or debtors' prisons: the master's, the knight's, the twopenny and the hole, in descending order of cost.

My husband's jealousy,
That masters him as he doth master me;
And as a keeper that locks prisoners up
Is himself prison'd under his own key,
Even so my husband, in restraining me,
With the same ward bars his own liberty.

COURTESAN. I'll tell him how you wish it, and I'll wear
My wits to the third pile, but all shall clear.

MISTRESS HAREBRAIN. I owe you more than thanks, but that I hope
My husband will requite you.

COURTESAN. Think you so, lady? He has small reason for't.

HAREBRAIN. [*joining them*] What, done so soon? Away, to't again, to't again, good wench, to't again; leave her not so. Where left you? Come –

COURTESAN. Faith, I am weary, sir.
I cannot draw her from her strict opinion
With all the arguments that sense can frame.

HAREBRAIN. No? Let me come. Fie, wife, you must consent! What opinion is't? Let's hear.

COURTESAN. Fondly and wilfully she retains that thought
That every sin is damn'd.

HAREBRAIN. Oh, fie, fie, wife! Pea, pea, pea, pea, how have you lost your time? For shame, be converted. There's a diabolical opinion indeed. Then you may think that usury were damn'd; you're a fine merchant, i'faith. Or bribery? You know the law well. Or sloth? Would some of the clergy heard you, i'faith. Or pride? You come at court. Or gluttony? You're not worthy to dine at an alderman's table.
Your only deadly sin's adultery,

---

119 *to the third pile*: 'to the bone'; 'three-pile' was velvet in which the loops of the pile-warp (forming the nap) were triple, forming a pile of treble thickness.

129 *sense*: the intellectual faculties/sensuality.

132 *fondly*: foolishly.

133 *every sin is damn'd*: The satire is directed against the views of the Familists, who regarded feelings of Divine love as having an importance that rendered doctrine essentially irrelevant, and who tended towards antinomianism on matters of conduct.

That villainous ringworm, woman's worst requital.
'Tis only lechery that's damn'd to th' pit-hole;
Ah, that's an arch-offence; believe it, squall,
All sins are venial but venereal.

COURTESAN. I've said enough to her.

HAREBRAIN. And she will be rul'd by you.

COURTESAN. Fah!

HAREBRAIN. I'll pawn my credit on't. Come hither, lady,
I will not altogether rest ingrateful; [*Offers ruby.*]
Here, wear this ruby for thy pains and counsel.

COURTESAN. It is not so much worth, sir. I am a very ill counsellor, truly.

HAREBRAIN. Go to, I say.

COURTESAN. Y'are to blame, i'faith, sir; I shall ne'er deserve it.

HAREBRAIN. Thou hast done't already. Farewell, sweet virgin, prithee let's see thee oft'ner.

COURTESAN. [*aside*] Such gifts will soon entreat me.

Exit.

HAREBRAIN. Wife, as thou lov'st the quiet of my breast,
Embrace her counsel, yield to her advices;
Thou wilt find comfort in 'em in the end,
Thou'lt feel an alteration; prithee think on't.
Mine eyes can scarce refrain.

MISTRESS HAREBRAIN. Keep in your dew, sir, lest when you would, you want it.

HAREBRAIN. I've pawn'd my credit on't. Ah, didst thou know
The sweet fruit once, thou'dst never let it go.

MISTRESS HAREBRAIN. 'Tis that I strive to get.

HAREBRAIN. And still do so.

Exeunt.

---

143 *ringworm*: The circular patches on the skin caused by this disease resembled the 'French crown' or *corona Veneris* caused by syphilis, woman's 'requital' for sin.

144 *pit-hole*: Hell/the female pudendum.

145 *squall*: a small insignificant person; but used as an endearment to a woman.

165 *refrain*: i.e. from weeping.

169 *sweet fruit*: fruits of repentance//of sexual pleasure (with allusion to Eve's apple).

ACT II

SCENE I

Enter SIR BOUNTEOUS *with two* KNIGHTS.

FIRST KNIGHT. You have been too much like your name, Sir Bounteous.

SIR BOUNTEOUS. Oh not so, good knights, not so, you know my humour; most welcome, good Sir Andrew Polcut, Sir Aquitaine Colewort, most welcome.

BOTH. Thanks, good Sir Bounteous. *Exeunt at one door.*

At the other, enter in haste a FOOTMAN.

FOOTMAN. Oh, cry your worship heartily mercy, sir.

SIR BOUNTEOUS. How now, linen stockings and three-score-mile-a-day, whose footman art thou?

FOOTMAN. Pray can your worship tell me [*Panting*] hoh, hoh, hoh – if my lord be come in yet?

SIR BOUNTEOUS. Thy lord! What lord?

FOOTMAN. My Lord Owemuch, sir.

SIR BOUNTEOUS. My Lord Owemuch! I have heard much speech of that lord; h'as great acquaintance i'th'city. That lord has been much followed.

FOOTMAN. And is still, sir; he wants no company when he's in London. He's free of the mercers, and there's none of 'em all dare cross him.

SIR BOUNTEOUS. And they did, he'd turn over a new leaf with 'em; he would make 'em all weary on't i'th' end.

---

4 *humour*: disposition.

5 *Polcut . . . Aquitaine Colewort*: 'Polecat' because of its fetid smell became a term of abuse, especially for the lecherous; presumably imported colewort, or cabbage, also smelt offensive.

8–9 *threescore-mile-a-day*: A running footman ran before his master's coach, covering considerable distances.

18 *free of the mercers*: literally, a freeman of the clothsellers' guild; but since 'being in the mercer's book' was used proverbially in the period of the debts of a gallant, the sense is that Owemuch is heavily in debt.

19 *cross him*: thwart him/cancel his debts by drawing lines across the page.

20 *turn over a new leaf*: make a new start/open a fresh account.

Much fine rumour have I heard of that lord, yet had I never the fortune to set eye upon him. Art sure he will alight here, footman? I am afraid thou'rt mistook.

FOOTMAN. Thinks your worship so, sir? By your leave, sir. [*He withdraws.*]

SIR BOUNTEOUS. Puh! Passion of me, footman! Why, pumps, I say, come back!

FOOTMAN. Does your worship call?

SIR BOUNTEOUS. Come hither, I say. I am but afraid on't; would it might happen so well. How dost know? Did he name the house with the great turret a'th' top?

FOOTMAN. No, faith, did he not, sir.

SIR BOUNTEOUS. Come hither, I say. Did he speak of a cloth a'gold chamber?

FOOTMAN. Not one word, by my troth, sir.

SIR BOUNTEOUS. Come again, you lousy seven-mile-an-hour.

FOOTMAN. I beseech your worship, detain me not.

SIR BOUNTEOUS. Was there no talk of a fair pair of organs, a great gilt candlestick, and a pair of silver snuffers?

FOOTMAN. 'Twere sin to belie my lord; I heard no such words, sir.

SIR BOUNTEOUS. A pox confine thee, come again! Puh!

FOOTMAN. Your worship will undo me, sir.

SIR BOUNTEOUS. Was there no speech of a long dining room, a huge kitchen, large meat, and a broad dresser board?

FOOTMAN. I have a greater maw to that, indeed, an't please your worship.

SIR BOUNTEOUS. Whom did he name?

FOOTMAN. Why, one Sir Bounteous Progress.

SIR BOUNTEOUS. Ah, a, a, I am that Sir Bounteous, you progressive roundabout rascal!

FOOTMAN. (*laughs*) Puh!

SIR BOUNTEOUS. I knew I should have him i'th' end; there's not a lord will miss me, I thank their good

---

28 *pumps*: alluding to the footman's running shoes.

40–1 *pair of organs . . . pair of silver snuffers*: a *single* organ . . . an instrument for snuffing candles.

47–8 *dresser board*: a kitchen table for the preparation of food.

49 *maw*: appetite, inclination.

54 *progressive*: because he accompanies his lord on 'progresses', tours in which the noble lives off friends and vassals.

honours; 'tis a fortune laid upon me, they can scent out their best entertainment; I have a kind of complimental gift given me above ordinary country knights, and how soon 'tis smelt out! I warrant ye, there's not one knight i'th' shire able to entertain a lord i'th' cue, or a lady i'th' nick like me, like me. There's a kind of grace belongs to't, a kind of art which naturally slips from me, I know not on't, I promise you, 'tis gone before I'm aware on't. Cuds me, I forget myself. Where?

[*Enter two* SERVANTS.]

FIRST SERVANT. Does your worship call?

SIR BOUNTEOUS. Run, sirrah, call in my chief gentleman i'th' chain of gold, expedite. [*Exit* FIRST SERVANT.] And how does my good lord? I never saw him before in my life. – A cup of bastard for this footman.

FOOTMAN. My lord has travell'd this five year, sir.

SIR BOUNTEOUS. Travail'd this five year? How many children has he? – Some bastard, I say!

FOOTMAN. No bastard, an't please your worship.

SIR BOUNTEOUS. A cup of sack to strengthen his wit.

[*Exit* SECOND SERVANT.]

The footman's a fool.

[*Enter* GUNWATER.]

Oh, come hither, Master Gunwater, come hither. Send presently to Master Pheasant for one of his hens; there's partridge i'th' house.

59–60 *complimental*: that which supplies all needs /complimentary.

62–3 *i'th'cue . . . i'th'nick*: *i'th'nick* = 'to perfection' and also 'at the critical moment', *i'th'cue* presumably has a similar meaning; but there are bawdy puns, since *cue* is the French 'queue', glossed by Cotgrave, *A Dictionarie of the French and English Tongues* (1611) as 'the bauble of a man', and *nick* is a variant of 'nock' = the female pudendum.

66 *Cuds me*: a mild oath.

70 *chain of gold*: the sign of the steward's office.

72–5 *bastard*: a sweet Spanish wine (the Footman misunderstands the call as an assertion that his master has illegitimate children).

73–4 *travell'd . . . Travail'd*: a frequent pun on 'travel' and 'to labour in childbirth'.

77 *sack*: white wine from Spain and the Canaries.

GUNWATER. And wild duck, an't please your worship.

SIR BOUNTEOUS. And woodcock, an't please thy worship.

GUNWATER. And woodcock, an't please your worship. I had thought to have spoke before you.

SIR BOUNTEOUS. Remember the pheasant, down with some plover, clap down six woodcocks: my lord's coming. Now, sir?

GUNWATER. An't please your worship, there's a lord and his followers newly alighted.

SIR BOUNTEOUS. Dispatch, I say, dispatch! Why, where's my music? He's come indeed.

Enter FOLLYWIT *like a lord with his comrades in blue coats.*

FOLLYWIT. Footman.

FOOTMAN. My lord?

FOLLYWIT. Run swiftly with my commendations to Sir Jasper Topaz; we'll ride and visit him i'th' morning, say.

FOOTMAN. Your lordship's charge shall be effected. *Exit.*

FOLLYWIT. That courtly, comely form should present to me Sir Bounteous Progress.

SIR BOUNTEOUS. Y'ave found me out, my lord; I cannot hide myself. Your honour is most spaciously welcome.

FOLLYWIT. In this forgive me, sir,
That being a stranger to your houses and you,
I make my way so bold, and presume
Rather upon your kindness than your knowledge;
Only your bounteous disposition
Fame hath divulg'd, and is to me well known.

SIR BOUNTEOUS. Nay, and your lordship know my disposition, you know me better than they that know my person; your honour is so much the welcomer for that.

FOLLYWIT. Thanks, good Sir Bounteous.

SIR BOUNTEOUS. Pray pardon me, it has been often my ambition, my lord, both in respect of your honourable presence, and the prodigal fame that keeps even stroke with your unbounded worthiness,

---

83 *woodcock*: a bird proverbial for its foolishness, and an epithet for a simpleton; hence Sir Bounteous's reply.

87 *lord's*: See Textual note, p. 400.

To have wish'd your lordship where your lordship is,
A noble guest in this unworthy seat.
Your lordship ne'er heard my organs?

FOLLYWIT. Heard of 'em, Sir Bounteous, but never heard 'em.

SIR BOUNTEOUS. They're but double gilt, my lord; some hundred and fifty pound will fit your lordship with such another pair.

FOLLYWIT. Indeed, Sir Bounteous?

SIR BOUNTEOUS. O my lord, I have a present suit to you.

FOLLYWIT. To me, Sir Bounteous? And you could ne'er speak at fitter time, for I'm here present to grant you.

SIR BOUNTEOUS. Your lordship has been a traveller?

FOLLYWIT. Some five year, sir.

SIR BOUNTEOUS. I have a grandchild, my lord. I love him, and when I die I'll do somewhat for him. I'll tell your honour the worst of him: a wild lad he has been.

FOLLYWIT. So we have been all, sir.

SIR BOUNTEOUS. So we have been all indeed, my lord; I thank your lordship's assistance. Some comic pranks he has been guilty of, but I'll pawn my credit for him, an honest, trusty bosom.

FOLLYWIT. And that's worth all, sir.

SIR BOUNTEOUS. And that's worth all indeed, my lord, for he's like to have all when I die. *Imberbis juvenis*, his chin has no more prickles yet than a midwife's; there's great hope of his wit, his hair's so long a-coming. Shall I be bold with your honour to prefer this aforesaid Ganymede to hold a plate under your lordship's cup?

FOLLYWIT. You wrong both his worth and your bounty, and you call that boldness. Sir, I have heard much good of that young gentleman.

---

127 *present suit*: immediate request.

142 *Imberbis juvenis*: 'beardless youth', a tag from Horace's *Ars Poetica*, line 161, where the context is appropriate: 'The beardless youth, free at last from his tutor, delights in horse and hound and in the grass of the sunny field'.

143 *midwife*: used of an effeminate man.

144–5 *great hope . . . long a-coming*: An allusion to the proverb 'Long hair and short wit', B.J. & H.W. Whiting, *Proverbs, Sentences and Proverbial Phrases* (Harvard, 1968), H 23.

146 *Ganymede*: the beautiful youth abducted by Zeus to serve as his cupbearer; hence, an effeminate youth.

SIR BOUNTEOUS. Nay, h'as a good wit, i'faith, my lord.

FOLLYWIT. H'as carried himself always generously.

SIR BOUNTEOUS. Are you advis'd of that, my lord? H'as carried many things cleanly. I'll show your lordship my will; I keep it above in an outlandish box. The whoreson boy must have all; I love him, yet he shall ne'er find it as long as I live.

FOLLYWIT. Well, sir, for your sake and his own deserving, I'll reserve a place for him nearest to my secrets.

SIR BOUNTEOUS. I understand your good lordship, you'll make him your secretary. My music, give my lord a taste of his welcome.

A strain play'd by the consort, SIR BOUNTEOUS *makes a courtly honour to that lord and seems to foot the tune.*

SIR BOUNTEOUS. So, how like you our airs, my lord? Are they choice?

FOLLYWIT. They're seldom match'd, believe it.

SIR BOUNTEOUS. The consort of mine own household.

FOLLYWIT. Yea, sir.

SIR BOUNTEOUS. The musicians are in ordinary, yet no ordinary musicians. Your lordship shall hear my organs now.

FOLLYWIT. Oh, I beseech you, Sir Bounteous.

SIR BOUNTEOUS. My organist!

The organs play, and cover'd dishes march over the stage.

Come, my lord, how does your honour relish my organ?

FOLLYWIT. A very proud air, i'faith, sir.

SIR BOUNTEOUS. Oh, how can't choose? A Walloon plays upon 'em, and a Welshman blows wind in their breech.

Exeunt.

A song to the organs.

---

155 *outlandish*: of foreign fashion.

159 *secrets*: private affairs/private parts.

s.d. *consort*: a company of musicians; *honour*: a bow.

168 *in ordinary*: part of the regular staff.

176–7 *Walloon . . . Welshman*: The Flemish were renowned for their musicianship, the Welsh for bragging (and for farting?).

SCENE II

Enter SIR BOUNTEOUS *with* FOLLYWIT *and his consorts* [MAWWORM, HOBOY *and others*] *toward his lodging.*

SIR BOUNTEOUS. You must pardon us, my lord, hasty cates. Your honour has had ev'n a hunting meal on't, and now I am like to bring your lordship to as mean a lodging: a hard down bed, i'faith, my lord, poor cambric sheets, and a cloth a' tissue canopy. The curtains indeed were wrought in Venice, with the story of the Prodigal child in silk and gold; only the swine are left out, my lord, for spoiling the curtains.

FOLLYWIT. 'Twas well prevented, sir.

SIR BOUNTEOUS. Silken rest, harmonious slumbers, and venereal dreams to your lordship.

FOLLYWIT. The like to kind Sir Bounteous.

SIR BOUNTEOUS. Fie, not to me, my lord. I'm old, past dreaming of such vanities.

FOLLYWIT. Old men should dream best.

SIR BOUNTEOUS. They're dreams indeed, my lord, y'ave gi'n't us. Tomorrow your lordship shall see my cocks, my fish ponds, my park, my champion grounds; I keep chambers in my house can show your lordship some pleasure.

FOLLYWIT. Sir Bounteous, you ev'n whelm me with delights.

SIR BOUNTEOUS. Once again a musical night to your honour; I'll trouble your lordship no more. *Exit.*

FOLLYWIT. Good rest, Sir Bounteous. – So, come, the vizards; where be the masquing suits?

MAWWORM. In your lordship's portmantua.

---

s.d. *consorts*: companions.

2 *cates*: provisions, food.
hunting meal: i.e. 'a rough-and-ready repast'; in fact, often lavish.

5 *cambric*: fine white linen; *cloth a'tissue*: a rich cloth, often interwoven with gold or silver.

7 *Prodigal child*: ironically appropriate, since the prodigal in Luke 15.11–32 'wasted his substance with riotous living'.

18–19 *champion grounds*: open fields; *chambers*: See Textual note, p. 400.

26 *vizards*: masks.

27 *portmantua*: portmanteau, travelling bag.

FOLLYWIT. Peace, lieutenant.
MAWWORM. I had rather have war, captain.
FOLLYWIT. Puh, the plot's ripe. Come, to our business, lad;
Though guilt condemns, 'tis gilt must make us glad.
MAWWORM. Nay, and you be at your distinctions, captain, I'll follow behind no longer.
FOLLYWIT. Get you before then, and whelm your nose with your vizard; go.

[*Exit* MAWWORM *and others.*]

Now, grandsire, you that hold me at hard meat
And keep me out at the dag's end, I'll fit you.
Under his lordship's leave, all must be mine,
He and his will confesses. What I take, then,
Is but a borrowing of so much beforehand.
I'll pay him again when he dies, in so many blacks;
I'll have the church hung round with a noble a yard,
Or requite him in scutcheons. Let him trap me
In gold, and I'll lap him in lead: *quid pro quo*. I
Must look none of his angels in the face, forsooth,
Until his face be not worth looking on. Tut, lads,
Let sires and grandsires keep us low, we must
Live when they're flesh as well as when they're dust.

Exit.

SCENE III

Enter COURTESAN *with her man.*

COURTESAN. Go, sirrah, run presently to Master Penitent Brothel; you know his lodging, knock him up; I know he cannot sleep for sighing.

---

31 *gilt*: gold, money.
32 *your distinctions*: punning on the nonce-word 'de-stink-shuns' = farts, and probably pointed by a gesture.
34 *whelm*: cover, engulf.
36 *dag's end*: at a distance (a dag was a heavy pistol).
40 *blacks*: funeral hangings.
41 *a noble a yard*: expensive cloth, since a gold noble was worth a third of £1.
42 *scutcheons*: hatchments, square or lozenge-shaped tablets for exhibiting the coat of arms of the deceased, and hung over his door; *trap*: adorn, clothe.
43 *lap him in lead*: wrap him in lead for burial; *quid pro quo*: tit for tat.

Tell him I've happily bethought a mean
To make his purpose prosper in each limb,
Which only rests to be approv'd by him.
Make haste, I know he thirsts for't.

Exeunt.

SCENE IV

[A CRY] WITHIN. Oh!

Enter, in a masquing suit with a vizard in his hand, FOLLYWIT.

FOLLYWIT. Hark, they're at their business.

FIRST [GENTLEMAN *within*]. Thieves, thieves!

FOLLYWIT. Gag that gaping rascal! Though he be my grandsire's chief gentleman i'th' chain of gold, I'll have no pity of him. How now, lads?

Enter the rest, [MAWWORM, HOBOY *and others*], *vizarded.*

MAWWORM. All's sure and safe. On with your vizard, sir; the servants are all bound.

FOLLYWIT. There's one care past, then. Come, follow me, lads, I'll lead you now to th' point and top of all your fortunes. Yon lodging is my grandsire's.

MAWWORM. So, so, lead on, on.

HOBOY. Here's a captain worth the following, and a wit worth a man's love and admiring.

[*Exeunt.*]

[*Re-*] *enter* [FOLLYWIT, MAWWORM, HOBOY *and others*] *with* SIR BOUNTEOUS *in his night-gown.*

SIR BOUNTEOUS. O gentlemen, and you be kind gentlemen, what countrymen are you?

FOLLYWIT. Lincolnshire men, sir.

SIR BOUNTEOUS. I am glad of that, i'faith.

FOLLYWIT. And why should you be glad of that?

SIR BOUNTEOUS. Oh, the honestest thieves of all come out of Lincolnshire, the kindest natur'd gentlemen;

20–1 *honestest thieves . . . out of Lincolnshire*: i.e. Robin Hood and his men, who though chiefly associated with Nottinghamshire, dressed in Lincoln green.

they'll rob a man with conscience, they have a feeling of what they go about, and will steal with tears in their eyes: ah, pitiful gentlemen.

FOLLYWIT. Push! Money, money, we come for money.

SIR BOUNTEOUS. Is that all you come for? Ah, what a beast was I to put out my money t'other day. Alas, good gentlemen, what shift shall I make for you? Pray come again another time.

FOLLYWIT. Tut, tut, sir, money.

SIR BOUNTEOUS. Oh, not so loud, sir, you're too shrill a gentleman. I have a lord lies in my house; I would not for the world his honour should be disquieted.

FOLLYWIT. Who, my Lord Owemuch? We have took order with him beforehand; he lies bound in his bed, and all his followers.

SIR BOUNTEOUS. Who? My lord? Bound my lord? Alas, what did you mean to bind my lord? He could keep his bed well enough without binding. Y'ave undone me in't already, you need rob me no farder.

FOLLYWIT. Which is the key, come?

SIR BOUNTEOUS. Ah, I perceive now y'are no true Lincolnshire spirits; you come rather out of Bedford-shire: we cannot lie quiet in our beds for you. So, take enough, my masters; spur a free horse, my name's Sir Bounteous. A merry world, i' faith; what knight but I keep open house at midnight? Well, there should be a conscience, if one could hit upon't.

FOLLYWIT. Away now; seize upon him, bind him.

SIR BOUNTEOUS. Is this your court of equity? Why should I be bound for mine own money? But come, come, bind me, I have need on't; I have been too liberal to-night. Keep in my hands; nay, as hard as you list. I am [not] too good to bear my lord company. You have watch'd your time, my masters; I was knighted at Westminster, but many of these nights will make me a

---

27 *put out*: invest.
28 *shift*: expedient provision.
34–5 *took order with*: taken care of.
45 *spur a free horse*: an allusion to the proverb 'Do not spur a free (i.e. willing) horse' (Tilley, H 638).
51 *bound*: tied up/put under legal obligation.
55–6 *at Westminster*: i.e. at Court rather than on the battlefield.

knight of Windsor. Y'ave deserv'd so well, my masters, I bid you all to dinner tomorrow; I would I might have your companies, i' faith; I desire no more.

FOLLYWIT. Oh ho, sir! [*Finds more treasure.*]

SIR BOUNTEOUS. Pray meddle not with my organs, to put 'em out of tune.

FOLLYWIT. Oh no, here's better music.

SIR BOUNTEOUS. Ah, pox feast you!

FOLLYWIT. Dispatch with him, away. [*Exeunt* HOBOY *and others carrying* SIR BOUNTEOUS] So, thank you, good grandsire; this was bounteously done of him, i' faith. It came somewhat hard from him at first, for indeed nothing comes stiff from an old man but money; and he may well stand upon that when he has nothing else to stand upon. Where's our portmantua?

MAWWORM. Here, bully captain.

FOLLYWIT. In with the purchase, 'twill lie safe enough there under's nose, I warrant you. What, is all sure?

Enter ANCIENT [HOBOY *and others*].

HOBOY. All's sure, captain.

FOLLYWIT. You know what follows now: one villain binds his fellows. Go, we must be all bound for our own securities, rascals, there's no dallying upo'th' point. You conceit me: there is a lord to be found bound in the morning, and all his followers; can you pick out that lord now?

MAWWORM. Oh admirable spirit!

FOLLYWIT. You ne'er plot for your safeties, so your wants be satisfied.

HOBOY. But if we bind one another, how shall the last man be bound?

FOLLYWIT. Pox on't, I'll have the footman 'scape.

FOOTMAN. That's I; I thank you, sir.

---

57 *knight of Windsor*: one of a body of military pensioners residing within the precincts of Windsor Castle.

70–1 *stand upon*: insist on/trust in, rely on (with an obscene innuendo, as in line 69).

73 *purchase*: booty.

77–8 *bound for our own securities*: punning on the meaning 'be placed under legal obligation on our own recognisances'.

79 *conceit*: understand.

FOLLYWIT. The footman, of all other, will be suppos'd to 'scape, for he comes in no bed all night, but lies in's clothes to be first ready i'th' morning. The horse and he lies in litter together; that's the right fashion of your bonny footman. And his freedom will make the better for our purpose, for we must have one i'th' morning to unbind the knight, that we may have our sport within ourselves. We now arrive at the most ticklish point, to rob and take our ease, to be thieves and lie by't. Look to't, lads, it concerns every man's gullet; I'll not have the jest spoil'd, that's certain, though it hazard a windpipe. I'll either go like a lord as I came, or be hang'd like a thief as I am; and that's my resolution.

MAWWORM. Troth, a match, captain, of all hands.

Exeunt.

SCENE V

Enter COURTESAN *with* MASTER PENITENT BROTHEL.

COURTESAN. Oh, Master Penitent Brothel!

PENITENT. What is't, sweet Lady Gullman, that so seizes on thee with rapture and admiration?

COURTESAN. A thought, a trick, to make you, sir, especially happy, and yet I myself a saver by it.

PENITENT. I would embrace that, lady, with such courage I would not leave you on the losing hand.

COURTESAN. I will give trust to you, sir, the cause then why I rais'd you from your bed so soon, wherein I know sighs would not let you sleep; thus understand it:
You love that woman, Master Harebrain's wife,
Which no invented means can crown with freedom
For your desires and her own wish but this,
Which in my slumbers did present itself.

PENITENT. I'm covetous, lady.

COURTESAN. You know her husband, ling'ring in suspect, Locks her from all society but mine.

PENITENT. Most true.

COURTESAN. I only am admitted, yet hitherto that has done you no real happiness: by my admittance I cannot perform that deed that should please you, you know. Wherefore thus I've convey'd it, I'll counterfeit a fit of violent sickness.

PENITENT. Good.

COURTESAN. Nay, 'tis not so good, by my faith, but to do you good.

PENITENT. And in that sense I call'd it. But take me with you, lady; would it be probable enough to have a sickness so suddenly violent?

COURTESAN. Puh, all the world knows women are soon down; we can be sick when we have a mind to't, catch an ague with the wind of our fans, surfeit upon the rump of a lark, and bestow ten pound in physic upon't; we're likest ourselves when we're down. 'Tis the easiest art and cunning for our sect to counterfeit sick, that are always full of fits when we are well; for since we were made for a weak, imperfect creature, we can fit that best that we are made for. I thus translated, and yourself slipp'd into the form of a physician –

PENITENT. I a physician, lady? Talk not on't, I beseech you; I shall shame the whole college.

COURTESAN. Tut, man, any quacksalving terms will serve for this purpose; for I am pitifully haunted with a brace of elder brothers, new perfum'd in the first of their fortunes, and I shall see how forward their purses will be to the pleasing of my palate, and restoring of my health. Lay on load enough upon 'em, and spare 'em not, for they're good, plump, fleshy asses, and may well enough bear it. Let gold, amber, and dissolved pearl be common ingrediences and that you cannot

---

23 *convey'd it*: craftily managed it.
28–9 *take me with you*: 'let me understand you'.
36 *sect*: sex.
37 *fits*: sudden seizures, probably hysterical, or moods.
39 *translated*: transformed.
43 *college*: the College of Physicians, founded 1518 to be an examining and qualifying body, so as to check superstition and quackery.

compose a cullis without 'em. Put but this cunningly in practice, it shall be both a sufficient recompense for all my pains in your love, and the ready means to make Mistress Harebrain way, by the visiting of me, to your mutual desired company.

PENITENT. I applaud thee, kiss thee, and will constantly embrace it.

Exeunt.

SCENE VI

Voices within. [FOLLYWIT *bound, behind curtains.*]

SIR BOUNTEOUS. Ho, Gunwater!
FOLLYWIT. Singlestone!
(WITHIN). Jenkin, wa, ha, ho!
(WITHIN). Ewen!
(WITHIN). Simcod!
FOLLYWIT. Footman! Whew!

Enter SIR BOUNTEOUS *with a cord, half unbound,* FOOTMAN *with him.*

FOOTMAN. Oh, good your worship, let me help your good old worship.

SIR BOUNTEOUS. Ah, poor honest footman, how didst thou 'scape this massacre?

FOOTMAN. E'en by miracle, and lying in my clothes, sir.

SIR BOUNTEOUS. I think so; I would I had lain in my clothes too, footman, so I had 'scap'd 'em; I could have but risse like a beggar then, and so I do now, till more money come in. But nothing afflicts me so much, my poor geometrical footman, as that the barbarous villains should lay violence upon my lord. Ah, the binding of my lord cuts my heart in two pieces. [*He is released*] So, so, 'tis well, I thank thee; run to thy fellows, undo 'em, undo 'em, undo 'em.

FOOTMAN. Alas, if my lord should miscarry, they're unbound already, sir; they have no occupation but

---

53 *cullis*: a strong meat broth, boiled and strained.
14 *risse*: a variant form of 'risen'.
16 *geometrical*: 'ground measuring'.
21–2 *unbound*: discharged from their employment.

sleep, feed, and fart. *Exit.*

SIR BOUNTEOUS. If I be not asham'd to look my lord i'th' face, I'm a Saracen. My lord –

FOLLYWIT. [*within curtains*] Who's that?

SIR BOUNTEOUS. One may see he has been scar'd. A pox on 'em for their labours!

FOLLYWIT. Singlestone!

SIR BOUNTEOUS. Singlestone? I'll ne'er answer to that, i'faith.

FOLLYWIT. Suchman!

SIR BOUNTEOUS. Suchman? Nor that neither, i' faith; I am not brought so low, though I be old.

FOLLYWIT. Who's that i'th' chamber?

SIR BOUNTEOUS. [*opens curtains*] Good morrow, my lord, 'tis I.

FOLLYWIT. Sir Bounteous, good morrow; I would give you my hand, sir, but I cannot come at it. Is this the courtesy a'th' country, Sir Bounteous?

SIR BOUNTEOUS. Your lordship grieves me more than all my loss;
'Tis the unnatural'st sight that can be found
To see a noble gentleman hard bound.

FOLLYWIT. Trust me, I thought you had been better belov'd, Sir Bounteous; but I see you have enemies, sir, and your friends fare the worse for 'em. I like your talk better than your lodging; I ne'er lay harder in a bed of down; I have had a mad night's rest on't. Can you not guess what they should be, Sir Bounteous?

SIR BOUNTEOUS. Faith, Lincolnshire men, my lord.

FOLLYWIT. How? Fie, fie, believe it not, sir; these lie not far off, I warrant you.

SIR BOUNTEOUS. Think you so, my lord?

FOLLYWIT. I'll be burnt and they do; some that use to your house, sir, and are familiar with all the conveyances.

---

29 *Singlestone*: i.e. 'One Testicle'.

32 *Suchman*: presumably meaning 'Impotent'; or perhaps foul case for 'Suckman', i.e. fellator, which makes better sense of Sir Bounteous's reply.

43 *hard bound*: tied fast//constipated.

55–6 *conveyances*: passages.

SIR BOUNTEOUS. This is the commodity of keeping open house, my lord, that makes so many shut their doors about dinner time.

FOLLYWIT. They were resolute villains. I made myself known to 'em, told 'em what I was, gave 'em my honourable word not to disclose 'em –

SIR BOUNTEOUS. Oh saucy, unmannerly villains!

FOLLYWIT. And think you the slaves would trust me upon my word?

SIR BOUNTEOUS. They would not?

FOLLYWIT. Forsooth, no. I must pardon 'em; they told me lords' promises were mortal, and commonly die within half an hour after they are spoken; they were but gristles, and not one amongst a hundred come to any full growth or perfection, and therefore though I were a lord, I must enter into bond.

SIR BOUNTEOUS. Insupportable rascals!

FOLLYWIT. Troth, I'm of that mind, Sir Bounteous. You far'd the worse for my coming hither.

SIR BOUNTEOUS. Ah, good my lord, but I'm sure your lordship far'd the worse.

FOLLYWIT. Pray pity not me, sir.

SIR BOUNTEOUS. Is not your honour sore about the brawn of the arm? A murrain meet 'em, I feel it.

FOLLYWIT. About this place, Sir Bounteous?

SIR BOUNTEOUS. You feel as it were a twinge, my lord?

FOLLYWIT. Ay, e'en a twinge; you say right.

SIR BOUNTEOUS. A pox discover 'em, that twinge I feel too.

FOLLYWIT. But that which disturbs me most, Sir Bounteous, lies here.

SIR BOUNTEOUS. True, about the wrist, a kind of tumid numbness.

FOLLYWIT. You say true, sir.

---

57 *commodity*: profit.

70 *gristles*: tender and delicate things, like children's bones.

72 *enter into bond*: be tied up/submit to a legal bond. As a peer, and therefore a member of the upper house of Parliament, a lord could not be summonsed to appear in court, be sued for debt or committed to prison for it.

80 *murrain*: plague.

SIR BOUNTEOUS. The reason of that, my lord, is the pulses had no play.
FOLLYWIT. Mass, so I guess'd it.
SIR BOUNTEOUS. A mischief swell 'em, for I feel that too.

[*Enter* MAWWORM.]

MAWWORM. 'Slid, here's a house haunted indeed.
SIR BOUNTEOUS. [*to* MAWWORM] A word with you, sir.
FOLLYWIT. How now, Singlestone?
MAWWORM. I'm sorry, my lord, your lordship has lost –
SIR BOUNTEOUS. Pup, pup, pup, pup, pup!
FOLLYWIT. What have I lost? Speak!
SIR BOUNTEOUS. A good night's sleep, say.
FOLLYWIT. Speak, what have I lost, I say.
MAWWORM. A good night's sleep, my lord, nothing else.
FOLLYWIT. That's true. My clothes, come!

Curtains drawn.

MAWWORM. My lord's clothes! His honour's rising.
SIR BOUNTEOUS. Hist, well said. [*Aside, to* MAWWORM] Come hither; what has my lord lost, tell me? Speak softly.
MAWWORM. His lordship must know that, sir.
SIR BOUNTEOUS. Hush, prithee tell me.
MAWWORM. 'Twill do you no pleasure to know't, sir.
SIR BOUNTEOUS. Yet again? I desire it, I say.
MAWWORM. Since your worship will needs know't, they have stol'n away a jewel in a blue silk riband of a hundred pound price, beside some hundred pounds in fair spur-royals.
SIR BOUNTEOUS. That's some two hundred i'th' total.
MAWWORM. Your worship's much about it, sir.
SIR BOUNTEOUS. Come, follow me; I'll make that whole again in so much money. Let not my lord know on't.
MAWWORM. Oh, pardon me, Sir Bounteous, that were a dishonour to my lord; should it come to his ear, I should hazard my undoing by it.
SIR BOUNTEOUS. How should it come to his ear? If you be my lord's chief man about him, I hope you do not use to speak unless you be paid for't; and I had rather

---

116 *spur-royals*: gold coins worth three quarters of £1, having a blazing sun on the reverse which resembled the rowel of a spur.

give you a counsellor's double fee to hold your peace. Come, go to; follow me, I say.

MAWWORM. There will be scarce time to tell it, sir; my lord will away instantly.

SIR BOUNTEOUS. His honour shall stay dinner, by his leave; I'll prevail with him so far. And now I remember a jest: I bade the whoreson thieves to dinner last night. I would I might have their companies, a pox poison 'em!

MAWWORM. [*aside*] Faith, and you are like to have no other guests, Sir Bounteous, if you have none but us; I'll give you that gift, i' faith.

Exeunt.

ACT III

SCENE I

Enter MASTER HAREBRAIN *with two elder brothers,* MASTER INESSE *and* MASTER POSSIBILITY.

POSSIBILITY. You see bold guests, Master Harebrain.

HAREBRAIN. You're kindly welcome to my house, good Master Inesse and Master Possibility.

INESSE. That's our presumption, sir.

HAREBRAIN. Rafe!

[*Enter* RAFE.]

RAFE. Here, sir.

HAREBRAIN. Call down your mistress to welcome these two gentlemen my friends.

RAFE. I shall, sir. *Exit.*

HAREBRAIN. [*aside*] I will observe her carriage, and watch
The slippery revolutions of her eye;
I'll lie in wait for every glance she gives,

127 *counsellor's double fee*: The chief counsel in legal actions took double fees; cf. Jonson, *Tale of a Tub*, I.v.54–6.

129 *tell*: count.

s.d. *Exeunt*: For directions for entertainment in the Act division from a Caroline performance, see Textual note, p. 400.

4 *That's our presumption*: 'So we presume'//'That's our arrogance.'

And poise her words i'th' balance of suspect.
If she but swag, she's gone: either on this hand
Overfamiliar, or this too neglectful;
It does behove her carry herself even.

POSSIBILITY. But Master Harebrain –

HAREBRAIN. True, I hear you, sir; was't you said?

POSSIBILITY. I have not spoke it yet, sir.

HAREBRAIN. Right, so I say.

POSSIBILITY. Is it not strange that in so short a time my little Lady Gullman should be so violently handled?

HAREBRAIN. Oh, sickness has no mercy, sir:
It neither pities ladies' lip, nor eye;
It crops the rose out of the virgin's cheek,
And so deflow'rs her that was ne'er deflowr'd.
Fools, then, are maids to lock from men that treasure
Which death will pluck, and never yield 'em pleasure.
Ah, gentlemen, though I shadow it, that sweet virgin's sickness grieves me not lightly; she was my wife's only delight and company. Did you not hear her, gentlemen, i'th' midst of her extremest fit, still how she call'd upon my wife, rememb'red still my wife, 'sweet Mistress Harebrain'? When she sent for me, a' one side of her bed stood the physician, the scrivener on the other; two horrible objects, but mere opposites in the course of their lives, for the scrivener binds folks, and the physician makes them loose.

POSSIBILITY. But not loose of their bonds, sir?

HAREBRAIN. No, by my faith, sir, I say not so. If the physician could make 'em loose of their bonds, there's many a one would take physic that dares not now for poisoning. But as I was telling of you, her will was fashioning, wherein I found her best and richest jewel given as a legacy unto my wife. When I read that, I could not refrain weeping. Well, of all other, my wife has most reason to visit her; if she have any good nature in her, she'll show it there.

---

14 *swag*: sway, sink down.

26 *deflow'rs . . . deflowr'd*: a reminiscence of *Romeo and Juliet*, IV.v.37.

29 *shadow*: hide.

35 *scrivener*: a scribe and notary, who drew up legal documents; many also served as money-lenders.

38 *loose*: i.e. by administering purgatives.

[*Enter* RAFE.]

Now, sir, where's your mistress?

RAFE. She desires you and the gentlemen your friends to hold her excused: sh'as a fit of an ague now upon her, which begins to shake her.

HAREBRAIN. Where does it shake her most?

RAFE. All over her body, sir.

HAREBRAIN. Shake all her body? 'Tis a saucy fit; I'm jealous of that ague. Pray walk in, gentlemen, I'll see you instantly.

[*Exeunt* INESSE *and* POSSIBILITY.]

RAFE. Now they are absent, sir, 'tis no such thing.

HAREBRAIN. What?

RAFE. My mistress has her health, sir,
But 'tis her suit she may confine herself
From sight of all men but your own dear self, sir;
For since the sickness of that modest virgin,
Her only company, she delights in none.

HAREBRAIN. No? Visit her again, commend me to her,
Tell her they're gone, and only I myself
Walk here to exchange a word or two with her.

RAFE. I'll tell her so, sir. *Exit.*

HAREBRAIN. Fool that I am, and madman, beast! What worse?
Suspicious o'er a creature that deserves
The best opinion and the purest thought;
Watchful o'er her that is her watch herself;
To doubt her ways, that looks too narrowly
Into her own defects. I, foolish-fearful,
Have often rudely, out of giddy flames,
Barr'd her those objects which she shuns herself.
Thrice I've had proof of her most constant temper;
Come I at unawares by stealth upon her,
I find her circled in with divine writs
Of heavenly meditations; here and there
Chapters with leaves tuck'd up, which when I see,
They either tax pride or adultery.
Ah, let me curse myself, that could be jealous
Of her whose mind no sin can make rebellious.

---

51 *a fit of an ague*: the paroxysm of acute fever.
75 *giddy flames*: insane passion.
79 *writs*: writings.

And here the unmatched comes.

[*Enter* MISTRESS HAREBRAIN.]

Now wife, i' faith they're gone.
Push, see how fearful 'tis; will you not credit me?
They're gone, i'faith; why, think you I'll betray you?
Come, come, thy delight and mine, thy only virtuous friend, thy sweet instructress, is violently taken, grievous sick, and which is worse, she mends not.

MISTRESS HAREBRAIN. Her friends are sorry for that, sir.

HAREBRAIN. She calls still upon thee, poor soul, remembers thee still, thy name whirls in her breath. 'Where's Mistress Harebrain?' says she.

MISTRESS HAREBRAIN. Alas, good soul!

HAREBRAIN. She made me weep thrice; sh'as put thee in a jewel in her will.

MISTRESS HAREBRAIN. E'en to th' last gasp, a kind soul.

HAREBRAIN. Take my man, go, visit her.

MISTRESS HAREBRAIN. Pray pardon me, sir; alas, my visitation cannot help her.

HAREBRAIN. Oh, yet the kindness of a thing, wife. [*Aside*] Still she holds the same rare temper. – Take my man, I say.

MISTRESS HAREBRAIN. I would not take your man, sir, though I did purpose going.

HAREBRAIN. No? Thy reason?

MISTRESS HAREBRAIN. The world's condition is itself so vild, sir,
'Tis apt to judge the worst of those deserve not;
'Tis an ill-thinking age, and does apply
All to the form of it own luxury.
This censure flies from one, that from another;
'That man's her squire', says he; 'Her pimp', the t'other;
'She's of the stamp', a third; fourth, 'I ha' known her.'
I've heard this, not without a burning cheek.
Then our attires are tax'd, our very gait

---

108 *vild*: vile.

110–11 *apply . . . luxury*: judge all by the standard of its own lecherousness.

114 *of the stamp*: loose (because she 'goes the rounds', like current coinage; 'to be stamped' = to engender, to take an 'impression' from the man).

Is call'd in question, where a husband's presence
Scatters such thoughts, or makes 'em sink for fear
Into the hearts that breed 'em.
Nay, surely, if I went, sir, I would entreat your company.

HAREBRAIN. Mine? Prithee, wife, I have been there already.

MISTRESS HAREBRAIN. That's all one; although you bring me but to th' door, sir, I would entreat no farther.

HAREBRAIN. Thou'rt such a wife! Why, I will bring thee thither, then, but not go up, I swear.

MISTRESS HAREBRAIN. I' faith, you shall not; I do not desire it, sir.

HAREBRAIN. Why then, content.

MISTRESS HAREBRAIN. Give me your hand you will do so, sir?

HAREBRAIN. Why, there's my lip I will [*Kisses her*].

MISTRESS HAREBRAIN. Why then, I go, sir.

HAREBRAIN. With me or no man; incomparable, such a woman.

Exeunt.

SCENE II

Vials, gallipots, plate, and an hourglass by her. The COURTESAN *on a bed for her counterfeit fit. To her,* MASTER PENITENT BROTHEL, *like a doctor of physic.*

PENITENT. Lady!

COURTESAN. Ha, what news?

PENITENT. There's one Sir Bounteous Progress newly alighted from his foot-cloth, and his mare waits at door, as the fashion is.

COURTESAN. 'Slid, 'tis the knight that privately main-

---

s.d. *Vials, gallipots*: medium-sized vessels for holding liquids, and small earthen glazed pots used by apothecaries for ointments; *plate*: metal utensils.

4 *foot-cloth*: a richly ornamented cloth laid over the back of a horse and hanging to the ground on each side; considered a mark of dignity.

tains me. A little short old spiny gentleman in a great doublet?

PENITENT. The same; I know'm.

COURTESAN. He's my sole revenue, meat, drink, and raiment. My good physician, work upon him; I'm weak.

PENITENT. Enough.

[*Enter* SIR BOUNTEOUS.]

SIR BOUNTEOUS. Why, where be these ladies, these plump, soft, delicate creatures? Ha?

PENITENT. Who would you visit, sir?

SIR BOUNTEOUS. Visit? Who? What are you with the plague in your mouth?

PENITENT. A physician, sir.

SIR BOUNTEOUS. Then you are a loose liver, sir; I have put you to your purgation.

PENITENT. [*aside*] But you need none, you're purg'd in a worse fashion.

COURTESAN. Ah, Sir Bounteous.

SIR BOUNTEOUS. How now? What art thou?

COURTESAN. Sweet Sir Bounteous.

SIR BOUNTEOUS. Passion of me, what an alteration's here! Rosamond sick, old Harry? Here's a sight able to make an old man shrink; I was lusty when I came in, but I am down now, i' faith. Mortality! Yea, this puts me in mind of a hole seven foot deep, my grave, my grave, my grave. Hist, master doctor, a word, sir: hark, 'tis not the plague, is't?

PENITENT. The plague, sir? No.

SIR BOUNTEOUS. Good.

PENITENT. [*aside*] He ne'er asks whether it be the pox or no, and of the twain that had been more likely.

SIR BOUNTEOUS. How now, my wench? How dost?

---

7 *spiny*: spindly, thin and dry.

19 *loose liver*: an immoral person/one with a disordered liver (regarded as the seat of passion). Physicians were often suspected of irreligion.

20 *put you to your purgation*: 'put you to inner cleansing'/'laid on you the onus of clearing yourself of the accusation'.

27 *Rosamond sick, old Harry*: apparently a quotation from a lost ballad or play on the story of 'Fair Rosamond', Rosamond Clifford, the mistress of Henry II, supposedly poisoned by Queen Eleanor at Woodstock.

COURTESAN. [*coughs*] Huh – weak, knight – huh.

PENITENT. [*aside*] She says true: he's a weak knight indeed.

SIR BOUNTEOUS. Where does it hold thee most, wench?

COURTESAN. All parts alike, sir.

PENITENT. [*aside*] She says true still, for it holds her in none.

SIR BOUNTEOUS. Hark in thine ear, thou'rt breeding of young bones; I am afraid I have got thee with child, i' faith.

COURTESAN. I fear that much, sir.

SIR BOUNTEOUS. Oh, oh, if it should! A young Progress, when all's done.

COURTESAN. You have done your good will, sir.

SIR BOUNTEOUS. I see by her 'tis nothing but a surfeit of Venus, i' faith, and though I be old, I have gi'n't her. But since I had the power to make thee sick, I'll have the purse to make thee whole, that's certain. – Master doctor.

PENITENT. Sir?

SIR BOUNTEOUS. Let's hear, I pray, what is't you minister to her.

PENITENT. Marry, sir, some precious cordial, some costly refocillation, a composure comfortable and restorative.

SIR BOUNTEOUS. Ay, ay, that, that, that.

PENITENT. No poorer ingrediences than the liquor of coral; clear amber, or *succinum*; unicorn's horn, six grains; *magisterium perlarum*, one scruple –

52–3 *surfeit of Venus*: i.e. too much sex.

61 *refocillation*: refreshment, tonic.
composure: composition.

63–5 *liquor of coral*: a solution of coral in water (See Textual note, p. 400); *clear amber, or succinum*: white amber (spermacete), or yellow amber, cited by Pliny as beneficial for stomach ailments, ear and eye diseases (*Natural History*, XXXVII, ch. 3); *unicorn's horn*: the horn of the rhinoceros, narwhal, or other animal, reputedly derived from the unicorn, and regarded as an antidote to poison; *magisterium perlarum*: precipitate of pearls from an acid solution; *magisterium* being also the alchemical term for a potent curative agency; *scruple*: 20 grains, 1/24 of an oz. The ingredients are taken from contemporary *materia medica*, and their rarity and richness inspired faith in their cure-all properties.

SIR BOUNTEOUS. Ah!

PENITENT. *Ossis de corde cervi*, half a scruple; *aurum potabile* or his tincture –

SIR BOUNTEOUS. Very precious, sir.

PENITENT. All which being finely contunded and mixed in a stone or glass mortar with the spirit of diamber –

SIR BOUNTEOUS. Nay, pray be patient, sir.

PENITENT. That's impossible; I cannot be patient and a physician too, sir.

SIR BOUNTEOUS. Oh, cry you mercy, that's true, sir.

PENITENT. All which aforesaid –

SIR BOUNTEOUS. Ay, there you left, sir.

PENITENT. When it is almost exsiccate or dry, I add thereto *olei succini*, *olei masi*, and *cinnamoni.*

SIR BOUNTEOUS. So, sir, *olei masi*; that same oil of mace is a great comfort to both the Counters.

PENITENT. And has been of a long time, sir.

SIR BOUNTEOUS. Well, be of good cheer, wench; there's gold for thee. [*Gives money*] – Huh, let her want for nothing, master doctor; a poor kinswoman of mine; nature binds me to have care of her. [*Aside*] There I gull'd you, master doctor. – Gather up a good spirit, wench, the fit will away; 'tis but a surfeit of gristles. – Ha, ha, I have fitted her; an old knight and a cock a'th' game still; I have not spurs for nothing, I see.

67–8 *Ossis de corde cervi*: small bones in the heart and womb of a hind, regarded as beneficial to pregnant women and those in labour (Pliny, XXVIII, ch. 19); *aurum potabile*: nitro-muriate of gold deoxydised in a volatile oil and drunk as a cordial; *tincture*: essence.

70 *contunded*: pounded.

71 *spirit of diamber*: a stomachic and cordial containing ambergris, musk and other aromatics.

79 *olei succini, olei masi, and cinnamoni*: oils of yellow amber, mace, cinnamon.

80 *oil of mace*: a pun alluding to the maces carried by the serjeants when they arrested debtors, who might replenish either of the Counters, City prisons under the jurisdiction of the Sheriffs of London; a parallel coinage is 'oil of whip', proverbially beneficial against idleness.

89 *I have fitted her*: 'I've caused this fit'/'I've served her appropriately.'

89–90 *cock a'th'game . . . not spurs for nothing*: an allusion to cockfighting and the metal spurs attached to the legs of the birds, with a pun on *cock a'th'game* = a sexual adept. Taylor suggests *spurs* also means 'testicles'.

PENITENT. No, by my faith, they're hatch'd; they cost you an angel, sir.

SIR BOUNTEOUS. Look to her, good master doctor, let her want nothing. I've given her enough already, ha, ha, ha! *Exit.*

COURTESAN. So, is he gone?

PENITENT. He's like himself, gone.

COURTESAN. Here's somewhat to set up with. How soon he took occasion to slip into his own flattery, soothing his own defects. He only fears he has done that deed which I ne'er fear'd to come from him in my life. This purchase came unlook'd for.

PENITENT. Hist! The pair of sons and heirs.

COURTESAN. Oh, they're welcome; they bring money.

Enter MASTER INESSE *and* POSSIBILITY.

POSSIBILITY. Master doctor.

PENITENT. I come to you, gentlemen.

POSSIBILITY. How does she now?

PENITENT. Faith, much after one fashion, sir.

INESSE. There's hope of life, sir?

PENITENT. I see no signs of death of her.

POSSIBILITY. That's some comfort. Will she take anything yet?

PENITENT. Yes, yes, yes, she'll take still; sh'as a kind of facility in taking. How comes your band bloody, sir?

INESSE. You may see I met with a scab, sir.

PENITENT. *Diversa genera scabierum*, as Pliny reports, 'there are divers kind[s] of scabs'.

INESSE. Pray let's hear 'em, sir.

PENITENT. An itching scab, that is your harlot; a sore

---

91 *hatch'd*: as a chick (alluding to the child)/engraved (alluding to a knight's spurs, which were gilt, excessively large, and often ornamented).

102 *purchase*: profit, booty.

114 *taking*: used of the female admitting the male; also, a 'taker-up' is one who in a gang of swindlers attracts and softens up the victim.

band: a wide collar often worn with the ruff.

116 *Diversa genera scabierum*: 'Ulcers as they be of many sorts, so are they cured after divers manners' (Pliny, *Natural History* XXVI, ch. 14, trans. P. Holland, 1601). *scab*: a low person, a scoundrel.

scab, your usurer; a running, your promoter; a broad scab, your intelligencer; but a white scab, that's a scald knave and a pander. But to speak truth, the only scabs we are nowadays troubled withal, are new officers.

INESSE. Why, now you come to mine, sir, for I'll be sworn one of them was very busy about my head this morning; and he should be a scab by that, for they are ambitious and covet the head.

PENITENT. Why, you saw I deriv'd him, sir.

INESSE. You physicians are mad gentlemen.

PENITENT. We physicians see the most sights of any men living. Your astronomers look upward into th' air, we look downward into th' body, and indeed we have power upward and downward.

INESSE. That you have, i' faith, sir.

POSSIBILITY. Lady, how cheer you now?

COURTESAN. The same woman still – huh.

POSSIBILITY. That's not good. [*Gives money.*]

COURTESAN. Little alteration. Fie, fie, you have been too lavish, gentlemen.

INESSE. Puh, talk not of that, lady, thy health's worth a million. Here, master doctor, spare for no cost. [*Gives money.*]

POSSIBILITY. Look what you find there, sir.

COURTESAN. What do you mean, gentlemen? Put up, put up; you see I'm down and cannot strive with you; I would rule you else. You have me at advantage, but if

---

120 *promoter*: informer (a *running* scab because he carries tales); *intelligencer*: a spy, one who gathers and distributes information (hence, *broad scab*).

122 *scald*: one affected with a scabby skin disease (here, the pox)/ contemptible.

124 *officers*: constables.

126 *busy about my head*: i.e. he was struck over the head.

128 *covet the head*: they aspire to the post of headborough, a minor parish official, (with an allusion to the tendency of skin complaints to afflict the scalp).

129 *deriv'd him*: traced his lineage, alluding also to the medical term 'derive' = to withdraw inflammation etc. from a diseased part of the body by blistering, cupping etc.

134 *power upward and downward*: i.e. by emetic, laxative and enema.

144 *Put up*: 'put your money away'. The speech also has obscene innuendoes.

ever I live, I will requite it deeply.

INESSE. Tut, an't come to that once, we'll requite ourselves well enough.

POSSIBILITY. Mistress Harebrain, lady, is setting forth to visit you too.

COURTESAN. Ha? – huh.

PENITENT. [*aside*] There struck the minute that brings forth the birth of all my joys and wishes. But see the jar now! How shall I rid these from her?

COURTESAN. Pray, gentlemen, stay not above an hour from my sight.

INESSE. 'Sfoot, we are not going, lady.

PENITENT. [*aside*] Subtilly brought about, yet 'twill not do: they'll stick by't. – A word with you, gentlemen.

BOTH. What says master doctor?

PENITENT. She wants but settling of her sense with rest. One hour's sleep, gentlemen, would set all parts in tune.

POSSIBILITY. He says true, i' faith.

INESSE. Get her to sleep, master doctor; we'll both sit here and watch by her.

PENITENT. [*aside*] Hell's angels watch you! No art can prevail with 'em. What with the thought of joys, and sight of crosses, my wits are at Hercules' Pillars, *non plus ultra.*

COURTESAN. Master doctor, master doctor!

PENITENT. Here, lady.

COURTESAN. Your physic works; lend me your hand.

[*A bed pan is produced, and she is lifted upon it.*]

POSSIBILITY. Farewell, sweet lady.

INESSE. Adieu, master doctor.

[*Exeunt* POSSIBILITY *and* INESSE.]

COURTESAN. So.

PENITENT. Let me admire thee!
The wit of man wanes and decreases soon,
But women's wit is ever at full moon.

Enter MISTRESS HAREBRAIN.

---

155 *jar*: discord, vibration of a clock.

170 *Hercules' Pillars*: Calpe (Gibraltar) and Mt Abyla, believed by the ancients to have been set up by Hercules as supports of the western boundary of the world, and therefore the limit of navigation (*non plus ultra*, 'no further').

There shot a star from heaven;
I dare not yet behold my happiness,
The splendour is so glorious and so piercing.

COURTESAN. Mistress Harebrain, give my wit thanks hereafter; your wishes are in sight, your opportunity spacious.

MISTRESS HAREBRAIN. Will you but hear a word from me?

COURTESAN. Whooh!

MISTRESS HAREBRAIN. My husband himself brought me to th' door, walks below for my return. Jealousy is prick-ear'd, and will hear the wagging of a hair.

COURTESAN. Pish, y'are a faint liver. Trust yourself with your pleasure, and me with your security; go.

PENITENT. The fullness of my wish!

MISTRESS HAREBRAIN. Of my desire!

PENITENT. Beyond this sphere I never will aspire.

Exeunt [PENITENT *and* MISTRESS HAREBRAIN.]

Enter MASTER HAREBRAIN *listening.*

HAREBRAIN. I'll listen, now the flesh draws nigh her end;
At such a time women exchange their secrets
And ransack the close corners of their hearts.
What many years hath whelm'd, this hour imparts.

COURTESAN. Pray sit down, there's a low stool. Good Mistress Harebrain, this was kindly done; – huh – give me your hand; – huh – alas, how cold you are. Ev'n so is your husband, that worthy, wise gentleman; as comfortable a man to woman in my case as ever trod – huh – shoe-leather. Love him, honour him, stick by him; he lets you want nothing that's fit for a woman; and to be sure on't, he will see himself that you want it not.

HAREBRAIN. And so I do, i' faith, 'tis right my humour.

COURTESAN. You live a lady's life with him, go where you will, ride when you will, and do what you will.

---

192 *prick-ear'd . . . hair*: i.e. has alert ears, but with obscene innuendos on *prick* = penis, *wagging* = copulation, *hair* = the female pudenda.

193 *faint liver*: i.e. a coward.

200 *whelm'd*: kept hidden.

212 *ride*: with a sexual innuendo; hence Harebrain's comment.

HAREBRAIN. Not so, not so neither; she's better look'd to.

COURTESAN. I know you do, you need not tell me that. 'Twere e'en pity of your life, i' faith, if ever you should wrong such an innocent gentleman. Fie, Mistress Harebrain, what do you mean? Come you to discomfort me? Nothing but weeping with you?

HAREBRAIN. She's weeping, 't'as made her weep. My wife shows her good nature already.

COURTESAN. Still, still weeping? [*Sobs*] Huff, huff, huff. – Why, how now, woman? Hey, hy, hy, for shame, leave. – Suh, suh. – She cannot answer me for snobbing.

HAREBRAIN. All this does her good. Beshrew my heart and I pity her; let her shed tears till morning. I'll stay for her. She shall have enough on't by my good will; I'll not be her hinderance.

COURTESAN. Oh, no, lay your hand here, Mistress Harebrain. Ay, there; oh, there, there lies my pain, good gentlewoman. Sore? Oh, ay, I can scarce endure your hand upon't.

HAREBRAIN. Poor soul, how she's tormented.

COURTESAN. Yes, yes, I eat a cullis an hour since.

HAREBRAIN. There's some comfort in that yet; she may 'scape it.

COURTESAN. Oh, it lies about my heart much.

HAREBRAIN. I'm sorry for that, i' faith; she'll hardly 'scape it.

COURTESAN. Bound? No, no, I'd a very comfortable stool this morning.

HAREBRAIN. I'm glad of that, i' faith, that's a good sign; I smell she'll 'scape it now.

COURTESAN. Will you be going then?

HAREBRAIN. Fall back, she's coming.

COURTESAN. Thanks, good Mistress Harebrain; welcome, sweet Mistress Harebrain; pray commend me to the good gentleman your husband –

HAREBRAIN. I could do that myself now.

---

222 *Hey, hy, hy*: See Textual note, p. 400.
224 *snobbing*: sobbing.
240 *bound*: constipated.

COURTESAN. And to my Uncle Winchcomb, and to my Aunt Lipsalve, and to my Cousin Falsetop, and to my Cousin Lickit, and to my Cousin Horseman, and to all my good cousins in Clerkenwell and St Jones's.

Enter WIFE *with* MASTER PENITENT.

MISTRESS HAREBRAIN. At three days' end my husband takes a journey.

PENITENT. Oh, thence I derive a second meeting.

MISTRESS HAREBRAIN. May it prosper still;
Till then I rest a captive to his will.
Once again, health, rest, and strength to thee, sweet lady. [*In an undertone*] Farewell, you witty squall. – Good master doctor, have a care to her body; if you stand her friend, I know you can do her good.

COURTESAN. Take pity of your waiter, go. Farewell, sweet Mistress Harebrain.

[*The curtains of the bed are drawn.*]

HAREBRAIN. Welcome, sweet wife, alight upon my lip.
Never was hour spent better.

MISTRESS HAREBRAIN. Why, were you within the hearing, sir?

HAREBRAIN. Ay, that I was, i' faith, to my great comfort;
I deceiv'd you there, wife, ha, ha!
I do entreat thee, nay, conjure thee, wife,
Upon my love or what can more be said,
Oft'ner to visit this sick, virtuous maid.

MISTRESS HAREBRAIN. Be not so fierce; your will shall be obey'd.

HAREBRAIN. Why then, I see thou lov'st me.

Exeunt [HAREBRAINS.]

250–2 *Uncle Winchcomb . . . Aunt Lipsalve . . . Cousin Falsetop . . . Lickit . . . Horseman*: of her 'relatives' the first two are bawds: *Winchcomb* presumably combs for wenches, *Lipsalve* soothes their chafed parts; among the whores, *Falsetop* wears a wig (a noted gambit) or a padded chest, *Lickit* fellates, and *Horseman* 'rides'.

253 *Clerkenwell and St Jones's*: The Priory of St John's was a major landmark in Clerkenwell, which was an area notorious for thieves and prostitutes.

263 *waiter*: ironic, for 'promoters' and 'waiters' kept watch at principal ports to search incoming vessels for Catholic recusants.

PENITENT. Art of ladies!
When plots are e'en past hope and hang their head,
Set with a woman's hand, they thrive and spread.
Exit.

SCENE III

Enter FOLLYWIT *with* LIEUTENANT MAWWORM, ANCIENT HOBOY, *and the rest of his consorts.*

FOLLYWIT. Was't not well manag'd, you necessary mischiefs? Did the plot want either life or art?

MAWWORM. 'Twas so well, captain, I would you could make such another muss at all adventures.

FOLLYWIT. Dost call't a muss? I am sure my grandsire ne'er got his money worse in his life than I got it from him. If ever he did cozen the simple, why, I was born to revenge their quarrel; if ever oppress the widow, I, a fatherless child, have done as much for him. And so 'tis through the world either in jest or earnest. Let the usurer look for't; for craft recoils in the end, like an overcharg'd musket, and maims the very hand that puts fire to't. There needs no more but a usurer's own blow to strike him from hence to hell; 'twill set him forward with a vengeance. But here lay the jest, whoresons: my grandsire, thinking in his conscience that we had not robb'd him enough o'ernight, must needs pity me i'th' morning and give me the rest.

MAWWORM. Two hundred pounds in fair rose nobles, I protest.

FOLLYWIT. Push, I knew he could not sleep quietly till he had paid me for robbing of him, too; 'tis his humour, and the humour of most of your rich men in the course of their lives; for you know they always

---

278–9 a metaphor from horticulture, but with bawdy innuendoes; cf. III.iii.41.

279 *Set*: transplanted, put in the ground to grow/arranged, adjusted.

4–5 *muss*: scramble; from 'muss', a game in which children competed for objects thrown down.

4 *at all adventures*: at any risk.

14–15 *set him forward*: advance him.

19 *rose nobles*: gold coins with a rose stamped on them, worth about sixteen shillings.

feast those mouths that are least needy, and give them more that have too much already. And what call you that but robbing of themselves a courtlier way? Oh!

MAWWORM. Cuds me, how now, captain?

FOLLYWIT. A cold fit that comes over my memory and has a shrode pull at my fortunes.

MAWWORM. What's that, sir?

FOLLYWIT. Is it for certain, lieutenant, that my grandsire keeps an uncertain creature, a quean?

MAWWORM. Ay, that's too true, sir.

FOLLYWIT. So much the more preposterous for me; I shall hop shorter by that trick: she carries away the thirds at least. 'Twill prove entail'd land, I am afraid, when all's done, i' faith. Nay, I have known a vicious, old, thought-acting father,
Damn'd only in his dreams, thirsting for game
(When his best parts hung down their heads for shame)
For his blanch'd harlot dispossess his son
And make the pox his heir; 'twas gravely done.
How hadst thou first knowledge on't, lieutenant?

MAWWORM. Faith, from discourse; yet all the policy
That I could use, I could not get her name.

FOLLYWIT. Dull slave, that ne'er couldst spy it!

MAWWORM. But the manner of her coming was describ'd to me.

FOLLYWIT. How is the manner, prithee?

MAWWORM. Marry, sir, she comes, most commonly, coach'd.

---

30 *shrode pull*: i.e. 'a shrewd pull', a fierce assault, but punning on 'shroud pall', 'shrode' being a variant of both words. Follywit affects a premonition of death.

33 *quean*: whore, mistress.

35 *preposterous*: placing last what should be first.

37 *thirds . . . entail'd*: She may get a widow's third of grandfather's estate while she lives, making it *entail'd land* (in a loose sense), since there will be a restriction on its alienation. The pun on 'in-tailed' = 'vested in a woman's privities' attracted Middleton.

39 *thought-acting*: capable of the sexual 'game' only in imagination.

42 *blanch'd*: i.e. whitened by cosmetics (but alluding to the practice of peeling skin by scalding it, and to the boiling which was part of the treatment for the 'pox', venereal disease, which itself caused 'a white scab' – see III.ii.121).

FOLLYWIT. Most commonly coach'd indeed; for coaches are as common nowadays as some that ride in 'em. She comes most commonly coach'd –

MAWWORM. True, there I left, sir; – guarded with some leash of pimps.

FOLLYWIT. Beside the coachman?

MAWWORM. Right, sir. Then alighting, she's privately receiv'd by Master Gunwater.

FOLLYWIT. That's my grandsire's chief gentleman i'th' chain of gold. That he should live to be a pander, and yet look upon his chain and his velvet jacket!

MAWWORM. Then is your grandsire rounded i'th' ear, the key given after the Italian fashion, backward, she closely convey'd into his closet, there remaining till either opportunity smile upon his credit, or he send down some hot caudle to take order in his performance.

FOLLYWIT. Peace, 'tis mine own, i' faith; I ha't!

MAWWORM. How now, sir?

FOLLYWIT. Thanks, thanks to any spirit
That mingled it 'mongst my inventions!

HOBOY. Why, Master Follywit!

ALL. Captain!

FOLLYWIT. Give me scope and hear me.
I have begot that means which will both furnish me
And make that quean walk under his conceit.

MAWWORM. That were double happiness, to put thyself into money and her out of favour.

FOLLYWIT. And all at one dealing!

53–4 *coaches . . . common*: Stow, *Annales* (1631), p. 867 remarks that in 1605 'began the ordinary use of Caroaches'; they were commonly used for prostitution.

57 *leash*: three (as of hunting dogs etc.).

64 *rounded*: whispered.

65 *after the Italian fashion, backward*: Italians were generally believed to favour anal intercourse.

67–9 *send down some hot caudle . . . performance*: order some caudle (a warm, spiced restorative drink) to set to rights his sexual performance.

70–2 A strikingly exact parallel is to be found in the anonymous *Revenger's Tragedy*, IV.ii.204 and leads many scholars to attribute that play to Middleton; alternatively, this passage may be a humorous echo.

77 *walk under his conceit*: sink in his opinion.

HOBOY. 'Sfoot, I long to see that hand play'd.

FOLLYWIT. And thou shalt see't quickly, i' faith; nay, 'tis in grain, I warrant it hold colour. Lieutenant, step behind yon hanging; if I mistook not at my entrance there hangs the lower part of a gentlewoman's gown, with a mask and a chin-clout; bring all this way. Nay, but do't cunningly now; 'tis a friend's house and I'd use it so – there's a taste for you.

[*Exit* MAWWORM.]

HOBOY. But prithee what wilt thou do with a gentlewoman's lower part?

FOLLYWIT. Why, use it.

HOBOY. Y'ave answered me indeed in that; I can demand no farder.

FOLLYWIT. Well said. Lieutenant –

[*Enter* MAWWORM, *with the clothes.*]

MAWWORM. What will you do now, sir?

FOLLYWIT. Come, come, thou shalt see a woman quickly made up here.

MAWWORM. But that's against kind, captain, for they are always long a-making ready.

FOLLYWIT. And is not most they do against kind, I prithee? To lie with their horse-keeper, is not that against kind? To wear half-moons made of another's hair, is not that against kind? To drink down a man, she that should set him up, pray is not that monstrously against kind, now? [MAWWORM *offers the gown to*

---

83 *'tis in grain*: 'It's dyed in a fast colour' (the expression derives ultimately from the granular appearance of dye from the *coccus* insect, cochineal); here it is used figuratively of a sound plan, and is almost exactly paralleled in *The Revenger's Tragedy*, IV.ii.225–6.

86 *chin-clout*: muffler, part of a prostitute's equipment, Masks had become fashionable for all women in public, but chin-clouts were chiefly worn by the lower classes.

87 *friend's house*: alluding to the clothing, as well as the locale.

98 *against kind*: against nature.

101 *horse-keeper*: Frances Brandon, Duchess of Suffolk, married her master of horse when her husband died in 1554; and Leicester was Master of the Queen's Horse!

102 *half-moons*: a wig in the shape of a half-moon, probably used to make the natural head of hair fuller.

104 *set him up*: stimulate him.

FOLLYWIT] Nay, over with it, lieutenant, over with it; ever while you live put a woman's clothes over her head. Cupid plays best at blindman buff.

MAWWORM. [*helping the gown over* FOLLYWIT*'s head*] You shall have your will, maintenance; I love mad tricks as well as you for your heart, sir. But what shift will you make for upper bodies, captain?

FOLLYWIT. I see now thou'rt an ass. Why, I'm ready.

MAWWORM. Ready?

FOLLYWIT. Why, the doublet serves as well as the best, and is most in fashion. We're all male to th' middle, mankind from the beaver to th' bum. 'Tis an Amazonian time; you shall have women shortly tread their husbands. I should have a couple of locks behind; prithee, lieutenant, find 'em out for me, and wind 'em about my hatband. Nay, you shall see, we'll be in fashion to a hair, and become all with probability; the most musty-visage critic shall not except against me.

MAWWORM. Nay, I'll give thee thy due behind thy back. [*He attaches the locks*] Thou art as mad a piece of clay –

FOLLYWIT. Clay! Dost call thy captain clay? Indeed, clay was made to stop holes, he says true. Did not I tell you rascals you should see a woman quickly made up?

HOBOY. I'll swear for't, captain.

FOLLYWIT. Come, come, my mask and my chin-clout. Come into th' court.

MAWWORM. Nay, they were both i'th' court long ago, sir.

FOLLYWIT. Let me see; where shall I choose two or three

---

109 *maintenance*: one who maintains servants; a 'meal-ticket'.

111 *upper bodies*: bodice. From the 1580s, the bodice was made very much like the masculine doublet.

116 *beaver to th'bum*: 'from top to tail', beaver being a hat made from beaver fur.

117 *Amazonian time*: i.e. an age of masculine women (from the name of a race of female warriors alleged to exist in Scythia); *tread*: mount sexually (as of birds).

118–19 *locks behind*: locks of false hair wound round the hatband, apparently indicating that the 'woman' is available (cf. III. iii.145).

122 *except against*: make objection to.

126 *clay*: human flesh/weak and cowardly substance/material for plastering/the penis.

131–2 *court*: courtyard//royal Court.

for pimps now? But I cannot choose amiss amongst you all, that's the best. Well, as I am a quean, you were best have a care of me and guard me sure; I give you warning beforehand, 'tis a monkey-tail'd age. Life, you shall go nigh to have half a dozen blithe fellows surprise me cowardly, carry me away with a pair of oars, and put in at Putney.

MAWWORM. We should laugh at that, i' faith.

FOLLYWIT. Or shoot in upo'th' coast of Cue.

MAWWORM. Two notable fit landing places for lechers, P. and C., Putney and Cue.

FOLLYWIT. Well, say you have fair warning on't. The hair about the hat is as good as a flag upo'th' pole at a common playhouse to waft company, and a chin-clout is of that powerful attraction, I can tell you, 'twill draw more linen to't.

MAWWORM. Fear not us, captain; there's none here but can fight for a whore as well as some Inns a' Court man.

FOLLYWIT. Why then, set forward; and as you scorn two-shilling brothel,
Twelve-penny panderism, and such base bribes,
Guard me from bonny scribs and bony scribes.

MAWWORM. Hang 'em, pensions and allowances, fourpence halfpenny a meal, hang 'em!

Exeunt.

---

137 *monkey-tail'd*: lecherous.

144 *P. and C., Putney and Cue*: 'Cue' is Kew (probably with a pun, as at II.i.62), and both places, west of London on the Surrey bank of the river, were notorious as pleasure haunts. Middleton makes obscene use of the initials.

145–6 *hair about the hat*: See note at III.iii.118–19.

151 *Inns a'Court*: law students, resident at one of the London Inns of Court.

152 *two-shilling*: the standard price for an ordinary whore.

154 *bonny scribs*: i.e. bonny scribblers, writers; *bony scribes*: starved professional penmen.

ACT IV

SCENE I

Enter in his chamber out of his study, MASTER PENITENT BROTHEL, *a book in his hand, reading.*

PENITENT. Ha! Read that place again. 'Adultery
Draws the divorce 'twixt heaven and the soul.'
Accursed man, that stand'st divorc'd from heaven,
Thou wretched unthrift, that hast play'd away
Thy eternal portion at a minute's game
To please the flesh, hast blotted out thy name;
Where were thy nobler meditations busied
That they durst trust this body with itself,
This natural drunkard that undoes us all
And makes our shame apparent in our fall?
Then let my blood pay for't, and vex and boil.
My soul, I know, would never grieve to th' death
The Eternal Spirit that feeds her with his breath.
Nay, I that knew the price of life and sin,
What crown is kept for continence, what for lust,
The end of man, and glory of that end
As endless as the giver,
To dote on weakness, slime, corruption, woman!
What is she, took asunder from her clothes?
Being ready, she consists of hundred pieces
Much like your German clock, and near allied:
Both are so nice they cannot go for pride,
Beside a greater fault, but too well known,
They'll strike to ten when they should stop at one.
Within these three days the next meeting's fix'd;
If I meet then, hell and my soul be mix'd.
My lodging, I know constantly, she not knows.
Sin's hate is the best gift that sin bestows;

---

s.d. PENITENT BROTHEL: See Textual note on DRAMATIS PERSONAE, p. 399.

21 *German clock*: The first clocks were imported from Germany and were notorious for their complicated mechanism, and their irregularity.

22 *nice*: delicate, over-refined.

24 *strike*: with an innuendo on the meaning 'copulate'.

I'll ne'er embrace her more; never, bear witness, never.

Enter the devil [*as* SUCCUBUS] *in her shape, claps him on the shoulder.*

SUCCUBUS. What, at a stand? The fitter for my company.
PENITENT. Celestial soldiers guard me!
SUCCUBUS. How now, man?
'Las, did the quickness of my presence fright thee?
PENITENT. Shield me, you ministers of faith and grace!
SUCCUBUS. Leave, leave! Are you not asham'd to use
Such words to a woman?
PENITENT. Th'art a devil.
SUCCUBUS. A devil?
Feel, feel, man. Has a devil flesh and bone?
PENITENT. I do conjure thee by that dreadful power –
SUCCUBUS. The man has a delight to make me tremble.
Are these the fruits of thy adventurous love?
Was I entic'd for this? To be soon rejected?
Come, what has chang'd thee so, delight?
PENITENT. Away!
SUCCUBUS. Remember –
PENITENT. Leave my sight!
SUCCUBUS. Have I this meeting wrought with cunning
Which, when I come, I find thee shunning?
Rouse thy amorous thoughts and twine me;
All my interest I resign thee.
Shall we let slip this mutual hour
Comes so seldom in our power?
Where's thy lip, thy clip, thy fadom?

29 *bear*: See Textual note, p. 400.

30 *at a stand*: in a state of perplexity/with *penis erectus*; but with a buried allusion to the proverb 'Idleness is the mother of all evil' (Tilley, I 13); no doubt pyrotechnics accompanied the entry, and account for Penitent's alarm.

36 *Has a devil flesh and bone*: A key question: 'the Platonists and some of the Christian Fathers . . . do give bodies both to good and ill angels. Aristotle and his Peripatetics, and our Schoolmen following them, hold that angels are simple and abstract intelligences, and substances altogether without bodies' (Fynes Moryson, *Itinerary* (1617), Part 3, Book I, p. 45).

46 *All my interest I resign*: 'Everything I possess I surrender'.

48 *our*: See Textual note, p. 400.

49 *clip . . . fadom*: embrace . . . encircling with the arms (but with additional suggestion of 'plumbing the depths').

Had women such loves, would't not mad 'em?
Art a man, or dost abuse one?
A love, and know'st not how to use one?
Come, I'll teach thee.

PENITENT. Do not follow!

SUCCUBUS. Once so firm, and now so hollow?
When was place and season sweeter?
Thy bliss in sight, and dar'st not meet her?
Where's thy courage, youth, and vigour?
Love's best pleas'd when't's seiz'd with rigour:
Seize me then with veins most cheerful;
Women love no flesh that's fearful.
'Tis but a fit, come, drink't away,
And dance and sing, and kiss and play.
Fa le la, le la, fa le la, le la la, [*Dances about him.*]
Fa le la, fa la le, la le la!

PENITENT. Torment me not!

SUCCUBUS. Fa le la, fa le la, fa la la loh!

PENITENT. Fury!

SUCCUBUS. Fa le la, fa le la, fa la la loh!

PENITENT. Devil! I do conjure thee once again,
By that soul-quaking thunder, to depart
And leave this chamber freed from thy damn'd art.

SUCCUBUS *stamps and exit.*

PENITENT. It has prevail'd. Oh, my sin-shaking sinews!
What should I think? Jasper, why, Jasper!

[*Enter* JASPER.]

JASPER. Sir! How now? What has disturb'd you, sir?

PENITENT. A fit, a qualm. Is Mistress Harebrain gone?

JASPER. Who, sir? Mistress Harebrain?

PENITENT. Is she gone, I say?

JASPER. Gone? Why, she was never here yet.

PENITENT. No?

JASPER. Why no, sir.

PENITENT. Art sure on't?

JASPER. Sure on't? If I be sure I breathe and am myself.

---

61 *fit*: passing mood.

s.d. SUCCUBUS *stamps and exit*: Probably through a trapdoor, whose opening was cued by stamping the feet. Cf. *Women Beware Women*, V.i.12.

76 *Harebrain*: See Textual note on DRAMATIS PERSONAE, p. 399.

PENITENT. I like it not. – Where kept'st thou?
JASPER. I'th' next room, sir.
PENITENT. Why, she struck by thee, man.
JASPER. You'd make one mad, sir; that a gentlewoman should steal by me and I not hear her! 'Sfoot, one may hear the rustling of their bums almost an hour before we see 'em.
PENITENT. I will be satisfied, although to hazard.
What though her husband meet me? I am honest.
When men's intents are wicked, their guilt haunts 'em,
But when they're just they're arm'd, and nothing daunts 'em.
JASPER. [*aside*] What strange humour call you this? He dreams of women and both his eyes broad open!
Exeunt.

SCENE II

Enter at one door SIR BOUNTEOUS, *at another* GUNWATER.

SIR BOUNTEOUS. Why, how now, Master Gunwater? What's the news with your haste?
GUNWATER. I have a thing to tell your worship.
SIR BOUNTEOUS. Why, prithee tell me; speak, man.
GUNWATER. Your worship shall pardon me, I have better bringing up than so.
SIR BOUNTEOUS. How, sir?
GUNWATER. 'Tis a thing made fit for your ear, sir.
SIR BOUNTEOUS. Oh, oh, oh, cry you mercy; now I begin to taste you. Is she come?
GUNWATER. She's come, sir.
SIR BOUNTEOUS. Recover'd, well and sound again?
GUNWATER. That's to be fear'd, sir.
SIR BOUNTEOUS. Why, sir?
GUNWATER. She wears a linen cloth about her jaw.

---

85 *struck by*: passed by (cf. *Women Beware Women*, III.ii.230).
88 *rustling*: See Textual note, p. 400. A *bum* was a French farthingale, stiffened by wire or stuffed with cotton, and worn as a roll about the hips.
90 *although to hazard*: even if at a risk.
10 *taste*: understand/relish.
13 *fear'd*: doubted. Gunwater believes she is disguising the effects of syphilis.

SIR BOUNTEOUS. Ha, ha, haw! Why, that's the fashion, you whoreson Gunwater.

GUNWATER. The fashion, sir?
Live I so long time to see that a fashion
Which rather was an emblem of dispraise?
It was suspected much in Monsieur's days.

SIR BOUNTEOUS. Ay, ay, in those days; that was a queasy time. Our age is better hard'ned now and put oft'ner in the fire: we are tried what we are. Tut, the pox is as natural now as an ague in the springtime; we seldom take physic without it. Here, take this key, you know what duties belong to't. Go, give order for a cullis; let there be a good fire made i'th' matted chamber, do you hear, sir?

GUNWATER. I know my office, sir. *Exit.*

SIR BOUNTEOUS. [*to the audience*] An old man's venery is very chargeable, my masters; there's much cookery belongs to't. *Exit.*

SCENE III

Enter GUNWATER *with* FOLLYWIT *in courtesan's disguise, and mask'd.*

GUNWATER. Come, lady, you know where you are now?

FOLLYWIT. Yes, good Master Gunwater.

GUNWATER. This is the old closet, you know.

FOLLYWIT. I remember it well, sir.

GUNWATER. There stands a casket. I would my yearly revenue were but worth the wealth that's lock'd in't, lady; yet I have fifty pound a year, wench.

FOLLYWIT. Beside your apparel, sir?

GUNWATER. Yes, faith, have I.

FOLLYWIT. But then you reckon your chain, sir.

GUNWATER. No, by my troth, do I not neither. Faith,

---

21 *Monsieur's days*: Francis, Duke of Anjou, brother of the French king Charles IX, sent Elizabeth a love-letter in 1572, and thrice visited England, the last visit being in 1579.

23–4 *put oft'ner in the fire*: Heat treatment was a frequent remedy for the pox. There is ironic allusion to Biblical metaphors of testing, especially Zechariah 13.9.

26 *physic*: a euphemism for 'coition'.

31 *venery*: lechery/hunting of game.

and you consider me rightly, sweet lady, you might admit a choice gentleman into your service.

FOLLYWIT. Oh, pray, away, sir.

GUNWATER. Pusha, come, come, you do but hinder your fortunes, i' faith. I have the command of all the house; I can tell you, nothing comes into th' kitchen but comes through my hands.

FOLLYWIT. Pray do not handle me, sir.

GUNWATER. Faith, y'are too nice, lady. And as for my secrecy, you know I have vow'd it often to you.

FOLLYWIT. Vow'd it? No, no, you men are fickle.

GUNWATER. Fickle? 'Sfoot, bind me, lady.

FOLLYWIT. Why, I bind you by virtue of this chain to meet me tomorrow at the Flower-de-luce yonder, between nine and ten.

GUNWATER. And if I do not, lady, let me lose it, thy love, and my best fortunes.

[*Gives* FOLLYWIT *the chain.*]

FOLLYWIT. Why now, I'll try you; go to!

GUNWATER. Farewell, sweet lady. *Kisses her. Exit.*

FOLLYWIT. Welcome, sweet coxcomb; by my faith, a good induction. I perceive by his overworn phrase, and his action toward the middle region, still there has been some saucy nibbling motion, and no doubt the cunning quean waited but for her prey; and I think 'tis better bestow'd upon me for his soul's health, and his body's too. I'll teach the slave to be so bold yet as once to offer to vault into his master's saddle, i' faith. Now, casket, by your leave; I have seen your outside oft, but that's no proof; some have fair outsides that are nothing worth. [*He opens the casket*] Ha! Now, by my faith, a gentlewoman of very good parts;

---

13 *admit . . . service*: accept as lover.

20 *nice*: coy.

25 *Flower-de-luce*: Fleur-de-Lis, a popular inn sign: there were two in Fleet Street (on the corners of Shoe Lane and Fetter Lane), one in Lombard Street, and one in Turnmill Street. Middleton probably means the latter, in a well-known brothel area.

diamond, ruby, sapphire, *onyx cum prole silexque*. If I do not wonder how the queen 'scap'd tempting, I'm an hermaphrodite! Sure she could lack nothing but the devil to point to't, and I wonder that he should be missing. Well, 'tis better as it is; this is the fruit of old grunting venery. Grandsire, you may thank your drab for this; oh fie, in your crinkling days, grandsire, keep a courtesan to hinder your grandchild! 'Tis against nature, i' faith, and I hope you'll be weary on't. Now to my villains that lurk close below.
Who keeps a harlot, tell him this from me,
He needs nor thief, disease, nor enemy. *Exit.*

Enter SIR BOUNTEOUS.

SIR BOUNTEOUS. Ah, sirrah, methink I feel myself well toasted, bumbasted, rubb'd, and refresh'd. But i' faith, I cannot forget to think how soon sickness has altered her, to my taste. I gave her a kiss at bottom o'th' stairs, and by th' mass, methought her breath had much ado to be sweet, like a thing compounded, methought, of wine, beer, and tobacco. I smelt much pudding in't.
It may be but my fancy, or her physic;
For this I know, her health gave such content,
The fault rests in her sickness, or my scent.
How dost thou now, sweet girl; what, well recover'd?
Sickness quite gone, ha? Speak! Ha? Wench? Frank Gullman! Why, body of me, what's here? My casket wide open, broke open, my jewels stol'n! Why,

---

43 *onyx cum prole silexque*: 'onyx with its compounds, and silica', part of a mnemonic quatrain in William Lily's Latin grammar, *Brevissima Institutio* (1540), 'The third Exception of Nouns increasing short, being the Doubtful Gender'. Onyx is a variety of quartz allied to agate, consisting of plane layers in different colours, much used for cameos; silica is also commonly found as quartz.

55 *sirrah*: Bounteous may be addressing Courtesan (lines 56–65 being an aside); more probably he believes Gunwater is still in the room.

56 *bumbasted*: roasted on the backside/thrashed/blown out (punning on 'bombasted').

62 *pudding*: a variety of tobacco, compacted into a wad, resembling a sausage.

65 *scent*: sense of smell.

Gunwater!

GUNWATER. [*within*] Anon, anon, sir.

SIR BOUNTEOUS. Come hither, Gunwater.

GUNWATER. [*within*] That were small manners, sir, i' faith; I'll find a time anon. Your worship's busy yet.

SIR BOUNTEOUS. Why, Gunwater!

GUNWATER. [*within*] Foh, nay then, you'll make me blush, i' faith, sir.

[*Enter* GUNWATER.]

SIR BOUNTEOUS. Where's this creature?

GUNWATER. What creature is't you'd have, sir?

SIR BOUNTEOUS. The worst that ever breathes.

GUNWATER. That's a wild boar, sir.

SIR BOUNTEOUS. That's a vild whore, sir. Where didst thou leave her, rascal?

GUNWATER. Who, your recreation, sir?

SIR BOUNTEOUS. My execration, sir!

GUNWATER. Where I was wont, in your worship's closet.

SIR BOUNTEOUS. A pox engross her, it appears too true. See you this casket, sir?

GUNWATER. My chain, my chain, my chain, my one and only chain! *Exit.*

SIR BOUNTEOUS. Thou run'st to much purpose now, Gunwater, yea? Is not a quean enough to answer for, but she must join a thief to't? A thieving quean! Nay, I have done with her, i' faith; 'tis a sign sh'as been sick a' late, for she's a great deal worse than she was. By my troth, I would have pawn'd my life upon't.
Did she want anything? Was she not supplied?
Nay, and liberally, for that's an old man's sin:
We'll feast our lechery though we starve our kin.
Is not my name Sir Bounteous? Am I not express'd there?
Ah, fie, fie, fie, fie, fie, but I perceive
Though she have never so complete a friend,
A strumpet's love will have a waft i'th' end

---

81 *wild boar*: the worst creature because it roots up the vineyard of Israel, Psalm 80.13, and therefore becomes an image of Satan.

87 *engross her*: wholly occupy her.

103 *waft*: ill-taste/passing breath of wind, and the odour carried on it.

And distaste the vessel. I can hardly bear this.
But say I should complain, perhaps she has pawn'd 'em.
'Sfoot, the judges will but laugh at it, and bid her
borrow more money of 'em. 'Make the old fellow pay
for's lechery', that's all the 'mends I get. I have seen
the same case tried at Newbury the last 'sizes. Well,
things must slip and sleep; I will dissemble it,
Because my credit shall not lose her lustre;
But whilst I live I'll neither love nor trust her.
I ha' done, I ha' done, I ha' done with her, i' faith.
Exit.

SCENE IV

MASTER PENITENT BROTHEL *knocking within; enter a* SERVANT.

SERVANT. Who's that knocks?
PENITENT. [*within*] A friend.

Enter MASTER PENITENT.

SERVANT. What's your will, sir?
PENITENT. Is Master Harebrain at home?
SERVANT. No, newly gone from it, sir.
PENITENT. Where's the gentlewoman his wife?
SERVANT. My mistress is within, sir.
PENITENT. When came she in, I pray?
SERVANT. Who, my mistress? She was not out these two days to my knowledge.
PENITENT. No? Trust me, I'd thought I'd seen her. I would request a word with her.
SERVANT. I'll tell her, sir. [*Exit.*]
PENITENT. I thank you. – It likes me worse and worse.

Enter MISTRESS HAREBRAIN.

MISTRESS HAREBRAIN. Why, how now, sir? 'Twas desperately adventur'd; I little look'd for you until the morrow.

---

104 *distaste*: render offensive.
109 *'sizes*: assizes.
s.d. PENITENT BROTHEL: See Textual note on DRAMATIS PERSONAE, p. 399.
4 *Harebrain*: See Textual note on DRAMATIS PERSONAE, p. 399.

PENITENT. No? Why, what made you at my chamber then even now?

MISTRESS HAREBRAIN. I, at your chamber?

PENITENT. Puh, dissemble not; come, come, you were there.

MISTRESS HAREBRAIN. By my life, you wrong me, sir.

PENITENT. What?

MISTRESS HAREBRAIN. First, y'are not ignorant what
watch keeps o'er me;
And for your chamber, as I live I know't not.

PENITENT. Burst into sorrow then, and grief's extremes,
Whilst I beat on this flesh!

MISTRESS HAREBRAIN. What is't disturbs you, sir?

PENITENT. Then was the devil in your likeness there.

MISTRESS HAREBRAIN. Ha?

PENITENT. The very devil assum'd thee formally,
That face, that voice, that gesture, that attire,
E'en as it sits on thee, not a pleat alter'd,
That beaver band, the colour of that periwig,
The farthingale above the navel, all,
As if the fashion were his own invention.

MISTRESS HAREBRAIN. Mercy defend me!

PENITENT. To beguile me more,
The cunning succubus told me that meeting
Was wrought o' purpose by much wit and art,
Wept to me, laid my vows before me, urg'd me,
Gave me the private marks of all our love,
Woo'd me in wanton and effeminate rhymes,
And sung and danc'd about me like a fairy;
And had not worthier cogitations bless'd me,
Thy form and his enchantments had possess'd me.

MISTRESS HAREBRAIN. What shall become of me? My own thoughts doom me!

PENITENT. Be honest; then the devil will ne'er assume
thee.
He has no pleasure in that shape to abide
Where these two sisters reign not, lust or pride.

---

18 *what made you*: 'What were you doing?'
31 *assum'd thee formally*: 'took on your shape'.
34 *beaver band*: hatband of beaver fur.
35 *farthingale above the navel*: the drum farthingale, which depended upon a hoop at waist level, and became popular in the last years of Elizabeth's reign.

He as much trembles at a constant mind
As looser flesh at him. Be not dismay'd:
Spring souls for joy, his policies are betray'd.
Forgive me, Mistress Harebrain, on whose soul
The guilt hangs double,
My lust and thy enticement; both I challenge,
And therefore of due vengeance it appear'd
To none but me, to whom both sins inher'd.
What knows the lecher when he clips his whore
Whether it be the devil his parts adore?
They're both so like, that in our natural sense,
I could discern no change nor difference.
No marvel then times should so stretch and turn;
None for religion, all for pleasure burn.
Hot zeal into hot lust is now transform'd,
Grace into painting, charity into clothes,
Faith into false hair, and put off as often.
There's nothing but our virtue knows a mean;
He that kept open house now keeps a quean.
He will keep open still that he commends,
And there he keeps a table for his friends;
And she consumes more than his sire could hoard,
Being more common than his house or board.

Enter HAREBRAIN [*unnoticed*].

Live honest, and live happy, keep thy vows;
She's part a virgin whom but one man knows.
Embrace thy husband, and beside him none;
Having but one heart, give it but to one.

MISTRESS HAREBRAIN. I vow it on my knees, with tears true bred,
No man shall ever wrong my husband's bed.

PENITENT. Rise, I'm thy friend forever.

HAREBRAIN. [*comes forward*] And I thine,
Forever and ever. Let me embrace thee, sir,
Whom I will love even next unto my soul:
And that's my wife;

---

54 *whose*: i.e. Penitent's.
56 *challenge*: claim.
68 *mean*: moderation.
70 *that*: i.e. his whore.
72 *his*: See Textual note, p. 400.

Two dear, rare gems this hour presents me with,
A wife that's modest, and a friend that's right.
Idle suspect and fear, now take your flight.
PENITENT. A happy inward peace crown both your joys.
HAREBRAIN. Thanks above utterance to you.

[*Enter* SERVANT.]

Now, the news?
SERVANT. Sir Bounteous Progress, sir,
Invites you and my mistress to a feast
On Tuesday next; his man attends without.
HAREBRAIN. Return both with our willingness and thanks.
[*Exit* SERVANT.]
I will entreat you, sir, to be my guest.
PENITENT. Who, I, sir?
HAREBRAIN. Faith, you shall.
PENITENT. Well, I'll break strife.
HAREBRAIN. A friend's so rare, I'll sooner part from life.
[*Exeunt.*]

SCENE V

Enter FOLLYWIT, *the* COURTESAN *striving from him.*

FOLLYWIT. What, so coy, so strict? Come, come.

COURTESAN. Pray change your opinion, sir; I am not for that use.

FOLLYWIT. Will you but hear me?

COURTESAN. I shall hear that I would not. *Exit.*

FOLLYWIT. 'Sfoot, this is strange. I've seldom seen a wench stand upon stricter points; life, she will not endure to be courted. Does she e'er think to prosper? I'll ne'er believe that tree can bring forth fruit that never bears a blossom; courtship's a blossom, and often brings forth fruit in forty weeks. 'Twere a mad part in me now to turn over; if ever there were any hope on't, 'tis at this instant. Shall I be madder now than ever I have been? I'm in the way, i' faith.
Man's never at high height of madness full
Until he love and prove a woman's gull.
I do protest in earnest, I ne'er knew

94 *break strife*: a conventional phrase for taking a meal.
12 *turn over*: reform.

At which end to begin to affect a woman
Till this bewitching minute; I ne'er saw
Face worth my object till mine eye met hers.
I should laugh and I were caught, i' faith; I'll see her again,
That's certain; whate'er comes on't.

Enter the MOTHER.

By your favour, lady.

MOTHER. You're welcome, sir.

FOLLYWIT. Know you the young gentlewoman that went in lately?

MOTHER. I have best cause to know her; I'm her mother, sir.

FOLLYWIT. Oh, in good time. I like the gentlewoman well; a pretty, contriv'd beauty.

MOTHER. Ay, nature has done her part, sir.

FOLLYWIT. But she has one uncomely quality.

MOTHER. What's that, sir?

FOLLYWIT. 'Sfoot, she's afraid of a man.

MOTHER. Alas, impute that to her bashful spirit; she's fearful of her honour.

FOLLYWIT. Of her honour? 'Slid, I'm sure I cannot get her maidenhead with breathing upon her, nor can she lose her honour in her tongue.

MOTHER. True, and I have often told her so. But what would you have of a foolish virgin, sir, a wilful virgin? I tell you, sir, I need not have been in that solitary estate that I am, had she had grace and boldness to have put herself forward. Always timorsome, always backward; ah, that same peevish honour of hers has undone her and me both, good gentleman. The suitors, the jewels, the jointures that has been offer'd her! We had been made women forever, but what was her fashion? She could not endure the sight of a man, forsooth, but run and hole herself presently. So

22 *By your favour, lady*: See Textual note, p. 401.
28 *in good time*: 'How fortunate!'
29 *contriv'd*: delicately made.
43 *timorsome*: fearful.
44 *peevish*: silly, perverse.
46 *jointures*: marriage settlements.

choice of her honour, I am persuaded whene'er she has husband
She will e'en be a precedent for all married wives,
How to direct their actions and their lives.

FOLLYWIT. Have you not so much power with her to command her presence?

MOTHER. You shall see straight what I can do, sir. *Exit.*

FOLLYWIT. Would I might be hang'd if my love do not stretch to her deeper and deeper; those bashful maiden humours take me prisoner. When there comes a restraint on't, upon flesh, we are always most greedy upon't, and that makes your merchant's wife oftentimes pay so dear for a mouthful. Give me a woman as she was made at first, simple of herself, without sophistication, like this wench; I cannot abide them when they have tricks, set speeches, and artful entertainments. You shall have some so impudently aspected they will outcry the forehead of a man, make him blush first, and talk him into silence, and this is counted manly in a woman. It may hold so; sure, womanly it is not; no,
If e'er I love, or anything move me,
'Twill be a woman's simple modesty.

Enter MOTHER *bringing in strivingly the* COURTESAN.

COURTESAN. Pray let me go; why, mother, what do you mean? I beseech you, mother! Is this your conquest now? Great glory 'tis to overcome a poor and silly virgin.

FOLLYWIT. The wonder of our time sits in that brow;
I ne'er beheld a perfect maid till now.

MOTHER. Thou childish thing, more bashful than thou'rt wise,
Why dost thou turn aside and drown thine eyes?

---

50 *choice of*: particular about.

60 *restraint . . . upon flesh*: An allusion to the Lenten prohibition against meat-eating, more strictly enforced to discourage the killing of livestock when fodder ran low.

63 *simple of herself*: pure and without adulteration.

69 *manly*: admirable/masculine.

75 *silly*: defenceless.

78 *maid*: See Textual note, p. 401.

Look, fearful fool, there's no temptation near thee;
Art not asham'd that any flesh should fear thee?
Why, I durst pawn my life the gentleman means no other but honest and pure love to thee. How say you, sir?

FOLLYWIT. By my faith, not I, lady.

MOTHER. Hark you there? What think you now, forsooth?
What grieves your honour now?
Or what lascivious breath intends to rear
Against that maiden organ, your chaste ear?
Are you resolv'd now better of men's hearts,
Their faiths, and their affections? With you none,
Or at most few, whose tongues and minds are one.
Repent you now of your opinion past;
Men love as purely as you can be chaste.
To her yourself, sir, the way's broke before you;
You have the easier passage.

FOLLYWIT. Fear not; come,
Erect thy happy graces in thy look.
I am no curious wooer, but, in faith,
I love thee honourably.

COURTESAN. How mean you that, sir?

FOLLYWIT. 'Sfoot, as one loves a woman for a wife.

MOTHER. Has the gentleman answered you, trow?

FOLLYWIT. I do confess it truly to you both,
My estate is yet but sickly; but I've a grandsire
Will make me lord of thousands at his death.

MOTHER. I know your grandsire well; she knows him better.

FOLLYWIT. Why then, you know no fiction. My state then
Will be a long day's journey 'bove the waste, wench.

MOTHER. Nay, daughter, he says true.

FOLLYWIT. And thou shalt often measure it in thy coach,
And with the wheels' tract make a girdle for't.

---

82 *fear*: frighten.
92 *With you none*: 'In your opinion there are none.'
96 *broke*: open (and with ironic allusion to the Courtesan's lack of a maidenhead).
99 *curious*: virtuoso/seeking to pry further than one should.
102 *trow*: 'do you think?'
108 *waste*: i.e. unproductive ground, and used of various barren regions, especially that about the Wash; but with a pun on 'waist'.
111 *tract*: track.

MOTHER. Ah, 'twill be a merry journey.

FOLLYWIT. What, is't a match? If't be, clap hands and lips. [*He clasps* COURTESAN*'s hand, kisses her.*]

MOTHER. 'Tis done, there's witness on't.

FOLLYWIT. Why then, mother, I salute you. [*Kisses her.*]

MOTHER. Thanks, sweet son. Son Follywit, come hither; if I might counsel thee, we'll e'en take her while the good mood's upon her. Send for a priest and clap't up within this hour.

FOLLYWIT. By my troth, agreed, mother.

MOTHER. Nor does her wealth consist all in her flesh,
Though beauty be enough wealth for a woman;
She brings a dowry of three hundred pound with her.

FOLLYWIT. 'Sfoot, that will serve till my grandsire dies; I warrant you he'll drop away at fall a'th' leaf. If ever he reach to All Hollantide, I'll be hang'd.

MOTHER. Oh yes, son, he's a lusty old gentleman.

FOLLYWIT. Ah, pox, he's given to women; he keeps a quean at this present.

MOTHER. Fie!

FOLLYWIT. Do not tell my wife on't.

MOTHER. That were needless, i' faith.

FOLLYWIT. He makes a great feast upon the 'leventh of this month, Tuesday next, and you shall see players there. [*Aside*] I have one trick more to put upon him. – My wife and yourself shall go thither before as my guests, and prove his entertainment; I'll meet you there at night. The jest will be here: that feast which he makes will, unknown to him, serve fitly for our wedding dinner. We shall be royally furnish'd, and get some charges by't.

MOTHER. An excellent course, i' faith, and a thrifty. Why, son, methinks you begin to thrive before y'are married.

---

113 *clap hands*: i.e. they join hands in a handfasting, a legally binding betrothal before a witness; hence Follywit addresses the bawd as 'mother'.

118 *clap't up*: stick it together hastily/conclude it.

126 *All Hollantide*: All Saints' Day, 1 November.

137 *prove*: test.

141 *get some charges by't*: 'and obtain our expenses by so doing'.

FOLLYWIT. We shall thrive one day, wench, and clip enough;
Between our hopes there's but a grandsire's puff.
Exit.

MOTHER. So, girl, here was a bird well caught.

COURTESAN. If ever, here;
But what for's grandsire? 'Twill scarce please him well.

MOTHER. Who covets fruit, ne'er cares from whence it fell;
Thou'st wedded youth and strength, and wealth will fall.
Last, thou'rt made honest.

COURTESAN. And that's worth 'em all.
Exeunt.

ACT V

SCENE I

Enter busily SIR BOUNTEOUS PROGRESS, [GUNWATER, SERVANTS] *for the feast.*

SIR BOUNTEOUS. Have a care, blue coats. Bestir yourself, Master Gunwater, cast an eye into th' kitchen, o'erlook the knaves a little. Every jack has his friend today, this cousin and that cousin puts in for a dish of meat; a man knows not till he make a feast how many varlets he feeds; acquaintances swarm in every corner like flies at Barthol'mew-tide that come up with drovers. 'Sfoot, I think they smell my kitchen seven mile about.

[*Enter* HAREBRAIN, MISTRESS HAREBRAIN, PENITENT BROTHEL.]

---

145 *clip enough*: embrace enough (possessions)/embrace one another enough.

1 *blue coats*: servants (who generally wore blue).

3 *jack*: fellow; glancing at the proverbial happy ending, 'All is well, Jack shall have Jill.'

7 *Barthol'mew-tide*: 24 August, the time of the annual fair held in West Smithfield.

Master Harebrain and his sweet bedfellow, y'are very copiously welcome.

HAREBRAIN. Sir, here's an especial dear friend of ours; we were bold to make his way to your table.

SIR BOUNTEOUS. Thanks for that boldness ever, good Master Harebrain. Is this your friend, sir?

HAREBRAIN. Both my wife's friend and mine, sir.

SIR BOUNTEOUS. Why then compendiously sir, y'are welcome.

PENITENT. In octavo I thank you, sir.

SIR BOUNTEOUS. Excellently retorted, i' faith; he's welcome for's wit. I have my sorts of salutes, and know how to place 'em courtly. Walk in, sweet gentlemen, walk in, there's a good fire i'th' hall. You shall have my sweet company instantly.

HAREBRAIN. Ay, good Sir Bounteous.

SIR BOUNTEOUS. You shall indeed, gentlemen.

[*Exeunt* HAREBRAINS, PENITENT.]

Enter SERVANT.

How now, what news brings thee in stumbling now?

SERVANT. There are certain players come to town, sir, and desire to interlude before your worship.

SIR BOUNTEOUS. Players? By the mass, they are welcome; they'll grace my entertainment well. But for certain players, there thou liest, boy; they were never more uncertain in their lives. Now up and now down, they know not when to play, where to play, nor what to play; not when to play for fearful fools, where to play for Puritan fools, nor what to play for critical fools. Go, call 'em in.

[*Exit* SERVANT.]

How fitly the whoresons come upo'th' feast; troth, I was e'en wishing for 'em.

10, 15 *Harebrain*: See Textual note on DRAMATIS PERSONAE, p. 399.

19 *in octavo*: briefly (octavo is a small size of book, where each sheet is folded into eight).

29 *interlude*: perform a play (in the interval of a feast).

35 *fearful fools*: When deaths from plague reached a certain number per week, dramatic performances (which might spread infection) were prohibited.

35–6 *where to play*: The City Fathers under Puritan influence constantly attempted to inhibit acting.

[*Re-enter* SERVANT *with* FOLLYWIT, MAWWORM, HOBOY *and others disguised as players.*]

Oh, welcome, welcome, my friends!

FOLLYWIT. The month of May delights not in her flowers
More than we joy in that sweet sight of yours.

SIR BOUNTEOUS. Well acted, a' my credit; I perceive he's your best actor.

SERVANT. He has greatest share, sir, and may live of himself, sir.

SIR BOUNTEOUS. [*to* FOLLYWIT, *who is removing his hat*] What, what? Put on your hat, sir, pray put on! Go to, wealth must be respected; let those that have least feathers stand bare. And whose men are you, I pray? Nay, keep on your hat still.

FOLLYWIT. We serve my Lord Owemuch, sir.

SIR BOUNTEOUS. My Lord Owemuch? By my troth, the welcom'st men alive! Give me all your hands at once. That honourable gentleman? He lay at my house in a robbery once, and took all quietly, went away cheerfully. I made a very good feast for him. I never saw a man of honour bear things bravelier away. Serve my Lord Owemuch? Welcome, i' faith. Some bastard for my lord's players!

[*Exit* SERVANT.]

Where be your boys?

FOLLYWIT. They come along with the wagon, sir.

SIR BOUNTEOUS. Good, good; and which is your politician amongst you? Now, i' faith, he that works out restraints, makes best legs at court, and has a suit made of purpose for the company's business, which is he? Come, be not afraid of him.

FOLLYWIT. I am he, sir.

SIR BOUNTEOUS. Art thou he? Give me thy hand. Hark

---

45 *He has greatest share*: He has the most shares in the actors' company (and can live off his income).

49 *feathers*: hat plumes (a sign of wealth).

63–4 *works out restraints*: gets out of prohibitions from playing (in Lent or time of plague); *legs*: bows.

in thine ear; thou rollest too fast to gather so much moss as thy fellow there; champ upon that. Ah, and what play shall we have, my masters?

FOLLYWIT. A pleasant witty comedy, sir.

SIR BOUNTEOUS. Ay, ay, ay, a comedy in any case, that I and my guests may laugh a little. What's the name on't?

FOLLYWIT. 'Tis call'd *The Slip.*

SIR BOUNTEOUS. *The Slip*? By my troth, a pretty name, and a glib one! Go all, and slip into't as fast as you can. – Cover a table for the players! – First take heed of a lurcher; he cuts deep, he will eat up all from you. – Some sherry for my lord's players there, sirrah! – Why, this will be a true feast, a right Mitre supper, a play, and all.

[*Exeunt* FOLLYWIT *and the others.*]

More lights!

Enter MOTHER *and* COURTESAN.

I call'd for light; here come in two are light enough for a whole house, i' faith. Dare the thief look me i'th' face? O impudent times! Go to, dissemble it!

MOTHER. Bless you, Sir Bounteous!

SIR BOUNTEOUS. Oh, welcome, welcome, thief, quean, and bawd, welcome all three!

MOTHER. Nay, here's but two on's, sir.

SIR BOUNTEOUS. A' my troth, I took her for a couple;

69–70 *thou rollest too fast . . . champ upon that*: An allusion to the proverb 'A rolling stone gathers no moss' (Tilley, S 885), intended as a gibe (*champ on that* = 'chew on that'); but its point is obscure. It is inappropriate addressed to Follywit, who has 'gathered moss' (= riches) according to line 45; perhaps Sir Bounteous turns to the over-active Footman of II.i and vi, whom he spots among Follywit's retinue, and contrasts with Follywit.

77 *The Slip*: Several of the many meanings of the word are alluded to in this scene: an act of evasion/ an act of falling down/ an error in conduct/ an unintentional error/ the skirt of a garment/ a counterfeit coin.

78 *glib*: smooth, slippery.

80 *lurcher*: a glutton, one who forestalls others of their fair share of food/a petty thief or swindler.

82 *Mitre*: a high-class tavern at the corner of Bread Street and Cheapside.

85 *light*: wanton, loose/light-fingered.

I'd have sworn there had been two faces there.
MOTHER. Not all under one hood, sir.
SIR BOUNTEOUS. Yes, faith, would I, to see mine eyes bear double.
MOTHER. I'll make it hold, sir; my daughter is a couple.
She was married yesterday.
SIR BOUNTEOUS. Buz!
MOTHER. Nay, to no buzzard neither; a right hawk
Whene'er you know him.
SIR BOUNTEOUS. Away! He cannot be but a rascal.
Walk in, walk in, bold guests that come unsent for.
[*Exit* MOTHER.]
Pox, I perceive how my jewels went now:
To grace her marriage.
COURTESAN. Would you with me, sir?
SIR BOUNTEOUS. Ay; how happ'd it, wench, you put the slip upon me
Not three nights since? I name it gently to you;
I term it neither pilfer, cheat, nor shark.
COURTESAN. Y'are past my reach.
SIR BOUNTEOUS. I'm old and past your reach, very good; but you will not deny this, I trust.
COURTESAN. With a safe conscience, sir.
SIR BOUNTEOUS. Yea? Give me thy hand; fare thee well. – I have done with her.
COURTESAN. Give me your hand, sir; you ne'er yet begun with me. *Exit.*
SIR BOUNTEOUS. Whew, whew! O audacious age!
She denies me and all, when on her fingers
I spied the ruby sit that does betray her
And blushes for her face. Well, there's a time for't,

---

94 *under one hood*: a denial of duplicity. Cf. the proverb 'He carries (bears) two faces under one hood' (Tilley, F 20).
96 *bear double*: obscure, perhaps proverbial. The sense seems to be 'Yes, I would swear that my eyes saw two faces.'
99 *Buz*: interjection of impatience, contempt – 'Tell me another!'
100 *buzzard*: a useless kind of hawk/a worthless person.
104 *Pox*: See Textual note, p. 401.
105 *Would you with me*: 'Do you want something from me?'
108 *shark*: petty swindle.
115–16 *begun with me*: a sneer at his impotence.
120 *face*: See Textual note, p. 401.

For all's too little now for entertainment,
Feast, mirth, ay, harmony, and the play to boot:
A jovial season.

Enter FOLLYWIT.

How now, are you ready?

FOLLYWIT. Even upon readiness, sir. [*Makes to take hat off.*]

SIR BOUNTEOUS. Keep you your hat on.

FOLLYWIT. I have a suit to your worship. *Takes it off.*

SIR BOUNTEOUS. Oh, cry you mercy; then you must stand bare.

FOLLYWIT. We could do all to the life of action, sir, both for the credit of your worship's house and the grace of our comedy –

SIR BOUNTEOUS. Cuds me, what else, sir?

FOLLYWIT. And for some defects, as the custom is, we would be bold to require your worship's assistance.

SIR BOUNTEOUS. Why, with all my heart. What is't you want? Speak.

FOLLYWIT. One's a chain for a justice's hat, sir.

SIR BOUNTEOUS. Why, here, here, here, here, whoreson, will this serve your turn? [*He takes off a chain*] What else lack you?

FOLLYWIT. We should use a ring with a stone in't.

SIR BOUNTEOUS. Nay, whoop, I have given too many rings already; talk no more of rings, I pray you. Here, here, here, make this jewel serve for once.

FOLLYWIT. Oh, this will serve, sir.

SIR BOUNTEOUS. What, have you all now?

FOLLYWIT. All now, sir. Only Time is brought i'th' middle of the play, and I would desire your worship's watch.

SIR BOUNTEOUS. My watch? With all my heart; only give Time a charge that he be not fiddling with it.

FOLLYWIT. You shall ne'er see that, sir.

SIR BOUNTEOUS. Well, now you are furnish'd, sir, make haste, away. [*Exit.*]

FOLLYWIT. E'en as fast as I can, sir. – I'll set my fellows going first; they must have time and leisure, or they're

---

139 *turn*: See Textual note, p. 401.
149 *watch*: See Textual note, p. 401.

dull else. I'll stay and speak a prologue, yet o'ertake 'em; I cannot have conscience, i' faith, to go away and speak ne'er a word to 'em. My grandsire has given me three shares here; sure I'll do somewhat for 'em. *Exit.*

SCENE II

Enter SIR BOUNTEOUS *and all the guests* [HAREBRAIN, MISTRESS HAREBRAIN, PENITENT BROTHEL, FRANK GULLMAN *and her* MOTHER *and* OTHER GUESTS, GUNWATER *and* SERVANTS].

SIR BOUNTEOUS. More lights! More stools! Sit, sit, the play begins.

HAREBRAIN. Have you players here, Sir Bounteous?

SIR BOUNTEOUS. We have 'em for you, sir; fine, nimble comedians, proper actors, most of them.

PENITENT. Whose men, I pray you, sir?

SIR BOUNTEOUS. Oh, there's their credit, sir; they serve an honourable, popular gentleman yclipped my Lord Owemuch.

HAREBRAIN. My Lord Owemuch? He was in Ireland lately.

SIR BOUNTEOUS. Oh, you ne'er knew any of the name but were great travellers.

HAREBRAIN. How is the comedy call'd, Sir Bounteous?

SIR BOUNTEOUS. Marry, sir, *The Slip.*

HAREBRAIN. *The Slip*?

SIR BOUNTEOUS. Ay, and here's the Prologue begins to slip in upon's.

HAREBRAIN. 'Tis so indeed, Sir Bounteous.

Enter, for a Prologue, FOLLYWIT.

Prologue

FOLLYWIT. *We sing of wand'ring knights, what them*
betide
Who nor in one place nor one shape abide;
They're here now, and anon no scouts can reach 'em,

---

2 s.h. HAREBRAIN: See Textual note, p. 399.
8 *yclipped*: named (an affected archaism).
10 *Owemuch . . . Ireland*: Ireland was notorious as a refuge for English debtors.

Being every man well-hors'd like a bold Beacham.
The play which we present no fault shall meet
But one: you'll say 'tis short, we'll say 'tis sweet.
'Tis given much to dumb shows, which some praise,
And like the Term, delights much in delays.
So to conclude, and give the name her due,
The play being call'd The Slip, *I vanish too.* *Exit.*

SIR BOUNTEOUS. Excellently well acted, and a nimble conceit.

HAREBRAIN. The Prologue's pretty, i' faith.

PENITENT. And went off well.

SIR BOUNTEOUS. Ay, that's the grace of all, when they go away well, ah!

COURTESAN. A' my troth, and I were not married I could find in my heart to fall in love with that player now, and send for him to a supper. I know some i'th' town that have done as much, and there took such a good concept of their parts into th' twopenny room that the actors have been found i'th' morning in a less compass than their stage, though 'twere ne'er so full of gentlemen.

SIR BOUNTEOUS. But, passion of me, where be these knaves? Will they not come away? Methinks they stay very long.

---

23 *bold Beacham*: Proverbial (see Tilley, B 162, 'As bold as Beauchamp'); it derived from the exploits of Thomas Beauchamp, first Earl of Warwick.

26 *dumb shows*: mimes anticipating or filling out the action of a play; some of the leading dramatists eschewed them.

27 *the Term*: the law term, in which actions were heard.

30–1 *nimble conceit*: witty invention.

36–43 Several tales were current of loose City women inviting favoured players (Burbage and Shakespeare among them) for 'entertainment'.

40 *good concept of their parts*: thorough understanding of their roles (with an innuendo on 'parts').

twopenny room: a covered upper room of the theatre, which had seats and could be used for entertainment after a performance; it was a disreputable part of the house, frequented by whores.

41–2 *a less compass*: a smaller circumference (gentlemen sitting on stage often restricted the playing area). For a similar innuendo, see *The Changeling*, IV.i.58–62.

PENITENT. Oh, you must bear a little, sir; they have many shifts to run into.

SIR BOUNTEOUS. Shifts call you 'em? They're horrible long things.

FOLLYWIT *returns in a fury.*

FOLLYWIT. [*aside*] A pox of such fortune! The plot's betray'd! All will come out; yonder they come, taken upon suspicion and brought back by a constable. I was accurs'd to hold society with such coxcombs! What's to be done? I shall be sham'd forever, my wife here and all. Ah, pox! – By light, happily thought upon: the chain! Invention, stick to me this once, and fail me ever hereafter. So, so.

SIR BOUNTEOUS. Life, I say, where be these players? – Oh, are you come? Troth, it's time; I was e'en sending for you.

HAREBRAIN. How moodily he walks! What plays he, trow?

SIR BOUNTEOUS. A justice, upon my credit; I know by the chain there.

FOLLYWIT. [*improvising*] *Unfortunate justice!*

SIR BOUNTEOUS. Ah, a, a.

FOLLYWIT. *In thy kin unfortunate!*
Here comes thy nephew now upon suspicion,
Brought by a constable before thee, his vild associates with him,
But so disguis'd none knows him but myself.
Twice have I set him free from officers' fangs,
And, for his sake, his fellows. Let him look to't;
My conscience will permit but one wink more.

SIR BOUNTEOUS. Yea, shall we take justice winking?

FOLLYWIT. *For this time I have bethought a means to work thy freedom, though hazarding myself; should the law seize him,*
Being kin to me, 'twould blemish much my name.
No, I'd rather lean to danger than to shame.

Enter CONSTABLE *with them* [MAWWORM, HOBOY, *and others, with* CITIZENS].

SIR BOUNTEOUS. A very explete justice.

48–9 *shifts*: changes of costume//linen smocks.
80 *explete*: complete/working to fill out a loss, to compensate.

CONSTABLE. Thank you, good neighbours, let me alone with 'em now.

[*Exeunt* CITIZENS.]

MAWWORM. 'Sfoot, who's yonder?

HOBOY. Dare he sit there?

SECOND [COMPANION]. Follywit!

THIRD [COMPANION]. Captain! Puh!

FOLLYWIT. *How now, constable, what news with thee?*

CONSTABLE. [*facing* SIR BOUNTEOUS] May it please your worship, sir, here are a company of auspicious fellows.

SIR BOUNTEOUS. To me? Puh! Turn to th' justice, you whoreson hobbyhorse! – This is some new player now; they put all their fools to the constable's part still.

FOLLYWIT. *What's the matter, constable, what's the matter?*

CONSTABLE. I have nothing to say to your worship. [*He turns to* SIR BOUNTEOUS] They were all riding a-horseback, an't please your worship.

SIR BOUNTEOUS. Yet again? A pox of all asses still! They could not ride afoot unless 'twere in a bawdy house.

CONSTABLE. The ostler told me they were all unstable fellows, sir.

FOLLYWIT. *Why, sure the fellow's drunk!*

MAWWORM. [*improvising also*] *We spied that weakness in him long ago, sir. Your worship must bear with him; the man's much o'erseen. Only in respect of his office we obey'd him, both to appear comformable to law, and clear of all offence. For I protest, sir, he found us but a-horseback.*

FOLLYWIT. *What, he did?*

MAWWORM. *As I have a soul, that's all, and all he can lay to us.*

CONSTABLE. I' faith, you were not all riding away, then?

---

89 *auspicious*: a malapropism for 'suspicious'. Cf. *Much Ado*, III.v.41–3.

92 *hobbyhorse*: the figure in morris dances who acted the part of the horse; hence, a buffoon.

101 *ride*: a pun on the sense 'to mount sexually'.

107 *o'erseen*: deluded/intoxicated with drink.

112–13 *lay to us*: charge us with.

MAWWORM. *'Sfoot, being a-horseback, sir, that must needs follow.*

FOLLYWIT. *Why true, sir.*

SIR BOUNTEOUS. Well said, justice. He helps his kinsman well.

FOLLYWIT. *Why, sirrah, do you use to bring gentlemen before us for riding away? What, will you have 'em stand still when they're up, like Smug upo'th' white horse yonder? Are your wits sleep'd? I'll make you an example for all dizzy constables! How they abuse justice! Here, bind him to this chair.*

[*They seize and bind him.*]

CONSTABLE. Ha, bind him? Ho!

FOLLYWIT. *If you want cords, use garters.*

CONSTABLE. Help, help, gentlemen!

MAWWORM. *As fast as we can, sir.*

CONSTABLE. Thieves, thieves!

FOLLYWIT. *A gag will help all this. Keep less noise, you knave!*

CONSTABLE. Oh help, rescue the constable! Oh, oh!

[*They gag him.*]

SIR BOUNTEOUS. Ho, ho, ho, ho!

FOLLYWIT. *Why, la you, who lets you now?*
You may ride quietly; I'll see you to
Take horse myself. I have nothing else to do.

Exit [FOLLYWIT *with* MAWWORM, HOBOY *and* OTHERS.]

CONSTABLE. Oh, oh, oh!

SIR BOUNTEOUS. Ha, ha, ha! By my troth, the maddest piece of justice, gentlemen, that ever was committed!

HAREBRAIN. I'll be sworn for the madness on't, sir.

SIR BOUNTEOUS. I am deceiv'd if this prove not a merry comedy and a witty.

PENITENT. Alas, poor constable, his mouth's open and ne'er a wise word.

SIR BOUNTEOUS. Faith, he speaks now e'en as many as he has done; he seems wisest when he gapes and says nothing. Ha, ha, he turns and tells his tale to me like

---

98 *Smug upo'th'white horse*: referring to a scene (missing from the printed version) of *The Merry Devil of Edmonton* in which Smug plays St George riding upon a white horse.

124 *dizzy*: foolish, giddy; but see Textual note, p. 401.

135 *lets*: hinders.

an ass. What have I to do with their riding away; They may ride for me, thou whoreson coxcomb, thou; nay, thou art well enough serv'd, i' faith.

PENITENT. But what follows all this while, sir? Methinks some should pass by before this time and pity the constable.

SIR BOUNTEOUS. By th' mass, and you say true, sir. – Go, sirrah, step in; I think they have forgot themselves. Call the knaves away; they're in a wood, I believe.

[*Exit* SERVANT.]

CONSTABLE. Ay, ay, ay!

SIR BOUNTEOUS. Hark, the constable says 'ay', they're in a wood! Ha, ha!

[HAREBRAIN]. He thinks long of the time, Sir Bounteous.

[*Enter* SERVANT.]

SIR BOUNTEOUS. How now? When come they?

SERVANT. Alas, an't please your worship, there's not one of them to be found, sir.

SIR BOUNTEOUS. How?

HAREBRAIN. What says the fellow?

SERVANT. Neither horse nor man, sir.

SIR BOUNTEOUS. Body of me, thou liest!

SERVANT. Not a hair of either, sir.

HAREBRAIN. How now, Sir Bounteous?

SIR BOUNTEOUS. Cheated and defeated! Ungag that rascal; I'll hang him for's fellows, I'll make him bring 'em out. [*The* CONSTABLE *is untied.*]

CONSTABLE. Did not I tell your worship this before? Brought 'em before you for suspected persons? Stay'd 'em at town's end upon warning given? Made signs that my very jawbone aches? Your worship would not hear me, call'd me ass, saving your worship's presence, laugh'd at me.

SIR BOUNTEOUS. Ha?

HAREBRAIN. I begin to taste it.

SIR BOUNTEOUS. Give me leave, give me leave. Why, art not thou the constable i'th' comedy?

---

157 *in a wood*: in some difficulty.

161 s.h. [HAREBRAIN]: See Textual note, p. 399.

CONSTABLE. I'th' comedy? Why, I am the constable i'th' commonwealth, sir.

SIR BOUNTEOUS. I am gull'd, i' faith, I am gull'd! When wast thou chose?

CONSTABLE. On Thursday last, sir.

SIR BOUNTEOUS. A pox go with't, there't goes!

PENITENT. I seldom heard jest match it.

HAREBRAIN. Nor I, i' faith.

SIR BOUNTEOUS. Gentlemen, shall I entreat a courtesy?

HAREBRAIN. What is't, sir?

SIR BOUNTEOUS. Do not laugh at me seven year hence.

PENITENT. We should betray and laugh at our own folly then, for of my troth none here but was deceiv'd in't.

SIR BOUNTEOUS. Faith, that's some comfort yet. Ha, ha, it was featly carried! Troth, I commend their wits! Before our faces make us asses, while we sit still and only laugh at ourselves.

PENITENT. Faith, they were some counterfeit rogues, sir.

SIR BOUNTEOUS. Why, they confess so much themselves; they said they'd play *The Slip*; they should be men of their words. I hope the justice will have more conscience, i' faith, than to carry away a chain of a hundred mark of that fashion.

HAREBRAIN. What, sir?

SIR BOUNTEOUS. Ay, by my troth, sir; besides a jewel and a jewel's fellow, a good fair watch that hung about my neck, sir.

HAREBRAIN. 'Sfoot, what did you mean, sir?

SIR BOUNTEOUS. Methinks my Lord Owemuch's players should not scorn me so, i' faith; they will come and bring all again, I know. Push, they will, i' faith; but a jest, certainly.

Enter FOLLYWIT *in his own shape, and all the rest* [MAWWORM, HOBOY *and others*].

FOLLYWIT. Pray, grandsire, give me your blessing. [*He kneels.*]

SIR BOUNTEOUS. Who? Son Follywit?

---

198 *featly*: deftly.
206 *mark*: two thirds of a £1; *of that fashion*: in that manner.

FOLLYWIT. [*aside*] This shows like kneeling after the play, I praying for my Lord Owemuch and his good countess, our honourable lady and mistress.

SIR BOUNTEOUS. Rise richer by a blessing; thou art welcome.

FOLLYWIT. Thanks, good grandsire. I was bold to bring those gentlemen, my friends.

SIR BOUNTEOUS. They're all welcome. Salute you that side, and I'll welcome this side. [BOUNTEOUS *and* FOLLYWIT *each greet the other's retinue*] Sir, to begin with you. [*Salutes* MAWWORM.]

HAREBRAIN. Master Follywit. [*Salutes* FOLLYWIT.]

FOLLYWIT. I am glad 'tis our fortune so happily to meet, sir.

SIR BOUNTEOUS. [*to* HOBOY] Nay, then you know me not, sir.

FOLLYWIT. Sweet Mistress Harebrain. [*Salutes her.*]

SIR BOUNTEOUS. [*to another of Follywit's men*] You cannot be too bold, sir.

FOLLYWIT. [*greeting the* COURTESAN] Our marriage known?

COURTESAN. [*in an undertone*] Not a word yet.

FOLLYWIT. The better.

SIR BOUNTEOUS. Faith, son, would you had come sooner with these gentlemen.

FOLLYWIT. Why, grandsire?

SIR BOUNTEOUS. We had a play here.

FOLLYWIT. A play, sir? No.

SIR BOUNTEOUS. Yes, faith, a pox a'th' author!

FOLLYWIT. [*aside*] Bless us all! – Why, were they such vild ones, sir?

SIR BOUNTEOUS. I am sure villainous ones, sir.

FOLLYWIT. Some raw, simple fools?

SIR BOUNTEOUS. Nay, by th' mass, these were enough for thievish knaves.

FOLLYWIT. What, sir?

SIR BOUNTEOUS. Which way came you, gentlemen? You could not choose but meet 'em.

---

218 *kneeling after the play*: It was the custom for players (who evaded being classed as vagabonds by being nominally the servants of a member of the aristocracy) to pray publicly for their patron at the close of a performance, though it probably was no longer done in the public theatres.

FOLLYWIT. We met a company with hampers after 'em.

SIR BOUNTEOUS. Oh, those were they, those were they, a pox hamper 'em!

FOLLYWIT. [*aside*] Bless us all again!

SIR BOUNTEOUS. They have hamper'd me finely, sirrah.

FOLLYWIT. How, sir?

SIR BOUNTEOUS. How, sir? I lent the rascals properties to furnish out their play, a chain, a jewel, and a watch, and they watch'd their time and rid quite away with 'em.

FOLLYWIT. Are they such creatures?

[*The watch rings in his pocket.*]

SIR BOUNTEOUS. Hark, hark, gentlemen! By this light, the watch rings alarum in his pocket! There's my watch come again, or the very cousin-german to't. Whose is't, whose is't? By th' mass, 'tis he; hast thou one, son? Prithee bestow it upon thy grandsire. I now look for mine again, i' faith. [*He delves in* FOLLYWIT*'s pocket*] Nay, come with a good will or not at all; I'll give thee a better thing. A prize, a prize, gentlemen!

HAREBRAIN. Great or small?

SIR BOUNTEOUS. At once I have drawn chain, jewel, watch, and all!

PENITENT. By my faith, you have a fortunate hand, sir.

HAREBRAIN. Nay, all to come at once.

MAWWORM. A vengeance of this foolery!

FOLLYWIT. Have I 'scap'd the constable to be brought in by the watch?

COURTESAN. O destiny! Have I married a thief, mother?

MOTHER. Comfort thyself; thou art beforehand with him, daughter.

SIR BOUNTEOUS. Why son, why gentlemen, how long have you been my Lord Owemuch his servants, i' faith?

FOLLYWIT. Faith, grandsire, shall I be true to you?

SIR BOUNTEOUS. I think 'tis time; thou'st been a thief already.

---

269 *cousin-german*: first cousin.

273 *come with a good will or not at all*: the last line of the nursery rhyme 'Girls and Boys Come Out to Play'.

274 *prize*: See Textual note, p. 401.

282 *watch*: punning on the body of citizens who policed the streets at night.

284–5 *thou art beforehand with him*: 'You've paid him in advance for it'.

FOLLYWIT. I, knowing the day of your feast and the natural inclination you have to pleasure and pastime, presum'd upon your patience for a jest, as well to prolong your days as –

SIR BOUNTEOUS. Whoop! Why, then you took my chain along with you to prolong my days, did you?

FOLLYWIT. Not so neither, sir; and that you may be seriously assured of my hereafter stableness of life, I have took another course.

SIR BOUNTEOUS. What?

FOLLYWIT. Took a wife.

SIR BOUNTEOUS. A wife? 'Sfoot, what is she for a fool would marry thee, a madman? When was the wedding kept in Bedlam?

FOLLYWIT. She's both a gentlewoman and a virgin.

SIR BOUNTEOUS. Stop there, stop there; would I might see her!

FOLLYWIT. You have your wish; she's here.

SIR BOUNTEOUS. Ah, ha, ha, ha! This makes amends for all.

FOLLYWIT. How now?

MAWWORM. Captain, do you hear? Is she your wife in earnest?

FOLLYWIT. How then?

MAWWORM. Nothing but pity you, sir.

SIR BOUNTEOUS. Speak, son, is't true?
Can you gull us, and let a quean gull you?

FOLLYWIT. Ha!

COURTESAN. What I have been is past; be that forgiven,
And have a soul true both to thee and heaven.

FOLLYWIT. Is't come about? Tricks are repaid, I see.

SIR BOUNTEOUS. The best is, sirrah, you pledge none
but me;
And since I drink the top, take her; and hark,
I spice the bottom with a thousand mark.

FOLLYWIT. By my troth, she is as good a cup of nectar as any bachelor needs to sip at.

---

302 *what is she for a fool*: 'What kind of fool is she?'

304 *Bedlam*: the hospital of St Mary of Bethlehem, a hospital for the mentally deranged in Bishopsgate, controlled by the Mayor and Corporation.

322 *you pledge*: i.e. 'you follow in drinking from this "cup" '.

Tut, give me gold, it makes amends for vice;
Maids without coin are caudles without spice.
SIR BOUNTEOUS. Come, gentlemen, to th' feast, let not time waste;
We have pleas'd our ear, now let us please our taste.
Who lives by cunning, mark it, his fate's cast;
When he has gull'd all, then is himself the last.

Finis

---

328 *caudles*: a warm drink; wine or ale mixed with gruel, sweetened and spiced.
Finis: For detail of a Caroline production, see Textual note, p. 401.

A

CHAST MAYD

IN

CHEAPE-SIDE.

A

Pleaſant conceited Comedy
neuer before printed.

As it hath beene often acted at the
Swan on the Banke-ſide, by the
Lady ELIZABETH her
Seruants.

By THOMAS MIDELTON Gent.

LONDON,
Printed for *Francis Conſtable* dwelling at the
ſigne of the *Crane* in *Pauls*
Church-yard.
1630.

Title-page of the 1630 Quarto of *A Chaste Maid in Cheapside*, reproduced by permission of the Trustees of the British Museum.

INTRODUCTORY NOTE

A British Museum copy (Ashley 5353) of the 1630 quarto served as copy text for this edition. Q is well printed with few important variants, and was probably set up from a scribal transcript of a Middleton fair copy. Besides being included in collections, the play has been edited as unpublished theses by M. Fisher (Oxford B.Litt., 1937), by R.J. Wall (Ph.D., University of Michigan, 1958) and D.F. George (M.A., University of Manchester, 1962). One-volume editions are by A. Brissenden for New Mermaid (1968), C. Barber for Fountainwell Drama Texts (1969) and R.B. Parker for the Revels (1969). Brissenden's text collated five copies and followed Q's lineation fairly closely; he offers a brief, sensible introduction but limited notes. Barber offers an old-spelling text with a modest introduction, notes and glossary. Much of their work has been superseded by Parker's collation of known copies of Q and later editions, by his exhaustive notes and introduction. However, Parker re-lineates extensively on very subjective criteria, departing wholly from Q and from what is known of Middleton's practice in the manuscript of *A Game at Chess*; some of his critical comments and annotation seem a little fanciful. The Scolar Press have published a facsimile of the 1630 quarto (1969).

There are no actual sources of Middleton's play but many analogues in his own work, in jest-books and contemporary anecdote, and in the drama and ballad traditions. Minor sources may be: the sixth chapter of Thomas Campion's *Observations in the Art of English Poesie* (1602), a nineteen-line poem entitled 'The Eighth Epigram' which parallels the Allwit sub-plot; the mock funeral in Beaumont's *Knight of the Burning Pestle*, acted in 1607 (though the episode was also conventional); the third chapter of *The Batchelar's Banquet* (1603), 'The humour of a woman lying in Child-bed' (though again the material is conventional).

The 1630 title-page says that the play 'hath been often acted at the Swan on the Bankside, by the Lady Elizabeth and her Servants'. The play does not seem to have been revived at the Restoration, and the first modern production appears to have been a snippet from the action entitled *A Posy on the Ring* which received one performance in a reconstructed Globe Theatre in the 'Shakespeare's England' Exhibition at Earls Court on 16 September 1912. Leverett House, Harvard University, acted a version directed by Alfred David at Christmas 1956. Frederick May produced the play for a season from 26 November 1956 for the Theatre Group of Leeds University

Students Union. William Gaskell produced a heavily cut version for the Central School of Speech and Drama at the Embassy Theatre, Swiss Cottage, London, 10 March 1961. In March 1962 the University of Southampton put on a version in Jacobean costume. In May Week 1964, on 14 and 15 June, Martin Short produced a heavily cut version at Jesus College, Cambridge, concentrating on the satire relevant to Cambridge and academics. A professional production by William Gaskell for the English Stage Society opened at the Royal Court Theatre, 13 January 1966, in Edwardian settings. St Michael's College, University of Toronto, under the direction of William Glassco, gave a conservative version from 2–4 February 1967. Oxford University Dramatic Society opened a production on 17 February 1970.

R.B. Parker's Revels edition of the play (pp. 128–37) contains seventeenth-century music for the songs at IV.i and V.ii.

[DRAMATIS PERSONAE]

The Names of the Principal Persons.

MASTER YELLOWHAMMER, a goldsmith.
MAUDLINE, his wife.
TIM, their son.
MOLL, their daughter [sometimes called MARY].
TUTOR to Tim.
SIR WALTER WHOREHOUND, a suitor to Moll.
SIR OLIVER KIX, and his WIFE, kin to Sir Walter.
MASTER ALLWIT, and his WIFE, whom Sir Walter keeps.
WELSH GENTLEWOMAN, Sir Walter's whore.
WAT and NICK, his bastards [by MISTRESS ALLWIT].
DAVY DAHUMMA, his man.
TOUCHWOOD SENIOR, and his WIFE, a decayed gentleman.
TOUCHWOOD JUNIOR, another suitor to Moll.
2 PROMOTERS.
SERVANTS.
WATERMEN.
[PORTER].
[GENTLEMAN].

---

1 YELLOWHAMMER: Besides indicating his profession as a goldsmith, the name can be slang for 'a gold coin' and for 'a fool'.

2 MAUDLINE: The spelling represents the English pronunciation of 'Magdalene'; according to Christian tradition, Mary Magdalene was a reformed prostitute.

4 MOLL: diminutive of 'Mary', but applied to whores and the women of criminals; it reflects the ambiguity of the author's attitude to the romantic sub-plot.

7 OLIVER KIX: 'Oliver' means fruitful, 'Kix' is a dry, hollow plant stalk and, figuratively, a dried-up, sapless person; Middleton was fond of oxymoron in names, a reflection of his ambiguous stance towards his characters.

8 ALLWIT: 'All Intellect', but also a transposition of 'wittol' = willing cuckold.

11 DAHUMMA: See Textual note, p. 401. It is a phonetic spelling of the Welsh for 'come here'.

12 TOUCHWOOD: tinder, especially that used to light the touchhold of a musket, and (figuratively) a passionate person; one who emotionally or sexually gives and takes 'fire' easily.

14 PROMOTERS: informers.

16 WATERMEN: boatmen, plying for hire on the Thames.

[COUNTRY WENCH, with a child.]
[JUGG, a maid to Lady Kix.]
[DRY NURSE.]
[WET NURSE.]
[2 MEN, with baskets.]
[MISTRESS UNDERMAN, a Puritan.]
[PURITANS and GOSSIPS.]
[MIDWIFE.]
[PARSON.]
[SUSAN, maid to Moll.]

A Chaste Maid in Cheapside: Cheapside, or West Cheap, ran east from the N.E. corner of St Paul's, and the shop would be in Goldsmith's Row on the south side; the paradoxical title may have been semi-proverbial, with similar implications to 'a nice girl in Soho'.

A CHASTE MAID IN CHEAPSIDE

ACT I

SCENE I

Enter MAUDLINE *and* MOLL, *a shop being discovered.*

MAUDLINE. Have you play'd over all your old lessons o'the virginals?

MOLL. Yes.

MAUDLINE. Yes! You are a dull maid a' late, methinks you had need have somewhat to quicken your green sickness (do you weep?) – a husband! Had not such a piece of flesh been ordained, what had us wives been good for? To make sallets, or else cried up and down for sampier. To see the difference of these seasons! When I was of your youth, I was lightsome, and quick, two years before I was married. You fit for a knight's bed! Drowsy-brow'd, dull-eyed, drossy-sprited – I hold my life you have forgot your dancing: when was the dancer with you?

MOLL. The last week.

MAUDLINE. Last week? When I was of your bord, he

---

s.d. *discovered*: This would suggest that a curtain was drawn back to reveal an inner stage or alcove (though s.d. at III.ii does not seem to imply such a facility).

2 *virginals*: a keyboard instrument, legless and housed in a case, whose strings were plucked like a spinet; the lady-like accomplishment of 'playing the virginals' is a recurrent metaphor for sexual stimulation (as also 'dancing' later).

5–6 *quicken*: make alive/make pregnant; *green sickness*: chlorosis, an anaemic sickness of girls at puberty, regarded as a sign of love-sickness or of desire for a man.

8 *to make sallets*: to become salads.

8–9 *cried up and down for sampier*: hawked in the street as samphire (Fr. 'herbe de Saint Pierre'), either marsh-samphire, used in salads or cooked like spinach, or the unrelated rock-samphire, which was pickled in brine and brought to London from the coast as a relish to meat.

9 *To see the difference of these seasons*: 'How times have changed!'

10 *quick*: lively//pregnant.

12 *drossy-sprited*: in foul spirits.

16 *bord*: bore, calibre (as of a gun); hence size, age (innuendos are maintained).

miss'd me not a night, I was kept at it; I took delight to learn, and he to teach me, pretty brown gentleman, he took pleasure in my company; but you are dull, nothing comes nimbly from you, you dance like a plumber's daughter, and deserve two thousand pounds in lead to your marriage, and not in goldsmith's ware.

Enter YELLOWHAMMER.

YELLOWHAMMER. Now what's the din betwixt mother and daughter, ha?

MAUDLINE. Faith, small, telling your daughter Mary of her errors.

YELLOWHAMMER. Errors! Nay, the city cannot hold you, wife, but you must needs fetch words from Westminster (I ha' done, i'faith): has no attorney's clerk been here a' late and changed his half-crown-piece his mother sent him, or rather cozen'd you with a gilded twopence, to bring the word in fashion for her faults or cracks in duty and obedience? Term 'em e'en so, sweet wife. As there is no woman made without a flaw, your purest lawns have frays, and cambrics bracks.

MAUDLINE. But 'tis a husband sowders up all cracks.

MOLL. What, is he come, sir?

YELLOWHAMMER. Sir Walter's come.
He was met at Holborn Bridge, and in his company
A proper fair young gentlewoman, which I guess
By her red hair, and other rank descriptions,
To be his landed niece brought out of Wales,
Which Tim our son (the Cambridge boy) must marry.

28–9 *Westminster*: Westminster Hall housed the courts of Common Pleas, King's Bench and Chancery, with other courts in the immediate neighbourhood; Yellowhammer objects to a term apparently derived from the Law French in which actions were conducted.

31–2 *gilded twopence*: i.e. counterfeit; the silver twopence is made to look like the gold half-crown, which was of similar size.

35–6 *lawns . . . cambrics*: fine white linens; *bracks*: flaws.

37 *sowders*: solders; *cracks*: also, the female genitals.

40 *Holborn Bridge*: over the Fleet Ditch at the eastern end of Holborn Hill; it carried the main road from the west to enter the City at Newgate.

42 *rank*: over-abundant/indicative of rank//corrupt, lecherous (red hair was held to indicate sexual vigour).

'Tis a match of Sir Walter's own making
To bind us to him, and our heirs for ever.

MAUDLINE. We are honour'd then, if this baggage would be humble,
And kiss him with devotion when he enters.
I cannot get her for my life
To instruct her hand thus, before and after,
Which a knight will look for, before and after.
I have told her still, 'tis the waving of a woman
Does often move a man, and prevails strongly.
But sweet, ha' you sent to Cambridge,
Has Tim word on't?

YELLOWHAMMER. Had word just the day after when you sent him the silver spoon to eat his broth in the hall amongst the gentlemen commoners.

MAUDLINE. Oh, 'twas timely.

Enter PORTER.

YELLOWHAMMER. How now?

PORTER. A letter from a gentleman in Cambridge.

YELLOWHAMMER. Oh, one of Hobson's porters, thou art welcome. – I told thee, Maud, we should hear from Tim. [*He reads the letter*] *Amantissimis carissimisque ambobus parentibus patri et matri.*

MAUDLINE. What's the matter?

YELLOWHAMMER. Nay, by my troth, I know not, ask not me, he's grown too verbal; this learning is a great witch.

MAUDLINE. Pray let me see it, I was wont to understand him. [*She reads*] *Amantissimus carissimus*, he has sent

---

50 *before and after*: Maudline indicates the affected carriage of the hands before and behind the waist, in making a curtsey; an innuendo is also intended.

52 *waving*: bodily movement/hand movements.

58 *gentlemen commoners*: wealthy undergraduates who bought certain privileges, including that of dining at a separate table from poorer students; Tim is a social climber.

62 *Hobson*: the famous Cambridge carrier Thomas Hobson, on whose death in January 1630/1 the student Milton wrote two epitaphs; his stables were probably on the site of the chapel of St Catherine's College.

64–5 Latin: 'To my two most loving and dearest parents, father and mother'.

66 *matter*: content; but Maudline probably expresses alarm at hearing her husband spout gibberish.

the carrier's man, he says; *ambobus parentibus*, for a pair of boots; *patri et matri*, pay the porter, or it makes no matter.

PORTER. Yes, by my faith! Mistress, there's no true construction in that; I have took a great deal of pains, and come from the Bell sweating. Let me come to't, for I was a scholar forty years ago. 'Tis thus, I warrant you: [*He takes the letter and reads*] *Matri*, it makes no matter; *ambobus parentibus*, for a pair of boots; *patri*, pay the porter; *amantissimis carissimis*, he's the carrier's man, and his name is Sims – and there he says true, forsooth, my name is Sims indeed. I have not forgot all my learning. – A money matter, I thought I should hit on't.

YELLOWHAMMER. Go, thou art an old fox, there's a tester for thee. [*Gives money.*]

PORTER. If I see your worship at Goose Fair, I have a dish of birds for you.

YELLOWHAMMER. Why, dost dwell at Bow?

PORTER. All my lifetime, sir, I could ever say Bo, to a goose.
Farewell to your worship. *Exit* PORTER.

YELLOWHAMMER. A merry porter.

MAUDLINE. How can he choose but be so, coming with Cambridge letters from our son Tim?

74–5 *no true construction*: no accurate construing, translating.

76 *the Bell*: Wagons and coaches came every Thursday and Friday to the Black Bull in Bishopsgate Street, so 'Bell' may be a compositor's error; however, Cambridge carriers are known to have lodged at the Bell in Coleman Street, off Moorgate.

86 *tester*: sixpence.

87 *Goose Fair*: fair held in Whitsun week at Stratford-le-Bow, then in Essex (4½ miles N.E. of St Paul's), where young ('green') geese were roasted and sold; 'green goose' also means 'a harlot', and 'goose' = a fool, so that there is probably an indecent suggestion in the offer of a 'dish of birds'.

90 *Bo to a goose*: Proverbial (Tilley, B 481); but as 'bow' = the female pudendum in *Michaelmas Term*, II.i.111–16, an indecent quibble is probably intended.

YELLOWHAMMER. What's here? [*Reads*] *Maximus diligo.* – Faith, I must to my learned counsel with this gear, 'twill ne'er be discern'd else.
MAUDLINE. Go to my cousin then, at Inns of Court.
YELLOWHAMMER. Fie, they are all for French, they speak no Latin.
MAUDLINE. The parson then will do it.

Enter a GENTLEMAN *with a chain.*

YELLOWHAMMER. Nay he disclaims it, calls Latin 'Papistry': he will not deal with it. What is't you lack, gentleman?
GENTLEMAN. Pray weigh this chain.
[YELLOWHAMMER *weighs it.*]

Enter SIR WALTER WHOREHOUND, WELSH GENTLEWOMAN *and* DAVY DAHUMMA.

SIR WALTER. Now, wench, thou art welcome to the heart of the city of London.
WELSH GENTLEWOMAN. *Dugat a whee.*
SIR WALTER. You can thank me in English, if you list.
WELSH GENTLEWOMAN. I can, sir, simply.
SIR WALTER. 'Twill serve to pass, wench; 'twas strange that I should lie with thee so often, to leave thee without English – that were unnatural.
I bring thee up to turn thee into gold, wench,
And make thy fortune shine like your bright trade;
A goldsmith's shop sets out a city maid.
Davy Dahumma, not a word!
DAVY. Mum, mum, sir.
SIR WALTER. Here you must pass for a pure virgin.

---

95 *Maximus diligo*: See Textual note, p. 402. Probably Tim means to say 'I esteem you most highly', but his schoolboy Latin makes him say 'I am the greatest and I love (you).'
97 *gear*: matter, stuff.
98–9 *Inns of Court*: London collegiate bodies of practitioners and students of law; *French*: Law French was much used by the students.
108 *Dugat a whee*: phonetic spelling for the Welsh for 'God keep you.'
111–12 *'twas strange that*: it would be strange if.
115 *your*: Probably impersonal, 'one's', referring to the goldsmith's trade.

DAVY. [*aside*] Pure Welsh virgin! She lost her maidenhead in Brecknockshire.

SIR WALTER. I hear you mumble, Davy.

DAVY. I have teeth, sir, I need not mumble yet this forty years.

SIR WALTER. [*aside*] The knave bites plaguily.

YELLOWHAMMER. [*to* GENTLEMAN] What's your price, sir?

GENTLEMAN. A hundred pound, sir.

YELLOWHAMMER. A hundred marks the utmost, 'tis not for me else.
– What, Sir Walter Whorehound.

[*Exit* GENTLEMAN.]

MOLL. Oh, death! *Exit* MOLL.

MAUDLINE. Why, daughter! Faith, the baggage!
– A bashful girl, sir; these young things are shamefast;
Besides you have a presence, sweet Sir Walter,
Able to daunt a maid brought up i'the city:

[*Re-*]*enter* [MOLL].

A brave Court spirit makes our virgins quiver,
And kiss with trembling thighs. Yet see, she comes, sir.

SIR WALTER. Why, how now, pretty mistress, now I have caught you. [*Catches* MOLL *by the hand*] What, can you injure so your time to stray thus from your faithful servant?

YELLOWHAMMER. Pish, stop your words, good knight, 'twill make her blush else, which wound too high for the daughters of the Freedom. 'Honour', and 'faithful

---

121 *Brecknockshire*: in S.E. Wales; a pun on 'break nock', 'nock' being the female pudendum.

125 *plaguily*: excessively, vexatiously. Davy presumably hits at his master's senility, or at the effects of veneral disease upon him.

129 *marks*: A mark was worth two-thirds of £1.

133 *shamefast*: bashful, modest.

135 s.d. See Textual note, p. 402. As the text stands, Moll's return seems to be voluntary; perhaps she is retrieved by Yellowhammer.

143 *wound*: go, proceed. See Textual note, p. 402.

144 *daughters of the Freedom*: i.e. daughters of London citizens, as opposed to the courtiers who frequented the royal palaces of Whitehall and Greenwich.

servant', they are compliments for the worthies of Whitehall, or Greenwich. E'en plain, sufficient, subsidy words serves us, sir. And is this gentlewoman your worthy niece?

SIR WALTER. You may be bold with her on these terms, 'tis she, sir, heir to some nineteen mountains.

YELLOWHAMMER. Bless us all! You overwhelm me, sir, with love and riches.

SIR WALTER. And all as high as Paul's.

DAVY. [*aside*] Here's work, i'faith.

SIR WALTER. How sayest thou, Davy?

DAVY. Higher, sir, by far; you cannot see the top of 'em.

YELLOWHAMMER. What, man? Maudline, salute this gentlewoman – our daughter, if things hit right.

[MAUDLINE *kisses* WELSH GENTLEWOMAN.]

Enter TOUCHWOOD JUNIOR.

TOUCHWOOD JUNIOR. [*aside*] My knight with a brace of footmen
Is come and brought up his ewe mutton
To find a ram at London; I must hasten it,
Or else pick a famine; her blood's mine,
And that's the surest. Well, knight, that choice spoil
Is only kept for me.

[*He attracts* MOLL*'s attention from behind.*]

MOLL. Sir?

TOUCHWOOD JUNIOR. Turn not to me till thou may'st lawfully, it but whets my stomach, which is too sharp set already. [*Gives her a letter*] Read that note carefully, keep me from suspicion still, nor know my zeal but in thy heart; read and send but thy liking in three words, I'll be at hand to take it.

146–7 *subsidy*: solid bourgeois, commercial.
153 *as high as Paul's*: Proverbial. The tower of Old St Paul's was 245 feet, and until the fire of 1561 had been surmounted by a steeple a further 205 feet high.
160 *mutton*: prostitute.
161 *hasten it*: 'act fast'.
162 *pick a famine*: choose to starve; but see Textual note, p. 402. *blood*: See Additional note, p. 402. 'Her sexual desire is towards me, and that is the surest way to be certain of her.'
167–8 *stomach . . . sharp set*: sexual appetite . . . keen.
170 *liking*: consent, approval.

YELLOWHAMMER. Oh, turn, sir, turn.
A poor plain boy, an university man,
Proceeds next Lent to a Bachelor of Art;
He will be call'd Sir Yellowhammer then
Over all Cambridge, and that's half a knight.
MAUDLINE. Please you draw near, and taste the welcome of the city, sir?
YELLOWHAMMER. Come, good Sir Walter, and your virtuous niece here.
SIR WALTER. 'Tis manners to take kindness.
YELLOWHAMMER. Lead 'em in, wife.
SIR WALTER. Your company, sir.
YELLOWHAMMER. I'll give't you instantly.
[*Exeunt* MAUDLINE, SIR WALTER, DAVY *and* WELSH GENTLEWOMAN; MOLL *is unwilling to follow*.]
TOUCHWOOD JUNIOR. [*aside*] How strangely busy is the devil and riches;
Poor soul kept in too hard, her mother's eye
Is cruel toward her, being to him.
'Twere a good mirth now to set him a-work
To make her wedding ring; I must about it.
Rather than the gain should fall to a stranger,
'Twas honesty in me to enrich my father.
YELLOWHAMMER. [*aside*] The girl is wondrous peevish; I fear nothing
But that she's taken with some other love;
Then all's quite dash'd. That must be narrowly look'd to;
We cannot be too wary in our children.
– What is't you lack?
TOUCHWOOD JUNIOR. [*aside*] Oh, nothing now, all that I wish is present.
– I would have a wedding ring made for a gentlewoman
With all speed that may be.

---

172 *Oh, turn, sir, turn*: See Textual note, p. 402.

175 *Sir*: a rendering of 'Dominus', the Latin title accorded to graduates at Oxford and Cambridge; used only with the surname, it was thus distinguished from the knightly title (hence 'half a knight').

187 *being to him*: perhaps 'being favourable to him'; or the MS may have read 'being *kind* to him', balancing the previous phrase.

191 *'Twas*: it would be.

YELLOWHAMMER. Of what weight, sir?
TOUCHWOOD JUNIOR. Of some half ounce,
Stand fair and comely with the spark of a diamond.
Sir, 'twere pity to lose the least grace.
YELLOWHAMMER. Pray let's see it; [*He takes the stone*] indeed, sir, 'tis a pure one.
TOUCHWOOD. So is the mistress.
YELLOWHAMMER. Have you the wideness of her finger, sir?
TOUCHWOOD JUNIOR. Yes, sure, I think I have her measure about me.
– Good faith, 'tis down; I cannot show't you,
I must pull too many things out to be certain.
Let me see: long, and slender, and neatly jointed;
Just such another gentlewoman that's your daughter, sir.
YELLOWHAMMER. And therefore, sir, no gentlewoman.
TOUCHWOOD JUNIOR. I protest I never saw two maids handed more alike;
I'll ne'er seek farther, if you'll give me leave, sir.
YELLOWHAMMER. If you dare venture by her finger, sir.
TOUCHWOOD JUNIOR. Ay, and I'll bide all loss, sir.
YELLOWHAMMER. Say you so, sir? Let's see hither, girl.
TOUCHWOOD JUNIOR. Shall I make bold with your finger, gentlewoman?
MOLL. Your pleasure, sir.
TOUCHWOOD JUNIOR. [*trying the ring on* MOLL*'s finger*]
That fits her to a hair, sir.
YELLOWHAMMER. What's your posy now, sir?

---

201 *Stand*: probably elliptic, 'that would stand'; *spark of a diamond*: with a small (sparkling) diamond. Wedding rings were often an enamelled hoop with small gems or took the form of two hands clasping a heart made from a jewel; a motto was engraved inside.

208 *measure*: the size of her finger/that capable of 'measuring' her (i.e. the phallus).

209 *down*: at the bottom of the pocket/detumescent.

212 *that's your daughter*: 'as is your daughter'; but see Textual note, p. 402.

217 *bide all loss*: pay for any mistakes.

222 *to a hair*: to perfection, but probably with an innuendo on 'hair' = female pubes.

223 *posy*: verse motto.

TOUCHWOOD. Mass, that's true, posy, i'faith. E'en thus, sir:
Love that's wise, blinds parents' eyes.
YELLOWHAMMER. How, how? If I may speak without offence, sir,
I hold my life –
TOUCHWOOD JUNIOR. What, sir?
YELLOWHAMMER. Go to, you'll pardon me?
TOUCHWOOD JUNIOR. Pardon you? Ay, sir.
YELLOWHAMMER. Will you, i'faith?
TOUCHWOOD JUNIOR. Yes, faith I will.
YELLOWHAMMER. You'll steal away some man's daughter, am I near you?
Do you turn aside? You gentlemen are mad wags!
I wonder things can be so warily carried,
And parents blinded so; but they're served right
That have two eyes, and wear so dull a sight.
TOUCHWOOD JUNIOR. [*aside*] Thy doom take hold of thee.
YELLOWHAMMER. Tomorrow noon shall show your ring well done.
TOUCHWOOD JUNIOR. Being so, 'tis soon. Thanks – and your leave, sweet gentlewoman. *Exit.*
MOLL. Sir, you are welcome.
[*Aside*] Oh, were I made of wishes, I went with thee.
YELLOWHAMMER. Come now, we'll see how the rules go within.
MOLL. [*aside*] That robs my joy, there I lose all I win.
Ex[*eunt*].

SCENE II

Enter DAVY *and* ALLWIT *severally.*

DAVY. Honesty wash my eyes, I have spied a wittol.
ALLWIT. What, Davy Dahumma? Welcome from North Wales,
I'faith; and is Sir Walter come?
DAVY. New come to town, sir.

---

233 *am I near you*: 'Do I guess correctly?' (but with unconscious irony).
246 *rules*: probably 'revels, frolicsome games'.
s.d. *severally*: from different directions.

ALLWIT. In to the maids, sweet Davy, and give order
His chamber be made ready instantly;
My wife's as great as she can wallow, Davy,
And longs for nothing but pickled cucumbers,
And his coming, and now she shall ha't, boy.
DAVY. She's sure of them, sir.
ALLWIT. Thy very sight will hold my wife in pleasure,
Till the knight come himself. Go in, in, in, Davy.
Exit [DAVY].
The founder's come to town; I am like a man
Finding a table furnish'd to his hand,
As mine is still to me, prays for the founder:
'Bless the right worshipful, the good founder's life.'
I thank him, h'as maintain'd my house this ten years,
Not only keeps my wife, but a keeps me,
And all my family; I am at his table,
He gets me all my children, and pays the nurse,
Monthly, or weekly, puts me to nothing,
Rent, nor church duties, not so much as the scavenger:
The happiest state that ever man was born to.
I walk out in a morning, come to breakfast,
Find excellent cheer, a good fire in winter;
Look in my coal house about midsummer eve,
That's full, five or six chaldron, new laid up;
Look in my back yard, I shall find a steeple
Made up with Kentish faggots, which o'erlooks
The waterhouse and the windmills; I say nothing,
But smile, and pin the door. When she lies in,
And now she's even upon the point of grunting,

---

17 *a*: he.

21 *church duties . . . scavenger*: Parish dues could be paid by service or by cash. The scavenger had to see that pavements were maintained and streets clean, and also that chimneys and furnaces were not a fire-risk.

26 *chaldron*: a dry measure of four quarters or thirty-two bushels.

28 *Kentish faggots*: bundles of brushwood, about eight foot long and a foot through; Kent supplied much of London's firewood.

29 *waterhouse and the windmills*: probably the six windmills in Finsbury Fields (½ mile N.E.), and the cistern at the head of the New River at Islington, completed in 1613 by Hugh Middleton to bring London fresh water (about 1 mile N.E.).

30 *pin*: bolt.

A lady lies not in like her: there's her embossings,
Embroid'rings, spanglings, and I know not what,
As if she lay with all the gaudy shops
In Gresham's Burse about her; then her restoratives,
Able to set up a young 'pothecary,
And richly stock the foreman of a drug shop;
Her sugar by whole loaves, her wines by rundlets.
I see these things, but like a happy man,
I pay for none at all, yet fools think's mine;
I have the name, and in his gold I shine;
And where some merchants would in soul kiss Hell
To buy a paradise for their wives, and dye
Their conscience in the bloods of prodigal heirs
To deck their night-piece, yet all this being done,
Eaten with jealousy to the inmost bone
(As what affliction nature more constrains
Than feed the wife plump for another's veins?),
These torments stand I freed of, I am as clear
From jealousy of a wife as from the charge:
Oh two miraculous blessings! 'Tis the knight
Hath took that labour all out of my hands:
I may sit still and play; he's jealous for me,
Watches her steps, sets spies. I live at ease,
He has both the cost and torment: when the strings
Of his heart frets, I feed, laugh, or sing,
La dildo, dildo la dildo, la dildo dildo de dildo.

---

32 *embossings*: ornaments in low relief (here probably upon cloth).

33 *spanglings*: material decorated with small spangles.

35 *Gresham's Burse*: the Royal Exchange, built by Sir Thomas Gresham from 1566–8 as a meeting place for merchants. In the covered walk on the south side were stalls selling trinkets, fine silks and draperies, finery or 'gaudy'.

38 *rundlets*: here, large barrels of 18½ gallons in capacity.

45 *night-piece*: properly, 'a painting depicting a night scene', but here used jocularly of a mistress, perhaps with the implication that she is painted.

47 *nature more constrains*: more oppresses nature.

48 *veins*: i.e. 'blood' = sexual desire.

55 *strings*: The heart was believed to be braced with strings which frayed and snapped under emotional stress; there is also allusion to musical strings and to the rings of gut which served as frets on the fingerboard, eventually fretting the strings.

57 *La dildo*: a meaningless refrain in songs, but also an artificial penis.

Enter two SERVANTS.

1 [SERVANT]. What has he got a-singing in his head now?

2 [SERVANT]. Now's out of work he falls to making dildoes.

ALLWIT. Now, sirs, Sir Walter's come.

1 [SERVANT]. Is our master come?

ALLWIT. Your master? What am I?

1 [SERVANT]. Do not you know, sir?

ALLWIT. Pray am not I your master?

1 [SERVANT]. Oh you are but our mistress's husband.

Enter SIR WALTER *and* DAVY.

ALLWIT. *Ergo* knave, your master.

1 [SERVANT]. *Negatur argumentum.* – Here comes Sir Walter. [*Aside to* 2 SERVANT] Now a stands bare as well as we; make the most of him, he's but one peep above a servingman, and so much his horns make him.

SIR WALTER. How dost, Jack?

ALLWIT. Proud of your worship's health, sir.

SIR WALTER. How does your wife?

ALLWIT. E'en after your own making, sir;
She's a tumbler, a' faith, the nose and belly meets.

SIR WALTER. They'll part in time again.

ALLWIT. At the good hour, they will, and please your worship.

SIR WALTER. [*to* 1 SERVANT] Here, sirrah, pull off my boots. [*To* ALLWIT] Put on, put on, Jack.

ALLWIT. I thank your kind worship, sir.

SIR WALTER. Slippers! [2 SERVANT *brings slippers*] Heart, you are sleepy.

ALLWIT. [*aside*] The game begins already.

SIR WALTER. Pish, put on, Jack.

---

58 *a-singing in his head*: a symptom of cuckoldry.

67–8 *Ergo . . . Negatur argumentum*: 'therefore' . . . 'I deny your proof'; both are standard tags from Latin disputations.

69 *bare*: bareheaded;
peep: degree (from 'pips', the spots on a playing-card which indicate its denomination); Allwit *peeps* over a servingman's head through the additional stature conferred by a cuckold's horns.

76 *tumbler*: acrobat//copulator.

81 *put on*: Allwit having deferentially taken off his hat, he is invited to resume it; hats were worn indoors.

ALLWIT. [*to audience*] Now I must do it, or he'll be as angry now as if I had put it on at first bidding; 'tis but observing, [*He puts on his hat*] 'tis but observing a man's humour once, and he may ha' him by the nose all his life.

SIR WALTER. What entertainment has lain open here?
No strangers in my absence?

1 SERVANT. Sure, sir, not any.

ALLWIT. [*aside*] His jealousy begins. Am not I happy now
That can laugh inward whilst his marrow melts?

SIR WALTER. How do you satisfy me?

1 SERVANT. Good sir, be patient.

SIR WALTER. For two months' absence I'll be satisfied.

1 SERVANT. No living creature ent'red –

SIR WALTER. Ent'red? Come, swear –

1 SERVANT. You will not hear me out, sir –

SIR WALTER. Yes, I'll hear't out, sir.

1 SERVANT. Sir, he can tell himself.

SIR WALTER. Heart, he can tell!
Do you think I'll trust him? – as a usurer
With forfeited lordships. Him? O monstrous injury!
Believe him? Can the devil speak ill of darkness?
What can you say, sir?

ALLWIT. Of my soul and conscience sir, she's a wife as honest of her body to me as any lord's proud lady can be.

SIR WALTER. Yet, by your leave, I heard you were once off'ring to go to bed to her.

ALLWIT. No, I protest, sir.

SIR WALTER. Heart if you do, you shall take all. I'll marry!

ALLWIT. Oh, I beseech you, sir –

SIR WALTER. [*aside*] That wakes the slave, and keeps his flesh in awe.

ALLWIT. [*aside*] I'll stop that gap

---

90 *humour*: disposition.

95 *marrow melts*: i.e. in the heat of his jealousy, which like other strong emotions was held to dry up the blood and other vital substances.

99 *hear me out . . . hear't out*: 'let me finish' . . . 'hear the whole story'.

102 *forfeited lordships*: mortgaged estates which are forfeit to the usurer on the non-repayment of the loan.

Where e'er I find it open; I have poisoned
His hopes in marriage already –
Some old rich widows, and some landed virgins,

Enter two CHILDREN [WAT *and* NICK].

And I'll fall to work still before I'll lose him;
He's yet too sweet to part from.

1 BOY [WAT]. God-den, father.

ALLWIT. Ha, villain, peace!

2 BOY [NICK]. God-den, father.

ALLWIT. Peace, bastard! [*Aside*] Should he hear 'em! [*Aloud*] These are two foolish children, they do not know the gentleman that sits there.

SIR WALTER. Oh, Wat! How dost, Nick? Go to school, ply your books, boys, ha?

ALLWIT. [*to the boys*] Where's your legs, whoresons? [*Aside*] They should kneel indeed if they could say their prayers.

SIR WALTER. [*aside*] Let me see, stay;
How shall I dispose of these two brats now
When I am married? For they must not mingle
Amongst my children that I get in wedlock;
'Twill make foul work that, and raise many storms.
I'll bind Wat 'prentice to a goldsmith – my father Yellowhammer,
As fit as can be! Nick with some vintner; good!
Goldsmith and vintner; there will be wine in bowls, i'faith.

Enter ALLWIT'S WIFE.

MISTRESS ALLWIT. Sweet knight,
Welcome; I have all my longings now in town,
Now well-come the good hour. [*She embraces him.*]

SIR WALTER. How cheers my mistress?

MISTRESS ALLWIT. Made lightsome, e'en by him that made me heavy.

SIR WALTER. Methinks she shows gallantly, like a moon at full, sir.

---

124 *God-den*: 'Good evening' (but used any time after noon).
130 *legs*: bows.
146 *heavy*: sad/pregnant.

ALLWIT. True, and if she bear a male child, there's the man in the moon, sir.
SIR WALTER. 'Tis but the boy in the moon yet, goodman calf.
ALLWIT. There was a man, the boy had never been there else.
SIR WALTER. It shall be yours, sir.
ALLWIT. No, by my troth, I'll swear it's none of mine, let him that got it keep it! [*Aside*] Thus do I rid myself of fear,
Lie soft, sleep hard, drink wine, and eat good cheer.
[*Exeunt.*]

ACT II

SCENE I

Enter TOUCHWOOD SENIOR *and his* WIFE.

MISTRESS TOUCHWOOD. 'Twill be so tedious, sir, to live from you,
But that necessity must be obeyed.
TOUCHWOOD SENIOR. I would it might not, wife, the tediousness
Will be the most part mine, that understand
The blessings I have in thee; so to part,
That drives the torment to a knowing heart.
But as thou say'st, we must give way to need
And live awhile asunder; our desires
Are both too fruitful for our barren fortunes.
How adverse runs the destiny of some creatures:
Some only can get riches and no children,
We only can get children and no riches!
Then 'tis the prudent'st part to check our wills
And, till our state rise, make our bloods lie still.

---

152 *calf*: idiot.
6 *knowing*: i.e. 'fully understanding the felicities I have in you'.
13 *wills*: sexual desires.
14 *bloods*: passions; see Additional note, p. 410.

Life, every year a child, and some years two,
Besides drinkings abroad, that's never reckon'd;
This gear will not hold out.

MISTRESS TOUCHWOOD. Sir, for a time, I'll take the courtesy of my uncle's house,
If you be pleas'd to like on't, till prosperity
Look with a friendly eye upon our states.

TOUCHWOOD SENIOR. Honest wife, I thank thee; I ne'er knew
The perfect treasure thou brought'st with thee more
Than at this instant minute. A man's happy
When he's at poorest that has match'd his soul
As rightly as his body. Had I married
A sensual fool now, as 'tis hard to 'scape it
'Mongst gentlewomen of our time, she would ha' hang'd
About my neck, and never left her hold
Till she had kiss'd me into wanton businesses,
Which at the waking of my better judgement
I should have curs'd most bitterly,
And laid a thicker vengeance on my act
Than misery of the birth; which were enough
If it were born to greatness, whereas mine
Is sure of beggary, though it were got in wine.
Fulness of joy showeth the goodness in thee;
Thou art a matchless wife. Farewell, my joy.

MISTRESS TOUCHWOOD. I shall not want your sight?

TOUCHWOOD SENIOR. I'll see thee often,
Talk in mirth, and play at kisses with thee,
Anything, wench, but what may beget beggars;
There I give o'er the set, throw down the cards,
And dare not take them up.

---

15 *Life*: abbreviation of 'by God's life'. In 1606 an Act for 'preventing . . . of the great abuse of the Holy Name of God in Stage plays' had been passed.

16 *drinkings abroad*: 'sips' at other women, away from home.

17 *gear*: business (perhaps with a pun on 'gear' = genitals).

33 *misery of the birth*: Man is born to sorrow and the agony of childbirth remains the penalty of Eve's sin, even in the great; but it is worse if the birth is into poverty.

41 *give o'er the set*: abandon the match, game ('set' is used of a game of cards or dice).

MISTRESS TOUCHWOOD. Your will be mine, sir.
Exit.

TOUCHWOOD SENIOR. This does not only make her honesty perfect,
But her discretion, and approves her judgement.
Had her desires been wanton, they'd been blameless
In being lawful ever, but of all creatures
I hold that wife a most unmatched treasure
That can unto her fortunes fix her pleasure,
And not unto her blood: this is like wedlock;
The feast of marriage is not lust but love,
And care of the estate. When I please blood,
Merely I sing, and suck out others'; then,
'Tis many a wise man's fault; but of all men
I am the most unfortunate in that game
That ever pleas'd both genders, I ne'er play'd yet
Under a bastard; the poor wenches curse me
To the Pit where e'er I come; they were ne'er served so,
But us'd to have more words than one to a bargain.
I have such a fatal finger in such business
I must forth with't, chiefly for country wenches,
For every harvest I shall hinder hay-making:

Enter a WENCH *with a child.*

I had no less than seven lay-in last progress,

---

44 *approves*: attests.

52 *sing, and suck out others'*: 'I only copulate, and draw out the blood of another (by firing it with my lust).' See also Textual note, p. 402.

56 *Under a bastard*: 'with a score against me less than a bastard' (a metaphor from card games where cards held at the end score against a player; a bastard would be somewhat less expensive to maintain than a legitimate child).

57 *Pit*: Hell (but with bawdy innuendo on 'pit' = the female pudendum); *served*: treated/sexually serviced.

58 *us'd to have more words than one to a bargain*: expect to have several sexual encounters before becoming pregnant; 'More words than one go to a bargain' is proverbial (Tilley, W 827), expressing unwillingness to agree easily.

59 *finger*: also, penis.

61 *every harvest I shall hinder hay-making*: i.e. by making the girls pregnant.

62 *lay-in last progress*: confined for childbirth last summer. King and Court undertook a royal journey in July or August, expecting lavish entertainment and often creating havoc in the districts visited.

Within three weeks of one another's time.
WENCH. O Snaphance, have I found you?
TOUCHWOOD SENIOR. How 'Snaphance'?
WENCH. [*showing the child*] Do you see your workmanship?
Nay turn not from it, nor offer to escape, for if you do,
I'll cry it through the streets, and follow you.
Your name may well be called Touchwood, a pox on you,
You do but touch and take; thou hast undone me;
I was a maid before, I can bring a certificate for it,
From both the churchwardens.
TOUCHWOOD SENIOR. I'll have the parson's hand too, or I'll not yield to't.
WENCH. Thou shalt have more, thou villain! Nothing grieves me
But Ellen, my poor cousin in Derbyshire;
Thou hast crack'd her marriage quite; she'll have a bout with thee.
TOUCHWOOD SENIOR. Faith, when she will, I'll have a bout with her.
WENCH. A law bout, sir, I mean.
TOUCHWOOD SENIOR. True, lawyers use such bouts as other men do.
And if that be all thy grief, I'll tender her a husband;
I keep of purpose two or three gulls in pickle
To eat such mutton with, and she shall choose one.
Do but in courtesy, faith, wench, excuse me

---

64 *Snaphance*: bandit, marauder/the flintlock of a gun, or the gun itself (every time he is 'struck', a spark of life results, igniting the 'touchwood' or tinder in the 'touchhole' (= female pudendum)).

69 *touch and take*: Proverbial (Tilley, T 447), indicating speed in laying one's hands on something.

70 *certificate*: a certificate of good conduct required of all who moved out of their own parish; but notoriously unreliable.

72 *hand*: signature.

75–8 *bout*: quarrel, lawsuit//sexual encounter.

80 *gulls in pickle*: punning on 'gulls' = cheated fools, who are being 'pickled' in the sweating tub by mercurial fumigation, as a remedy for syphilis.

81 *mutton*: whore.

Of this half yard of flesh, in which I think it wants
A nail or two.
WENCH. No, thou shalt find, villain,
It hath right shape, and all the nails it should have.
TOUCHWOOD SENIOR. Faith, I am poor; do a charitable deed, wench;
I am a younger brother, and have nothing.
WENCH. Nothing! Thou hast too much, thou lying villain,
Unless thou wert more thankful.
TOUCHWOOD SENIOR. I have no dwelling,
I brake up house but this morning. Pray thee pity me;
I am a good fellow, faith, have been too kind
To people of your gender: if I ha't
Without my belly, none of your sex shall want it;
[*Aside*] That word has been of force to move a woman.
– There's tricks enough to rid thy hand on't, wench:
Some rich man's porch, tomorrow before day,
Or else anon i'th evening; twenty devices.
[*Gives money*] Here's all I have, i'faith, take purse and all;
[*Aside*] And would I were rid of all the ware i'the shop so.
WENCH. Where I find manly dealings, I am pitiful:
[*She gestures towards the child*] This shall not trouble you.
TOUCHWOOD SENIOR. And I protest, wench, the next I'll keep myself.
WENCH. Soft, let it be got first.
[*Aside*] This is the fifth; if e'er I venture more,
Where I now go for a maid, may I ride for a whore.
Exit.

83–4 *half yard of flesh . . . wants/A nail or two*: i.e. the baby, which seems to be some inches shorter than half a yard (a 'nail' was a cloth measure of 2¼ inches). The children of syphilitics sometimes lacked nails, as well as being stunted, hence the Country Wench's reply.

92–3 *if I ha't/Without my belly*: 'If I have unconsumed food'/ 'While I have a phallus'.

99 *ware*: commonly used in Middleton of a dissolute female.

105 *go for a maid . . . ride for a whore*: walk/pass as a virgin . . . be taken as/be exhibited in a cart as a strumpet (with an additional pun on 'ride' = straddle sexually).

TOUCHWOOD SENIOR. What shift she'll make now with this piece of flesh
In this strict time of Lent, I cannot imagine;
Flesh dare not peep abroad now; I have known
This city now above this seven years,
But I protest in better state of government
I never knew it yet, nor ever heard of;
There has been more religious, wholesome laws
In the half circle of a year erected
For common good, than memory ever knew of,

Enter SIR OLIVER KIX *and his* LADY.

Setting apart corruption of promoters,
And other poisonous officers that infect,
And with a venomous breath taint every goodness.

LADY KIX. Oh that e'er I was begot, or bred, or born!

SIR OLIVER. Be content, sweet wife.

TOUCHWOOD SENIOR. [*aside*] What's here to do, now?
I hold my life she's in deep passion
For the imprisonment of veal and mutton
Now kept in garrets, weeps for some calf's head now;
Methinks her husband's head might serve, with bacon.

Enter TOUCHWOOD JUNIOR.

LADY KIX. Hist!

SIR OLIVER. Patience, sweet wife. [*They walk aside.*]

TOUCHWOOD JUNIOR. Brother, I have sought you strangely.

TOUCHWOOD SENIOR. Why, what's the business?

TOUCHWOOD JUNIOR. With all speed thou canst, procure a licence for me.

TOUCHWOOD SENIOR. How, a licence?

TOUCHWOOD JUNIOR. Cud's foot, she's lost else, I shall miss her ever.

---

106 *flesh*: jocularly, the child.

106–14 From 1608 onwards Acts which forbade the killing and eating of meat in Lent were more strictly enforced, and the law was tightened further in 1613 by forbidding even the killing of meat for sale to invalids or pregnant women.

115 *promoters*: informers. In 1613 the Privy Council appointed 'messengers' to spy out abuses of the Lenten regulations, such as secret butchering in 'garrets'.

124 s.h. LADY KIX: See Textual note, p. 402.

131 *Cud's foot*: a corruption of 'By God's foot'.

TOUCHWOOD SENIOR. Nay, sure, thou shalt not miss so fair a mark
For thirteen shillings fourpence.
TOUCHWOOD JUNIOR. Thanks by hundreds.
Exit.
SIR OLIVER. Nay, pray thee cease, I'll be at more cost yet;
Thou know'st we are rich enough.
LADY KIX. All but in blessings,
And there the beggar goes beyond us. Oh, oh, oh!
To be seven years a wife and not a child, oh, not a child!
SIR OLIVER. Sweet wife, have patience.
LADY KIX. Can any woman have a greater cut?
SIR OLIVER. I know 'tis great, but what of that, wife?
I cannot do withal; there's things making
By thine own doctor's advice at 'pothecary's;
I spare for nothing, wife; no, if the price
Were forty marks a spoonful,
I'd give a thousand pound to purchase fruitfulness;
'Tis but bating so many good works
In the erecting of Bridewells and spital-houses,
And so fetch it up again; for, having none,
I mean to make good deeds my children.
LADY KIX. Give me but those good deeds, and I'll find children.
[TOUCHWOOD SENIOR *smiles, and goes out.*]
SIR OLIVER. Hang thee, thou hast had too many!
LADY KIX. Thou li'st, brevity!
SIR OLIVER. Oh horrible! Dar'st thou call me 'brevity'?
Dar'st thou be so short with me?

---

132 *mark*: target/female pudendum/two thirds of £1, the price of the special licence required from the bishop to marry without the calling of banns.

139 *cut*: misfortune//pudendum//gelding (with reference to Sir Oliver).

141 *cannot do withal*: cannot help it//cannot copulate.

146 *bating*: diminishing.

147 *Bridewells and spital-houses*: houses of correction for prostitutes and hospitals for treating venereal disease.

148 *fetch it up again*: make good the financial loss/make up the number of good works (by producing children, as an alternative to leaving buildings to posterity)/become tumescent.

150 *good deeds*: sexual acts.

153 *brevity*: i.e. 'short tool'.

LADY KIX. Thou deservest worse.
Think but upon the goodly lands and livings
That's kept back through want on't.
SIR OLIVER. Talk not on't, pray thee;
Thou'lt make me play the woman and weep too.
LADY KIX. 'Tis our dry barrenness puffs up Sir Walter;
None gets by your not-getting, but that knight;
He's made by th'means, and fats his fortune shortly
In a great dowry with a goldsmith's daughter.
SIR OLIVER. They may all be deceived;
Be but you patient, wife.
LADY KIX. I have suff'red a long time.
SIR OLIVER. Suffer thy heart out, a pox suffer thee!
LADY KIX. Nay thee, thou desertless slave!
SIR OLIVER. Come, come, I ha' done.
You'll to the gossiping of Master Allwit's child?
LADY KIX. Yes, to my much joy!
Everyone gets before me: there's my sister
Was married but at Barthol'mew eve last,
And she can have two children at a birth.
Oh, one of them, one of them would ha' serv'd my turn.
SIR OLIVER. Sorrow consume thee, thou art still crossing me,
And know'st my nature –

Enter a MAID.

MAID. O mistress! [*Aside*] Weeping or railing,
That's our house harmony.
LADY KIX. What say'st, Jugg?
MAID. The sweetest news.
LADY KIX. What is't, wench?

---

163 *by th'means*: i.e. by this means, that Sir Oliver cannot beget; presumably Sir Walter 'gets', gains, because an estate has been entailed to pass to him in default of children being born to the Kixes. He has raised money on his expectations.

171 *gossiping*: christening; *Master*: See Textual note, p. 402.

174 *Barthol'mew eve*: 23 August; since it is not yet mid-Lent Sunday (II.ii.207), the twins were conceived out of wedlock.

180 *Jugg*: a familiar substitute for 'Joan', commonly applied to any maidservant.

MAID. Throw down your doctor's drugs,
They're all but heretics; I bring certain remedy
That has been taught, and proved, and never fail'd.
SIR OLIVER. Oh that, that, that or nothing.
MAID. There's a gentleman,
I haply have his name, too, that has got
Nine children by one water that he useth:
It never misses; they come so fast upon him,
He was fain to give it over.
LADY KIX. His name, sweet Jugg?
MAID. One Master Touchwood, a fine gentleman,
But run behind hand much with getting children.
SIR OLIVER. Is't possible?
MAID. Why, sir, he'll undertake,
Using that water, within fifteen year,
For all your wealth, to make you a poor man,
You shall so swarm with children.
SIR OLIVER. I'll venture that, i'faith.
LADY KIX. That shall you, husband.
MAID. But I must tell you first, he's very dear.
SIR OLIVER. No matter, what serves wealth for?
LADY KIX. True, sweet husband.
[SIR OLIVER]. There's land to come. Put case his water stands me
In some five hundred pound a pint,
'Twill fetch a thousand, and a Kersten soul.
[LADY KIX]. And that's worth all, sweet husband.
[SIR OLIVER]. I'll about it.
Ex[*eunt*].

---

184 *all but heretics*: Compare *Oxford Dictionary of Proverbs*, 'Where there are three physicians there are two atheists.' Some were rightly suspected of indulging in white magic.
188 *haply*: by chance; or perhaps a contraction of 'happily'.
193 *behind hand*: in debt.
201–4 See Textual note, p. 402, for arrangement of lines and their assignation.
201–2 *Put case his water stands me/In*: 'Suppose his water costs me'. *Water* = medicine//semen.
203 *Kersten*: Christian.

SCENE II

Enter ALLWIT.

ALLWIT. I'll go bid gossips presently myself,
That's all the work I'll do; nor need I stir,
But that it is my pleasure to walk forth
And air myself a little; I am tied to nothing
In this business, what I do is merely recreation,
Not constraint.
Here's running to and fro, nurse upon nurse,
Three charwomen, besides maids and neighbours' children.
Fie, what a trouble have I rid my hands on!
It makes me sweat to think on't.

Enter SIR WALTER WHOREHOUND.

SIR WALTER. How now, Jack?
ALLWIT. I am going to bid gossips for your worship's child, sir.
A goodly girl, i'faith, give you joy on her;
She looks as if she had two thousand pound to her portion
And run away with a tailor; a fine, plump, black-eyed slut;
Under correction, sir,
I take delight to see her. – Nurse!

Enter DRY NURSE.

DRY NURSE. Do you call, sir?
ALLWIT. I call not you, I call the wet nurse hither.
Exit [DRY NURSE].
Give me the wet nurse.

Enter WET NURSE [*carrying baby*].

Ay, 'tis thou.
Come hither, come hither,
Let's see her once again; I cannot choose

---

1 *gossips*: strictly, godparents, but extended to cover midwives and friends at a christening; *presently*: immediately.
14 *run away with a tailor*: i.e. because her clothes are so fine.
16–18 *DRY NURSE . . . wet nurse*: the former generally looked after the child, the latter was employed to suckle it.

But buss her thrice an hour.
WET NURSE. You may be proud on't, sir;
'Tis the best piece of work that e'er you did.
ALLWIT. Think'st thou so, nurse? What sayest to Wat
and Nick?
WET NURSE. They're pretty children both, but here's a
wench
Will be a knocker.
ALLWIT. Pup! – Say'st thou me so? – Pup, little countess;
– Faith, sir, I thank your worship for this girl,
Ten thousand times, and upward.
SIR WALTER. I am glad I have her for you, sir.
ALLWIT. Here, take her in, nurse; wipe her, and give her
spoon-meat.
WET NURSE. [*aside*] Wipe your mouth, sir.
Exit [*with child*].
ALLWIT. And now about these gossips.
SIR WALTER. Get but two, I'll stand for one myself.
ALLWIT. To your own child, sir?
SIR WALTER. The better policy, it prevents suspicion;
'Tis good to play with rumour at all weapons.
ALLWIT. Troth, I commend your care, sir; 'tis a thing
That I should ne'er have thought on.
SIR WALTER. [*aside*] The more slave!
When man turns base, out goes his soul's pure flame;
The fat of ease o'erthrows the eyes of shame.
ALLWIT. I am studying who to get for godmother
Suitable to your worship. Now I ha' thought on't.
SIR WALTER. I'll ease you of that care, and please my-
self in't.
[*Aside*] My love, the goldsmith's daughter, if I send,

---

21 *buss*: kiss.
26 *knocker*: a 'smasher' (but also 'a notable copulator').
27 *Pup*: an all-purpose exclamation popular with Middleton; *countess*: See Additional note, p. 411; there may also be a bawdy pun.
31 *spoon-meat*: i.e. the child is to be weaned onto soft food given with a spoon.
32 *Wipe your mouth*: i.e. 'Slobberchops!' There may just be an allusion to the adulterous woman of Proverbs 30.20 who 'eateth, and wipeth her mouth, and saith, I have done no wickedness'.
37 *play . . . at all weapons*: engage in combat with all weapons.

Her father will command her. – Davy Dahumma!

Enter DAVY.

ALLWIT. I'll fit your worship then with a male partner.
SIR WALTER. What is he?
ALLWIT. A kind, proper gentleman, brother to Master Touchwood.
SIR WALTER. I know Touchwood. Has he a brother living?
ALLWIT. A neat bachelor.
SIR WALTER. Now we know him, we'll make shift with him.
Dispatch, the time draws near. – Come hither, Davy.

Exit [*with* DAVY].

ALLWIT. In troth, I pity him, he ne'er stands still.
Poor knight, what pains he takes: sends this way one,
That way another, has not an hour's leisure.
I would not have thy toil, for all thy pleasure.

Enter two PROMOTERS.

[*Aside*] Ha, how now? What are these that stand so close
At the street corner, pricking up their ears,
And snuffing up their noses, like rich men's dogs
When the first course goes in? By the mass, promoters!
'Tis so, I hold my life; and planted there
To arrest the dead corpse of poor calves and sheep,
Like ravenous creditors that will not suffer
The bodies of their poor departed debtors
To go to th' grave, but e'en in death to vex
And stay the corpse, with bills of Middlesex.
This Lent will fat the whoresons up with sweetbreads
And lard their whores with lamb-stones; what their golls

---

51 *neat*: elegant.

67 *bills of Middlesex*: a subterfuge by which a plaintiff in a civil action before the King's Bench could secure the arrest of his opponent for a supposed offence committed in Middlesex, the county in which Westminster was; when arrested, the real action was proceeded with. A writ of *latitat* could extend the bill to cover the rest of the country.

69 *lard . . . with lamb-stones*: fatten . . . with lambs' testicles (these and sweetbreads were thought to be aphrodisiac).

69 *golls*: hands.

Can clutch goes presently to their Molls and Dolls:
The bawds will be so fat with what they earn
Their chins will hang like udders by Easter eve,
And, being strok'd, will give the milk of witches.
How did the mongrels hear my wife lies in?
Well, I may baffle 'em gallantly. – By your favour, gentlemen,
I am a stranger both unto the city
And to her carnal strictness.

1 PROMOTER. Good; your will, sir?

ALLWIT. Pray tell me where one dwells that kills this Lent.

1 PROMOTER. How, kills? [*Aside*] Come hither, Dick; a bird, a bird!

2 PROMOTER. What is't that you would have?

ALLWIT. Faith, any flesh,
But I long especially for veal and green sauce.

1 PROMOTER. [*aside*] Green goose, you shall be sauc'd.

ALLWIT. I have half a scornful stomach, no fish will be admitted.

1 PROMOTER. Not this Lent, sir?

ALLWIT. Lent? What cares colon here for Lent?

[*He slaps his belly.*]

1 PROMOTER. You say well, sir;
Good reason that the colon of a gentleman
(As you were lately pleas'd to term your worship, sir)
Should be fulfill'd with answerable food,
To sharpen blood, delight health, and tickle nature.
Were you directed hither to this street, sir?

ALLWIT. That I was, ay, marry.

---

70 *Molls and Dolls*: both names used of whores, and consorts of criminals.

72–3 *udders . . . milk of witches*: Double-chins were considered the hallmark of bawds, and witches were held to nourish their familiars at unusually sited teats.

75 *baffle*: hoodwink, disgrace. The informers hang about the house of a pregnant woman, knowing she has odd and urgent tastes.

81–2 *veal and green sauce*: veal with a sauce made from vinegar or verjuice, spiced but with no garlic; metaphorically, 'to eat veal and green sauce' is to be cheated, hence the Promotor's reply; *green goose* = naive idiot; *be sauc'd* = made to pay dearly.

89 *answerable*: suitable.

2 PROMOTER. And the butcher, belike,
Should kill and sell close in some upper room?
ALLWIT. Some apple loft, as I take it, or a coal house;
I know not which, i'faith.
2 PROMOTER. Either will serve;
[*Aside*] This butcher shall kiss Newgate, 'less he turn up
The bottom of the pocket of his apron.
– You go to seek him?
ALLWIT. Where you shall not find him;
I'll buy, walk by your noses with my flesh,
Sheep-biting mongrels, hand-basket freebooters!
My wife lies in; a foutra for promoters! *Exit.*
1 PROMOTER. That shall not serve your turn. – What a rogue's this! How cunningly he came over us!

Enter a MAN *with meat in a basket.*

2 PROMOTER. Hush't, stand close.
MAN. I have 'scap'd well thus far; they say the knaves are wondrous hot and busy.
1 PROMOTER. By your leave, sir,
We must see what you have under your cloak there.
MAN. Have? I have nothing.
1 PROMOTER. No, do you tell us that? What makes this lump stick out then? We must see, sir.
MAN. What will you see, sir? A pair of sheets, and two of my wife's foul smocks, going to the washers?
2 PROMOTER. Oh, we love that sight well, you cannot please us better! [*He searches the basket.*]
–What, do you gull us? Call you these 'shirts and smocks'?

---

93 *close*: secretly.
96 *kiss Newgate*: go to prison, Newgate being used as a prison for freemen of the City guilty of criminal offences.
96–7 *turn up . . . his apron*: i.e. give all he has in a bribe.
100 *Sheep-biting*: slang for 'whoring'; *hand-basket freebooters*: 'shopping-bag pirates'.
101 *foutra*: obscene oath (French 'foutre').
102 *That shall not serve your turn*: 'That excuse won't do.' The total prohibition of meat-eating in Lent 1613 meant that even pregnant women and invalids were denied their usual exemption from the restrictions.

MAN. Now a pox choke you!
You have cozen'd me and five of my wife's kin'red
Of a good dinner; we must make it up now
With herrings and milk-pottage. *Exit.*

1 PROMOTER. 'Tis all veal.

2 PROMOTER. All veal? Pox, the worse luck! I promis'd faithfully to send this morning a fat quarter of lamb to a kind gentlewoman in Turnbull Street that longs; and how I'm cross'd!

1 PROMOTER. Let's share this, and see what hap comes next then.

Enter another [MAN] *with a basket.*

2 PROMOTER. Agreed. Stand close again; another booty. What's he?

1 PROMOTER. Sir, by your favour.

[2] MAN. Meaning me, sir?

1 PROMOTER. Good Master Oliver? Cry thee mercy, i'faith!
What hast thou there?

[2] MAN. A rack of mutton, sir, and half a lamb;
You know my mistress's diet.

1 PROMOTER. Go, go, we see thee not; away, keep close!
– Heart, let him pass! Thou'lt never have the wit
To know our benefactors.

[*Exit* 2 MAN.]

2 PROMOTER. I have forgot him.

1 PROMOTER. 'Tis Master Beggarland's man, the wealthy merchant
That is in fee with us.

2 PROMOTER. Now I have a feeling of him.

1 PROMOTER. You know he purchas'd the whole Lent together,
Gave us ten groats a-piece on Ash Wednesday.

---

123 *Turnbull Street*: a corruption of Turnmill Street, a notorious brothel area near Clerkenwell Green; the whore *longs* because she is pregnant.

133 *rack*: neck.

139 *in fee*: in league (having paid a bribe).

141 *purchas'd the whole Lent together*: bought immunity for the whole of Lent.

142 *groats*: coins originally worth fourpence, but used of any small sum after 1600.

2 PROMOTER. True, true.

Enter a WENCH *with a basket, and a child in it under a loin of mutton.*

1 PROMOTER. A wench.
2 PROMOTER. Why then, stand close indeed.
WENCH. [*aside*] Women had need of wit, if they'll shift here;
And she that hath wit may shift anywhere.
1 PROMOTER. Look, look! Poor fool,
She has left the rump uncover'd too,
More to betray her; this is like a murd'rer
That will outface the deed with a bloody band.
2 PROMOTER. What time of the year is't, sister?
WENCH. O sweet gentlemen, I am a poor servant,
Let me go.
1 PROMOTER. You shall, wench, but this must stay with us.
WENCH. Oh you undo me, sir!
'Tis for a wealthy gentlewoman that takes physic, sir;
The doctor does allow my mistress mutton.
Oh, as you tender the dear life of a gentlewoman!
I'll bring my master to you; he shall show you
A true authority from the higher powers,
And I'll run every foot.
2 PROMOTER. Well, leave your basket then,
And run and spare not.
WENCH. Will you swear then to me
To keep it till I come.
1 PROMOTER. Now by this light, I will.
WENCH. What say you, gentleman?
2 PROMOTER. What a strange wench 'tis!
Would we might perish else.
WENCH. Nay then I run, sir. *Exit.*
1 PROMOTER. And ne'er return, I hope.

146–7 *shift*: succeed, 'get by'/live by fraud/palm off something on someone.

151 *outface the deed with a bloody band*: brazenly pretend innocence, when all the while there is blood on his collar (the fashion was for high-standing collars, often with a ruff).

161 *authority*: official permission for exemption (which in view of the 1613 regulations would have to be specially given).

2 PROMOTER. A politic baggage,
She makes us swear to keep it;
I prithee, look what market she hath made.
1 PROMOTER. [*unpacking the basket*] *Imprimis*, sir, a good fat loin of mutton;
What comes next under this cloth?
Now for a quarter of lamb.
2 PROMOTER. Now for a shoulder of mutton.
1 PROMOTER. Done.
2 PROMOTER. Why, done, sir!
1 PROMOTER. [*feeling in the basket*] By the mass, I feel I have lost:
'Tis of more weight, i'faith.
2 PROMOTER. Some loin of veal?
1 PROMOTER. No, faith, here's a lamb's head,
I feel that plainly. Why yet [I'll] win my wager.
[*Takes out child.*]
2 PROMOTER. Ha?
1 PROMOTER. Swounds, what's here?
2 PROMOTER. A child!
1 PROMOTER. A pox of all dissembling cunning whores!
2 PROMOTER. Here's an unlucky breakfast!
1 PROMOTER. What shall's do?
2 PROMOTER. The quean made us swear to keep it too.
1 PROMOTER. We might leave it else.
2 PROMOTER. Villainous strange!
Life, had she none to gull but poor promoters,
That watch hard for a living?
1 PROMOTER. Half our gettings must run in sugar-sops
And nurses' wages now, besides many a pound of soap,
And tallow; we have need to get loins of mutton still,
To save suet to change for candles.

---

173 *politic*: crafty.
175 *market*: purchase.
176 *Imprimis*: 'first', a Latin tag introducing an inventory.
179 *Now*: See Textual note, p. 402. They wager on the contents.
193 *quean*: whore.
198 *sugar-sops*: bread soaked in sugar water.
200 *tallow*: used for soap and candles, but here probably for greasing the baby's bottom.
201 *change for candles*: exchange for candles, since the baby will need attention at night; cheap candles were made of suet or animal fat.

2 PROMOTER. Nothing mads me but this was a lamb's head with you, you felt it. She has made calves' heads of us.

1 PROMOTER. Prithee, no more on't.
There's time to get it up; it is not come
To mid-Lent Sunday yet.

2 PROMOTER. I am so angry, I'll watch no more today.

1 PROMOTER. Faith, nor I neither.

2 PROMOTER. Why then I'll make a motion.

1 PROMOTER. Well, what is't?

2 PROMOTER. Let's e'en go to the Checker at Queen-hive and roast the loin of mutton, till young flood; then send the child to Brainford.

[*Exeunt.*]

SCENE III

Enter ALLWIT *in one of Sir Walter's suits, and* DAVY *trussing him.*

ALLWIT. 'Tis a busy day at our house, Davy.

DAVY. Always the kurs'ning day, sir.

ALLWIT. Truss, truss me, Davy.

DAVY. [*aside*] No matter and you were hang'd, sir.

ALLWIT. How does this suit fit me, Davy?

DAVY. Excellent neatly; my master's things were ever fit for you, sir, e'en to a hair, you know.

---

203 *calves' heads*: fools.

206 *get it up*: make up the loss.

212–13 *Checker at Queen-hive*: an inn with the sign of a chess board at Queenhithe, a large quay just west of Southwark Bridge; Stowe, *Survey of London* (1633), p. 248 places it in Chequer Lane in Downgate Ward, but as the privileges of Queenhithe had extended to Downgate (p. 38), Middleton may have thought of it as in Queenhithe.

213 *young flood*: when the tide begins to flow up-river.

214 *Brainford*: Brentford, a Middlesex town on the north side of the Thames, opposite Kew; it was a favourite place for whores and for putting children out to nurse.

s.d. *trussing*: tying the 'points' or laces of the hose to the doublet// stringing up for hanging.

2 *kurs'ning day*: christening day.

7 *e'en to a hair*: exactly/even to the female pudendum.

ALLWIT. Thou has hit it right, Davy,
We ever jump'd in one, this ten years, Davy.

Enter a SERVANT *with a box.*

So, well said. What art thou?
SERVANT. Your comfit-maker's man, sir.
ALLWIT. O sweet youth, into the nurse quick,
Quick, 'tis time, i'faith;
Your mistress will be here?
SERVANT. She was setting forth, sir.

Enter two PURITANS.

ALLWIT. Here comes our gossips now. Oh I shall have such kissing work today. – Sweet Mistress Underman, welcome, i'faith.
1 PURITAN. Give you joy of your fine girl, sir.
Grant that her education may be pure,
And become one of the faithful.
ALLWIT. Thanks to your sisterly wishes, Mistress Underman.
2 PURITAN. Are any of the brethren's wives yet come?
ALLWIT. There are some wives within, and some at home.
1 PURITAN. Verily, thanks, sir.
Ex [*eunt* PURITANS].
ALLWIT. 'Verily', you are an ass, forsooth;
I must fit all these times, or there's no music.

Enter two GOSSIPS.

Here comes a friendly and familiar pair;
Now I like these wenches well.
1 GOSSIP. How dost, sirrah?
ALLWIT. Faith, well, I thank you, neighbour; and how dost thou?
2 GOSSIP. Want nothing, but such getting, sir, as thine.
ALLWIT. My gettings, wench? They are poor.

---

9 *jump'd in one*: agreed exactly/swived the same woman.
11 *comfit-maker*: confectioner, producing sweetmeats, crystallised fruits.
25 *Verily*: Allwit mocks the Puritans' 'scriptural' style of speech.
27 *I must fit all these times, or there's no music*: 'I must fall in with all these rhythms/occasions, or the 'music' (the easy life) will stop.'
33 *gettings*: begettings/earnings.

1 GOSSIP. Fie that thou'lt say so!
Th'ast as fine children as a man can get.
DAVY. [*aside*] Ay, as a man can get,
And that's my master.
ALLWIT. They are pretty, foolish things.
Put to making in minutes;
I ne'er stand long about 'em.
Will you walk in, wenches?

[*Exeunt* GOSSIPS.]

Enter TOUCHWOOD JUNIOR *and* MOLL.

TOUCHWOOD JUNIOR. The happiest meeting that our souls could wish for. Here's the ring ready; I am beholding unto your father's haste, h'as kept his hour.
MOLL. He never kept it better.

Enter SIR WALTER WHOREHOUND.

TOUCHWOOD JUNIOR. Back, be silent.
SIR WALTER. Mistress and partner, I will put you both into one cup. [*Drinks to them.*]
DAVY. [*aside*] Into one cup! Most proper:
A fitting compliment for a goldsmith's daughter.
ALLWIT. Yes, sir, that's he must be your worship's partner
In this day's business, Master Touchwood's brother.
SIR WALTER. I embrace your acquaintance, sir.
TOUCHWOOD JUNIOR. It vows your service, sir.
SIR WALTER. It's near high time. Come, Master Allwit.
ALLWIT. Ready, sir.
SIR WALTER. Will't please you walk?
TOUCHWOOD JUNIOR. Sir, I obey your time.

Ex[*eunt*].

Enter MIDWIFE *with the child,* [MAUDLINE, *two* PURITANS] *and the* GOSSIPS *to the kurs'ning.*

[*Exit* MIDWIFE *with child.*]

---

40 *stand*: delay/remain erect.
47–8 *put you both into one cup*: i.e. he pledges them together in a single toast (with unconscious irony, since they are to be one, and a betrothed couple drank from a loving-cup after the betrothal ceremony).
55 *high time*: the appropriate time; or possibly, 'noon'.
58 *obey your time*: 'follow your beat' (a musical image).

1 GOSSIP. [*offering precedence*] Good Mistress Yellowhammer.
MAUDLINE. In faith, I will not.
1 GOSSIP. Indeed, it shall be yours.
MAUDLINE. I have sworn, i'faith.
1 GOSSIP. I'll stand still then.
MAUDLINE. So will you let the child go without company
And make me forsworn.
1 GOSSIP. You are such another creature.
[*Exeunt* 1 GOSSIP *and* MAUDLINE.]
2 GOSSIP. Before me? I pray come down a little.
3 GOSSIP. Not a whit; I hope I know my place.
2 GOSSIP. Your place? Great wonder, sure! Are you any better than a comfit-maker's wife?
3 GOSSIP. And that's as good at all times as a 'pothecary's.
2 GOSSIP. Ye lie. Yet I forbear you too.
[*Exeunt* 2 *and* 3 GOSSIPS.]
1 PURITAN. Come, sweet sister, we go in unity, and show the fruits of peace like children of the spirit.
2 PURITAN. I love lowliness.
[*Exeunt* PURITANS.]
4 GOSSIP. True, so say I: though they strive more,
There comes as proud behind, as goes before.
5 GOSSIP. Every inch, i'faith.
Exit [4 GOSSIP *and* 5 GOSSIP].

ACT III

SCENE I

Enter TOUCHWOOD JUNIOR *and a* PARSON.

TOUCHWOOD JUNIOR. O sir, if ever you felt the force of love, pity it in me!
PARSON. Yes, though I ne'er was married, sir,
I have felt the force of love from good men's daughters,

68 *come down a little*: be socially humbler.
78 *There comes as proud behind as goes before*: Proverbial; cf. Tilley, C 536. The meaning 'proud' = sexually excited is perhaps taken up in the next line.

And some that will be maids yet three years hence.
Have you got a licence?
TOUCHWOOD JUNIOR. Here, 'tis ready, sir.
PARSON. That's well.
TOUCHWOOD JUNIOR. The ring and all things perfect, she'll steal hither.
PARSON. She shall be welcome, sir; I'll not be long
A-clapping you together.

Enter MOLL *and* TOUCHWOOD SENIOR.

TOUCHWOOD JUNIOR. Oh, here she's come, sir.
PARSON. What's he?
TOUCHWOOD JUNIOR. My honest brother.
TOUCHWOOD SENIOR. Quick, make haste, sirs!
MOLL. You must dispatch with all the speed you can,
For I shall be miss'd straight; I made hard shift
For this small time I have.
PARSON. Then I'll not linger;
Place that ring upon her finger:
[TOUCHWOOD JUNIOR *places the ring on* MOLL*'s finger.*]
This the finger plays the part,
Whose master-vein shoots from the heart;
Now join hands –

Enter YELLOWHAMMER *and* SIR WALTER.

YELLOWHAMMER. Which I will sever,
And so ne'er again meet never!
MOLL. Oh, we are betray'd.
TOUCHWOOD JUNIOR. Hard fate!
SIR WALTER. I am struck with wonder.
YELLOWHAMMER. Was this the politic fetch, thou mystical baggage,
Thou disobedient strumpet?

---

13 *made hard shift*: contrived with difficulty.

18 *master-vein*: an artery, which was supposed to run directly from the heart to the third finger of the left hand.

19 *join hands*: This, the 'handfasting', was the legally binding part of the contract, and it is interrupted. The doggerel ceremony is Middleton's substitute for the Prayer Book marriage service, which it would be dangerous to echo in a stage play.

25 *politic fetch*: cunning trick; *mystical*: secret.

[*To* SIR WALTER] And were so wise to send for her to such an end?

SIR WALTER. Now I disclaim the end; you'll make me mad.

YELLOWHAMMER. [*to* TOUCHWOOD JUNIOR] And what are you, sir?

TOUCHWOOD JUNIOR. And you cannot see with those two glasses, put on a pair more.

YELLOWHAMMER. I dreamt of anger still! Here, take your ring, sir; [*Takes ring off* MOLL*'s finger.*]
Ha! This? Life, 'tis the same. Abominable!
Did not I sell this ring?

TOUCHWOOD JUNIOR. I think you did, you received money for 't.

YELLOWHAMMER. Heart, hark you, knight;
Here's no inconscionable villainy!
Set me a-work to make the wedding ring,
And come with an intent to steal my daughter:
Did ever runaway match it?

SIR WALTER. [*to* TOUCHWOOD SENIOR] This your brother, sir?

TOUCHWOOD SENIOR. He can tell that as well as I.

YELLOWHAMMER. The very posy mocks me to my face:
'Love that's wise, blinds parents' eyes.'
I thank your wisdom, sir, for blinding of us;
We have good hope to recover our sight shortly.
In the meantime, I will lock up this baggage
As carefully as my gold: she shall see as little sun,
If a close room or so can keep her from the light on't.

MOLL. O sweet father, for love's sake, pity me.

YELLOWHAMMER. Away!

MOLL. [*to* TOUCHWOOD JUNIOR] Farewell, sir, all content bless thee,
And take this for comfort:
Though violence keep me, thou canst lose me never;
I am ever thine although we part for ever.

---

32 *glasses*: spectacles.

39 *no inconscionable*: probably, 'not having regard to conscience', since in Jacobean English a double negative may be used merely for emphasis. Or Yellowhammer may mean 'no unconscious'.

52 *close*: confined, shut-up.

YELLOWHAMMER. Ay, we shall part you, minx.
Exit [*with* MOLL].
SIR WALTER. [*to* TOUCHWOOD JUNIOR] Your acquaintance, sir, came very lately,
Yet it came too soon;
I must hereafter know you for no friend,
But one that I must shun like pestilence,
Or the disease of lust.
TOUCHWOOD JUNIOR. Like enough, sir; you h' ta'en me at the worst time for words that e'er ye pick'd out; faith, do not wrong me, sir.
Exit [*with* PARSON].
TOUCHWOOD SENIOR. Look after him and spare not: there he walks
That never yet received baffling; you're bless'd
More than e'er I knew. Go take your rest. *Exit.*
SIR WALTER. I pardon you, you are both losers. *Exit.*

SCENE II

A bed thrust out upon the stage, ALLWIT'S WIFE *in it. Enter all the* GOSSIPS [*including* MAUDLINE, LADY KIX, *the* PURITANS, *also* DRY NURSE *with the child*].

1 GOSSIP. How is't, woman? We have brought you home
A Kursen soul.
MISTRESS ALLWIT. Ay, I thank your pains.
[1] PURITAN. And verily well kursen'd, i'the right way,
Without idolatry or superstition,
After the pure manner of Amsterdam.
MISTRESS ALLWIT. Sit down, good neighbours. – Nurse!
NURSE. At hand, forsooth.
MISTRESS ALLWIT. Look they have all low stools.
NURSE. They have, forsooth.
2 GOSSIP. Bring the child hither, Nurse. How say you now,

---

68 *Look after him*: 'Watch out for him.'

69–70 *baffling*: public humiliation; *you're bless'd/More than e'er I knew*: 'You are luckier than any I've known (i.e. to escape being killed).'

3–5 *kursen'd*: christened; but since it was *after the pure manner of Amsterdam*, the pun on 'cursen'd' becomes more obvious. Amsterdam was a refuge for European dissenters, and hence symbolic of Puritanism.

Gossip, is't not a chopping girl, so like the father?
3 GOSSIP. As if it had been spit out of his mouth,
Eyed, nos'd and brow'd as like a girl can be;
Only, indeed, it has the mother's mouth.
2 GOSSIP. The mother's mouth up and down, up and down!
3 GOSSIP. 'Tis a large child; she's but a little woman.
[1] PURITAN. No believe me, a very spiny creature, but all heart,
Well mettl'd, like the faithful, to endure
Her tribulation here, and raise up seed.
2 GOSSIP. She had a sore labour on't, I warrant you, you can tell, neighbour.
3 GOSSIP. Oh, she had great speed;
We were afraid once,
But she made us all have joyful hearts again;
'Tis a good soul, i'faith;
The midwife found her a most cheerful daughter.
[1] PURITAN. 'Tis the Spirit; the sisters are all like her.

Enter SIR WALTER *with two spoons and plate and* ALLWIT.

2 GOSSIP. Oh, here comes the chief gossip, neighbours.
[*Exit* NURSE *with child*.]
SIR WALTER. The fatness of your wishes to you all, ladies.
3 GOSSIP. Oh, dear, sweet gentleman, what fine words he has:
'The fatness of our wishes'.
2 GOSSIP. Calls us all 'ladies'!
4 GOSSIP. I promise you, a fine gentleman, and a courteous.
2 GOSSIP. Methinks her husband shows like a clown to him.
3 GOSSIP. I would not care what clown my husband were too, so I had such fine children.

---

9 *chopping*: vigorous, strapping.
13 *up and down*: exactly//top and bottom.
15 *spiny*: thin, spindly.
16 *mettl'd*: spirited/with natural ardour.
25 *the Spirit*: the Holy Spirit//alcohol. See Textual note, p. 402. Millenial sects of the period frequently claimed the guidance of the Spirit, which for them replaced concern with New Testament doctrine and ethics. Their antinomianism sometimes led to debauchery.
s.d. *plate*: gold or silver ware.

2 GOSSIP. She's all fine children, gossip.
3 GOSSIP. Ay, and see how fast they come.
[1] PURITAN. Children are blessings, if they be got with zeal,
By the brethren, as I have five at home.
SIR WALTER. [*to* MISTRESS ALLWIT] The worst is past, I hope now, gossip.
MISTRESS ALLWIT. So I hope too, good sir.
ALLWIT. [*aside*] Why then, so hope I too, for company!
I have nothing to do else.
SIR WALTER. [*giving cup and spoons*] A poor remembrance, lady,
To the love of the babe; I pray accept of it.
MISTRESS ALLWIT. Oh, you are at too much charge, sir.
2 GOSSIP. Look, look, what has he given her? What is't, gossip?
3 GOSSIP. Now, by my faith, a fair high standing cup, and two great 'postle spoons, one of them gilt.
1 PURITAN. Sure that was Judas then with the red beard.
2 PURITAN. I would not feed my daughter with that spoon for all the world, for fear of colouring her hair; red hair the brethren like not, it consumes them much: 'tis not the sisters' colour.

Enter NURSE *with comfits and wine.*

ALLWIT. Well said, Nurse;
About, about with them amongst the gossips.
[*Aside*] Now out comes all the tassell'd handkerchers,
They are spread abroad between their knees already;
Now in goes the long fingers that are wash'd
Some thrice a day in urine (my wife uses it).

---

36 *zeal*: religious enthusiasm/sexual gusto.
45 *charge*: expense.
47–8 *standing cup . . . 'postle spoons*: a stemmed goblet and spoons whose handles end in the figure of an apostle; though a common christening gift, the spoons would be idolatrous images to Puritans, hence their comments.
49 *red beard*: Judas was red-bearded by tradition. Red hair was held to denote lasciviousness, hence lines 50–3. 'Gilt', being silver covered by gold, is deceiving, and therefore appropriate to Judas' spoon.
52 *consumes*: eats them up (with anger, with sexual lust).
54 *Well said*: 'Well done!'
59 *urine*: used as a cleansing lotion.

Now we shall have such pocketing;
See how they lurch at the lower end.
[1] PURITAN. Come hither, Nurse.
ALLWIT. [*aside*] Again! She has taken twice already.
[1] PURITAN. I had forgot a sister's child that's sick.
[*Taking comfits.*]
ALLWIT. [*aside*] A pox! It seems your purity loves sweet things well that puts in thrice together. Had this been all my cost now I had been beggar'd. These women have no consciences at sweetmeats, where e'er they come; see and they have not cull'd out all the long plums too, they have left nothing here but short wriggle-tail comfits, not worth mouthing; no mar'l I heard a citizen complain once that his wife's belly only broke his back: mine had been all in fitters seven years since, but for this worthy knight that with a prop upholds my wife and me, and all my estate buried in Bucklersberry.
MISTRESS ALLWIT. [*pledging them*] Here, Mistress Yellowhammer, and neighbours,
To you all that have taken pains with me,
All the good wives at once. [*Wine is taken round.*]
[1] PURITAN. I'll answer for them.
They wish all health and strength,
And that you may courageously go forward,
To perform the like and many such,
Like a true sister with motherly bearing. [*She drinks.*]
ALLWIT. [*aside*] Now the cups troll about to wet the gossips' whistles;

---

61 *lurch*: filch, steal; *lower end*: far end of the room (with a probable innuendo).
65–6 *sweet things*: There is a further allusion to sexual pleasure, less muted than in Allwit's preceding and subsequent speeches.
70 *plums*: i.e. sugar plums.
70–1 *short wriggle-tail comfits*: sweetmeats with twisted tails (which resembled small phalluses, and have therefore been rejected).
73 *broke his back*: i.e. by her weight, and by her demands for food and sex; *in fitters*: in small pieces.
75 *prop*: This has a phallic suggestion.
76 *Bucklersberry*: a street running from the Poultry to Walbrook, inhabited by grocers and apothecaries.
84 *troll about*: go the round.

It pours down, i'faith; they never think of payment.

[1] PURITAN. Fill again, nurse. [*She drinks again.*]

ALLWIT. [*aside*] Now bless thee, two at once! I'll stay no longer;
It would kill me and if I paid for't.
[*To* SIR WALTER] Will it please you to walk down and leave the women?

SIR WALTER. With all my heart, Jack.

ALLWIT. Troth, I cannot blame you.

SIR WALTER. Sit you all, merry ladies.

ALL GOSSIPS. Thank your worship, sir.

[1] PURITAN. Thank your worship, sir.

ALLWIT. [*aside*] A pox twice tipple ye, you are last and lowest!

Exit [ALLWIT *with* SIR WALTER].

[1] PURITAN. Bring hither that same cup, Nurse, I would fain drive away this-hup!-antichristian grief. [*Drinks*]

3 GOSSIP. See, gossip, and she lies not in like a countess;
Would I had such a husband for my daughter!

4 GOSSIP. Is not she toward marriage?

3 GOSSIP. Oh, no, sweet gossip!

4 GOSSIP. Why, she's nineteen?

3 GOSSIP. Ay, that she was last Lammas;
But she has a fault, gossip, a secret fault.

[NURSE *fills the glass, then exit.*]

4 GOSSIP. A fault, what is't?

3 GOSSIP. I'll tell you when I have drunk.

[*Drinks.*]

4 GOSSIP. [*aside*] Wine can do that, I see, that friendship cannot.

3 GOSSIP. And now I'll tell you, gossip; she's too free.

4 GOSSIP. Too free?

3 GOSSIP. Oh, ay, she cannot lie dry in her bed.

4 GOSSIP. What, and nineteen?

3 GOSSIP. 'Tis as I tell you, gossip.

[*Enter* NURSE *and speaks to* MAUDLINE.]

MAUDLINE. Speak with me, Nurse? Who is't?

---

95 *tipple*: topple, tumble.
98 *countess*: See Additional note, p. 411.
101 *Lammas*: 1 August, harvest festival of the early English church.

NURSE. A gentleman from Cambridge;
I think it be your son, forsooth.
MAUDLINE. 'Tis my son Tim, i'faith.
Prithee call him up among the women;
[*Exit* NURSE.]
'Twill embolden him well,
For he wants nothing but audacity.
Would the Welsh gentlewoman at home were here now.
LADY [KIX]. Is your son come, forsooth?
MAUDLINE. Yes, from the university, forsooth.
LADY [KIX]. 'Tis great joy on ye.
MAUDLINE. There's a great marriage towards for him.
LADY [KIX]. A marriage?
MAUDLINE. Yes, sure, a huge heir in Wales,
At least to nineteen mountains,
Besides her goods and cattle.

Enter [NURSE *with*] TIM.

TIM. Oh, I'm betray'd! *Exit.*
MAUDLINE. What, gone again? – Run after him, good
Nurse; [*Exit* NURSE.]
He's so bashful, that's the spoil of youth:
In the university they're kept still to men,
And ne'er train'd up to women's company.
LADY [KIX]. 'Tis a great spoil of youth, indeed.

Enter NURSE *and* TIM.

NURSE. Your mother will have it so.
MAUDLINE. Why, son, why, Tim!
What, must I rise and fetch you? For shame, son!
TIM. Mother you do intreat like a freshwoman;
'Tis against the laws of the university

123 *cattle*: Q spells 'Cattell' = property (some of which is 'cattle', her two thousand runts).

133 *freshwoman*: Tim's coinage on the analogy of 'freshman'; but since 'fresh' = new/impudent, it probably means also 'an inexperienced whore'.

For any that has answered under bachelor
To thrust 'mongst married wives.
MAUDLINE. Come, we'll excuse you here.
TIM. Call up my tutor, mother, and I care not.
MAUDLINE. What is your tutor come? Have you brought him up?
TIM. I ha' not brought him up, he stands at door:
Negatur. There's logic to begin with you, mother.
MAUDLINE. Run, call the gentleman, Nurse, he's my son's tutor.

[*Exit* NURSE.]

Here, eat some plums.
TIM. Come I from Cambridge, and offer me six plums?
MAUDLINE. Why, how now, Tim,
Will not your old tricks yet be left?
TIM. Serv'd like a child,
When I have answer'd under bachelor?
MAUDLINE. You'll never lin till I make your tutor whip you; you know how I serv'd you once at the free school in Paul's churchyard?
TIM. Oh monstrous absurdity!
Ne'er was the like in Cambridge since my time;
'Life, whip a bachelor? You'd be laugh'd at soundly;
Let not my tutor hear you!
'Twould be a jest through the whole university;
No more words, mother.

Enter TUTOR.

MAUDLINE. Is this your tutor, Tim?
TUTOR. Yes surely, lady, I am the man that brought him in league with logic, and read the Dunces to him.

135, 148 *answered under bachelor*: satisfied the requirements for the degree of Bachelor of Arts.
139–40 *up . . . up*: up to London . . . upstairs.
141 *Negatur*: 'It is denied', part of the Latin formula for denying an opponent's position in an academic disputation.
149 *lin*: cease.
150 *free school*: St Paul's School, re-endowed by John Colet, Dean of St Paul's in 1512, for 153 poor scholars.
160 *Dunces*: schoolmen, followers of Duns Scotus (1265?–1308?). These scholastic philosophers had been under attack from the humanists and reformers, so that 'dunce' means also 'fool, pedant'. In place of the arithmetic and music in Middleton's undergraduate course at Oxford, Cambridge men substituted philosophy.

TIM. That did he, mother, but now I have 'em all in my own pate, and can as well read 'em to others.

TUTOR. That can he, mistress, for they flow naturally from him.

MAUDLINE. I'm the more beholding to your pains, sir.

TUTOR. *Non ideo sane.*

MAUDLINE. True, he was an idiot indeed
When he went out of London, but now he's well mended.
Did you receive the two goose pies I sent you?

TUTOR. And eat them heartily, thanks to your worship.

MAUDLINE. 'Tis my son Tim: I pray bid him welcome, gentlewomen.

TIM. 'Tim'? Hark you, 'Timothius', mother, 'Timothius'.

MAUDLINE. How, shall I deny your name? 'Timothius', quoth he?
Faith, there's a name! 'Tis my son Tim, forsooth.

LADY KIX. You're welcome, Master Tim. *Kiss.*

TIM. [*aside to* TUTOR] Oh, this is horrible, she wets as she kisses!
Your handkercher, sweet tutor, to wipe them off as fast as they come on.

2 GOSSIP. Welcome from Cambridge. *Kiss.*

TIM. [*aside to* TUTOR] This is intolerable! This woman has a villainous sweet breath, did she not stink of comfits. Help me, sweet tutor, or I shall rub my lips off.

TUTOR. I'll go kiss the lower end the whilst.

TIM. Perhaps that's the sweeter, and we shall dispatch the sooner.

[1] PURITAN. Let me come next. Welcome from the wellspring of discipline, that waters all the brethren.

Reels and falls.

TIM. Hoist, I beseech thee.

---

166 *Non ideo sane*: 'Not on that account indeed' (disputants' Latin tag).

180–1 *sweet breath . . . stink of comfits*: In fact 'kissing comfits' were taken to sweeten the breath.

183 *lower end*: those at the end of the room (or table)//the backside.

186–7 *wellspring of discipline*: Cambridge was the intellectual centre of Puritanism.

188 *Hoist*: Lift up (addressed to the woman, or the Tutor).

3 GOSSIP. Oh bless the woman! – Mistress Underman!
[1] PURITAN. 'Tis but the common affliction of the faithful;
We must embrace our falls.
TIM. [*aside to* TUTOR] I'm glad I 'scap'd it, it was some rotten kiss, sure:
It dropp'd down before it came at me.

Enter ALLWIT *and* DAVY.

ALLWIT. [*aside*] Here's a noise! Not parted yet?
Hyda, a looking glass! They have drunk so hard in plate
That some of them had need of other vessels.
[*Aloud*] Yonder's the bravest show.
ALL GOSSIPS. Where? Where, sir?
ALLWIT. Come along presently by the Pissing-conduit,
With two brave drums and a standard bearer.
ALL GOSSIPS. Oh brave!
TIM. Come, tutor.
Ex[*eunt*].
ALL GOSSIPS. Farewell, sweet gossip. *Ex*[*eunt*].
MISTRESS ALLWIT. I thank you all for your pains.
[1] PURITAN. Feed and grow strong. *Exit.*
[*The curtains around* MISTRESS ALLWIT*'s bed are drawn. Exeunt* MAUDLINE, LADY KIX *and* PURITANS.]
ALLWIT. You had more need to sleep than eat;
Go take a nap with some of the brethren, go,
And rise up a well edified, boldified sister!
Oh here's a day of toil well pass'd o'er,
Able to make a citizen hare mad!

---

191 *embrace our falls*: 'accept our moral (and sexual) lapses'; a travesty of Calvin's teaching that the fallen state of Man must be humbly accepted.

195 *Hyda*: an exclamation; *a looking glass*: a piss-pot; *in plate*: i.e. in the silver vessels brought out for the christening.

199 *Pissing-conduit*: a little conduit close to the Royal Exchange, at the junction of Threadneedle Street and Cornhill.

200 *two brave drums and a standard bearer*: The phallic appearance of this 'show' or procession provokes the women's enthusiasm.

207–8 An allusion to the Anabaptist contention that any man and woman could lie together if they were asleep.

210 *hare mad*: Hares become wilder around March, the breeding season.

How hot they have made the room with their thick
bums.
Dost not feel it, Davy?
DAVY. Monstrous strong, sir.
ALLWIT. What's here under the stools?
DAVY. Nothing but wet, sir; some wine spilt here, belike.
ALLWIT. Is't no worse, think'st thou?
Fair needlework stools cost nothing with them, Davy.
DAVY. [*aside*] Nor you neither, i'faith.
ALLWIT. Look how they have laid them,
E'en as they lie themselves, with their heels up;
How they have shuffled up the rushes too, Davy,
With their short, figging, little shittle-cork heels!
These women can let nothing stand as they find it.
But what's the secret thou'st about to tell me,
My honest Davy?
DAVY. If you should disclose it, sir –
ALLWIT. Life, rip my belly up to the throat then, Davy.
DAVY. My master's upon marriage.
ALLWIT. Marriage, Davy? Send me to hanging rather.
DAVY. [*aside*] I have stung him.
ALLWIT. When, where? What is she, Davy?
DAVY. E'en the same was gossip, and gave the spoon.
ALLWIT. I have no time to stay, nor scarce can speak;
I'll stop those wheels, or all the work will break. *Exit.*
DAVY. I knew t'would prick. Thus do I fashion still
All mine own ends by him and his rank toil:
'Tis my desire to keep him still from marriage;
Being his poor nearest kinsman, I may fare

---

211 *bums*: cushion-rolls under the skirt to extend it/rumps.
217 *needlework stools*: stools with embroidered padded seats, which were in vogue.
221 *rushes*: used as floor covering both in houses and on the public stage.
222 *short, figging, little shittle-cork heels*: 'jigging feet' (wedge-heels and soles of cork were fashionable), but with innuendoes, since 'figging' = copulating, and 'shuttle-cock' = a whore; 'short-heel'd' also indicated 'light', 'loose'.
223 *stand*: with obscene innuendo.
233–4 *speak . . . break*: These rhyme, 'speak' being pronounced 'spake'.
236 *rank*: excessive/sweaty/corrupt.

The better at his death; there my hopes build,
Since my Lady Kix is dry, and hath no child. *Exit.*

SCENE III

Enter both the TOUCHWOODS.

TOUCHWOOD JUNIOR. Y'are in the happiest way to enrich yourself
And pleasure me, brother, as man's feet can tread in;
For though she be lock'd up, her vow is fix'd
Only to me: then time shall never grieve me,
For by that vow e'en absent [I] enjoy her,
Assuredly confirm'd that none else shall,
Which will make tedious years seem gameful to me.
In the mean space, lose you no time, sweet brother;
You have the means to strike at this knight's fortunes
And lay him level with his bankrout merit;
Get but his wife with child, perch at tree top,
And shake the golden fruit into her lap.
About it before she weep herself to a dry ground,
And whine out all her goodness.
TOUCHWOOD SENIOR. Prithee, cease;
I find a too much aptness in my blood
For such a business, without provocation;
You might'well spar'd this banket of eryngoes,
Hartichokes, potatoes, and your butter'd crab:
They were fitter kept for your own wedding dinner.

239–40 *build . . . child*: another rhyme, 'child' being pronounced by some as in modern 'children'.

7 *gameful*: joyful/full of sexual pleasure.

10 *bankrout*: bankrupt.

11 *perch at tree top*: alluding to Satan's first entry to Paradise, when he roosts in the forbidden tree (cf. Milton, *Paradise Lost*, IV, 194–6).

12 *golden fruit*: the apples of the Hesperides, a symbol of sexual delight; the image of the harvester shaking down fruit from a forbidden tree seems to be combined with another favoured Middletonian reference, to Danae impregnated by Jove in a shower of gold. Cf. *Women Beware Women*, V.ii.122.

13 *weep herself to a dry ground*: i.e. before she makes herself too dry and barren to bear 'fruit'.

17–18 *eryngoes . . . crab*: all thought to be aphrodisiac; 'eryngo' was the candied root of sea-holly, 'potatoes' are probably sweet potatoes or yams; *banket*: banquet.

TOUCHWOOD JUNIOR. Nay and you'll follow my suit,
and save my purse too,
Fortune dotes on me: he's in happy case
Finds such an honest friend i'the common place.
TOUCHWOOD SENIOR. Life, what makes thee so merry?
Thou hast no cause
That I could hear of lately since thy crosses,
Unless there be news come, with new additions.
TOUCHWOOD JUNIOR. Why there thou hast it right:
I look for her this evening, brother.
TOUCHWOOD SENIOR. How's that, 'look for her'?
TOUCHWOOD JUNIOR. I will deliver you of the wonder
straight, brother:
By the firm secrecy and kind assistance
Of a good wench i'the house (who, made of pity,
Weighing the case her own) she's led through gutters,
Strange hidden ways, which none but love could find,
Or ha'the heart to venture; I expect her
Where you would little think.
TOUCHWOOD SENIOR. I care not where,
So she be safe, and yours.
TOUCHWOOD JUNIOR. Hope tells me so;
But from your love and time my peace must grow.
Exit.
TOUCHWOOD SENIOR. You know the worst then, brother.
Now to my Kix,
The barren he and she; they're i'the next room;
But to say which of their two humours hold them
Now at this instant, I cannot say truly.
SIR OLIVER. Thou liest, barrenness!
KIX *to his* LADY *within.*
TOUCHWOOD SENIOR. Oh, is't that time of day? Give
you joy of your tongue,
There's nothing else good in you: this their life

---

22 *i'the common place*: at the Court of Common Pleas at Westminster, literally/also used of the 'common land'. 'If you will promote my cause and save me money, I am lucky to find such an advocate in the wicked world.'

24 *crosses*: setbacks/deletions.

25 *new additions*: further news/augmentations to a text.

32 *gutters*: house gutters; Moll escapes over the roofs (see IV.i. 303).

40 *humours*: moods.

The whole day, from eyes open to eyes shut,
Kissing or scolding, and then must be made friends,
Then rail the second part of the first fit out,
And then be pleas'd again, no man knows which way;
Fall out like giants, and fall in like children;
Their fruit can witness as much.

Enter SIR OLIVER KIX *and his* LADY.

SIR OLIVER. 'Tis thy fault.
LADY KIX. Mine, drouth and coldness?
SIR OLIVER. Thine, 'tis thou art barren.
LADY KIX. I barren! Oh life, that I durst but speak now,
In mine own justice, in mine own right! I barren!
'Twas otherways with me when I was at court;
I was ne'er call'd so till I was married.
SIR OLIVER. I'll be divorc'd.
LADY KIX. Be hang'd! I need not wish it,
That will come too soon to thee: I may say
'Marriage and hanging goes by destiny',
For all the goodness I can find in't yet.
SIR OLIVER. I'll give up house, and keep some fruitful whore,
Like an old bachelor, in a tradesman's chamber;
She and her children shall have all.
LADY KIX. Where be they?
TOUCHWOOD SENIOR. [*coming forward*] Pray cease;
When there are friendlier courses took for you
To get and multiply within your house,
At your own proper costs in spite of censure,
Methinks an honest peace might be establish'd.

---

47 *fit*: large division of a poem/struggle/paroxysm or seizure.

49 *fall in*: make up/copulate. They 'make up' like children, without sexual contact.

52 *drouth*: drought.

58 *I'll be divorc'd*: Divorce was possible for the rich who could afford the necessary Act of Parliament; but barrenness would not be sufficient matrimonial offence. Perhaps he thinks he could seek a decree of nullity for non-consummation.

60 Proverbial: Tilley, W 232: 'Wedding and hanging go by destiny.'

69 *proper costs in spite of censure*: own expense, in defiance of criticism (for being infertile?). For an alternative interpretation see Textual note, p. 402.

SIR OLIVER. What, with her? Never.
TOUCHWOOD SENIOR. Sweet sir!
SIR OLIVER. You work all in vain.
LADY KIX. Then he doth all like thee.
TOUCHWOOD SENIOR. Let me intreat, sir.
SIR OLIVER. Singleness confound her!
I took her with one smock.
LADY KIX. But indeed you came not so single,
When you came from shipboard.
SIR OLIVER. [*aside*] Heart, she bit sore there!
[*To* TOUCHWOOD SENIOR] Prithee, make's friends.
TOUCHWOOD SENIOR. [*aside*] Is't come to that? The peal begins to cease.
SIR OLIVER. [*to* LADY KIX] I'll sell all at an outcry.
LADY KIX. Do thy worst, slave!
[*To* TOUCHWOOD SENIOR] Good sweet sir, bring us into love again.
TOUCHWOOD SENIOR. [*aside*] Some would think this impossible to compass.
– Pray let this storm fly over.
SIR OLIVER. Good sir, pardon me: I'm master of this house,
Which I'll sell presently, I'll clap up bills this evening.
TOUCHWOOD SENIOR. Lady, friends – come?
LADY KIX. If e'er ye lov'd woman, talk not on't, sir.
What, friends with him? Good faith, do you think I'm mad?
With one that's scarce the hinder quarter of a man?
SIR OLIVER. Thou art nothing of a woman.
LADY KIX. Would I were less than nothing. *Weeps.*
SIR OLIVER. Nay, prithee, what dost mean?
LADY KIX. I cannot please you.
SIR OLIVER. I'faith, thou art a good soul, he lies that says it;
Buss, buss, pretty rogue. [*Kisses her.*]
LADY KIX. You care not for me.

---

76 *Singleness*: i.e. the state of being divorced.
78 *not so single*: not so poorly equipped (compare 'Singlestone' at *A Mad World*, II.vi.29)/not so celibate (suggesting he brought several 'smocks' or loose women with him).
83 *outcry*: auction.
89 *clap up bills*: put up advertisements.

TOUCHWOOD SENIOR. [*aside*] Can any man tell now which way they came in?
By this light, I'll be hang'd then!
SIR OLIVER. Is the drink come?
TOUCHWOOD SENIOR. (*aside*) Here's a little vial of almond-milk
That stood me in some three pence.
SIR OLIVER. I hope to see thee, wench, within these few years,
Circled with children, pranking up a girl,
And putting jewels in their little ears;
Fine sport, i'faith!
LADY KIX. Ay, had you been aught, husband,
It had been done ere this time.
SIR OLIVER. 'Had I been aught'! Hang thee, hadst thou been aught!
But a cross thing I ever found thee.
LADY KIX. Thou art a grub to say so.
SIR OLIVER. A pox on thee!
TOUCHWOOD SENIOR. [*aside*] By this light they are out again at the same door,
And no man can tell which way.
– Come, here's your drink, sir.
SIR OLIVER. I will not take it now, sir,
And I were sure to get three boys ere midnight.
LADY KIX. Why there thou show'st now of what breed thou com'st,
To hinder generation! O thou villain,
That knows how crookedly the world goes with us
For want of heirs, yet put by all good fortune.
SIR OLIVER. Hang, strumpet, I will take it now in spite!
TOUCHWOOD SENIOR. Then you must ride upon't five hours.
SIR OLIVER. I mean so. – Within there?

Enter a SERVANT.

SERVANT. Sir?

---

104 *almond-milk*: made from sweet almonds pounded with water.
105 *stood me in*: cost me.
107 *pranking up*: dressing up, titivating.
114 *grub*: maggot/short, thick-set person (with probable allusion to his sexual inadequacy).
124 *put by*: neglect.

SIR OLIVER. Saddle the white mare;
I'll take a whore along, and ride to Ware.
LADY KIX. Ride to the devil!
SIR OLIVER. I'll plague you every way.
Look ye, do you see, 'tis gone. *Drinks.*
LADY KIX. A pox go with it!
SIR OLIVER. Ay, curse and spare not now.
TOUCHWOOD SENIOR. Stir up and down, sir, you must not stand.
SIR OLIVER. Nay, I'm not given to standing.
TOUCHWOOD SENIOR. So much the better, sir, for the –
SIR OLIVER. I never could stand long in one place yet;
I learnt it of my father, ever figient.
How if I cross'd this, sir? *Capers.*
TOUCHWOOD SENIOR. Oh, passing good, sir, and would show well a'horseback; when you come to your inn, if you leap'd over a joint-stool or two 'twere not amiss; (*Aside*) – although you brake your neck, sir.
SIR OLIVER. [*still capering*] What say you to a table thus high, sir?
TOUCHWOOD SENIOR. Nothing better, sir [*aside*] – if it be furnished with good victuals. You remember how the bargain runs about this business?
SIR OLIVER. Or else I had a bad head; you must receive, sir, four hundred pounds of me at four several payments: one hundred pound now in hand.
TOUCHWOOD SENIOR. Right, that I have, sir.
SIR OLIVER. Another hundred when my wife is quick; the third when she's brought a-bed; and the last hundred when the child cries, for if it should be stillborn, it doth no good, sir.
TOUCHWOOD SENIOR. All this is even still; a little faster, sir.

---

130 *Ware*: a town in Hertfordshire, 20 miles north of London, a place for amorous rendezvous.
137 *standing*: staying still/staying sexually erect.
139 See Textual note, p. 403.
141 *figient*: fidgety (but see note on III.ii.222).
142 *cross'd this*: jumped over this (presumably a joint-stool, about two feet high); there was a fashion for stool-leaping.
156 *quick*: pregnant.
160 *even*: exact; *faster*: he is still jigging to activate the medicine.

SIR OLIVER. Not a whit, sir,
I'm in an excellent pace for any physic.

Enter a SERVANT.

SERVANT. Your white mare's ready.
SIR OLIVER. I shall up presently.
[*Exit* SERVANT.]
– One kiss, and farewell.
LADY KIX. Thou shalt have two, love.
SIR OLIVER. Expect me about three. *Exit.*
LADY KIX. With all my heart, sweet.
TOUCHWOOD SENIOR. [*aside*] By this light they have forgot their anger since,
And are as far in again as e'er they were.
Which way the devil came they? Heart, I saw 'em not,
Their ways are beyond finding out. – Come, sweet lady.
LADY KIX. How must I take mine, sir?
TOUCHWOOD SENIOR. Clean contrary, yours must be taken lying.
LADY KIX. Abed, sir?
TOUCHWOOD SENIOR. Abed, or where you will for your own ease;
Your coach will serve.
LADY KIX. The physic must needs please.
Ex[*eunt*].

ACT IV

SCENE I

Enter TIM *and* TUTOR.

TIM. *Negatur argumentum*, tutor.
TUTOR. *Probo tibi*, pupil, *stultus non est animal rationale.*
TIM. *Falleris sane.*

---

171 *Which way the devil came they*: 'How on earth did they get into this mood?'

178 *coach*: Closed coaches were notorious as places for sexual encounters.

TUTOR. *Quaeso ut taceas: probo tibi –*

TIM. *Quomodo probas, domine?*

TUTOR. *Stultus non habet rationem, ergo non est animal rationale.*

TIM. *Sic argumentaris, domine: stultus non habet rationem, ergo non est animal rationale. Negatur argumentum* again, tutor.

TUTOR. *Argumentum iterum probo tibi, domine: qui non participat de ratione nullo modo potest vocari rationalibus*; but *stultus non participat de ratione, ergo stultus nullo modo potest dicere rationalis.*

TIM. *Participat.*

TUTOR. *Sic disputas; qui participat, quomodo participat?*

TIM. *Ut homo; probabo tibi in silagismo.*

TUTOR. *Hunc proba.*

TIM. *Sic probo, domine: stultus est homo sicut tu et ego sum, homo est animal rationale, sicut stultus est animal rationale.*

Enter MAUDLINE.

MAUDLINE. Here's nothing but disputing all the day long with 'em.

1–26 This is a Latin disputation of the type customary at the Universities, and hinges on both parties accepting unquestioningly the traditional definition of man as a 'rational animal'. See Textual note, p. 403.
Tim. 'I deny your proof, tutor.' *Tutor.* 'I am proving to you, pupil, that a fool is not a rational animal.' *Tim.* 'You are certainly mistaken.' *Tutor.* 'Please be silent: I am demonstrating to you –' *Tim.* 'How do you prove it, sir?' *Tutor.* 'A fool does not have reason, therefore he is not a rational animal.' *Tim.* 'You argue thus, sir: a fool does not have reason, therefore he is not a rational animal. I deny your proof again, tutor.' *Tutor.* 'I will demonstrate the proof to you again, sir: he who has no share of reason cannot by any means be called rational; but a fool has no share of reason, therefore a fool cannot by any means be said to be rational.' *Tim.* 'He does share it.' *Tutor.* 'So you maintain: but in what way does he who shares have a share?' *Tim.* 'As a man; I will prove it to you by a syllogism.' *Tutor.* 'Prove it.' *Tim.* 'I prove it thus, sir: a fool is a man just as you and I are, a man is a rational animal, just as a fool is a rational animal.' . . . *Tutor.* 'So you maintain: a fool is a man just as you and I are, a man is a rational animal, just as a fool is a rational animal.'

TUTOR. *Sic disputas: stultus est homo sicut tu et ego sum, homo est animal rationale, sicut stultus est animal rationale.*

MAUDLINE. Your reasons are both good, what e'er they be;
Pray, give them o'er; faith, you'll tire yourselves.
What's the matter between you?

TIM. Nothing but reasoning about a fool, mother.

MAUDLINE. About a fool, son? Alas, what need you trouble your heads about that? None of us all but knows what a fool is.

TIM. Why, what's a fool, mother?
I come to you now.

MAUDLINE. Why, one that's married before he has wit.

TIM. 'Tis pretty, i'faith, and well guess'd of a woman never brought up at the university; but bring forth what fool you will, mother, I'll prove him to be as reasonable a creature as myself or my tutor here.

MAUDLINE. Fie, 'tis impossible.

TUTOR. Nay, he shall do't, forsooth.

TIM. 'Tis the easiest thing to prove a fool by logic;
By logic I'll prove anything.

MAUDLINE. What, thou wilt not?

TIM. I'll prove a whore to be an honest woman.

MAUDLINE. Nay, by my faith, she must prove that herself, or logic will never do't.

TIM. 'Twill do't, I tell you.

MAUDLINE. Some in this street would give a thousand pounds that you could prove their wives so.

TIM. Faith, I can, and all their daughters too, though they had three bastards. When comes your tailor hither?

MAUDLINE. Why what of him?

TIM. By logic I'll prove him to be a man,
Let him come when he will.

MAUDLINE. How hard at first was learning to him? Truly, sir, I thought he would never a' took the Latin tongue.

---

29 *matter*: issue.

35 *I come to you now*: A disputation term for 'I pose the question to you.'

56 *a man*: Tailors were frequently regarded as cowardly; cf. Tilley, T 23: 'Nine tailors make but one man'.

How many Accidences do you think he wore out ere he came to his Grammar?

TUTOR. Some three or four?

MAUDLINE. Believe me, sir, some four and thirty.

TIM. Pish, I made haberdines of 'em in church porches.

MAUDLINE. He was eight years in his Grammar, and stuck horribly at a foolish place there call'd *as in presenti.*

TIM. Pox, I have it here now. [*Taps his head.*]

MAUDLINE. He so sham'd me once before an honest gentleman that knew me when I was a maid.

TIM. These women must have all out.

MAUDLINE. '*Quid est grammatica?*' says the gentleman to him (I shall remember by a sweet, sweet token), but nothing could he answer.

TUTOR. How now, pupil, ha? *Quid est grammatica?*

TIM. *Grammatica?* Ha, ha, ha!

MAUDLINE. Nay, do not laugh, son, but let me hear you say it now: there was one word went so prettily off the gentleman's tongue, I shall remember it the longest day of my life.

TUTOR. Come, *quid est grammatica?*

TIM. Are you not asham'd, tutor? *Grammatica?* Why, *recte scribendi atque loquendi ars*, sir-reverence of my mother.

60–1 *Accidences . . . Grammar*: The former contained Latin inflexions, the latter syntax; the first may have been William Lily's *Short Introduction*, the second was certainly his *Brevissima Institutio* (1540).

64 *haberdines*: Haberdines are dried salt cod, but this game is unknown. Probably it was like the modern children's game 'Kippers', in which fish cut out of paper are fanned along a confined course, the first 'kipper' wafted across the line being the winner.

66–7 *as in presenti*: the beginning of Lily's didactic poem on the endings of verbs of the first conjugation in his *Brevissima Institutio*, Part II, 'De Verbo'. Q prints 'Asse' to point the joke: 'An ass/arse in the presence'.

73 *token*: the word 'ars'; there are obscene innuendoes on 'knew' (line 70) and 'have all out' (line 71) also.

75–83 *Quid est grammatica? . . . recte scribendi . . . ars*: 'What is grammar? The art of writing and speaking correctly' – the opening sentences of Part II of Lily's grammar.

83 *sir-reverence*: 'save your reverence' (an apology for an indelicacy)/excrement (so that the phrase may be taken as an insult to the Tutor).

MAUDLINE. That was it, i'faith! Why now, son, I see you are a deep scholar; and, master tutor, a word I pray. [*Aside to* TUTOR] Let us withdraw a little into my husband's chamber; I'll send in the North Wales gentlewoman to him, she looks for wooing. I'll put together both, and lock the door.

TUTOR. I give great approbation to your conclusion.

Exit [*with* MAUDLINE].

TIM. I mar'l what this gentlewoman should be
That I should have in marriage: she's a stranger to me;
I wonder what my parents mean, i'faith,
To match me with a stranger so:
A maid that's neither kiff nor kin to me.
'Life, do they think I have no more care of my body
Than to lie with one that I ne'er knew,
A mere stranger,
One that ne'er went to school with me neither,
Nor ever playfellows together?
They're mightily o'erseen in't, methinks.
They say she has mountains to her marriage;
She's full of cattle, some two thousand runts:
Now what the meaning of these runts should be,
My tutor cannot tell me;
I have look'd in *Rider's Dictionary* for the letter R,
And there I can hear no tidings of these runts neither;
Unless they should be Rumford hogs,
I know them not.

Enter WELSH GENTLEWOMAN.

And here she comes.
If I know what to say to her now
In the way of marriage, I'm no graduate!
Methinks, i'faith, 'tis boldly done of her
To come into my chamber, being but a stranger;
She shall not say I'm so proud yet, but I'll speak to her:

---

96 *kiff*: kith, neighbour.
102 *o'erseen*: mistaken, imprudent.
103 *to her marriage*: i.e. as dowry.
104 *runts*: a small breed of Welsh and Highland cattle.
107 *Rider's Dictionary*: a Latin/English, English/Latin dictionary, published in 1589 by John Rider, Bishop of Killaloe.
109 *Rumford hogs*: Romford, Essex, twelve miles north-east of London, held a famous hog market each Tuesday.

Marry as I will order it,
She shall take no hold of my words, I'll warrant her.
[*She curtseys.*]
She looks and makes a cur'sey.
[*To her*] *Salve tu quoque, puella pulcherima,*
Quid vis nescio nec sane curo.
– Tully's own phrase to a heart!
WELSH GENTLEWOMAN. [*aside*] I know not what he means;
A suitor, quotha?
I hold my life he understands no English.
TIM. *Fertur me hercule tu virgo,*
Wallia ut opibus abundis maximis.
WELSH GENTLEWOMAN. [*aside*] What's this *fertur* and *abundundis*?
He mocks me sure, and calls me a bundle of farts.
TIM. [*aside*] I have no Latin word now for their runts;
I'll make some shift or other: [*To her*] *Iterum dico, opibus abundat maximis montibus et fontibus et, ut ita dicam, rontibus; attamen vero homunculus ego sum natura simule arte bachalarius lecto profecto non parata.*
WELSH GENTLEWOMAN. [*aside*] This is most strange.
May be he can speak Welsh.
– *Avedera whee comrage, derdue cog foginis?*
TIM. [*aside*] *Cog foggin?* I scorn to cog with her; I'll tell her so too, in a word near her own language: – *Ego non cogo.*

120–1 'Greetings to you also, most beautiful maiden; what you want I do not know, nor indeed do I care.'

122 *Tully*: Cicero; *to a heart*: to perfection (but see Textual note, p. 403).

126–7 Dog-Latin: 'By Hercules, it is said, young lady, that in Wales you abound in great riches.' See Textual note, p. 403.

131–5 'Again I say, it abounds in great riches, in mountains and fountains and (to coin a phrase) in runts; but truly, I am a little man by nature and a bachelor by art, not really ready for bed.' See Textual note, p. 403.

138 *Avedera . . . foginis*: The first phrase is phonetically spelt Welsh for 'Can you speak Welsh?', the second has not been convincingly interpreted.

139 *cog*: cheat, lie/lie sexually; *Ego non cogo*: 'I won't come together with you.'

WELSH GENTLEWOMAN. *Rhegosin a whiggin harle ron corid ambre.*
TIM. By my faith, she's a good scholar, I see that already:
She has the tongues plain; I hold my life she has travell'd.
What will folks say? 'There goes the learned couple!'
Faith, if the truth were known, she hath proceeded.

Enter MAUDLINE.

MAUDLINE. How now, how speeds your business?
TIM. [*aside*] I'm glad my mother's come to part us.
MAUDLINE. How do you agree, forsooth?
WELSH GENTLEWOMAN. As well as e'er we did before we met.
MAUDLINE. How's that?
WELSH GENTLEWOMAN. You put me to a man I understand not;
Your son's no Englishman methinks.
MAUDLINE. No Englishman! Bless my boy,
And born i'the heart of London?
WELSH GENTLEWOMAN. I ha' been long enough in the chamber with him,
And I find neither Welsh nor English in him.
MAUDLINE. Why, Tim, how have you us'd the gentlewoman?
TIM. As well as a man might do, mother, in modest Latin.
MAUDLINE. Latin, fool?
TIM. And she recoil'd in Hebrew.
MAUDLINE. In Hebrew, fool? 'Tis Welsh.
TIM. All comes to one, mother.
MAUDLINE. She can speak English too.
TIM. Who told me so much?
Heart, and she can speak English, I'll clap to her;
I thought you'd marry me to a stranger.

141–2 *Rhegosin . . . ambre*: Perhaps this represents *Rhyw gosyn a chwigyn ar ôl bod yn cerdedd am dro*, 'Some cheese and whey after taking a walk'. Cheese and whey were supposed to be the favourite diet of the Welsh.
146 *proceeded*: taken a degree//gone beyond virginity.
161 *recoil'd*: responded.
166 *clap*: stick/ clasp hands on the contract/seize vigorously. The 'clap' being the pox, there is probably an unconscious irony.

MAUDLINE. You must forgive him, he's so inur'd to Latin,
He and his tutor, that he hath quite forgot
To use the Protestant tongue.
WELSH GENTLEWOMAN. 'Tis quickly pardon'd, forsooth.
MAUDLINE. Tim, make amends and kiss her.
– He makes towards you, forsooth.
[TIM *kisses* WELSH GENTLEWOMAN.]

TIM. Oh, delicious! One may discover her country by her kissing. 'Tis a true saying, 'There's nothing tastes so sweet as your Welsh mutton.' [*To* GENTLEWOMAN] It was reported you could sing.

MAUDLINE. Oh, rarely, Tim, the sweetest British songs.
TIM. And 'tis my mind, I swear, before I marry,
I would see all my wife's good parts at once,
To view how rich I were.
MAUDLINE. Thou shalt hear sweet music, Tim.
– Pray, forsooth.

Music and Welsh Song.

THE SONG

[WELSH GENTLEWOMAN]. Cupid is Venus' only joy,
But he is a wanton boy,
A very, very wanton boy;
He shoots at ladies' naked breasts,
He is the cause of most men's crests,
I mean upon the forehead,
Invisible but horrid;
'Twas he first taught upon the way
To keep a lady's lips in play.

Why should not Venus chide her son
For the pranks that he hath done,

---

170 *Protestant tongue*: i.e. the vernacular, the liturgical language of the reformers.
176 *mutton*: with a pun on the slang meaning, 'whore'.
178 *British*: i.e. Welsh.
180 *good parts*: attainments/physical attributes (suggested perhaps by the custom of seeing fiancées naked in More's *Utopia*). There are perhaps innuendoes also on 'country' (line 174) and 'sing' (line 177).
184–210 See Textual notes, p. 403.
188 *crests*: heraldic crests/cuckold's horns.
192, 201 *lips*: upper and lower (see line 210).

The wanton pranks that he hath done?
He shoots his fiery darts so thick,
They hurt poor ladies to the quick,
Ah me, with cruel wounding!
His darts are so confounding
That life and sense would soon decay,
But that he keeps their lips in play.

Can there be any part of bliss
In a quickly fleeting kiss,
A quickly, [quickly] fleeting kiss?
To one's pleasure, leisures are but waste,
The slowest kiss makes too much haste,
[We always are behind it,]
And lose it ere we find it;
The pleasing sport they only know
That close above and close below.

TIM. I would not change my wife for a kingdom;
I can do somewhat too in my own lodging.

Enter YELLOWHAMMER *and* ALLWIT [*disguised*].

YELLOWHAMMER. Why well said, Tim! The bells go merrily;
I love such peals a'life; wife, lead them in a while;
Here's a strange gentleman desires private conference.

[*Exeunt* MAUDLINE, TIM *and* WELSH GENTLEWOMAN.]

You're welcome, sir, the more for your name's sake,
Good Master Yellowhammer, I love my name well;
And which a'the Yellowhammers take you descent from,
If I may be so bold with you? Which, I pray?

---

197 *quick*: the tenderest part (with bawdy implication).
199–200 *darts . . . decay*: 'Dart of love' = the penis, and the allusion is to the belief that each act of sexual intercourse shortened one's life by one day.
205 *leisures are but waste*: intermissions are a waste of time.
210 *close*: unite in an embrace.
212 *in my own lodging*: on my own account (with obscene innuendo).
213 *The bells go merrily*: probably proverbial; cf. modern 'I hear wedding bells.'
214 *a'life*: as life itself.

ALLWIT. The Yellowhammers in Oxfordshire,
Near Abbington.
YELLOWHAMMER. And those are the best Yellowhammers, and truest bred: I came from thence myself, though now a citizen. I'll be bold with you; you are most welcome.
ALLWIT. I hope the zeal I bring with me shall deserve it.
YELLOWHAMMER. I hope no less; what is your will, sir?
ALLWIT. I understand by rumours, you have a daughter,
Which my bold love shall henceforth title 'cousin'.
YELLOWHAMMER. I thank you for her, sir.
ALLWIT. I heard of her virtues, and other confirm'd graces.
YELLOWHAMMER. A plaguy girl, sir.
ALLWIT. Fame sets her out with richer ornaments
Than you are pleas'd to boast of; 'tis done modestly.
I hear she's towards marriage.
YELLOWHAMMER. You hear truth, sir.
ALLWIT. And with a knight in town, Sir Walter Whorehound.
YELLOWHAMMER. The very same, sir.
ALLWIT. I am the sorrier for't.
YELLOWHAMMER. The sorrier? Why, cousin?
ALLWIT. 'Tis not too far past, is't? It may be yet recall'd?
YELLOWHAMMER. Recall'd? Why, good sir?
ALLWIT. Resolve me in that point, ye shall hear from me.
YELLOWHAMMER. There's no contract pass'd.
ALLWIT. I am very joyful, sir.
YELLOWHAMMER. But he's the man must bed her.
ALLWIT. By no means, cuz; she's quite undone then,
And you'll curse the time that e'er you made the match;
He's an arrant whoremaster, consumes his time and state,
[*Whispers*] – whom in my knowledge he hath kept this seven years;
Nay, cuz, another man's wife too.
YELLOWHAMMER. Oh abominable!
ALLWIT. Maintains the whole house, apparels the husband,

---

221 *Abbington*: Abingdon in Berkshire, on the Thames five miles south of Oxford.
231 *confirm'd*: established.
232 *plaguy*: troublesome.
243 *resolve me . . . point*: 'satisfy me on that question'.
250 See Textual note, p. 403.

Pays servants' wages, not so much but – [*Whispers*]
YELLOWHAMMER. Worse and worse! And doth the husband know this?
ALLWIT. Knows? Ay, and glad he may too, 'tis his living:
As other trades thrive, butchers by selling flesh,
Poulters by venting conies, or the like, cuz.
YELLOWHAMMER. What an incomparable wittol's this!
ALLWIT. Tush, what cares he for that?
Believe me, cuz, no more than I do.
YELLOWHAMMER. What a base slave is that!
ALLWIT. All's one to him: he feeds and takes his ease,
Was ne'er the man that ever broke his sleep
To get a child yet, by his own confession,
And yet his wife has seven.
YELLOWHAMMER. What, by Sir Walter?
ALLWIT. Sir Walter's like to keep 'em, and maintain 'em,
In excellent fashion; he dares do no less, sir.
YELLOWHAMMER. Life, has he children too?
ALLWIT. Children? Boys thus high,
In their Cato and Cordelius.
YELLOWHAMMER. What! You jest, sir!
ALLWIT. Why, one can make a verse,
And is now at Eton College.
YELLOWHAMMER. Oh, this news has cut into my heart, cuz!
ALLWIT. It had eaten nearer if it had not been prevented:
One Allwit's wife.
YELLOWHAMMER. Allwit? Foot, I have heard of him;
He had a girl kurs'ned lately?
ALLWIT. Ay, that work did cost the knight above a hundred mark.

---

254 See Textual note, p. 403.

258 *venting conies*: selling rabbits. Probably *Poulters* are intended to suggest 'pimps', and *conies* 'whores'.

259 *wittol*: acquiescent cuckold.

272 *Cato and Cordelius*: 'Dionysius Cato's' *Disticha de Moribus* (third or fourth century) and Mathurin Cordier's *Colloquia Scholastica* (1564), both moralising schoolbooks widely used at the time.

275 *Eton College*: founded by Henry VI as a school in 1440, situated in Buckinghamshire about twenty-three miles west of London. The composition of Latin verses was a regular school exercise.

YELLOWHAMMER. I'll mark him for a knave and villain for't;
A thousand thanks and blessings! I have done with him.
ALLWIT. [*aside*] Ha, ha, ha! This knight will stick by my ribs still;
I shall not lose him yet, no wife will come;
Where'er he woos, I find him still at home. Ha, ha!
Exit.
YELLOWHAMMER. Well grant all this, say now his deeds are black,
Pray what serves marriage, but to call him back;
I have kept a whore myself, and had a bastard,
By Mistress Anne, in *Anno* –
I care not who knows it; he's now a jolly fellow,
H'as been twice warden; so many his fruit be:
They were but base begot, and so was he;
The knight is rich, he shall be my son-in-law.
No matter, so the whore he keeps be wholesome:
My daughter takes no hurt then, so let them wed;
I'll have him sweat well e'er they go to bed.

Enter MAUDLINE.

MAUDLINE. O husband, husband!
YELLOWHAMMER. How now, Maudline?
MAUDLINE. We are all undone! She's gone, she's gone!
YELLOWHAMMER. Again? Death! Which way?
MAUDLINE. Over the houses.
Lay the waterside; she's gone forever, else.
YELLOWHAMMER. Oh vent'rous baggage!
Exit [*with* MAUDLINE.]

Enter TIM *and* TUTOR.

---

285 *stick by my ribs*: 'stick to me like my skin'. But Middleton may have written 'my rib' = 'my wife'.
289 *call him back*: reform him.
291 *in Anno*: See Textual note, p. 403: 'in the year . . . '.
293 *warden*: member of the governing body of a City Company/ warden pear (hence the pun on 'fruit').
296 *wholesome*: free of the pox.
298 *sweat*: i.e. undergo mercurial fumigation in the sweating-tub, the remedy for venereal disease.
303 *Over the houses*: i.e. over the roofs.
304 *Lay*: search, set watch on.
305 *vent'rous*: bold.

TIM. Thieves, thieves! My sister's stol'n!
Some thief hath got her.
Oh how miraculously did my father's plate 'scape!
'Twas all left out, tutor.
TUTOR. Is't possible?
TIM. Besides three chains of pearl and a box of coral.
My sister's gone, let's look at Trig stairs for her;
My mother's gone to lay the Common stairs
At Puddle wharf, and at the dock below
Stands my poor silly father. Run, sweet tutor, run.
Exit [*with* TUTOR].

SCENE II

Enter both the TOUCHWOODS.

TOUCHWOOD SENIOR. I had been taken, brother, by eight sergeants,
But for the honest watermen; I am bound to them;
They are the most requiteful'st people living:
For as they get their means by gentlemen,
They are still the forwardest to help gentlemen.
You heard how one 'scap'd out of the Blackfriars,
But a while since, from two or three varlets
Came into the house with all their rapiers drawn,
As if they'd dance the sword-dance on the stage,
With candles in their hands, like chandlers' ghosts,
Whilst the poor gentleman so pursued and bandied
Was by an honest pair of oars safely landed.
TOUCHWOOD JUNIOR. I love them with my heart for't.

Enter three or four WATERMEN.

313–15 *Trig stairs . . . Common stairs . . . Puddle wharf . . . dock below*: They mark the possible embarkation points: Trig stairs, a landing place at the bottom of Trig Lane; the 'common' or public stairs about 300 yards upstream from Trig stairs at Puddle wharf, where the Mermaid theatre now stands; at Dung wharf 'below', i.e. downstream.

1 *sergeants*: officers of the sheriff.

2 *watermen*: boatmen running a taxi-service on the Thames.

3 *requiteful'st*: most eager to pay back favours.

6 *Blackfriars*: indoor private theatre, since 1609 occupied by the King's Men, and lit by candles.

10 *chandlers*: candle-makers.

11 *bandied*: struck to and fro.

1 [WATERMAN]. Your first man, sir.
2 [WATERMAN]. Shall I carry you gentlemen with a pair of oars?
TOUCHWOOD SENIOR. These be the honest fellows.
Take one pair, and leave the rest for her.
TOUCHWOOD JUNIOR. Barn Elms.
TOUCHWOOD SENIOR. No more, brother.
1 [WATERMAN]. Your first man.
2 [WATERMAN]. Shall I carry your worship?
[*Exit* TOUCHWOOD SENIOR *with* 1 WATERMAN.]
TOUCHWOOD JUNIOR. Go.
And you honest watermen that stay,
Here's a French crown for you; [*Gives money.*]
There comes a maid with all speed to take water;
Row her lustily to Barn Elms after me.
2 [WATERMAN]. To Barn Elms, good sir. –Make ready the boat, Sam.
We'll wait below.
Exit [2 WATERMAN, *and* OTHERS].

Enter MOLL.

TOUCHWOOD JUNIOR. What made you stay so long?
MOLL. I found the way more dangerous than I look'd for.
TOUCHWOOD JUNIOR. Away, quick! There's a boat waits for you;
And I'll take water at Paul's wharf, and overtake you.
MOLL. Good sir, do; we cannot be too safe.
[*Exeunt.*]

SCENE III

Enter SIR WALTER, YELLOWHAMMER, TIM *and* TUTOR.

SIR WALTER. Life, call you this close keeping?

---

14 *Your first man*: the trade-cry of the watermen: 'I'm first in the queue.'
18 *Barn Elms*: a manor house and park on the south bank of the Thames opposite Hammersmith; a favourite place for assignations and duelling.
24 *French crown*: the écu, a French silver coin accepted as equivalent to the English five-shilling piece.
25 *water*: note also the meaning at II.i.189ff.
32 *Paul's wharf*: between Puddle wharf and Trig stairs, due south of St Paul's.

YELLOWHAMMER. She was kept under a double lock.
SIR WALTER. A double devil!
TIM. That's a buff sergeant, tutor, he'll ne'er wear out.
YELLOWHAMMER. How would you have women lock'd?
TIM. With padlocks, father, the Venetian uses it; my tutor reads it.
SIR WALTER. Heart, if she were so lock'd up, how got she out?
YELLOWHAMMER. There was a little hole, look'd into the gutter;
But who would have dreamt of that?
SIR WALTER. A wiser man would.
TIM. He says true, father, a wise man for love will seek every hole; my tutor knows it.
TUTOR. *Verum poeta dicit.*
TIM. *Dicit Virgilius*, father.
YELLOWHAMMER. Prithee, talk of thy gills somewhere else, she's play'd the gill with me. Where's your wise mother now?
TIM. Run mad, I think; I thought she would have drown'd herself; she would not stay for oars, but took a smelt boat: sure, I think she be gone a-fishing for her!
YELLOWHAMMER. She'll catch a goodly dish of gudgeons now,
Will serve us all to supper.

---

4 *buff sergeant*: officer responsible for making arrests; 'buff', the tough ox-hide leather from which their jerkins were made, became a symbol of their obduracy.

6 *Venetian*: Venetians were commonly believed to restrict their lascivious womenfolk by means of chastity-belts.

7 *reads*: has read it (perhaps with a pun on the more archaic meaning, 'advises').

13 *knows it*: ironic, since the Tutor has probably cuckolded Yellowhammer.

14–15 *Verum poeta dicit . . . Dicit Virgilius*: 'The poet says true . . . Virgil says it, father' (Latin). Tim ludicrously misattributes this vulgarity to a poet known for his high-mindedness.

16 *gills*: wantons, wenches.

21 *smelt boat*: boat for fishing smelts or sparlings, small fish used metaphorically (like 'gudgeon') for 'fools'.

23 *gudgeon*: small freshwater fish, easily caught and used chiefly as bait. 'To gape after, swallow gudgeons' was proverbial for being deceived (Tilley, G 473).

Enter MAUDLINE *drawing* MOLL *by the hair, and* WATERMEN.

MAUDLINE. I'll tug thee home by the hair.

WATERMEN. Good mistress, spare her.

MAUDLINE. Tend your own business.

WATERMEN. You are a cruel mother.

Ex[*eunt* WATERMEN].

MOLL. Oh, my heart dies!

MAUDLINE. I'll make thee an example for all the neighbours' daughters.

MOLL. Farewell, life!

MAUDLINE. You that have tricks can counterfeit.

YELLOWHAMMER. Hold, hold, Maudline!

MAUDLINE. I have brought your jewel by the hair.

YELLOWHAMMER. She's here, knight.

SIR WALTER. Forbear or I'll grow worse.

TIM. Look on her, tutor, she hath brought her from the water like a mermaid: she's but half my sister now, as far as the flesh goes; the rest may be sold to fishwives.

MAUDLINE. Dissembling, cunning baggage!

YELLOWHAMMER. Impudent strumpet!

SIR WALTER. Either give over both, or I'll give over!
– Why have you us'd me thus, unkind mistress?
Wherein have I deserved?

YELLOWHAMMER. You talk too fondly, sir. We'll take another course and prevent all; we might have done't long since; we'll lose no time now, nor trust to't any longer: tomorrow morn as early as sunrise, we'll have you join'd.

MOLL. O, bring me death tonight, love-pitying Fates;
Let me not see tomorrow up upon the world.

YELLOWHAMMER. Are you content, sir, till then she shall be watch'd?

MAUDLINE. Baggage, you shall!

Exit [*with* MOLL *and* YELLOWHAMMER].

---

37 *worse*: i.e. more angry.

39–40 *mermaid . . . fishwives*: 'Mermaid' is used elsewhere by Middleton to mean 'enticing whore', and 'fishmonger', 'oyster-wife' and 'fishwife' were synonyms for 'bawd'.

53 See Textual note, p. 404.

TIM. Why, father, my tutor and I will both watch in armour.

TUTOR. How shall we do for weapons?

TIM. Take you no care for that, if need be I can send for conquering metal, tutor, ne'er lost day yet; 'tis but at Westminster: I am acquainted with him that keeps the monuments; I can borrow Harry the Fifth's sword, 'twill serve us both to watch with.

Exit [*with* TUTOR].

SIR WALTER. I never was so near my wish, as this chance
Makes me; ere tomorrow noon,
I shall receive two thousand pound in gold,
And a sweet maidenhead
Worth forty.

Enter TOUCHWOOD JUNIOR *with a* WATERMAN.

TOUCHWOOD JUNIOR. Oh, thy news splits me!

WATERMAN. Half drown'd, she cruelly tugg'd her by the hair,
Forc'd her disgracefully, not like a mother.

TOUCHWOOD JUNIOR. Enough, leave me, like my joys.

Exit WATERMAN.

– Sir, saw you not a wretched maid pass this way?
Heart, villain, is that thou?

SIR WALTER. Yes, slave, 'tis I! *Both draw and fight.*

TOUCHWOOD JUNIOR. I must break through thee then: there is no stop
That checks my tongue and all my hopeful fortunes,
That breast excepted, and I must have way.

SIR WALTER. Sir, I believe 'twill hold your life in play.

[*He wounds* TOUCHWOOD JUNIOR.]

---

55 *in armour*: also slang for 'emboldened by drinking'.

60–1 *him that keeps the monuments*: the master of the monuments at Westminster Abbey, who for one penny acted as official guide.

61 *Harry the Fifth's sword*: Henry V's armour and silver head had been stolen; Tim probably means the seven foot sword of Edward III.

67 *forty*: i.e. the price of a virgin in the prostitution market.

76 *checks my tongue*: 'prevents me speaking on my own behalf' (because Sir Walter is the accepted suitor).

78 *life in play*: life at risk, hazard (the first of a succession of gaming images).

TOUCHWOOD JUNIOR. Sir, you'll gain the heart in my breast at first?
SIR WALTER. There is no dealing then? Think on the dowry for two thousand pounds.
TOUCHWOOD JUNIOR. [*striking at* SIR WALTER] Oh now 'tis quit, sir.
SIR WALTER. And being of even hand, I'll play no longer.
TOUCHWOOD JUNIOR. No longer, slave?
SIR WALTER. I have certain things to think on
Before I dare go further.
TOUCHWOOD JUNIOR. But one bout?
I'll follow thee to death, but ha't out.

Ex[*eunt*].

ACT V

SCENE I

Enter ALLWIT, *his* WIFE, *and* DAVY DAHUMMA.

MISTRESS ALLWIT. A misery of a house!
ALLWIT. What shall become of us?
DAVY. I think his wound be mortal.
ALLWIT. Think'st thou so, Davy?
Then am I mortal too, but a dead man, Davy;
This is no world for me, when e'er he goes;
I must e'en truss up all, and after him, Davy;
A sheet with two knots, and away!

Enter SIR WALTER, *led in hurt* [*by two* SERVANTS].

DAVY. Oh see, sir,

---

80 *Sir . . . at first*: See Textual note, p. 404. 'Do you think you'll kill me with the first thrust?'
81 *dealing*: compromising (Sir Walter offers him a cut of the dowry.)
84 *quit*: paid back, requited.
85 *of even hand*: 'all square'.
87 *certain things to think on*: i.e. the religious considerations of V.i.
7 *truss up all*: pack up everything (as in a winding sheet).
8 *sheet with two knots*: the shroud was knotted at head and foot.

How faint he goes! Two of my fellows lead him.
MISTRESS ALLWIT. [*fainting*] Oh me!
ALLWIT. Hyday, my wife's laid down too! Here's like to be
A good house kept, when we are altogether down.
Take pains with her, good Davy, cheer her up there.
Let me come to his worship, let me come.
[*Exeunt* SERVANTS.]
SIR WALTER. Touch me not, villain! My wound aches at thee,
Thou poison to my heart!
ALLWIT. He raves already,
His senses are quite gone, he knows me not.
– Look up, an't like your worship; heave those eyes;
Call me to mind; is your remembrance left?
Look in my face: who am I, an't like your worship?
SIR WALTER. If any thing be worse than slave or villain,
Thou art the man.
ALLWIT. Alas, his poor worship's weakness!
He will begin to know me by little and little.
SIR WALTER. No devil can be like thee!
ALLWIT. Ah, poor gentleman,
Methinks the pain that thou endurest –
SIR WALTER. Thou know'st me to be wicked, for thy baseness
Kept the eyes open still on all my sins;
None knew the dear account my soul stood charg'd with
So well as thou, yet like Hell's flattering angel
Would'st never tell me on't, let'st me go on,
And join with death in sleep: that if I had not wak'd
Now by chance, even by a stranger's pity,
I had everlastingly slept out all hope
Of grace and mercy.
ALLWIT. Now he is worse and worse.
Wife, to him, wife; thou wast wont to do good on him.
MISTRESS ALLWIT. How is't with you, sir?
SIR WALTER. Not as with you,
Thou loathsome strumpet! Some good pitying man
Remove my sins out of my sight a little;

19 *left*: departed; but see Textual note, p. 404.
25 See Textual note, p. 404.
35 *do good on*: benefit/copulate with.

I tremble to behold her, she keeps back
All comfort while she stays. Is this a time,
Unconscionable woman, to see thee?
Art thou so cruel to the peace of man,
Not to give liberty now? The devil himself
Shows a far fairer reverence and respect
To goodness than thyself: he dares not do this,
But part[s] in time of penitence, hides his face;
When man withdraws from him, he leaves the place.
Hast thou less manners, and more impudence,
Than thy instructor? Prithee show thy modesty,
If the least grain be left, and get thee from me.
Thou should'st be rather lock'd many rooms hence
From the poor miserable sight of me,
If either love or grace had part in thee.

MISTRESS ALLWIT. He is lost for ever.

ALLWIT. Run, sweet Davy, quickly,
And fetch the children hither; sight of them
Will make him cheerful straight.

[*Exit* DAVY.]

SIR WALTER. [*to* MISTRESS ALLWIT] Oh death! Is this
A place for you to weep? What tears are those?
Get you away with them, I shall fare the worse
As long as they are a-weeping; they work against me;
There's nothing but thy appetite in that sorrow,
Thou weep'st for lust; I feel it in the slackness
Of comforts coming towards me:
I was well till thou began'st to undo me.
This shows like the fruitless sorrow of a careless
mother
That brings her son with dalliance to the gallows,
And then stands by, and weeps to see him suffer.

Enter DAVY *with the* CHILDREN.

DAVY. There are the children, sir, an't like your worship;
Your last fine girl: in troth she smiles!
Look, look, in faith, sir.

SIR WALTER. Oh my vengeance!

---

41 *unconscionable*: having no conscience/insensitive, unthinking (see III.i.39).

65 *dalliance*: indulgence/sexual sport.

69 *vengeance*: i.e. the pledge of God's vengeance upon him (the children).

Let me for ever hide my cursed face
From sight of those, that darkens all my hopes,
And stands between me and the sight of Heaven.
Who sees me now, he too and those so near me,
May rightly say, I am o'er-grown with sin.
Oh, how my offences wrestle with my repentance!
It hath scarce breath;
Still my adulterous guilt hovers aloft,
And with her black wings beats down all my prayers
Ere they be half way up. What's he knows now
How long I have to live? Oh, what comes then?
My taste grows bitter; the round world, all gall now;
Her pleasing pleasures now hath poison'd me,
Which I exchang'd my soul for.
Make way a hundred sighs at once for me.

ALLWIT. Speak to him, Nick.

NICK. I dare not, I am afraid.

ALLWIT. Tell him he hurts his wounds, Wat, with making moan.

SIR WALTER. Wretched, death of seven.

ALLWIT. Come, let's be talking somewhat to keep him alive.
Ah, sirrah Wat, and did my lord bestow that jewel on thee,
For an epistle thou mad'st in Latin?
Thou art a good forward boy, there's great joy on thee.

SIR WALTER. Oh sorrow!

ALLWIT. [*aside*] Heart, will nothing comfort him?
If he be so far gone, 'tis time to moan.
– Here's pen, and ink, and paper, and all things ready;
Will't please your worship for to make your will?

---

73 *he too*: i.e. God ('Heaven' in the previous line); but see Textual note, p. 404.

84 'May the hundred sighs (of repentance) I now breathe out clear me a path (to Heaven).'

87 *death of seven*: Sir Walter means he has been the spiritual destruction of the seven bastards he has got on Mistress Allwit (Middleton seems to treat the misfortune of being the victim of sexual sin (e.g. rape) as being damnable).

89 *my lord*: not an appropriate title for Sir Walter. Some unspecified lord or bishop has rewarded the child for a composition, perhaps a message of greeting on a visit to Eton (see IV.i.274–5).

SIR WALTER. My will? Yes, yes, what else? Who writes
apace now?
ALLWIT. That can your man Davy, an't like your worship,
A fair, fast, legible hand.
SIR WALTER. Set it down then: [DAVY *writes.*]
Imprimis, I bequeath to yonder wittol
Three times his weight in curses –
ALLWIT. How?
SIR WALTER. All plagues of body and of mind –
ALLWIT. Write them not down, Davy.
DAVY. It is his will; I must.
SIR WALTER. Together also
With such a sickness, ten days ere his death.
ALLWIT. [*aside*] There's a sweet legacy,
I am almost chok'd with't.
SIR WALTER. Next I bequeath to that foul whore his wife
All barrenness of joy, a drouth of virtue,
And dearth of all repentance; for her end,
The common misery of an English strumpet,
In French and Dutch: beholding ere she dies
Confusion of her brats before her eyes,
And never shed a tear for it.

Enter a SERVANT.

SERVANT. Where's the knight?
O sir, the gentleman you wounded is newly departed!
SIR WALTER. Dead? Lift, lift! Who helps me?
ALLWIT. Let the law lift you now, that must have all;
I have done lifting on you, and my wife too.
SERVANT. You were best lock yourself close.
ALLWIT. Not in my house, sir,
I'll harbour no such persons as men-slayers;
Lock yourself where you will.
SIR WALTER. What's this?
MISTRESS ALLWIT. Why, husband!

---

114 *In French and Dutch*: the 'French disease' is syphilis, and since 'Dutch widow' = a whore, the 'Dutch disease' may be gonorrhoea; or it may merely be 'drunkenness'.

115 *Confusion*: i.e. death, either from starvation or hereditary syphilis.

119 *lift*: lift up (on the gallows)/rob, plunder (the goods of murderers were forfeit).

120 *lifting*: helping/plundering, robbing/copulating.

ALLWIT. I know what I do, wife.
MISTRESS ALLWIT. You cannot tell yet;
For having kill'd the man in his defence,
Neither his life nor estate will be touch'd, husband.
ALLWIT. Away, wife! Hear a fool! His lands will hang him.
SIR WALTER. Am I denied a chamber?
– What say you, forsooth?
MISTRESS ALLWIT. Alas, sir, I am one that would have all well,
But must obey my husband. – Prithee, love,
Let the poor gentleman stay, being so sore wounded;
There's a close chamber at one end of the garret
We never use, let him have that, I prithee.
ALLWIT. We never use? You forget sickness then,
And physic times: is't not a place for easement?

Enter a [*nother*] SERVANT.

SIR WALTER. Oh death! Do I hear this with part
Of former life in me? – What's the news now?
SERVANT. Troth, worse and worse; you're like to lose your land
If the law save your life, sir, or the surgeon.
ALLWIT. [*aside*] Hark you there, wife.
SIR WALTER. Why how, sir?
SERVANT. Sir Oliver Kix's wife is new quick'ned;
That child undoes you, sir.
SIR WALTER. All ill at once!
ALLWIT. I wonder what he makes here with his consorts?
Cannot our house be private to ourselves,
But we must have such guests? I pray depart, sirs,
And take your murtherer along with you;
Good he were apprehended ere he go,
H'as kill'd some honest gentleman. Send for officers.
SIR WALTER. I'll soon save you that labour.
ALLWIT. I must tell you, sir,
You have been somewhat bolder in my house
Than I could well like of; I suff'red you

---

127 *Hear a fool*: 'You're talking nonsense.'
136 *physic . . . easement*: I.e. the private room is used as a lavatory by those who have taken 'physic', purges.
143 *quick'ned*: made pregnant.
145 *consorts*: companions (i.e. servants).

Till it stuck here at my heart; I tell you truly
I thought you had been familiar with my wife once.
MISTRESS ALLWIT. With me? I'll see him hang'd first: I defy him,
And all such gentlemen in the like extremity.
SIR WALTER. If ever eyes were open, these are they;
Gamesters, farewell, I have nothing left to play. *Exit.*
ALLWIT. And therefore get you gone, sir.
DAVY. Of all wittols
Be thou the head! [*To* MISTRESS ALLWIT] Thou, the grand whore of spitals!
Exit [*with* SERVANTS].
ALLWIT. So, since he's like now to be rid of all,
I am right glad I am so well rid of him.
MISTRESS ALLWIT. I knew he durst not stay when you nam'd officers.
ALLWIT. That stopp'd his spirits straight.
What shall we do now, wife?
MISTRESS ALLWIT. As we were wont to do.
ALLWIT. We are richly furnish'd, wife, with household stuff.
MISTRESS ALLWIT. Let's let out lodgings then,
And take a house in the Strand.
ALLWIT. In troth, a match, wench:
We are simply stock'd with cloth-of-tissue cushions,
To furnish out bay windows; push, what not that's quaint
And costly, from the top to the bottom.
'Life, for furniture, we may lodge a countess!
There's a close-stool of tawny velvet too,
Now I think on't wife,
MISTRESS ALLWIT. There's that should be, sir;
Your nose must be in every thing!
ALLWIT. I have done, wench;
And let this stand in every gallant's chamber:

---

159 *Gamesters*: gamblers/lechers.
161 *spitals*: hospitals for venereal diseases.
170 *Strand*: the fashionable residential area, from Temple Bar to Charing Cross; but also notorious for high-class prostitutes; *a match*: a deal, bargain.
171 *cloth-of-tissue*: cloth interwoven with gold and silver thread.
175 *close-stool*: a commode, chamber-pot in a box or stool.

'There's no gamester like a politic sinner,
For who e'er games, the box is sure a winner.'
Exit [*with* MISTRESS ALLWIT].

SCENE II

Enter YELLOWHAMMER *and his* WIFE.

MAUDLINE. Oh, husband, husband, she will die, she will die!
There is no sign but death.
YELLOWHAMMER. 'Twill be our shame then.
MAUDLINE. Oh, how she's chang'd in compass of an hour!
YELLOWHAMMER. Ah, my poor girl! Good faith, thou wert too cruel
To drag her by the hair.
MAUDLINE. You would have done as much, sir,
To curb her of her humour.
YELLOWHAMMER. 'Tis curb'd sweetly, she catch'd her bane o'th' water!

Enter TIM.

MAUDLINE. How now, Tim?
TIM. Faith, busy, mother, about an epitaph
Upon my sister's death.
MAUDLINE. Death! She is not dead, I hope?
TIM. No, but she means to be, and that's as good,
And when a thing's done, 'tis done;
You taught me that, mother.
YELLOWHAMMER. What is your tutor doing?
TIM. Making one too, in principal pure Latin,
Cull'd out of *Ovid de Tristibus*.

---

180 *box*: Money was placed by gamesters in the box as they drew their first hand, in payment of the house charges. There are the usual puns on *gamester*, *games* (= sexual sport), and perhaps a play on *box* = coffin.

9 *water*: a pun, since 'Walter' was a homophone, the *l* not being pronounced.

15 *when a thing's done, 'tis done*: Proverbial; Tilley, T 200, 'Things done cannot be undone.' There was also a game, rather like the modern 'consequences', called 'A thing done', as in Jonson's *Cynthia's Revels*, IV.iii.160–70.

18 *principal*: excellent, choice.

19 *Ovid de Tristibus*: Ovid's *Tristia*, five books of mournful poems, used as a third form text book in grammar schools.

YELLOWHAMMER. How does your sister look? Is she not chang'd?
TIM. Chang'd? Gold into white money was never so chang'd
As is my sister's colour into paleness.

Enter MOLL [*led in by* SERVANTS].

YELLOWHAMMER. Oh, here she's brought; see how she looks like death!
TIM. Looks she like death, and ne'er a word made yet?
I must go beat my brains against a bed post,
And get before my tutor. [*Exit.*]
YELLOWHAMMER. Speak, how dost thou?
MOLL. I hope I shall be well, for I am as sick at heart
As I can be.
YELLOWHAMMER. 'Las, my poor girl!
The doctor's making a most sovereign drink for thee,
The worst ingredience, dissolv'd pearl and amber;
We spare no cost, girl.
MOLL. Your love comes too late;
Yet timely thanks reward it. What is comfort,
When the poor patient's heart is past relief?
It is no doctor's art can cure my grief.
YELLOWHAMMER. All is cast away then.
Prithee, look upon me cheerfully.
MAUDLINE. Sing but a strain or two, thou wilt not think
How 'twill revive thy spirits: strive with thy fit,
Prithee, sweet Moll.
MOLL. You shall have my good will, mother.
MAUDLINE. Why, well said, wench.

THE SONG

[MOLL *sings.*] Weep eyes, break heart,
My love and I must part;
Cruel fates true love do soonest sever;
Oh, I shall see thee never, never, never!

---

21 *white money*: silver.

26 *get before*: precede/beget (poesy) before.

30 *pearl and amber*: See note to *A Mad World, My Masters*, III. ii.63–5. Marston's *Fawn*, II.i.163, refers to 'cullesses made of dissolved pearl and bruis'd amber' as aphrodisiac.

38 *fit*: attack of illness/strain of music.

Oh, happy is the maid whose life takes end,
Ere it knows parent's frown, or loss of friend.
Weep eyes, break heart,
My love and I must part.

Enter TOUCHWOOD SENIOR *with a letter.*

MAUDLINE. Oh, I could die with music! Well sung, girl.
MOLL. If you call it so, it was.
YELLOWHAMMER. She plays the swan, and sings herself to death.
TOUCHWOOD SENIOR. By your leave, sir.
YELLOWHAMMER. What are you, sir? Or what's your business, pray?
TOUCHWOOD SENIOR. I may be now admitted, though the brother
Of him your hate pursu'd. It spreads no further,
Your malice sets in death, does it not, sir?
YELLOWHAMMER. In death?
TOUCHWOOD SENIOR. He's dead: 'twas a dear love to him,
It cost him but his life, that was all, sir:
He paid enough, poor gentleman, for his love.
YELLOWHAMMER. [*aside*] There's all our ill remov'd, if she were well now.
– Impute not, sir, his end to any hate
That sprung from us; he had a fair wound brought that.
TOUCHWOOD SENIOR. That help'd him forward, I must needs confess;
But the restraint of love, and your unkindness,
Those were the wounds that from his heart drew blood;
But being past help, let words forget it too.
Scarcely three minutes ere his eyelids clos'd
And took eternal leave of this world's light,
He wrote this letter, which by oath he bound me
To give to her own hands: that's all my business.
YELLOWHAMMER. You may perform it then; there she sits.

---

52 *swan*: The swan was believed to sing whilst dying.
57 *sets*: declines, rests.

TOUCHWOOD SENIOR. Oh, with a following look.
YELLOWHAMMER. Ay, trust me, sir, I think she'll follow him quickly.
TOUCHWOOD SENIOR. Here's some gold
He will'd me to distribute faithfully amongst your servants. [*He distributes the gold.*]
YELLOWHAMMER. 'Las, what doth he mean, sir?
TOUCHWOOD SENIOR. [*to* MOLL] How cheer you, mistress?
MOLL. I must learn of you, sir.
TOUCHWOOD SENIOR. [*giving letter*] Here's a letter from a friend of yours,
And where that fails in satisfaction,
I have a sad tongue ready to supply.
MOLL. How does he, ere I look on't?
TOUCHWOOD SENIOR. Seldom better, h'as a contented health now.
MOLL. I am most glad on't. [*She reads.*]
MAUDLINE. [*to* TOUCHWOOD SENIOR] Dead, sir?
YELLOWHAMMER. He is. [*Aside*] Now, wife, let's but get the girl
Upon her legs again, and to church roundly with her.
MOLL. Oh, sick to death, he tells me.
How does he after this?
TOUCHWOOD SENIOR. Faith, feels no pain at all; he's dead, sweet mistress.
MOLL. Peace close mine eyes! [*She faints.*]
YELLOWHAMMER. The girl, look to the girl, wife!
MAUDLINE. Moll, daughter, sweet girl, speak!
Look but once up, thou shalt have all the wishes of thy heart
That wealth can purchase.
YELLOWHAMMER. Oh, she's gone for ever! That letter broke her heart.
TOUCHWOOD SENIOR. As good now, then, as let her lie in torment,
And then break it.

Enter SUSAN.

MAUDLINE. O Susan, she thou loved'st so dear is gone!
SUSAN. Oh, sweet maid!

---

73 *following*: about to follow/resembling.
82 *roundly*: promptly.

TOUCHWOOD SENIOR. This is she that help'd her still.
I've a reward here for thee. [*He gives* SUSAN *a note.*]
YELLOWHAMMER. Take her in,
Remove her from our sight, our shame, and sorrow.
TOUCHWOOD SENIOR. Stay, let me help thee; 'tis the last cold kindness
I can perform for my sweet brother's sake.
[*Exeunt* TOUCHWOOD SENIOR *and* SUSAN, *with* SERVANTS *carrying* MOLL.]
YELLOWHAMMER. All the whole street will hate us, and the world
Point me out cruel. It is our best course, wife,
After we have given order for the funeral,
To absent ourselves, till she be laid in ground.
MAUDLINE. Where shall we spend that time?
YELLOWHAMMER. I'll tell thee where, wench: go to some private church,
And marry Tim to the rich Brecknock gentlewoman.
MAUDLINE. Mass, a match!
We'll not lose all at once, somewhat we'll catch.
Exit [*with* YELLOWHAMMER].

SCENE III

Enter SIR OLIVER *and* SERVANTS.

SIR OLIVER. Ho, my wife's quick'ned; I am a man for ever!
I think I have bestirr'd my stumps, i'faith.
Run, get your fellows all together instantly,
Then to the parish church, and ring the bells.
[1] SERVANT. It shall be done, sir. [*Exit.*]
SIR OLIVER. Upon my love I charge you, villain, that you make a bonfire before the door at night.
[2] SERVANT. A bonfire, sir?
SIR OLIVER. A thwacking one, I charge you.
[2] SERVANT. [*aside*] This is monstrous. [*Exit.*]

---

114 *private church*: secluded church; or perhaps a private chapel where licensed marriages might be celebrated without the publicity of a parish church.
116 *a match*: agreed/a wedding.
2 *bestirr'd my stumps*: been busy (with obscene innuendo).

SIR OLIVER. Run, tell a hundred pound out for the gentleman
That gave my wife the drink, the first thing you do.
[3] SERVANT. A hundred pounds, sir?
SIR OLIVER. A bargain! As our joys grows,
We must remember still from whence it flows,
Or else we prove ungrateful multipliers;
The child is coming, and the land comes after;
The news of this will make a poor Sir Walter.
I have strook it home, i'faith.
[3] SERVANT. That you have, marry, sir.
But will not your worship go to the funeral
Of both these lovers?
SIR OLIVER. Both? Go both together?
[3] SERVANT. Ay, sir, the gentleman's brother will have it so;
'Twill be the pitifullest sight; there's such running,
Such rumours, and such throngs, a pair of lovers
Had never more spectators, more men's pities,
Or women's wet eyes.
SIR OLIVER. My wife helps the number then?
[3] SERVANT. There's such a drawing out of handkerchers;
And those that have no handkerchers, lift up aprons.
SIR OLIVER. Her parents may have joyful hearts at this!
I would not have my cruelty so talk'd on,
To any child of mine, for a monopoly.
[3] SERVANT. I believe you, sir.
'Tis cast so too, that both their coffins meet,
Which will be lamentable.
SIR OLIVER. Come, we'll see't.

Ex[*eunt*].

---

11 *tell*: count.

17–18 *after . . . Walter*: a rhyme; see E.J. Dobson, *English Pronunciation* (Oxford, 1957) II, 532–4, 984–5.

19 *strook it home*: given a winning blow (with a pun on 'strike' = copulate).

29 *helps the number*: increases the number (of mourners).

34 *monopoly*: a royal grant of exclusive rights to deal in a given commodity (ironic, since he has surrendered his marital 'monopoly').

36 *cast*: arranged.

SCENE IV

Recorders dolefully playing. Enter at one door the coffin of the gentleman, solemnly deck'd, his sword upon it, attended by many in black, his brother being the chief mourner. At the other door, the coffin of the virgin, with a garland of flowers, with epitaphs pinn'd on it, attended by maids and women. Then set them down one right over against the other, while all the company seem to weep and mourn; there is a sad song in the music room. [*The company includes* SIR OLIVER *and* LADY KIX, MASTER *and* MISTRESS ALLWIT, SUSAN *and a* PARSON.]

TOUCHWOOD SENIOR. Never could death boast of a richer prize
From the first parent; let the world bring forth
A pair of truer hearts. To speak but truth
Of this departed gentleman, in a brother
Might, by hard censure, be call'd flattery,
Which makes me rather silent in his right
Than so to be deliver'd to the thoughts
Of any envious hearer starv'd in virtue,
And therefore pining to hear others thrive.
But for this maid, whom envy cannot hurt
With all her poisons, having left to ages
The true, chaste monument of her living name,
Which no time can deface, I say of her
The full truth freely, without fear of censure:
What nature could there shine, that might redeem
Perfection home to woman, but in her
Was fully glorious; beauty set in goodness
Speaks what she was, that jewel so infix'd;
There was no want of any thing of life

---

s.d. *over against*: alongside; *music room*: a room for the theatre's musicians, probably situated in the public theatres in a curtained gallery above the main stage.

2 *first parent*: Adam.

5 *censure*: critical opinion.

15–16 *redeem/Perfection home to woman*: bring back to woman what was lost by the Fall.

16 *but*: only.

18 *infix'd*: firmly fixed.

To make these virtuous precedents man and wife.
ALLWIT. Great pity of their deaths!
ALL. Ne'er more pity!
LADY KIX. It makes a hundred weeping eyes, sweet gossip.
TOUCHWOOD SENIOR. I cannot think there's any one amongst you
In this full fair assembly, maid, man, or wife,
Whose heart would not have sprung with joy and gladness
To have seen their marriage day?
ALL. It would have made a thousand joyful hearts.
TOUCHWOOD SENIOR. Up then apace, and take your fortunes!
Make these joyful hearts, here's none but friends.
[MOLL *and* TOUCHWOOD JUNIOR *rise from their coffins.*]
ALL. Alive, sir? Oh, sweet, dear couple!
TOUCHWOOD SENIOR. Nay, do not hinder 'em now, stand from about 'em;
If she be caught again, and have this time,
I'll ne'er plot further for 'em, nor this honest chambermaid
That help'd all at a push.
TOUCHWOOD JUNIOR. [*to* PARSON] Good sir, apace!
PARSON. Hands join now, but hearts for ever,
Which no parent's mood shall sever.
[*To* TOUCHWOOD JUNIOR] You shall forsake all widows, wives, and maids;
[*To* MOLL] You, lords, knights, gentlemen, and men of trades;
And if, in haste, any article misses
Go interline it with a brace of kisses.
TOUCHWOOD SENIOR. Here's a thing troll'd nimbly. – Give you joy, brother!

---

20 *precedents*: examples.
34 *at a push*: at a crisis.
36 *Hands join*: I.e. he continues with the interrupted 'hand-fasting', which since it is a contract before witnesses and is in terms *de praesenti* (taking the spouse 'now') would be treated as a binding marriage. See note to III.i.19 also.
40 *article*: clause of the contract.
41 *interline it*: write it in.
42 *troll'd*: rolled off the tongue.

Were't not better thou should'st have her,
Than the maid should die?

MISTRESS ALLWIT. To you, sweet mistress bride.

ALL. Joy, joy to you both.

TOUCHWOOD SENIOR. Here be your wedding sheets you brought along with you; you may both go to bed when you please to.

TOUCHWOOD JUNIOR. My joy wants utterance.

TOUCHWOOD SENIOR. Utter all at night then, brother.

MOLL. I am silent with delight.

TOUCHWOOD SENIOR. Sister, delight will silence any woman;
But you'll find your tongue again, among maidservants,
Now you keep house, sister.

ALL. Never was hour so fill'd with joy and wonder.

TOUCHWOOD SENIOR. To tell you the full story of this chambermaid,
And of her kindness in this business to us,
'Twould ask an hour's discourse. In brief, 'twas she
That wrought it to this purpose cunningly.

ALL. We shall all love her for't.

Enter YELLOWHAMMER *and his* WIFE.

ALLWIT. See who comes here now.

TOUCHWOOD SENIOR. A storm, a storm, but we are shelt'red for it.

YELLOWHAMMER. I will prevent you all, and mock you thus,
You, and your expectations: I stand happy,
Both in your lives, and your hearts' combination.

TOUCHWOOD SENIOR. Here's a strange day again!

YELLOWHAMMER. The knight's prov'd villain,
(All's come out now) his niece an arrant baggage;
My poor boy Tim is cast away this morning,
Even before breakfast, married a whore
Next to his heart.

ALL. A whore?

---

47 *wedding sheets*: i.e. the shrouds (a favourite Middleton equation, cf. *Women Beware Women*, I.i.20–4).

51 *utter*: say/ejaculate.

71 *Next to his heart*: closest to his affections/on an empty stomach.

YELLOWHAMMER. His 'niece', forsooth!
ALLWIT. [*aside*] I think we rid our hands in good time of him.
MISTRESS ALLWIT. [*aside*] I knew he was past the best, when I gave him over.
– What is become of him pray, sir?
YELLOWHAMMER. Who, the knight? He lies i'th' knight's ward now.
[*To* LADY KIX] Your belly, lady, begins to blossom, there's no peace for him,
His creditors are so greedy.
SIR OLIVER. [*to* TOUCHWOOD SENIOR] Master Touchwood, hear'st thou this news?
I am so endear'd to thee for my wife's fruitfulness
That I charge you both, your wife and thee,
To live no more asunder for the world's frowns:
I have purse, and bed, and board for you;
Be not afraid to go to your business roundly;
Get children, and I'll keep them.
TOUCHWOOD SENIOR. Say you so, sir?
SIR OLIVER. Prove me, with three at a birth, and thou dar'st now.
TOUCHWOOD SENIOR. Take heed how you dare a man, while you live, sir,
That has good skill at his weapon.

Enter TIM *and* WELSH GENTLEWOMAN [*and* TUTOR].

SIR OLIVER. 'Foot, I dare you, sir!
YELLOWHAMMER. Look, gentlemen, if ever you say the picture
Of the unfortunate marriage, yonder 'tis.
WELSH GENTLEWOMAN. Nay, good sweet Tim –
TIM. Come from the university,
To marry a whore in London, with my tutor too?

---

75 *th'knight's ward*: the second of four grades of accommodation in the two Counters and the Fleet (all used for debtors); the grades were: the master's side, the knight's ward, the twopenny ward, and the hole (for those who could pay nothing).

83 *roundly*: thoroughly/punning on 'round' = pregnant.

89–90 *say*: obsolete past tense of 'to see'; but see Textual note, p. 404.

O tempora! O mors!
TUTOR. Prithee, Tim, be patient!
TIM. I bought a jade at Cambridge;
I'll let her out to execution, tutor,
For eighteen pence a day, or Brainford horse races;
She'll serve to carry seven miles out of town well.
Where be these mountains? I was promis'd mountains,
But there's such a mist, I can see none of 'em.
What are become of those two thousand runts?
Let's have a bout with them in the meantime.
A vengeance runt thee!
MAUDLINE. Good sweet Tim, have patience.
TIM. *Flectere si nequeo superos Acheronta movebo,*
mother.
MAUDLINE. I think you have married her in logic, Tim.
You told me once, by logic you would prove
A whore an honest woman; prove her so, Tim,
And take her for thy labour.
TIM. Troth, I thank you.
I grant you I may prove another man's wife so,
But not mine own.
MAUDLINE. There's no remedy now, Tim,
You must prove her so as well as you may.
TIM. Why then, my tutor and I will about her
As well as we can.
Uxor non est meretrix, ergo falacis.

---

94 *O tempora, O mors*: A (deliberate or ignorant) variation of the tag 'O tempora, O mores', 'O times, O manners!' from Cicero, *Catiline*, I.i; *mors*: death.

96 *jade*: ill-conditioned horse/whore (Tim implies he will rent out his wife, since he has no need of a second jade).

97 *execution*: for hire/for 'execution', the sexual act.

98 *Brainford*: Brentford, Middlesex, a notorious place for assignations, where horse-racing (and 'whores' races') were part of the entertainment.

104 *runt*: probably 'reduce you to nothing' (from 'runt' = a stunted animal), though there is a rare usage of 'runt' to mean 'reprove, admonish'.

105 *Flectere . . . movebo*: Virgil, *Aeneid*, VII, 312: 'Since I cannot move the powers above, I shall work on the lower regions.' See also Textual note, p. 404.

110 *for thy labour*: for your pains/for your sexual effort.

114 *about her*: with innuendo.

116 *Uxor . . . falacis*: 'A wife is not a whore, therefore you are wrong.' See also Textual note, p. 404.

WELSH GENTLEWOMAN. Sir, if your logic cannot prove me honest,
There's a thing call'd marriage, and that makes me honest.

MAUDLINE. Oh, there's a trick beyond your logic, Tim.

TIM. I perceive then a woman may be honest according to the English print, when she is a whore in the Latin. So much for marriage and logic! I'll love her for her wit, I'll pick out my runts there; and for my mountains, I'll mount upon –

YELLOWHAMMER. So fortune seldom deals two marriages
With one hand, and both lucky; the best is,
One feast will serve them both! Marry, for room
I'll have the dinner kept in Goldsmiths' Hall.
To which, kind gallants, I invite you all.

[*Exeunt.*]

Finis

119–21 *trick . . . English print*: The Latin *meretrix*, meaning 'a whore', is in English spelling 'merry tricks'; the joke was common.

124 *mount upon*: ride on/mount sexually on; see Textual note, p. 404.

128 *Goldsmiths' Hall*: hall of the Goldsmiths' Company, on the east side of Foster Lane, north of Cheapside, at the end of Engain or Maiden Lane.

WOMEN

BEWARE

WOMEN.

A

TRAGEDY;

BY

Tho. Middleton, Gent.

LONDON:

Printed for *Humphrey Moſeley*, 1657.

Title-page of the 1657 Octavo of *Women Beware Women*, reproduced by permission of the Master and Fellows, Trinity College, Cambridge.

INTRODUCTORY NOTE

The Trinity College, Cambridge octavo of *Two New Plays* (containing *More Dissemblers Besides Women* and *Women Beware Women*), printed for Humphrey Moseley in 1657, has served as copy-text for this edition, except for the missing part of the O gathering, where the British Museum copy 643b.37 was used. The play was well printed, probably from a scribal transcript related to a Middleton holograph, and only three press variants affect meaning to any significant degree. Two unpublished doctoral dissertations, by E.R. Jacobs (University of Wisconsin, 1941) and J.R. Mulryne (University of Cambridge, 1963), have contributed much to the study of the play, and R.B. Parker also edited the play as an M.A. thesis (University of Liverpool, 1957). Mulryne's work eventually formed the basis of his Revels edition of the play (London, 1975), edited to the usual high standard of the series, collating twenty known copies of the octavo, and offering an extensive introduction to the play. The play had previously appeared in several anthologies, and Roma Gill edited it for the New Mermaid series (1968), using the Bodleian Library copy as foundation text; she offers a reasonable critical introduction but only moderate annotation, and her text has inaccuracies. C. Barber has edited a good old-spelling edition (with tidied punctuation) for Fountainwell Drama Texts (1969); he has undertaken collation of copies of O in the British Museum (2), Trinity College, Cambridge, and Worcester College, Oxford, relying on Jacobs and Mulryne for information about the Library of Congress copy. Barber gives a full textual apparatus, together with a modest introduction, commentary and glossary.

The main plot of Middleton's play is based on the history of Bianca Capello (b. 1548), a Venetian girl of noble family who in 1563 eloped with Pietro Buonaventuri, a Florentine gentleman of the Salvati family. Though she married Pietro and had a daughter by him, Bianca became the secret mistress of Francesco de' Medici, and was openly acknowledged by him after the assassination of her husband in 1569. Francesco became Grand Duke of Tuscany in 1574. In 1579 the death of his wife left him free to marry Bianca, despite the opposition of his brother, the Cardinal Ferdinando. Francesco died suddenly of a fever in 1587, and Bianca a few hours after; Ferdinando succeeded as Grand Duke. The history of Bianca circulated widely in manuscript accounts, and the first part of her story was contained in Celio Malespini's *Ducento Novelle* (Venice, 1609), the 84th and 85th stories, where Buonaventuri is a bank clerk who connives at his wife's adultery and later boasts himself to be the lover of a rich Florentine widow, whose family is provoked to murder the boaster. Despite similarities, it is not certain that Middleton used Malespini, and he would have needed to supplement the tale from his own imagination or from other sources, especially for the end of the story: Mulryne suggests that he may have seen a manuscript of the unpublished portion of Fynes Moryson's *Itinerary* written 1619–20. The sub-plot of Middleton's play clearly derives from the *Histoire Veritable des Infortunees et Tragiques Amours d'Hypolite & d'Isabella, Neapolitains* (Rouen, 1597), though an English version was not published till 1628, after Middleton's death.

Nathaniel Richards's prefatory verses are our only evidence that the play was well-received in the pre-Commonwealth period, and it was not revived after the Restoration. No eighteenth- or nineteenth-century performances are known, and it may be that a student production at Reading University in March 1962 was the first revival since Middleton's own day. On 4 July 1962 a professional production by Anthony Page with the Royal Shakespeare Company opened at the New Arts Theatre, London. Philip McKie produced and Gordon Flemyng directed a heavily cut version for Granada Television, 11 January 1965. In March 1967 the play was produced by the University Alumnae Club at the Coach House Theatre, Toronto, directed by Brian Meeson. A production at the Traverse Theatre Club, Edinburgh ran from 20 February to 16 March 1968, and was produced by Gordon McDougall. Terry Hands directed a highly successful production for the Royal Shakespeare Company at Stratford-upon-Avon in July 1969. The Lady Margaret Players, directed by Neil Coulbeck, put on a curtailed version (omitting the final masque) in the School of Pythagoras, St John's College, Cambridge, December 1972.

[PREFATORY MATERIAL TO THE FIRST EDITION]

TO THE READER

When these amongst others of Mr Thomas Middleton's excellent poems came to my hands, I was not a little confident but that his name would prove as great an inducement for thee to read, as me to print them, since those issues of his brain that have already seen the sun have by their worth gained themselves a free entertainment amongst all that are ingenious; and I am most certain that these will no way lessen his reputation, nor hinder his admission to any noble and recreative spirits. All that I require at thy hands, is to continue the author in his deserved esteem, and to accept of my endeavours which have ever been to please thee.

Farewell.

[THE PUBLISHER]

UPON THE TRAGEDY OF MY FAMILIAR ACQUAINTANCE, THO. MIDDLETON

Women beware Women: 'tis a true text
Never to be forgot. Drabs of state vex'd
Have plots, poisons, mischiefs that seldom miss,
To murther virtue with a venom kiss.
Witness this worthy tragedy, express'd
By him that well deserv'd among the best
Of poets in his time. He knew the rage,
Madness of women cross'd; and for the stage
Fitted their humours, hell-bred malice, strife
Acted in state, presented to the life.
I that have seen't can say, having just cause,
Never came tragedy off with more applause.

NATH. RICHARDS

---

2 *drabs of state*: the whores of great men (quoted from *The Revenger's Tragedy*, IV.iv.80, which Richards cites in full in *Messalina*, lines 1778–9).

10 *in state*: with great pomp and ceremony.

13 NATH. RICHARDS: Nathaniel Richards (fl. 1630–54), chiefly noted for his play *The Tragedy of Messalina, the Roman Empress* (published 1640).

[DRAMATIS PERSONAE]

DUKE OF FLORENCE.
LORD CARDINAL, brother to the DUKE.
TWO CARDINALS more.
A LORD.
FABRITIO, father to ISABELLA [brother to LIVIA].
HIPPOLITO, brother to FABRITIO [and LIVIA].
GUARDIANO, uncle to the foolish WARD [brother-in-law to LIVIA].
THE WARD, a rich young heir [resident with GUARDIANO at LIVIA's house].
LEANTIO, a factor, husband to BIANCA.
SORDIDO, the WARD's man.

LIVIA, sister to FABRITIO.
ISABELLA, niece to LIVIA.
BIANCA, LEANTIO's wife.
WIDOW, his [LEANTIO's] mother.
STATES OF FLORENCE.
CITIZENS.
A 'PRENTICE.
BOYS.
MESSENGER.
[KNIGHTS.]
SERVANTS.
[TWO LADIES.]
[LORDS.]
[PAGES.]
[GUARD.]
[*Figures in the Masque:* HYMEN, GANYMEDE, HEBE, CUPIDS.]

The Scene: FLORENCE.

---

11 *factor*: agent or deputy in commercial dealings.
15 BIANCA: See Textual note, p. 404.
17 STATES: nobility.

WOMEN BEWARE WOMEN

ACT I

SCENE I

Enter LEANTIO *with* BIANCA *and* MOTHER.
[BIANCA *stands apart.*]

MOTHER. Thy sight was never yet more precious to me;
Welcome, with all the affection of a mother
That comfort can express from natural love:
Since thy birth-joy (a mother's chiefest gladness
After sh'as undergone her curse of sorrows)
Thou wast not more dear to me than this hour
Presents thee to my heart. Welcome again.
LEANTIO. [*aside*] 'Las, poor affectionate soul, how her joys speak to me!
I have observ'd it often, and I know it is
The fortune commonly of knavish children
To have the loving'st mothers.
MOTHER. What's this gentlewoman?
LEANTIO. Oh, you have nam'd the most unvalued'st purchase
That youth of man had ever knowledge of.
As often as I look upon that treasure
And know it to be mine (there lies the blessing)
It joys me that I ever was ordain'd
To have a being, and to live 'mongst men;
Which is a fearful living, and a poor one,
Let a man truly think on't;
To have the toil and griefs of fourscore years
Put up in a white sheet, tied with two knots.
Methinks it should strike earthquakes in adulterers,
When ev'n the very sheets they commit sin in
May prove, for aught they know, all their last garments.

---

3 *That comfort can express from natural love*: 'that pleasure and relief (at your return) can evoke from a mother's natural feelings'.

5 *curse of sorrows*: child-birth, an allusion to Genesis 3.16, God's infliction of birth pangs on Eve in punishment for her primal sin.

12 *unvalued'st purchase*: inestimable acquisition/plunder.

21 *two knots*: the knots at head and foot of a death-shroud.

Oh, what a mark were there for women then!
But beauty able to content a conqueror,
Whom earth could scarce content, keeps me in compass;
I find no wish in me bent sinfully
To this man's sister, or to that man's wife;
In love's name let 'em keep their honesties,
And cleave to their own husbands, 'tis their duties.
Now when I go to church, I can pray handsomely;
Not come like gallants only to see faces,
As if lust went to market still on Sundays.
I must confess I am guilty of one sin, mother,
More than I brought into the world with me;
But that I glory in: 'tis theft, but noble
As ever greatness yet shot up withal.

MOTHER. How's that?

LEANTIO. Never to be repented, mother,
Though sin be death; I had died, if I had not sinn'd,
And here's my masterpiece. Do you now behold her!
Look on her well, she's mine. Look on her better.
Now say, if't be not the best piece of theft
That ever was committed. And I have my pardon for't:
'Tis seal'd from Heaven by marriage.

MOTHER. Married to her!

LEANTIO. You must keep counsel, mother, I am undone else;
If it be known, I have lost her. Do but think now
What that loss is: life's but a trifle to't.
From Venice her consent and I have brought her
From parents great in wealth, more now in rage;
But let storms spend their furies. Now we have got
A shelter o'er our quiet, innocent loves

---

25 *mark*: sign.

26–7 Alexander the Great was alleged to have wept because there were no more worlds to conquer; he was also known to have been resistant to feminine charms.

27 *in compass*: within due limits.

30 *honesties*: chastities.

32 *handsomely*: decently.

37–8 *noble/As ever greatness yet shot up withal*: as noble as ever helped to bring a great man up (from nothing).

40 *Though sin be death*: alluding to Romans 6.23, 'the wages of sin is death'.

We are contented. Little money sh'as brought me:
View but her face, you may see all her dowry,
Save that which lies lock'd up in hidden virtues,
Like jewels kept in cabinets.

MOTHER. Y'are to blame,
If your obedience will give way to a check,
To wrong such a perfection.

LEANTIO. How?

MOTHER. Such a creature,
To draw her from her fortune, which no doubt,
At the full time, might have prov'd rich and noble:
You know not what you have done. My life can give you
But little helps, and my death lesser hopes;
And hitherto your own means has but made shift
To keep you single, and that hardly too.
What ableness have you to do her right, then,
In maintenance fitting her birth and virtues,
Which ev'ry woman of necessity looks for,
And most to go above it, not confin'd
By their conditions, virtues, bloods, or births,
But flowing to affections, wills and humours?

LEANTIO. Speak low, sweet mother; you are able to spoil as many
As come within the hearing; if it be not
Your fortune to mar all, I have much marvel.
I pray do not you teach her to rebel,
When she's in a good way to obedience:
To rise with other women in commotion
Against their husbands, for six gowns a year,
And so maintain their cause, when they're once up,
In all things else that require cost enough.
They are all of 'em a kind of spirits soon rais'd,

---

57 *check*: reproof.

64 *hardly*: in poor circumstances.

68–70 i.e. 'not restrained by their circumstances, by moral considerations or qualities, by their lineage or the station to which they are born, but overflowing (these limits) in the direction of private inclinations, self-will and mere whim'. 'Affection', 'will', and 'humours' have the further suggestion of 'passion', 'sexual desire' and 'displays of ill-temper' respectively.

80 *a kind of spirits soon rais'd*: a type of temperament easily incited/a sort of demon easily called up. See Additional note, p. 410.

But not so soon laid, mother. As, for example,
A woman's belly is got up in a trice;
A simple charge ere it be laid down again;
So ever in all their quarrels, and their courses.
And I'm a proud man I hear nothing of 'em;
They're very still, I thank my happiness,
And sound asleep; pray let not your tongue wake 'em.
If you can but rest quiet, she's contented
With all conditions that my fortunes bring her to:
To keep close as a wife that loves her husband;
To go after the rate of my ability,
Not the licentious swindge of her own will,
Like some of her old schoolfellows. She intends
To take out other works in a new sampler,
And frame the fashion of an honest love,
Which knows no wants, but, mocking poverty,
Brings forth more children, to make rich men wonder
At divine Providence, that feeds mouths of infants,
And sends them none to feed, but stuffs their rooms
With fruitful bags, their beds with barren wombs.
Good mother, make not you things worse than they
are,
Out of your too much openness (pray take heed on't)
Nor imitate the envy of old people,
That strive to mar good sport, because they are perfit;
I would have you more pitiful to youth,
Especially to your own flesh and blood.
I'll prove an excellent husband (here's my hand)

---

83 *a simple charge*: a sheer expense (for midwife's fees etc.).
84 *courses*: actions/combative encounters.
85 *of 'em*: i.e. of a woman's rebellious spirits.
91–2 i.e. 'to live according to my means and not the free range of her own desires', but with a further implication: 'to make love according to my sexual powers, and not the lawless drive of her own appetite'.
93–5 Bianca intends to act quite differently, according to a novel pattern, and give form to/make fashionable an ideal of chaste love. The metaphor seems to be suggested by the practice of undertaking home embroidery for an entrepreneur who supplied the design to be copied; Leantio perhaps has such cottage industry in mind for Bianca.
100 *bags*: i.e. money-bags.
104 *perfit*: See Textual note, p. 404. They are 'of full age' and therefore 'past it', perfect in the grammatical rather than the moral sense.

Lay in provision, follow my business roundly,
And make you a grandmother in forty weeks.
Go, pray salute her, bid her welcome cheerfully.
MOTHER. Gentlewoman, thus much is a debt of courtesy
[*She kisses* BIANCA.]
Which fashionable strangers pay each other
At a kind meeting; then there's more than one,
Due to the knowledge I have of your nearness;
[*Kisses again.*]
I am bold to come again, and now salute you
By th'name of daughter, which may challenge more
Than ordinary respect. [*Kisses again.*]
LEANTIO. [*aside*] Why, this is well now,
And I think few mothers of threescore will mend it.
MOTHER. What I can bid you welcome to is mean,
But make it all your own; we are full of wants,
And cannot welcome worth.
LEANTIO. [*aside*] Now this is scurvy,
And spake as if a woman lack'd her teeth.
These old folks talk of nothing but defects,
Because they grow so full of 'em themselves.
BIANCA. Kind mother, there is nothing can be wanting
To her that does enjoy all her desires.
Heaven send a quiet peace with this man's love,
And I am as rich as virtue can be poor;
Which were enough, after the rate of mind,
To erect temples for content plac'd here.
I have forsook friends, fortunes, and my country;
And hourly I rejoice in't. Here's my friends,
And few is the good number. [*To* LEANTIO] Thy successes,
Howe'er they look, I will still name my fortunes;
Hopeful or spiteful, they shall all be welcome.
Who invites many guests has of all sorts,

---

108 *roundly*: briskly, wholeheartedly. 'Business' has a secondary implication of 'sexual activity'.
122 One symptom of scurvy was the loss of teeth.
127 *send*: See Textual note, p. 405.
129 *after the rate of mind*: 'according to my mind's reckoning'/'If we adopt the standard of the contented mind' (the mind being able to contain all things within itself). Virtue is sometimes poor, in that it fails to 'enjoy all its desires'.
133 *successes*: future fortunes.

As he that trafficks much drinks of all fortunes;
Yet they must all be welcome, and us'd well.
I'll call this place the place of my birth now,
And rightly too: for here my love was born,
And that's the birthday of a woman's joys.
You have not bid me welcome since I came.

LEANTIO. That I did, questionless.

BIANCA. No sure, how was't?
I have quite forgot it.

LEANTIO. Thus. [*Kisses her.*]

BIANCA. Oh sir, 'tis true,
Now I remember well: I have done thee wrong;
Pray take't again, sir. [*Kisses him.*]

LEANTIO. How many of these wrongs
Could I put up in an hour, and turn up the glass
For twice as many more.

MOTHER. Will't please you to walk in, daughter?

BIANCA. Thanks, sweet mother;
The voice of her that bare me is not more pleasing.

Exeunt [MOTHER *and* BIANCA.]

LEANTIO. Though my own care and my rich master's trust
Lay their commands both on my factorship,
This day and night I'll know no other business
But her and her dear welcome. 'Tis a bitterness
To think upon tomorrow, that I must leave her
Still to the sweet hopes of the week's end.
That pleasure should be so restrain'd and curb'd
After the course of a rich workmaster,
That never pays till Saturday night!
Marry, it comes together in a round sum then,
And does more good, you'll say. O fair-eyed Florence!
Didst thou but know what a most matchless jewel
Thou now art mistress of, a pride would take thee
Able to shoot destruction through the bloods
Of all thy youthful sons! But 'tis great policy
To keep choice treasures in obscurest places:

---

137 *trafficks*: trades.

147 *turn up the glass*: reverse the hour glass (to gain a further hour).

158 *After the course of*: according to the practice of.

163 *pride*: pride/sexual heat.

Should we show thieves our wealth, 'twould make 'em bolder.
Temptation is a devil will not stick
To fasten upon a saint; take heed of that.
The jewel is cas'd up from all men's eyes;
Who could imagine now a gem were kept,
Of that great value, under this plain roof?
But how in times of absence? What assurance
Of this restraint then? Yes, yes, there's one with her!
Old mothers know the world; and such as these,
When sons lock chests, are good to look to keys. *Exit.*

SCENE II

Enter GUARDIANO, FABRITIO, *and* LIVIA [*with* SERVANT].

GUARDIANO. What, has your daughter seen him yet? Know you that?
FABRITIO. No matter, she shall love him.
GUARDIANO. Nay, let's have fair play!
He has been now my ward some fifteen year,
And 'tis my purpose, as time calls upon me,
By custom seconded, and such moral virtues,
To tender him a wife. Now, sir, this wife
I'd fain elect out of a daughter of yours:
You see my meaning's fair. If now this daughter,
So tendered (let me come to your own phrase, sir)
Should offer to refuse him, I were hansell'd.

---

168 *stick*: hesitate, scruple.

3–10 The King became guardian of minors whose deceased fathers had held lands from him under feudal tenure, but in the Jacobean period there was an extensive sale of the royal rights of guardianship to speculators. The guardian had the right to propose a match and to levy a fine if his ward refused it; but when the Ward reached majority, these and other rights lapsed. Guardiano is therefore anxious to marry off his ward, who approaches twenty; presumably the guardian can expect a payment from Fabritio. But were Isabella to refuse the Ward, Guardiano would not even collect the fine due if the Ward had refused her.

10 *I were hansell'd*: A 'handsell' was an auspicious first-fruit, a first return, a New Year gift, a token of good luck. Guardiano uses the phrase ironically: 'I'd be left with the sixpence in the Christmas pudding.'

[*Aside*] Thus am I fain to calculate all my words
For the meridian of a foolish old man,
To take his understanding! – What do you answer, sir?

FABRITIO. I say still, she shall love him.

GUARDIANO. Yet again?
And shall she have no reason for this love?

FABRITIO. Why, do you think that women love with reason?

GUARDIANO. [*aside*] I perceive fools are not at all hours foolish,
No more than wise men wise.

FABRITIO. I had a wife;
She ran mad for me; she had no reason for't
For aught I could perceive. What think you,
Lady sister?

GUARDIANO. [*aside*] 'Twas a fit match that,
Being both out of their wits! – A loving wife, it seem'd,
She strove to come as near you as she could.

FABRITIO. And if her daughter prove not mad for love too,
She takes not after her; nor after me,
If she prefer reason before my pleasure.
– You're an experienc'd widow, lady sister;
I pray let your opinion come amongst us.

LIVIA. I must offend you then, if truth will do't,
And take my niece's part, and call't injustice
To force her love to one she never saw.
Maids should both see and like; all little enough;
If they love truly after that, 'tis well.
Counting the time, she takes one man till death;
That's a hard task, I tell you; but one may
Enquire at three years' end amongst young wives,
And mark how the game goes.

FABRITIO. Why, is not man
Tied to the same observance, lady sister,
And in one woman?

---

12 *meridian*: furthest stretch of mental faculties.

34 *counting the time*: 'if one reckons up the length of her commitment'.

37 *mark how the game goes*: 'see how things go', but with an innuendo on 'game' = sexual sport.

38 *observance*: rule, duty.

LIVIA. 'Tis enough for him;
Besides, he tastes of many sundry dishes
That we poor wretches never lay our lips to:
As obedience, forsooth, subjection, duty, and such kickshaws,
All of our making, but serv'd in to them;
And if we lick a finger then, sometimes,
We are not to blame: your best cooks use it.
FABRITIO. Th'art a sweet lady, sister, and a witty –
LIVIA. A witty! Oh, the bud of commendation
Fit for a girl of sixteen! I am blown, man!
I should be wise by this time; and, for instance,
I have buried my two husbands in good fashion,
And never mean more to marry.
GUARDIANO. No, why so, lady?
LIVIA. Because the third shall never bury me.
I think I am more than witty. How think you, sir?
FABRITIO. I have paid often fees to a counsellor
Has had a weaker brain.
LIVIA. Then I must tell you,
Your money was soon parted.
GUARDIANO. Light her now, brother!
LIVIA. Where is my niece? Let her be sent for straight.
[*Exit* SERVANT.]
If you have any hope 'twill prove a wedding,
'Tis fit, i'faith, she should have one sight of him,
And stop upon't, and not be join'd in haste,
As if they went to stock a new-found land.

---

42 *kickshaws*: fancy dishes in cookery.
45 *use it*: are accustomed to do it (alluding to the proverb 'He is an ill cook who cannot lick his own fingers', M.P. Tilley, *Dictionary of Proverbs in England*, C 636).
48 *blown*: fully flowered/past my best.
54 *counsellor*: advocate.
55 An allusion to the proverb 'A fool and his money are soon parted' (Tilley, F 452).
56 *Light her now, brother*: See Textual note, p. 405. Guardiano is the brother of Livia's dead husband, and seems to incite his brother-in-law to 'come back at her', though the exact meaning is obscure.
61 *a new-found land*: one of the territories in the New World, Virginia, Massachusetts, or Newfoundland itself. Middleton elsewhere comments on the hastily arranged marriages of colonists setting out.

FABRITIO. Look out her uncle, and y'are sure of her;
Those two are nev'r asunder: they've been heard
In argument at midnight, moonshine nights
Are noondays with them; they walk out their sleeps,
Or rather at those hours appear like those
That walk in 'em, for so they did to me.
Look you, I told you truth; they're like a chain:
Draw but one link, all follows.

Enter HIPPOLITO *and* ISABELLA *the niece.*

GUARDIANO. O affinity,
What piece of excellent workmanship art thou!
'Tis work clean wrought; for there's no lust, but love in't,
And that abundantly; when in stranger things
There is no love at all, but what lust brings.
FABRITIO. [*to* ISABELLA] On with your mask, for 'tis your part to see now,
And not be seen. Go to, make use of your time;
See what you mean to like; nay, and I charge you,
Like what you see. Do you hear me? There's no dallying;
The gentleman's almost twenty, and 'tis time
He were getting lawful heirs, and you a-breeding on 'em.
ISABELLA. Good father!
FABRITIO. Tell not me of tongues and rumours!
You'll say the gentleman is somewhat simple;
The better for a husband, were you wise:
For those that marry fools, live ladies' lives.
On with the mask, I'll hear no more; he's rich:
The fool's hid under bushels.
LIVIA. Not so hid neither,
But here's a foul great piece of him, methinks;

---

71 *clean wrought*: perfectly made.
72 *stranger*: less closely related.
75 *not be seen*: The Italian custom was for the prospective bride not to be seen by the husband before betrothal.
85 *bushels*: eight gallon measures of capacity, used for grain etc., also vessels used for measuring; there is an ironic allusion to Matthew 5.15, the injunction not to hide lights under bushels. A piece of the Ward's anatomy (his rump?) is visible before his entry.

What will he be, when he comes altogether?

Enter the WARD *with a trapstick, and* SORDIDO *his man.*

WARD. Beat him?
I beat him out o'th'field with his own cat-stick,
Yet gave him the first hand.
SORDIDO. Oh strange!
WARD. I did it,
Then he set jacks on me.
SORDIDO. What, my lady's tailor?
WARD. Ay, and I beat him too.
SORDIDO. Nay, that's no wonder,
He's us'd to beating.
WARD. Nay, I tickl'd him
When I came once to my tippings.
SORDIDO. Now you talk on 'em, there was a poulterer's wife made a great complaint of you last night to your guardianer, that you struck a bump in her child's head, as big as an egg.

WARD. An egg may prove a chicken then, in time; the poulterer's wife will get by't. When I am in game, I am furious: came my mother's eyes in my way, I would not lose a fair end; no, were she alive, but with one tooth in her head, I should venture the striking out of that. I think of nobody when I am in play, I am so earnest. Coads me, my guardiner! Prithee lay up my cat and cat-stick safe.

SORDIDO. Where, sir, i'th'chimney-corner?

---

s.d. *trapstick*: used in the games of Tip-Cat and Trap; for details see Additional note, p. 411.
90 *first hand*: first turn.
91 *jacks*: fellows. But 'Jacks' may be a proper name, known to the audience.
93 *beating*: blows/silk embroidered by having gold and silver beaten into it.
94 *tippings*: the knocking up of the 'cat' at tip-cat.
99 *get*: gain.
101 *a fair end*: a good result.
104 *Coads me*: a mild oath, a variant of 'Ecod', 'Egad'.

WARD. Chimney-corner!

SORDIDO. Yes, sir, your cats are always safe i'th'chimney-corner, unless they burn their coats.

WARD. Marry, that I am afraid on.

SORDIDO. Why then, I will bestow your cat i'th'gutter, and there she's safe, I am sure.

WARD. If I but live to keep a house, I'll make thee a great man if meat and drink can do't. I can stoop gallantly, and pitch out when I list; I'm dog at a hole. I mar'l my guardiner does not seek a wife for me; I protest, I'll have a bout with the maids else, or contract myself at midnight to the larder-woman in presence of a fool or a sack-posset.

GUARDIANO. Ward!

WARD. I feel myself after any exercise horribly prone: let me but ride, I'm lusty; a cockhorse straight, i'faith

GUARDIANO. Why, ward, I say!

WARD. I'll forswear eating eggs in moon-shine nights;

107–9 *chimney-corner . . . cats . . . coats*: Obscene: *cats* = whores, the *chimney-corner* = (?) a brothel (cf. Overbury, *Characters*, 11th imp., 1623, v. 1, where 'a young fellow fallen in love with a whore is said to have fallen asleep in the chimney-corner'), and *burning* was a common term for venereal disease.

114–15 *stoop gallantly . . . pitch out . . . I'm a dog at a hole*: 'I bend elegantly, bowl when I choose, I'm adept at scoring.' The 'hole' is the cavity into which the ball or marble must be got in various games, and the allusion may be to Hole or Troll Madam, in which bowls were rolled through arches. There are obscene innuendoes: 'stoop gallant' is a term for venereal disease and for sexual bending (cf. Chapman, *Widow's Tears*, I.i.82), *pitch out* = to ejaculate, and *hole* = the female pudendum.

115 *mar'l*: marvel.

119 *a fool or a sack-posset*: 'Fool' is a dish of cooked, crushed fruit mixed with cream or custard, but there may be a pun on the Jacobean homophone 'fowl'. 'Sack-posset' is hot milk curdled by the addition of dry, white wine, with sugar, spices etc. Such will serve as the witness at the betrothal.

121 *prone*: i.e. to lechery.

122 *ride*: ride/mount sexually; *cockhorse*: the child's toy/one sexually aroused.

124 *eggs in moon-shine nights*: i.e. eggs (thought to be aphrodisiac) on nights when the moon anyway stimulated madness. Or Middleton may mean 'eggs-in-moonshine' (poached eggs in onion sauce) 'a'nights', at night.

there's nev'r a one I eat, but turns into a cock in four-and-twenty hours; if my hot blood be not took down in time, sure 'twill crow shortly.

GUARDIANO. Do you hear, sir? Follow me; I must new school you.

WARD. School me? I scorn that now; I am past schooling. I am not so base to learn to write and read; I was born to better fortunes in my cradle.

Exit [WARD, SORDIDO *and* GUARDIANO].

FABRITIO. How do you like him, girl? This is your husband.
Like him or like him not, wench, you shall have him,
And you shall love him.

LIVIA. Oh soft there, brother! Though you be a justice,
Your warrant cannot be serv'd out of your liberty.
You may compel, out of the power of father,
Things merely harsh to a maid's flesh and blood;
But when you come to love, there the soil alters;
Y'are in another country, where your laws
Are no more set by, than the cacklings of geese
In Rome's great Capitol.

FABRITIO. Marry him she shall then;
Let her agree upon love afterwards. *Exit.*

LIVIA. You speak now, brother, like an honest mortal
That walks upon th'earth with a staff;
You were up i'th'clouds before. You'd command love!
And so do most old folks that go without it.
– My best and dearest brother, I could dwell here;

[*She embraces* HIPPOLITO]

There is not such another seat on earth
Where all good parts better express themselves.

HIPPOLITO. You'll make me blush anon.

---

125 *cock*: cockerel/penis.
127 *crow*: orgasm.
137 *out of your liberty*: out of the area of your jurisdiction (a 'liberty' was an area within a county, but having its own commission of the peace).
142 *set by*: here, 'set store by', 'observed'. Juno's sacred geese on the Capitol by their cackling successfully alerted Rome to a secret attack from the Gauls: Middleton perhaps misunderstood the legend.
150 *seat*: dwelling, local situation/Hippolito's person.
151 *parts*: qualities of mind and body/features of a landscape.

LIVIA. 'Tis but like saying grace before a feast, then,
And that's most comely; thou art all a feast,
And she that has thee, a most happy guest.
Prithee cheer up that niece with special counsel.
[*Exit.*]
HIPPOLITO. [*aside*] I would 'twere fit to speak to her what I would, but
'Twas not a thing ordain'd, Heaven has forbid it;
And 'tis most meet that I should rather perish
Than the decree divine receive least blemish.
Feed inward, you my sorrows, make no noise;
Consume me silent, let me be stark dead
Ere the world know I'm sick. You see my honesty;
If you befriend me, so.
ISABELLA. [*aside*] Marry a fool!
Can there be greater misery to a woman
That means to keep her days true to her husband,
And know no other man, so virtue wills it!
Why, how can I obey and honour him,
But I must needs commit idolatry?
A fool is but the image of a man,
And that but ill made, neither. Oh the heartbreakings
Of miserable maids, where love's enforc'd!
The best condition is but bad enough:
When women have their choices, commonly
They do but buy their thraldoms, and bring great portions
To men to keep 'em in subjection;
As if a fearful prisoner should bribe
The keeper to be good to him, yet lies in still,
And glad of a good usage, a good look
Sometimes, by'r Lady. No misery surmounts a woman's:
Men buy their slaves, but women buy their masters.
Yet honesty and love makes all this happy,

163–4 *You see my honesty,/If you befriend me, so*: The appeal is addressed to his sorrows, who are called to witness his honest intentions and befriend him by killing him.

169 *idolatry*: Woman is created to honour and obey the image of God in her husband; to honour a fool is to commit '*idio*latry' therefore, by worshipping a worthless imitation.

175 *portions*: dowries.

178 *lies in still*: remains imprisoned.

And, next to angels', the most blest estate.
That Providence that has made ev'ry poison
Good for some use, and sets four warring elements
At peace in man, can make a harmony
In things that are most strange to human reason.
Oh but this marriage! – What, are you sad too, uncle?
'Faith, then there's a whole household down together!
Where shall I go to seek my comfort now
When my best friend's distressed? What is't afflicts
you, sir?

HIPPOLITO. 'Faith, nothing but one grief that will not
leave me,
And now 'tis welcome; ev'ry man has something
To bring him to his end, and this will serve,
Join'd with your father's cruelty to you.
That helps it forward.

ISABELLA. Oh be cheer'd, sweet uncle!
How long has't been upon you? I nev'r spied it;
What a dull sight have I! How long, I pray, sir?

HIPPOLITO. Since I first saw you, niece, and left Bologna.

ISABELLA. And could you deal so unkindly with my
heart,
To keep it up so long hid from my pity?
Alas, how shall I trust your love hereafter!
Have we pass'd through so many arguments,
And miss'd of that still, the most needful one?
Walk'd out whole nights together in discourses,
And the main point forgot? We are to blame both:
This is an obstinate, wilful forgetfulness,
And faulty on both parts. Let's lose no time now.
Begin, good uncle, you that feel't. What is it?

HIPPOLITO. You of all creatures, niece, must never hear
on't;
'Tis not a thing ordain'd for you to know.

ISABELLA. Not I, sir! All my joys that word cuts off.
You made profession once you lov'd me best:
'Twas but profession!

---

185 *warring elements*: Earth, water, air and fire, the basic constituents of matter are held in balanced tension in the ideal human temperament. There is a likely reminiscence of Marlowe's *Tamburlaine*, Part I, II.vii.18–20. For details of the theory, see Additional note, p. 410.

203 *arguments*: topics for discussion.

HIPPOLITO. Yes, I do't too truly,
And fear I shall be chid for't. Know the worst then:
I love thee dearlier than an uncle can.
ISABELLA. Why, so you ever said, and I believ'd it.
HIPPOLITO. [*aside*] So simple is the goodness of her thoughts
They understand not yet th'unhallowed language
Of a near sinner; I must yet be forced
(Though blushes be my venture) to come nearer.
– As a man loves his wife, so love I thee.
ISABELLA. What's that?
Methought I heard ill news come toward me,
Which commonly we understand too soon,
Than over-quick at hearing. I'll prevent it,
Though my joys fare the harder. Welcome it?
It shall nev'r come so near mine ear again.
Farewell all friendly solaces and discourses;
I'll learn to live without ye, for your dangers
Are greater than your comforts. What's become
Of truth in love, if such we cannot trust,
When blood that should be love is mix'd with lust?
Exit.
HIPPOLITO. The worst can be but death, and let it come;
He that lives joyless, ev'ry day's his doom. *Exit.*

SCENE III

Enter LEANTIO *alone.*

LEANTIO. Methinks I'm ev'n as dull now at departure
As men observe great gallants the next day
After a revels: you shall see 'em look
Much of my fashion, if you mark 'em well.
'Tis ev'n a second hell to part from pleasure

220–1 *near*: related/almost; *come nearer*: be more explicit/get into an even closer relationship.

223–7 She thought she heard bad news, which is generally understood only too easily, rather than over-hastily mis-heard; she will therefore anticipate his full declaration (despite the cost to herself), and, rather than welcome it, ensure that he never has the chance to speak further. For alternative interpretations, see Additional note, p. 411.

224 *Welcome it?*: See also Textual note, p. 405.

When man has got a smack on't. As many holidays
Coming together makes your poor heads idle
A great while after, and are said to stick
Fast in their fingers' ends, ev'n so does game
In a new-married couple for the time;
It spoils all thrift, and indeed lies a-bed
To invent all the new ways for great expenses.

[*Enter*] BIANCA *and* MOTHER *above.*

See, and she be not got on purpose now
Into the window to look after me!
I have no power to go now and I should be hang'd.
Farewell all business, I desire no more
Than I see yonder. Let the goods at quay
Look to themselves; why should I toil my youth out?
It is but begging two or three year sooner,
And stay with her continually. Is't a match?
Oh fie, what a religion have I leap'd into!
Get out again, for shame! The man loves best
When his care's most; that shows his zeal to love.
Fondness is but the idiot to affection,
That plays at hot-cockles with rich merchants' wives;
Good to make sport withal when the chest's full,
And the long warehouse cracks. 'Tis time of day
For us to be more wise: 'tis early with us,
And if they lose the morning of their affairs
They commonly lose the best part of the day.
Those that are wealthy and have got enough,
'Tis after sunset with 'em; they may rest,
Grow fat with ease, banket, and toy and play,

---

6 *smack*: taste.

8–9 *are said to stick/Fast in their fingers' ends*: i.e. aching head in hand.

9 *game*: sexual pleasure.

12 *new ways for great expenses*: new grounds for lavish spending/ new methods of sexual 'spending'.

20 *match*: bargain.

24 *Fondness is but the idiot to affection*: 'Infatuation is a foolish parody of love.'

25 *hot-cockles*: a country game in which a blindfolded player has to guess who struck him, and a common euphemism for intimate sexual handling.

27 *cracks*: i.e. because full to bursting.

33 *banket*: banquet.

When such as I enter the heat o'th'day;
And I'll do't cheerfully.

BIANCA. I perceive, sir,
Y'are not gone yet; I have good hope you'll stay now.

LEANTIO. Farewell, I must not.

BIANCA. Come, come; pray return.
Tomorrow, adding but a little care more,
Will dispatch all as well; believe me, 'twill, sir.

LEANTIO. I could well wish myself where you would have me;
But love that's wanton must be rul'd awhile
By that that's careful, or all goes to ruin.
As fitting is a government in love
As in a kingdom: where 'tis all mere lust
'Tis like an insurrection in the people
That, rais'd in self-will, wars against all reason;
But love that is respective for increase
Is like a good king, that keeps all in peace.
Once more, farewell.

BIANCA. But this one night, I prithee.

LEANTIO. Alas, I'm in for twenty if I stay,
And then for forty more, I have such luck to flesh:
I never bought a horse but he bore double.
If I stay any longer, I shall turn
An everlasting spendthrift; as you love
To be maintain'd well, do not call me again,
For then I shall not care which end goes forward.
Again, farewell to thee. *Exit.*

BIANCA. Since it must, farewell too.

MOTHER. 'Faith, daughter, y'are to blame: you take the course
To make him an ill husband, troth you do,
And that disease is catching, I can tell you;

---

47 *respective for increase*: careful about the increase of worldly goods.

52 *I never bought a horse, but he bore double*: (?) was doubly fruitful. A 'double horse' in Middle English is any horse above the size of a hackney, and in the eighteenth century, it refers to a horse with a pillion rider; but neither meaning seems primary here. See Additional note, p. 411.

56 *I shall not care which end goes forward*: 'I won't care how things go'. The expression is proverbial, implying negligence (Tilley, E 130).

Ay, and soon taken by a young man's blood,
And that with little urging. Nay, fie, see now,
What cause have you to weep? Would I had no more,
That have liv'd threescore years; there were a cause,
And 'twere well thought on. Trust me, y'are to blame;
His absence cannot last five days at utmost.
Why should those tears be fetch'd forth? Cannot love
Be ev'n as well express'd in a good look,
But it must see her face still in a fountain?
It shows like a country maid dressing her head
By a dish of water. Come, 'tis an old custom
To weep for love.

Enter two or three BOYS, *and a* CITIZEN *or two, with an* APPRENTICE.

BOYS. Now they come, now they come!
2 [BOY]. The duke!
3 [BOY]. The state!
CITIZEN. How near, boy?
1 BOY. I'th'next street, sir, hard at hand.
CITIZEN. You, sirrah, get a standing for your mistress,
The best in all the city.
APPRENTICE. I have't for her, sir.
'Twas a thing I provided for her over-night;
'Tis ready at her pleasure.
CITIZEN. Fetch her to't then; away, sir!
BIANCA. What's the meaning of this hurry?
Can you tell, mother?
MOTHER. What a memory
Have I! I see by that years come upon me.
Why, 'tis a yearly custom and solemnity,
Religiously observ'd by th'duke and state,
To St Mark's temple, the fifteenth of April.
See if my dull brains had not quite forgot it!

---

69 *in a fountain*: in tears/reflected in a fountain (an idea suggested by statues of love).

70–1 The country maid arranges her hair by a saucer of water serving as mirror.

73 *the state*: the nobles, the ruling body.

85 *fifteenth of April*: St Mark's Day, if the Gregorian calendar were adjusted to the current English (Julian) calendar, though 25 April is the actual feast day in both.

'Twas happily question'd of thee; I had gone down
else,
Sat like a drone below, and never thought on't.
I would not to be ten years younger again
That you had lost the sight. Now you shall see
Our duke, a goodly gentleman of his years.
BIANCA. Is he old then?
MOTHER. About some fifty-five.
BIANCA. That's no great age in man: he's then at best
For wisdom and for judgement.
MOTHER. The lord cardinal,
His noble brother, there's a comely gentleman,
And greater in devotion than in blood.
BIANCA. He's worthy to be mark'd.
MOTHER. You shall behold
All our chief states of Florence; you came fortunately
Against this solemn day.
BIANCA. I hope so always. *Music.*
MOTHER. I hear 'em near us now. Do you stand easily?
BIANCA. Exceeding well, good mother.
MOTHER. Take this stool.
BIANCA. I need it not, I thank you.
MOTHER. Use your will, then.

Enter in great solemnity six KNIGHTS *bare-headed, then two* CARDINALS, *and then the* LORD CARDINAL, *then the* DUKE [*with* GUARDIANO]; *after him the* STATES OF FLORENCE *by two and two, with variety of music and song. Exit* [*procession, followed by* CITIZENS, APPRENTICES *and* BOYS.]

MOTHER. How like you, daughter?
BIANCA. 'Tis a noble state.
Methinks my soul could dwell upon the reverence
Of such a solemn and most worthy custom.
Did not the duke look up? Methought he saw us.

---

88 *drone*: idler or sluggard/(from the bass of the bag-pipe) a moaning misery.
92 *fifty-five*: James I was fifty-five on 19 June 1621, and it is likely that this passage was intended as a compliment.
98 *chief states*: leading nobility, chief dignitaries.
103 *state*: ruling body.

MOTHER. That's ev'ryone's conceit that sees a duke:
If he look steadfastly, he looks straight at them;
When he perhaps, good careful gentleman,
Never minds any; but the look he casts
Is at his own intentions, and his object
Only the public good.
BIANCA. Most likely so.
MOTHER. Come, come, we'll end this argument below.
Exeunt.

ACT II

SCENE I

Enter HIPPOLITO *and* LADY LIVIA *the widow.*

LIVIA. A strange affection, brother, when I think on't!
I wonder how thou cam'st by't.
HIPPOLITO. Ev'n as easily
As man comes by destruction, which oft-times
He wears in his own bosom.
LIVIA. Is the world
So populous in women, and creation
So prodigal in beauty and so various,
Yet does love turn thy point to thine own blood?
'Tis somewhat too unkindly. Must thy eye
Dwell evilly on the fairness of thy kin'red,
And seek not where it should? It is confined
Now in a narrower prison than was made for't:
It is allow'd a stranger; and where bounty
Is made the great man's honour, 'tis ill husbandry
To spare, and servants shall have small thanks for't.
So he Heaven's bounty seems to scorn and mock,
That spares free means, and spends of his own stock.

---

107 *conceit*: thought, opinion, but with a likely pun on the modern sense, 'self-conceit'.
7 *turn thy point*: i.e. as the needle of the compass is attracted, but with an innuendo.
8 *unkindly*: cruelly/unnaturally.
16 *stock*: goods, capital/family, kin.

HIPPOLITO. Never was man's misery so soon sew'd up,
Counting how truly.
LIVIA. Nay, I love you so,
That I shall venture much to keep a change from you
So fearful as this grief will bring upon you.
'Faith, it even kills me, when I see you faint
Under a reprehension; and I'll leave it,
Though I know nothing can be better for you.
Prithee, sweet brother, let not passion waste
The goodness of thy time, and of thy fortune;
Thou keep'st the treasure of that life I love
As dearly as mine own; and if you think
My former words too bitter, which were minist'red
By truth and zeal, 'tis but a hazarding
Of grace and virtue, and I can bring forth
As pleasant fruits as sensuality wishes
In all her teeming longings. This I can do.
HIPPOLITO. Oh nothing that can make my wishes perfect!
LIVIA. I would that love of yours were pawn'd to't, brother,
And as soon lost that way as I could win.
Sir, I could give as shrewd a lift to chastity
As any she that wears a tongue in Florence:
Sh'ad need be a good horsewoman and sit fast
Whom my strong argument could not fling at last.
Prithee take courage, man; though I should counsel
Another to despair, yet I am pitiful
To thy afflictions, and will venture hard.
I will not name for what, 'tis not handsome;
Find you the proof, and praise me.
HIPPOLITO. Then I fear me,
I shall not praise you in haste.

---

17 *sew'd up*: perhaps a metaphor analogous to the modern 'buttoned up' = completed; or from surgical sewing, and meaning 'closed up', 'healed'. But see Textual note, p. 405.
22 *reprehension*: reprimand.
24 *passion*: sorrow.
34 *pawn'd to't*: pledged as a surety against Livia's success.
36 *as shrewd a lift to chastity*: 'as cunning/dangerous a blow at female honour'.
37 *wears a tongue*: The odd phrase for 'an articulate woman' probably reflects the fashion for wearing jewellery in the shape of tongues.
43 *handsome*: decent.

LIVIA. This is the comfort:
You are not the first, brother, has attempted
Things more forbidden than this seems to be.
I'll minister all cordials now to you,
Because I'd cheer you up, sir.
HIPPOLITO. I am past hope.
LIVIA. Love, thou shalt see me do a strange cure then,
As e'er was wrought on a disease so mortal
And near akin to shame. When shall you see her?
HIPPOLITO. Never in comfort more.
LIVIA. Y'are so impatient too.
HIPPOLITO. Will you believe? Death, sh'as forsworn my company,
And seal'd it with a blush.
LIVIA. So, I perceive
All lies upon my hands, then; well, the more glory
When the work's finish'd.

Enter SERVANT.

How now, sir, the news?
SERVANT. Madam, your niece, the virtuous Isabella,
Is 'lighted now to see you.
LIVIA. That's great fortune.
Sir, your stars bless. – You simple, lead her in!
Exit SERVANT.
HIPPOLITO. What's this to me?
LIVIA. Your absence, gentle brother;
I must bestir my wits for you.
HIPPOLITO. Ay, to great purpose.
Exit HIPPOLITO.
LIVIA. Beshrew you, would I lov'd you not so well!
I'll go to bed, and leave this deed undone.
I am the fondest where I once affect,
The carefull'st of their healths, and of their ease, forsooth,
That I look still but slenderly to mine own;

---

48 *cordials*: medicines or beverages which stimulate the action of the heart.
54 *death*: an exclamation contracted from 'God's death!'.
60 *You simple*: 'You fool!' But see Textual note, p. 405.
65 *fondest*: most foolishly doting.
65 *affect*: love.

I take a course to pity him so much now
That I have none left for modesty and myself;
This 'tis to grow so liberal. Y'have few sisters
That love their brother's ease 'bove their own honesties;
But if you question my affections,
That will be found my fault.

Enter ISABELLA *the niece.*

Niece, your love's welcome.
Alas, what draws that paleness to thy cheeks?
This enforc'd marriage towards?

ISABELLA. It helps, good aunt,
Amongst some other griefs; but those I'll keep
Lock'd up in modest silence, for they're sorrows
Would shame the tongue more than they grieve the thought.

LIVIA. Indeed, the ward is simple.

ISABELLA. 'Simple'! That were well:
Why, one might make good shift with such a husband.
But he's a fool entail'd, he halts downright in't.

LIVIA. And knowing this, I hope 'tis at your choice
To take or refuse, niece.

ISABELLA. You see it is not.
I loathe him more than beauty can hate death,
Or age, her spiteful neighbour.

LIVIA. Let 't appear, then.

ISABELLA. How can I, being born with that obedience
That must submit unto a father's will?
If he command, I must of force consent.

LIVIA. Alas, poor soul! Be not offended, prithee,
If I set by the name of niece awhile,
And bring in pity in a stranger fashion.
It lies here in this breast would cross this match.

ISABELLA. How, cross it, aunt?

LIVIA. Ay, and give thee more liberty

---

70 *liberal*: generous/tending to licence.
75 *towards*: in preparation, imminent.
81 *entail'd*: unavoidably endowed with hereditary qualities (the Ward is a congenital idiot).
81 *he halts downright in't*: 'he stops completely at "fool" and his capacities stretch no further'.
88 *of force*: of necessity.

Than thou hast reason yet to apprehend.
ISABELLA. Sweet aunt, in goodness keep not hid from me
What may befriend my life.
LIVIA. Yes, yes, I must,
When I return to reputation,
And think upon the solemn vow I made
To your dead mother, my most loving sister . . .
As long as I have her memory 'twixt mine eyelids,
Look for no pity now.
ISABELLA. Kind, sweet, dear aunt –
LIVIA. No, 'twas a secret I have took special care of,
Delivered by your mother on her deathbed
(That's nine years now) and I'll not part from 't yet,
Though nev'r was fitter time nor greater cause for 't.
ISABELLA. As you desire the praises of a virgin –
LIVIA. Good sorrow! I would do thee any kindness
Not wronging secrecy or reputation.
ISABELLA. Neither of which, as I have hope of fruit[ful]-ness,
Shall receive wrong from me.
LIVIA. Nay, 'twould be your own wrong
As much as any's, should it come to that once.
ISABELLA. I need no better means to work persuasion then.
LIVIA. Let it suffice, you may refuse this fool,
Or you may take him, as you see occasion
For your advantage; the best wits will do't.
Y'have liberty enough in your own will,
You cannot be enforc'd; there grows the flower,
If you could pick it out, makes whole life sweet to you.
That which you call your father's command's nothing;
Then your obedience must needs be as little.
If you can make shift here to taste your happiness,
Or pick out aught that likes you, much good do you.
You see your cheer, I'll make you no set dinner.

---

100 *'twixt mine eyelids*: 'in my (mind's) eye'.
122 *likes*: pleases.
123 *I'll make you no set dinner*: i.e. 'I won't make a meal of it', 'I won't spell it out'. The 'cheer' (entertainment) is offered for Isabella's choice like a buffet lunch.

ISABELLA. And trust me, I may starve for all the good
I can find yet in this! Sweet aunt, deal plainlier.
LIVIA. Say I should trust you now upon an oath,
And give you in a secret that would start you;
How am I sure of you, in faith and silence?
ISABELLA. Equal assurance may I find in mercy,
As you for that in me.
LIVIA. It shall suffice.
Then know, however custom has made good,
For reputation's sake, the names of niece
And aunt 'twixt you and I, w'are nothing less.
ISABELLA. How's that?
LIVIA. I told you I should start your blood.
You are no more allied to any of us,
Save what the courtesy of opinion casts
Upon your mother's memory and your name,
Than the mer'st stranger is, or one begot
At Naples, when the husband lies at Rome:
There's so much odds betwixt us. Since your knowledge
Wish'd more instruction, and I have your oath
In pledge for silence, it makes me talk the freelier.
Did never the report of that fam'd Spaniard,
Marquis of Coria, since your time was ripe
For understanding, fill your ear with wonder?
ISABELLA. Yes, what of him? I have heard his deeds of honour
Often related when we liv'd in Naples.
LIVIA. You heard the praises of your father then.
ISABELLA. My father!
LIVIA. That was he; but all the business
So carefully and so discreetly carried
That fame receiv'd no spot by't, not a blemish.
Your mother was so wary to her end;

---

129 *mercy*: i.e. the confident expectation of God's mercy at the Day of Judgement.

133 *w'are nothing less*: 'we are nothing related/we are less related than we seem' (two negative statements in Jacobean English may make an emphatic affirmative).

134 *start your blood*: 'surprise you'/'kindle your passions'.

144 *Marquis of Coria*: The title was established in 1465 by Henry IV of Castille, and was held by the Dukes of Alva.

152 *to her end*: till her death.

None knew it but her conscience, and her friend,
Till penitent confession made it mine,
And now my pity, yours; it had been long else,
And I hope care and love alike in you,
Made good by oath, will see it take no wrong now.
How weak his commands now, whom you call father!
How vain all his enforcements, your obedience!
And what a largeness in your will and liberty
To take or to reject, or to do both,
For fools will serve to father wise men's children.
All this y'have time to think on. O my wench,
Nothing o'erthrows our sex but indiscretion!
We might do well else of a brittle people
As any under the great canopy.
I pray forget not but to call me aunt still;
Take heed of that, it may be mark'd in time else.
But keep your thoughts to yourself, from all the world,
Kin'red, or dearest friend, nay, I entreat you,
From him that all this while you have call'd uncle;
And though you love him dearly, as I know
His deserts claim as much ev'n from a stranger,
Yet let not him know this, I prithee do not;
As ever thou hast hope of second pity
If thou shouldst stand in need on't, do not do't.

ISABELLA. Believe my oath, I will not.

LIVIA. Why, well said.
[*Aside*] Who shows more craft t'undo a maidenhead,
I'll resign my part to her.

Enter HIPPOLITO.

She's thine own, go. *Exit.*

HIPPOLITO. [*aside*] Alas, fair flattery cannot cure my sorrows!

---

153 *friend*: lover.

160 *will and liberty*: These words have connotations of sexual desire and licence.

165–6 'We might otherwise have as good a reputation with the fickle people as those who live under the great canopy of state (i.e. kings).' 'Great canopy' might here be used figuratively of the sky, but this is less likely.

175 *second pity*: i.e. more help from Livia.

ISABELLA. [*aside*] Have I pass'd so much time in ignorance,
And never had the means to know myself
Till this blest hour? Thanks to her virtuous pity
That brought it now to light! Would I had known it
But one day sooner! He had then receiv'd
In favours what, poor gentleman, he took
In bitter words: a slight and harsh reward
For one of his deserts.
HIPPOLITO. [*aside*] There seems to me now
More anger and distraction in her looks.
I'm gone, I'll not endure a second storm;
The memory of the first is not past yet.
ISABELLA. Are you return'd, you comforts of my life,
In this man's presence? I will keep you fast now,
And sooner part eternally from the world
Than my good joys in you. Prithee, forgive me.
I did but chide in jest; the best loves use it
Sometimes; it sets an edge upon affection.
When we invite our best friends to a feast
'Tis not all sweetmeats that we set before them;
There's somewhat sharp and salt, both to whet appetite,
And make 'em taste their wine well: so, methinks,
After a friendly, sharp and savoury chiding,
A kiss tastes wondrous well and full o'th'grape.
[*She kisses him.*]
How think'st thou, does't not?
HIPPOLITO. 'Tis so excellent,
I know not how to praise it, what to say to't!
ISABELLA. This marriage shall go forward.
HIPPOLITO. With the ward!
Are you in earnest?
ISABELLA. 'Twould be ill for us else.
HIPPOLITO. [*aside*] For us! How means she that?
ISABELLA. [*aside*] Troth, I begin
To be so well, methinks, within this hour!
For all this match able to kill one's heart,
Nothing can pull me down now; should my father
Provide a worse fool yet (which I should think
Were a hard thing to compass) I'd have him either:

---

213 *compass*: achieve.

The worse the better; none can come amiss now
If he want wit enough. So discretion love me,
Desert and judgement, I have content sufficient.
– She that comes once to be a housekeeper
Must not look every day to fare well, sir,
Like a young waiting-gentlewoman in service;
For she feeds commonly as her lady does,
No good bit passes her but she gets a taste on't;
But when she comes to keep house for herself,
She's glad of some choice cates then once a week,
Or twice at most, and glad if she can get 'em:
So must affection learn to fare with thankfulness.
Pray make your love no stranger, sir, that's all.
[*Aside*] Though you be one yourself, and know not on't,
And I have sworn you must not. *Exit.*

HIPPOLITO. This is beyond me!
Never came joys so unexpectedly
To meet desires in man. How came she thus?
What has she done to her, can any tell?
'Tis beyond sorcery, this, drugs, or love-powders;
Some art that has no name, sure; strange to me
Of all the wonders I e'er met withal
Throughout my ten years' travels. But I'm thankful for't.
This marriage now must of necessity forward:
It is the only veil wit can devise
To keep our acts hid from sin-piercing eyes. *Exit.*

SCENE II

Enter GUARDIANO *and* LIVIA.

LIVIA. How, sir, a gentlewoman so young, so fair
As you set forth, spied from the widow's window?

GUARDIANO. She!

LIVIA. Our Sunday-dinner woman?

215–16 *discretion . . . Desert and judgement*: These qualities are attributed to Hippolito.

217–25 A succession of metaphors relate sexual activity in the play to 'feeding' or to commerce.

223 *cates*: delicacies, usually elaborate, and purchased rather than made at home.

GUARDIANO. And Thursday-supper woman, the same
still.
I know not how she came by her, but I'll swear
She's the prime gallant for a face in Florence;
And no doubt other parts follow their leader.
The duke himself first spied her at the window;
Then in a rapture, as if admiration
Were poor when it were single, beck'ned me,
And pointed to the wonder warily,
As one that fear'd she would draw in her splendour
Too soon, if too much gaz'd at. I nev'r knew him
So infinitely taken with a woman;
Nor can I blame his appetite, or tax
His raptures of slight folly: she's a creature
Able to draw a state from serious business,
And make it their best piece to do her service.
What course shall we devise? H'as spoke twice now.
LIVIA. Twice?
GUARDIANO. 'Tis beyond your apprehension
How strangely that one look has catch'd his heart!
'Twould prove but too much worth in wealth and
favour
To those should work his peace.
LIVIA. And if I do't not,
Or at least come as near it (if your art
Will take a little pains and second me)
As any wench in Florence of my standing,
I'll quite give o'er, and shut up shop in cunning.
GUARDIANO. 'Tis for the duke; and if I fail your purpose,
All means to come, by riches or advancement,
Miss me and skip me over!
LIVIA. Let the old woman then
Be sent for with all speed; then I'll begin.
GUARDIANO. A good conclusion follow, and a sweet one,
After this stale beginning with old ware.
Within there!

---

7 *prime gallant*: an outstanding and fashionable beauty.
16–17 *or tax/His raptures of slight folly*: reproach his passion as trivial, foolish.
19 *piece*: work; but with a probable pun on the homophone 'peace'.
22 *strangely*: extremely//oddly. But see Textual note, p. 405.
34 *old ware*: stale (female) 'goods', i.e. the Mother.

Enter SERVANT.

SERVANT. Sir, do you call?
GUARDIANO. Come near, list hither.
[*Talks aside with* SERVANT.]
LIVIA. I long myself to see this absolute creature
That wins the heart of love and praise so much.
GUARDIANO. Go sir, make haste.
LIVIA. Say I entreat her company;
Do you hear, sir?
SERVANT. Yes, madam. *Exit.*
LIVIA. That brings her quickly.
GUARDIANO. I would 'twere done; the duke waits the good hour,
And I wait the good fortune that may spring from't.
I have had a lucky hand these fifteen year
At such court-passage with three dice in a dish.

Enter FABRITIO.

Seignior Fabritio!
FABRITIO. Oh sir, I bring an alteration in my mouth now.
GUARDIANO. [*aside*] An alteration! No wise speech, I hope;
He means not to talk wisely, does he, trow?
– Good! What's the change, I pray, sir?
FABRITIO. A new change.
GUARDIANO. [*aside*] Another yet! 'Faith, there's enough already.
FABRITIO. My daughter loves him now.
GUARDIANO. What, does she, sir?
FABRITIO. Affects him beyond thought, who but the ward, forsooth!
No talk but of the ward; she would have him
To choose 'bove all the men she ever saw.

---

43 *court-passage with three dice in a dish*: Passage is a gambling game played by two players with three dice. 'Court-passage' suggests amorous encounters at Court, and 'three dice in a dish' is a metaphor for sexual intercourse.

49 Guardiano's remark probably alludes to the 'New 'Change', opened in the Strand in 1609 as a meeting-place for merchants; being in addition to the Royal Exchange, its existence was not felt to be justified, and 'another yet' would be wholly redundant.

My will goes not so fast as her consent now:
Her duty gets before my command still.
GUARDIANO. Why then, sir, if you'll have me speak my thoughts,
I smell 'twill be a match.
FABRITIO. Ay, and a sweet young couple,
If I have any judgement.
GUARDIANO. [*aside*] 'Faith, that's little.
– Let her be sent tomorrow before noon,
And handsomely trick'd up, for 'bout that time
I mean to bring her in and tender her to him.
FABRITIO. I warrant you for handsome; I will see
Her things laid ready, every one in order,
And have some part of her trick'd up tonight.
GUARDIANO. Why, well said.
FABRITIO. 'Twas a use her mother had,
When she was invited to an early wedding:
She'd dress her head o'ernight, sponge up herself,
And give her neck three lathers.
GUARDIANO. [*aside*] Ne'er a halter?
FABRITIO. On with her chain of pearl, her ruby bracelets,
Lay ready all her tricks and jiggambobs.
GUARDIANO. So must your daughter.
FABRITIO. I'll about it straight, sir. *Exit* FABRITIO.
LIVIA. How he sweats in the foolish zeal of fatherhood
After six ounces an hour, and seems
To toil as much as if his cares were wise ones!
GUARDIANO. Y'have let his folly blood in the right vein, lady.
LIVIA. And here comes his sweet son-in-law that shall be.
They're both allied in wit before the marriage;
What will they be hereafter, when they are nearer?

---

60 *trick'd up*: adorned, dressed up.
62 *I warrant you for handsome*: 'I guarantee she will look good.'
68 *Ne'er a halter*: The halter would be made of leather, of which 'lather' is a variant form, and an anagram of *halter*.
70 *tricks and jiggambobs*: trinkets and knick-knacks.
73 *After six ounces an hour*: losing weight at the rate of six ounces an hour.
75 The reference is to blood-letting as a medical cure; a superflux of blood would result in over-emotional behaviour; see Additional note, p. 410.

Yet they can go no further than the fool:
There's the world's end in both of 'em.

Enter WARD *and* SORDIDO, *one with a shittlecock, the other a battledore.*

GUARDIANO. Now, young heir!

WARD. What's the next business after shittlecock, now?

GUARDIANO. Tomorrow you shall see the gentlewoman must be your wife.

WARD. There's ev'n another thing too must be kept up with a pair of battledores. My wife! What can she do?

GUARDIANO. Nay, that's a question you should ask yourself, ward, when y'are alone together.

[LIVIA *and* GUARDIANO *talk apart*.]

WARD. That's as I list! A wife's to be ask['d] anywhere, I hope; I'll ask her in a congregation, if I have a mind to't, and so save a licence. [*To* SORDIDO] My guardiner has no more wit than an herb-woman, that sells away all her sweet herbs and nosegays, and keeps a stinking breath for her own pottage.

SORDIDO. Let me be at the choosing of your beloved, if you desire a woman of good parts.

WARD. Thou shalt, sweet Sordido.

SORDIDO. I have a plaguey guess; let me alone to see what she is. If I but look upon her – 'way, I know all the faults to a hair that you may refuse her for.

WARD. Dost thou? I prithee let me hear 'em, Sordido.

SORDIDO. Well, mark 'em then; I have 'em all in rhyme:
The wife your guardiner ought to tender,

---

80 *world's end*: See Textual note, p. 405.

84–5 Women are 'Shittlecocks' = whores, because they shuttle to and fro; they must be satisfied with two men at least ('battledores' are the rackets in the game of Battledore and Shuttlecock, a precursor of badminton).

89–90 The Ward will have banns read in church, and thus avoid the expense of a special licence from the Archbishop of Canterbury or his surrogate.

91 *guardiner*: The context and the spelling suggest that a pun is intended on 'gardener'.

93 *breath . . . pottage*: an allusion to the proverbial 'Save your breath to cool your porridge' (Tilley, W 422).

97 *plaguey guess*: 'shrewd (capacity for) conjecture'; or perhaps 'disturbing apprehension'.

98 *'way*: straightway.

Should be pretty, straight and slender;
Her hair not short, her foot not long,
Her hand not huge, nor too too loud her tongue;
No pearl in eye nor ruby in her nose,
No burn or cut but what the catalogue shows.
She must have teeth, and that no black ones,
And kiss most sweet when she does smack once;
Her skin must be both white and plump,
Her body straight, not hopper-rump'd,
Or wriggle sideways like a crab;
She must be neither slut nor drab,
Nor go too splay-foot with her shoes,
To make her smock lick up the dews.
And two things more which I forgot to tell ye:
She neither must have bump in back, nor belly.
These are the faults that will not make her pass.

WARD. And if I spy not these, I am a rank ass!

SORDIDO. Nay, more; by right, sir, you should see her naked,
For that's the ancient order.

WARD. See her naked?
That were good sport, i'faith. I'll have the books turn'd over,
And if I find her naked on record,
She shall not have a rag on. But stay, stay!
How if she should desire to see me so too?
I were in a sweet case then; such a foul skin!

---

106 *pearl in eye*: a cataract, or whitish spot in the eye left by smallpox and other diseases.

106 *ruby in her nose*: a 'ruby' can be merely a red pimple; but probably some kind of tumorous growth is meant here.

107 *No burn or cut but what the catalogue shows*: 'cut' puns on the word for the female pudendum, 'burning' was a term for venereal disease.

111 *hopper-rump'd*: i.e. with a large rump that has a sideways and up-and-down wobble like that of the hopper (funnel) which feeds grain into a mill.

113 *drab*: slattern, whore.

117 I.e. she must be neither hunchbacked nor pregnant.

121 *the ancient order*: It was a custom in More's *Utopia*, and More himself observed it before the nuptials of both his daughters.

123 *naked on record*: 'if I find in the old records that my betrothed should be shown to me naked'.

126 *case*: situation/covering, clothing.

SORDIDO. But y'have a clean shirt, and that makes amends, sir.

WARD. I will not see her naked for that trick, though.

Exit.

SORDIDO. Then take her with all faults with her clothes on!
And they may hide a number with a bum-roll.
'Faith, choosing of a wench in a huge farthingale
Is like the buying of ware under a great penthouse:
What with the deceit of one,
And the false light of th'other (mark my speeches),
He may have a diseas'd wench in's bed
And rotten stuff in's breeches. *Exit.*

GUARDIANO. It may take handsomely.

LIVIA. I see small hindrance.
– How now, so soon return'd?

Enter [SERVANT *with*] MOTHER.

GUARDIANO. She's come.

LIVIA. That's well.
Widow, come, come; I have a great quarrel to you;
'Faith, I must chide you, that you must be sent for!
You make yourself so strange, never come at us;
And yet so near a neighbour, and so unkind!
Troth, y'are to blame; you cannot be more welcome
To any house in Florence, that I'll tell you.

MOTHER. My thanks must needs acknowledge so much, madam.

LIVIA. How can you be so strange then? I sit here
Sometime whole days together without company,
When business draws this gentleman from home,
And should be happy in society
Which I so well affect as that of yours.
I know y'are alone too. Why should not we,
Like two kind neighbours, then, supply the wants
Of one another, having tongue-discourse,

---

130 *bum-roll*: a cushion round the hips which held out the skirt.

131 *farthingale*: a framework of hoops, usually whalebone, which extended a woman's dress.

132 *penthouse*: a sloping roof over a door or window. It was complained that the loss of light from a draper's window when so fitted made it impossible to judge his goods.

136 *rotten stuff*: bad cloth/flesh afflicted with veneral disease.

Experience in the world, and such kind helps
To laugh down time, and meet age merrily?
MOTHER. Age, madam! You speak mirth; 'tis at my door,
But a long journey from your ladyship yet.
LIVIA. My faith, I'm nine-and-thirty, ev'ry stroke, wench;
And 'tis a general observation
'Mongst knights' wives or widows, we accompt
Ourselves then old, when young men's eyes leave looking at's:
'Tis a true rule amongst us, and ne'er fail'd yet
In any but in one that I remember;
Indeed, she had a friend at nine-and-forty!
Marry, she paid well for him; and in th'end
He kept a quean or two with her own money,
That robb'd her of her plate and cut her throat.
MOTHER. She had her punishment in this world, madam;
And a fair warning to all other women
That they live chaste at fifty.
LIVIA. Ay, or never, wench.
Come, now I have thy company I'll not part with't
Till after supper,
MOTHER. Yes, I must crave pardon, madam.
LIVIA. I swear you shall stay supper. We have no strangers, woman;
None but my sojourners and I: this gentleman
And the young heir, his ward; you know our company.
MOTHER. Some other time I will make bold with you, madam.
GUARDIANO. Nay, pray stay, widow.
LIVIA. 'Faith, she shall not go.
Do you think I'll be forsworn?
Table and chess [*are got ready*].
MOTHER. 'Tis a great while
Till supper-time; I'll take my leave then, now, madam,
And come again i'th'evening, since your ladyship
Will have it so.
LIVIA. I'th'evening! By my troth, wench,

---

155 *merrily*: See Textual note, p. 405.
166 *quean*: whore.
174 *sojourners*: guests, lodgers.

I'll keep you while I have you. You have great business, sure,
To sit alone at home; I wonder strangely
What pleasure you take in't! Were't to me now,
I should be ever at one neighbour's house
Or other all day long. Having no charge,
Or none to chide you if you go or stay,
Who may live merrier; ay, or more at heart's ease?
Come, we'll to chess, or draughts; there are an hundred tricks
To drive out time till supper, never fear't, wench.

MOTHER. I'll but make one step home and return straight, madam.

LIVIA. Come, I'll not trust you; you use more excuses
To your kind friends than ever I knew any.
What business can you have, if you be sure
Y'have lock'd the doors? And that being all you have,
I know y'are careful on't. One afternoon
So much to spend here! Say I should entreat you now
To lie a night or two, or a week, with me,
Or leave your own house for a month together,
It were a kindness that long neighbourhood
And friendship might well hope to prevail in.
Would you deny such a request? I'faith,
Speak truth, and freely.

MOTHER. I were then uncivil, madam.

LIVIA. Go to then, set your men; we'll have whole nights
Of mirth together ere we be much older, wench.

MOTHER. [*aside*] As good now tell her, then, for she will know't;
I have always found her a most friendly lady.

LIVIA. Why, widow, where's your mind?

MOTHER. Troth, ev'n at home, madam.
To tell you truth, I left a gentlewoman
Ev'n sitting all alone, which is uncomfortable,
Especially to young bloods.

LIVIA. Another excuse!

MOTHER. No, as I hope for health, madam, that's a truth;
Please you to send and see.

LIVIA. What gentlewoman? Pish!

---

186 *no charge*: no responsibilities or duties.
204 *your men*: i.e. the chessmen.

MOTHER. Wife to my son indeed, but not known, madam,
To any but yourself.
LIVIA. Now I beshrew you!
Could you be so unkind to her and me
To come and not bring her? 'Faith, 'tis not friendly!
MOTHER. I fear'd to be too bold.
LIVIA. Too bold? Oh what's become
Of the true hearty love was wont to be
'Mongst neighbours in old time?
MOTHER. And she's a stranger, madam.
LIVIA. The more should be her welcome. When is courtesy
In better practice than when 'tis employ'd
In entertaining strangers? I could chide, i'faith.
Leave her behind, poor gentlewoman, alone too!
Make some amends, and send for her betimes; go.
MOTHER. Please you command one of your servants, madam.
LIVIA. Within there!

Enter SERVANT.

SERVANT. Madam?
LIVIA. Attend the gentlewoman.
MOTHER. It must be carried wondrous privately
From my son's knowledge; he'll break out in storms else
– Hark you, sir.
[*She gives instructions; exit* SERVANT.]
LIVIA. [*aside*] Now comes in the heat of your part.
GUARDIANO. [*aside*] True, I know it, lady; and if I be out,
May the duke banish me from all employments,
Wanton or serious.
LIVIA. – So, have you sent, widow?
MOTHER. Yes, madam, he's almost at home by this.

---

225 *betimes*: at once.
228 *carried . . . privately*: kept secret.
231 *if I be out*: 'If I forget my lines'. Guardiano interprets Livia's last aside as being an acting metaphor ('Now comes the climax of your role'), and continues it.

LIVIA. And 'faith, let me entreat you, that henceforward
All such unkind faults may be swept from friendship,
Which does but dim the lustre. And think thus much:
It is a wrong to me, that have ability
To bid friends welcome, when you keep 'em from me;
You cannot set greater dishonour near me,
For bounty is the credit and the glory
Of those that have enough. I see y'are sorry,
And the good 'mends is made by't.
MOTHER. Here she's, madam.

Enter BIANCA, *and* SERVANT [*who shows her in, then goes off*].

BIANCA. [*aside*] I wonder how she comes to send for me now?
LIVIA. Gentlewoman, y'are most welcome, trust me y'are,
As courtesy can make one, or respect
Due to the presence of you.
BIANCA. I give you thanks, lady.
LIVIA. I heard you were alone, and 't had appear'd
An ill condition in me, though I knew you not,
Nor ever saw you (yet humanity
Thinks ev'ry case her own), to have kept your company
Here from you and left you all solitary.
I rather ventur'd upon boldness then
As the least fault, and wish'd your presence here:
A thing most happily motion'd of that gentleman,
Whom I request you, for his care and pity,
To honour and reward with your acquaintance;
A gentleman that ladies' rights stands for:
That's his profession.
BIANCA. 'Tis a noble one,
And honours my acquaintance.

---

247 *presence*: impressive demeanour and appearance.
249 *ill condition*: ill-nature *or* 'bad manners'.
250 *humanity*: the humane nature.
255 *motion'd of*: proposed by.
258–9 This seems to be an ironic reference to Guardiano's guardianships. He perhaps makes a 'profession' of seeking the wardship of young propertied ladies, 'standing' for them legally. *Profession* may also mean 'role', 'pose', 'assertion'.

GUARDIANO. All my intentions
Are servants to such mistresses.
BIANCA. 'Tis your modesty,
It seems, that makes your deserts speak so low, sir.
LIVIA. Come, widow. – Look you, lady, here's our
business; [*Points to chess table.*]
Are we not well employ'd, think you? An old quarrel
Between us, that will never be at an end.
BIANCA. No?
And methinks there's men enough to part you, lady.
LIVIA. Ho! But they set us on, let us come off
As well as we can, poor souls; men care no farther.
I pray sit down, forsooth, if you have the patience
To look upon two weak and tedious gamesters.
GUARDIANO. 'Faith, madam, set these by till evening;
You'll have enough on't then. The gentlewoman,
Being a stranger, would take more delight
To see your rooms and pictures.
LIVIA. Marry, good sir,
And well rememb'red! I beseech you show 'em her,
That will beguile time well; pray heartily, do, sir.
I'll do as much for you. Here, take these keys,
Show her the monument too – and that's a thing
Everyone sees not; you can witness that, widow.
MOTHER. And that's worth sight indeed, madam.
BIANCA. Kind lady,
I fear I came to be a trouble to you.
LIVIA. Oh, nothing less, forsooth.
BIANCA. And to this courteous gentleman,
That wears a kindness in his breast so noble
And bounteous to the welcome of a stranger.
GUARDIANO. If you but give acceptance to my service,
You do the greatest grace and honour to me
That courtesy can merit.
BIANCA. I were to blame else,
And out of fashion much. I pray you lead, sir.
LIVIA. After a game or two, w'are for you, gentlefolks.

---

267 *set us on*: encourage us/sexually excite us. *Come off*: get free/orgasm.

278 *monument*: any memorial, but commonly used of a carved figure in wood or stone.

282 *nothing less*: 'by no means', 'not at all'.

GUARDIANO. We wish no better seconds in society
Than your discourses, madam, and your partner's
there.
MOTHER. I thank your praise. I listen'd to you, sir,
Though when you spoke there came a paltry rook
Full in my way, and chokes up all my game.
Exit GUARDIANO *and* BIANCA.
LIVIA. Alas, poor widow, I shall be too hard for thee.
MOTHER. Y'are cunning at the game, I'll be sworn,
madam.
LIVIA. It will be found so, ere I give you over.
She that can place her man well –
MOTHER. As you do, madam.
LIVIA. As I shall, wench, can never lose her game.
Nay, nay, the black king's mine.
MOTHER. Cry you mercy, madam.
LIVIA. And this my queen.
MOTHER. I see't now.
LIVIA. Here's a duke
Will strike a sure stroke for the game anon;
Your pawn cannot come back to relieve itself.
MOTHER. I know that, madam.
LIVIA. You play well the whilst;
How she belies her skill! I hold two ducats

---

294 *rook*: a chess piece now often called the 'castle', but frequently called the 'duke' in the seventeenth century. See Additional note, p. 411.

297 *cunning at the game*: i.e. skilful at chess. Livia gives this the further meaning 'adept at sexual intrigue'. Innuendoes on *game* = chess/sexual play and *gamester* = player/sexual sportsman are maintained throughout this scene.

301 *the black king*: the chess piece. But as in Middleton's *Game at Chess*, the colours represent the contest between good and evil, Satan the black king, and the 'saintish' white king representing Innocence, 'Simplicity'. The Mother inadvertently touches an opposing piece, and makes the formal apology; Livia is made to verbally identify herself with the satanic party.

303 *strike a sure stroke*: 'strike' has the additional connotation of sexual thrusting: Livia's comment relates both to the game and to the Duke's impending sexual assault. The 'pawn' (Bianca) cannot move backwards, and so cannot escape being taken.

306 *hold*: wager, bet.

I give you check and mate to your white king,
Simplicity itself, your saintish king there.

MOTHER. Well, ere now, lady,
I have seen the fall of subtlety. Jest on.

LIVIA. Ay, but simplicity receives two for one.

MOTHER. What remedy but patience!

Enter above GUARDIANO *and* BIANCA.

BIANCA. Trust me, sir,
Mine eye nev'r met with fairer ornaments.

GUARDIANO. Nay, livelier, I'm persuaded, neither Florence
Nor Venice can produce.

BIANCA. Sir, my opinion
Takes your part highly.

GUARDIANO. There's a better piece
Yet than all these.

[*Enter*] DUKE *above.*

BIANCA. Not possible, sir!

GUARDIANO. Believe it;
You'll say so when you see't. Turn but your eye now,
Y'are upon it presently. *Exit.*

BIANCA. Oh sir!

DUKE. He's gone, beauty!
Pish, look not after him; he's but a vapour
That, when the sun appears, is seen no more.
[*He embraces her.*]

BIANCA. Oh treachery to honour!

DUKE. Prithee, tremble not.
I feel thy breast shake like a turtle panting
Under a loving hand that makes much on't.
Why art so fearful? As I'm friend to brightness,
There's nothing but respect and honour near thee.
You know me, you have seen me; here's a heart
Can witness I have seen thee.

BIANCA. The more's my danger.

---

311 *simplicity receives two for one*: Presumably the white faction (in the person of the king, 'Simplicity') has taken a piece, but Livia replies by inflicting the loss of two white pieces; 'innocence always gets the worst of it'.

323 *turtle*: turtle-dove.

DUKE. The more's thy happiness. Pish, strive not, sweet!
This strength were excellent employ'd in love, now,
But here 'tis spent amiss. Strive not to seek
Thy liberty and keep me still in prison.
I'faith, you shall not out till I'm releas'd now;
We'll both be freed together, or stay still by't;
So is captivity pleasant.
BIANCA. Oh my lord!
DUKE. I am not here in vain; have but the leisure
To think on that, and thou'lt be soon resolv'd.
The lifting of thy voice is but like one
That does exalt his enemy, who, proving high,
Lays all the plots to confound him that rais'd him.
Take warning, I beseech thee; thou seem'st to me
A creature so compos'd of gentleness
And delicate meekness, such as bless the faces
Of figures that are drawn for goddesses
And makes art proud to look upon her work;
I should be sorry the least force should lay
An unkind touch upon thee.
BIANCA. Oh my extremity!
My lord, what seek you?
DUKE. Love.
BIANCA. 'Tis gone already;
I have a husband.
DUKE. That's a single comfort;
Take a friend to him.
BIANCA. That's a double mischief,
Or else there's no religion.
DUKE. Do not tremble
At fears of thine own making.
BIANCA. Nor, great lord,
Make me not bold with death and deeds of ruin

---

332 *and keep me still in prison*: 'and so leave me locked in frustration'.

339 *exalt*: raise/praise/sexually arouse. If Bianca shouts, it will make her enemy more 'high', and so hasten her destruction, just as raising a political rival to greatness (by praising him) will make him more capable of destroying the one who 'exalted' him.

350 *a friend to him*: a lover in addition to him.

353 *bold with*: familiarly acquainted with (and therefore insensitive to).

Because they fear not you; me they must fright;
Then am I best in health. Should thunder speak
And none regard it, it had lost the name,
And were as good be still. I'm not like those
That take their soundest sleeps in greatest tempests;
Then wake I most, the weather fearfullest,
And call for strength to virtue.

DUKE. Sure I think
Thou know'st the way to please me: I affect
A passionate pleading 'bove an easy yielding;
But never pitied any: they deserve none
That will not pity me. I can command;
Think upon that. Yet if thou truly knewest
The infinite pleasure my affection takes
In gentle, fair entreatings, when love's businesses
Are carried courteously 'twixt heart and heart,
You'd make more haste to please me.

BIANCA. Why should you seek, sir,
To take away that you can never give?

DUKE. But I give better in exchange: wealth, honour.
She that is fortunate in a duke's favour
Lights on a tree that bears all women's wishes;
If your own mother saw you pluck fruit there,
She would commend your wit, and praise the time
Of your nativity. Take hold of glory.
Do not I know y'have cast away your life
Upon necessities, means merely doubtful
To keep you in indifferent health and fashion
(A thing I heard too lately and soon pitied);
And can you be so much your beauty's enemy
To kiss away a month or two in wedlock,

---

354 *fear*: frighten.

355 *Then am I best in health*: She is in her best state of health when she pays attention to the 'thunder' of moral prohibition in the 'tempest' of strong temptation. Her appeal for aid is to the social code ('virtue'), and the imagery indicates the extent to which her standards are fear-based taboos.

373–6 The image recalls the fatal tree of Genesis 3, from which Eve plucked fruit, aspiring (like Bianca) to *take hold of glory*, i.e. to become 'like God, knowing good and evil'. The Duke casts himself in the role of the Serpent, perhaps unconsciously.

378 *necessities*: unavoidable privations/mere necessities.

And weep whole years in wants for ever after?
Come, play the wise wench, and provide for ever:
Let storms come when they list, they find thee
shelter'd.
Should any doubt arise, let nothing trouble thee;
Put trust in our love for the managing
Of all to thy heart's peace. We'll walk together,
And show a thankful joy for both our fortunes.
Exit [*both*] *above.*

LIVIA. Did not I say my duke would fetch you over,
widow?

MOTHER. I think you spoke in earnest when you said it,
madam.

LIVIA. And my black king makes all the haste he can, too.

MOTHER. Well, madam, we may meet with him in time
yet!

LIVIA. I have given thee blind mate twice.

MOTHER. You may see, madam,
My eyes begin to fail.

LIVIA. I'll swear they do, wench.

Enter GUARDIANO.

GUARDIANO. [*aside*] I can but smile as often as I think
on't:
How prettily the poor fool was beguil'd,
How unexpectedly! It's a witty age;
Never were finer snares for women's honesties
Than are devis'd in these days; no spider's web
Made of a daintier thread than are now practis'd
To catch love's flesh-fly by the silver wing.
Yet to prepare her stomach by degrees
To Cupid's feast, because I saw 'twas queasy,
I show'd her naked pictures by the way:

---

390 *fetch you over*: 'get the better of you'.

392–3 Behind the conscious reference to the chess game is the ironic implication that Satan hastens to his victory as the Duke seduces Bianca, and will await both the Mother and Livia at the last.

394 *blind mate*: checkmate, but unperceived by the opponent, who calls only 'check', where she could have claimed the game. Probably there is ironic allusion to the 'blind mating' taking place above.

402 *flesh-fly*: the blow-fly, which plants its maggots in flesh.

A bit to stay the appetite. Well, advancement,
I venture hard to find thee; if thou com'st
With a greater title set upon thy crest,
I'll take that first cross patiently, and wait
Until some other comes greater than that.
I'll endure all.

LIVIA. The game's ev'n at the best now; you may see, widow,
How all things draw to an end.

MOTHER. Ev'n so do I, madam.

LIVIA. I pray take some of your neighbours along with you.

MOTHER. They must be those are almost twice your years, then,
If they be chose fit matches for my time, madam.

LIVIA. Has not my duke bestirr'd himself?

MOTHER. Yes, 'faith, madam,
H'as done me all the mischief in this game.

LIVIA. H'as show'd himself in's kind.

MOTHER. In's kind, call you it?
I may swear that.

LIVIA. Yes, 'faith, and keep your oath.

GUARDIANO. [*aside*] Hark, list! There's somebody coming down; 'tis she.

Enter BIANCA.

---

406 *stay*: appease/steady/settle/strengthen.

406–10 'Crest' is in heraldry the figure or device surmounting the helmet and shield, and is used on its own as a cognisance; 'title' is the inscription on or over the crest, giving the name of the owner. The passage seems to mean: 'If honours (symbolised by the heraldic crest) come destined for a more elevated recipient, I'll endure that first thwarting, and wait patiently for an even greater promotion to come my way.'

412–16 Livia's remark refers ostensibly to the chess game, but alludes to the sexual encounter, now reaching its climax. The Mother applies the remark to her own death, and Livia insists that she also (one of the Mother's 'neighbours') draws towards her life's end.

418 There is, of course, unconscious ironic reference to the activities of the real Duke. See Additional note, p. 411.

419 *in's kind*: in his true nature.

BIANCA. [*aside*] Now bless me from a blasting! I saw that now
Fearful for any woman's eye to look on.
Infectious mists and mildews hang at's eyes,
The weather of a doomsday dwells upon him.
Yet since mine honour's leprous, why should I
Preserve that fair that caus'd the leprosy?
Come, poison all at once! [*To* GUARDIANO] Thou in whose baseness
The bane of virtue broods, I'm bound in soul
Eternally to curse thy smooth-brow'd treachery
That wore the fair veil of a friendly welcome,
And I a stranger; think upon't, 'tis worth it.
Murders pil'd up upon a guilty spirit
At his last breath will not lie heavier
Than this betraying act upon thy conscience.
Beware of off'ring the first-fruits to sin:
His weight is deadly who commits with strumpets
After they have been abas'd and made for use;
If they offend to th'death, as wise men know,
How much more they, then, that first make 'em so?
I give thee that to feed on. I'm made bold now,
I thank thy treachery; sin and I'm acquainted,
No couple greater; and I'm like that great one
Who, making politic use of a base villain,
He likes the treason well, but hates the traitor;
So I hate thee, slave.

GUARDIANO Well, so the duke love me,
I fare not much amiss then; two great feasts
Do seldom come together in one day,
We must not look for 'em.

BIANCA. What, at it still, mother?

---

422 *bless me*: keep me; *blasting*: withering, shrivelling. See Additional note, p. 412.

427 *that*: her beauty, which according to Neo-Platonic doctrine is the physical manifestation of her spiritual condition.

429 *bane*: poison; *broods*: hatches.

437 *His weight is deadly who commits with strumpets*: 'One who sins with whores bears a guilt mortal to his soul.'

440 *How much more they, then, that first make 'em so*: 'How much more guilty those who first make women whores.'

445 *He likes the treason well, but hates the traitor*: Proverbial; see Tilley, K 64.

MOTHER. You see we sit by't. Are you so soon return'd?
LIVIA. [*aside*] So lively and so cheerful? A good sign, that.
MOTHER. You have not seen all since, sure?
BIANCA. That have I, mother,
The monument and all: I'm so beholding
To this kind, honest, courteous gentleman,
(You'd little think it, mother) show'd me all,
Had me from place to place so fashionably;
The kindness of some people, how't exceeds!
'Faith, I have seen that I little thought to see
I'th'morning when I rose.
MOTHER. Nay, so I told you
Before you saw't, it would prove worth your sight.
I give you great thanks for my daughter, sir,
And all your kindness towards her.
GUARDIANO. Oh good widow!
Much good may ['t] do her – [*Aside*] forty weeks hence, i'faith.

Enter SERVANT.

LIVIA. Now, sir?
SERVANT. May't please you, madam, to walk in?
Supper's upon the table.
LIVIA. Yes, we come.
[*Exit* SERVANT.]
Will't please you, gentlewoman?
BIANCA. Thanks, virtuous lady.
[*Softly to her*] Y'are a damn'd bawd! – I'll follow you, forsooth;
Pray take my mother in. [*Aside*] An old ass go with you!
– This gentleman and I vow not to part.
LIVIA. Then get you both before.
BIANCA. [*aside*] There lies his art.
Exeunt [BIANCA *and* GUARDIANO].

---

468 *An old ass go with you*: primarily, a formulaic insult to the Mother; but also an insult to Livia, since Bianca sees an old idiot as a suitable companion to the bawd. There is also the usual pun on ass/arse.

470 *There lies his art*: Guardiano's skill as a pandar lies in 'getting before', getting in first to prepare the way or to achieve an advantage; Bianca may also intend this aside in an obscene sense.

LIVIA. Widow, I'll follow you.
[*Exit* MOTHER.]
Is't so: 'damn'd bawd'!
Are you so bitter? 'Tis but want of use;
Her tender modesty is sea-sick a little,
Being not accustom'd to the breaking billow
Of woman's wavering faith, blown with temptations.
'Tis but a qualm of honour, 'twill away;
A little bitter for the time, but lasts not.
Sin tastes at the first draught like wormwood water,
But drunk again, 'tis nectar ever after. *Exit.*

ACT III

SCENE I

Enter MOTHER.

MOTHER. I would my son would either keep at home
Or I were in my grave!
She was but one day abroad, but ever since
She's grown so cutted, there's no speaking to her.
Whether the sight of great cheer at my lady's,
And such mean fare at home, work discontent in her,
I know not; but I'm sure she's strangely alter'd.
I'll nev'r keep daughter-in-law i'th'house with me
Again, if I had a hundred. When read I of any
That agreed long together, but she and her mother
Fell out in the first quarter? – nay, sometime
A grudging of a scolding the first week, by'r Lady;

---

478 *wormwood water*: a cordial prepared (like vermouth and absinthe) from the herb wormwood, proverbial for its bitterness.

4 *cutted*: curt, snappish.

12 *A grudging of a scolding*: probably, 'the resentment of a ticking-off (from the mother-in-law)'; but see Textual note, p. 406.

So takes the new disease, methinks, in my house.
I'm weary of my part, there's nothing likes her;
I know not how to please her here a' late.
And here she comes.

Enter BIANCA.

BIANCA. This is the strangest house
For all defects, as ever gentlewoman
Made shift withal, to pass away her love in!
Why is there not a cushion-cloth of drawn work,
Or some fair cut-work pinn'd up in my bed-chamber,
A silver-and-gilt casting-bottle hung by't?
Nay, since I am content to be so kind to you
To spare you for a silver basin and ewer,
Which one of my fashion looks for of duty:
She's never offered under, where she sleeps –
MOTHER. [*aside*] She talks of things here my whole state's not worth.
BIANCA. Never a green silk quilt is there i'th'house, mother,
To cast upon my bed?
MOTHER. No, by troth, is there!
Nor orange-tawny neither!
BIANCA. Here's a house
For a young gentlewoman to be got with child in!
MOTHER. Yes, simple though you make it, there has been three

---

13 *the new disease*: (metaphorically) 'this new vice of insubordination in the young'. The term was applied literally to a variety of undiagnosed fevers appearing in the latter half of the sixteenth century and causing headaches, disturbance of memory and judgement, followed by a general disorder of mental faculties.

14 *likes*: pleases.

19 *cushion-cloth of drawn work*: a cushion-case made from a fabric ornamented by drawing out some of the threads from warp and woof to form a pattern.

20 *cut-work*: open-work embroidery or lace, the pattern being cut rather than woven into the material.

21 *casting-bottle*: a bottle for sprinkling perfumed water.

25 *under*: less.

27–9 *green silk . . . orange tawny*: Green tended to be associated with courtesans, and orange-tawny was 'Colour de Roy' (Cotgrave, *Dictionary* (1611)), a royal colour, and denoted social aspiration.

Got in a year in't (since you move me to't),
And all as sweet-fac'd children and as lovely
As you'll be mother of; I will not spare you.
What, cannot children be begot, think you,
Without gilt casting-bottles? Yes, and as sweet ones:
The miller's daughter brings forth as white boys
As she that bathes herself with milk and bean-flour.
'Tis an old saying, 'one may keep good cheer
In a mean house': so may true love affect
After the rate of princes, in a cottage.

BIANCA. Troth, you speak wondrous well for your old house here;
'Twill shortly fall down at your feet to thank you,
Or stoop when you go to bed, like a good child,
To ask you blessing. Must I live in want,
Because my fortune match'd me with your son?
Wives do not give away themselves to husbands
To the end to be quite cast away; they look
To be the better us'd and tender'd rather,
Highlier respected, and maintain'd the richer;
They're well rewarded else for the free gift
Of their whole life to a husband. I ask less now
Than what I had at home when I was a maid
And at my father's house; kept short of that
Which a wife knows she must have, nay, and will,
Will, mother, if she be not a fool born;
And report went of me that I could wrangle
For what I wanted when I was two hours old;
And by that copy, this land still I hold.
You hear me, mother. *Exit.*

MOTHER. Ay, too plain, methinks;
And were I somewhat deafer when you spake
'Twere nev'r a whit the worse for my quietness.

---

37 *white boys*: 'darlings'. The expression points the irony that bastards of this traditionally promiscuous pleb are born to the same cosmetic luxuries as are employed by the women of the idle rich.

40–1 *affect/After the rate of princes*: love on a princely scale.

49 *tender'd*: cherished.

59 *copy*: copyhold. Under copyhold tenure, land was held by custom, and claims justified by production of a copy of the court-rolls of the manor. Bianca's right to wrangle for what she wants is established by the report of her earliest behaviour.

'Tis the most sudden'st, strangest alteration,
And the most subtilest that ev'r wit at threescore
Was puzzled to find out. I know no cause for't; but
She's no more like the gentlewoman at first
Than I am like her that nev'r lay with man yet
(And she's a very young thing, where'er she be).
When she first lighted here, I told her then
How mean she should find all things; she was pleas'd,
forsooth,
None better. I laid open all defects to her;
She was contented still. But the devil's in her,
Nothing contents her now. Tonight my son
Promis'd to be at home; would he were come once,
For I'm weary of my charge, and life too.
She'd be serv'd all in silver, by her good will,
By night and day; she hates the name of pewterer
More than sick men the noise, or diseas'd bones
That quake at fall o'th'hammer, seeming to have
A fellow-feeling with't at every blow.
What course shall I think on? She frets me so.
[*She stands aside.*]

Enter LEANTIO.

LEANTIO. How near am I now to a happiness
That earth exceeds not! Not another like it!
The treasures of the deep are not so precious
As are the conceal'd comforts of a man
Lock'd up in woman's love. I scent the air
Of blessings when I come but near the house.
What a delicious breath marriage sends forth!
The violet-bed's not sweeter. Honest wedlock
Is like a banqueting-house built in a garden,
On which the spring's chaste flowers take delight
To cast their modest odours; when base lust,

---

77 *pewterer*: a maker of inferior kitchen ware, pewter usually being an alloy of tin and lead. See Textual note, p. 406.

78 *the noise*: perhaps 'noise', or 'a band of musicians'.

86ff There is a general reminiscence of *Macbeth* I.vi.1–10.

90 *banqueting-house*: This was a favourite feature of Jacobean gardens, usually a semi-permanent structure in wood. The image is ironically appropriate, for the structures were notorious as places for illicit sexual encounters.

With all her powders, paintings and best pride,
Is but a fair house built by a ditch side.
When I behold a glorious dangerous strumpet,
Sparkling in beauty and destruction too,
Both at a twinkling, I do liken straight
Her beautified body to a goodly temple
That's built on vaults where carcasses lie rotting;
And so by little and little I shrink back again,
And quench desire with a cool meditation;
And I'm as well, methinks. Now for a welcome
Able to draw men's envies upon man:
A kiss now that will hang upon my lip
As sweet as morning dew upon a rose,
And full as long. After a five days' fast
She'll be so greedy now, and cling about me,
I take care how I shall be rid of her;
And here't begins.

[*Enter* BIANCA; MOTHER *comes forward.*]

BIANCA. Oh, sir, y'are welcome home.
MOTHER. Oh, is he come? I am glad on't.
LEANTIO. Is that all?
Why this as dreadful now as sudden death
To some rich man that flatters all his sins
With promise of repentance when he's old,
And dies in the midway before he comes to't.
Sure, y'are not well. Bianca! How dost, prithee?
BIANCA. I have been better than I am at this time.
LEANTIO. Alas, I thought so.
BIANCA. Nay, I have been worse too
Than now you see me, sir.
LEANTIO. I'm glad thou mend'st yet;
I feel my heart mend too. How came it to thee?

---

93 *pride*: finery.
94 *ditch side*: Both Moorditch and the City Ditch were clogged and stinking by the early seventeenth century.
98–9 The image derives from Matthew 23.27.
100 *shrink back again*: The allusion is to detumescence.
111 *this*: this is. See Textual note, p. 406. Middleton sometimes elided 'is' after 'this'.
116–17 *better . . . worse*: Beatrice alludes ironically to her spiritual health: 'better' before her seduction, 'worse' when she was in the act of adultery.

Has anything dislik'd thee in my absence?
BIANCA. No, certain; I have had the best content
That Florence can afford.
LEANTIO. Thou makest the best on't.
Speak, mother, what's the cause? You must needs know.
MOTHER. Troth, I know none, son; let her speak herself;
[*Aside*] Unless it be the same gave Lucifer
A tumbling-cast: that's pride.
BIANCA. Methinks this house stands nothing to my mind;
I'd have some pleasant lodging i'th'high street, sir,
Or if 'twere near the court, sir, that were much better:
'Tis a sweet recreation for a gentlewoman
To stand in a bay-window and see gallants.
LEANTIO. Now I have another temper, a mere stranger
To that of yours, it seems: I should delight
To see none but yourself.
BIANCA. I praise not that;
Too fond is as unseemly as too churlish;
I would not have a husband of that proneness
To kiss me before company, for a world!
Beside, 'tis tedious to see one thing still, sir,
Be it the best that ever heart affected;
Nay, were't yourself, whose love had power, you know,
To bring me from my friends, I would not stand thus
And gaze upon you always; troth, I could not, sir.
As good be blind and have no use of sight
As look on one thing still. What's the eye's treasure
But change of objects? You are learned, sir,
And know I speak not ill. 'Tis full as virtuous

---

120 *dislik'd*: displeased.
121–2 *the best content/That Florence can afford*: 'Florence' being the Duke, she suggests that she has had the highest quality of sexual satisfaction to be found.
126 *tumbling-cast*: wrestling throw.
127 *stands nothing to my mind*: 'is not situated as I would wish'.
131 *stand in a bay-window*: Italian women were known to be forbidden appearance near windows, and the stance Bianca proposes is notoriously that of whores.
136 *proneness*: tendency/lustful eagerness.
144–5 The doctrine is commonplace, and found in a variety of sources: Aristotle, *Rhetoric* I.ii.20 and Erasmus, *Adagia* I.vii.63; also Euripides, *Orestes*, line 234, Plutarch, *Moralia*, chap. 9, sec. 7c.

For woman's eye to look on several men,
As for her heart, sir, to be fixed on one.
LEANTIO. Now thou com'st home to me; a kiss for that word.
BIANCA. No matter for a kiss, sir; let it pass,
'Tis but a toy, we'll not so much as mind it;
Let's talk of other business and forget it.
What news now of the pirates; any stirring?
Prithee, discourse a little.
MOTHER. [*aside*] I am glad he's here yet
To see her tricks himself; I had lied monstrously
If I had told 'em first.
LEANTIO. Speak, what's the humour, sweet,
You make your lip so strange? This was not wont.
BIANCA. Is there no kindness betwixt man and wife
Unless they make a pigeon-house of friendship,
And be still billing? 'Tis the idlest fondness
That ever was invented, and 'tis pity
It's grown a fashion for poor gentlewomen;
There's many a disease kiss'd in a year by't,
And a French cur'sey made to't. Alas, sir,
Think of the world, how we shall live; grow serious;
We have been married a whole fortnight now.
LEANTIO. How? A whole fortnight! Why, is that so long?
BIANCA. 'Tis time to leave off dalliance; 'tis a doctrine
Of your own teaching, if you be rememb'red,
And I was bound to obey it.
MOTHER. Here's one fits him!
This was well catch'd, i'faith, son; like a fellow
That rids another country of a plague
And brings it home with him to his own house.
Knock within.

---

153 *pirates*: The Duke of Florence undertook to guard the coasts against African pirates; but the reference is topical, since piracy was rife on English shipping routes, and on 12 October 1620 a fleet under Sir Robert Mansell had set out in an attempt to scatter the pirates.

160 *fondness*: foolishness, foolish affection.

164 *French cur'sey*: The 'French disease' was syphilis, and the French were notorious for excessive courtesy; this is probably analogous to 'stoop gallant', I.ii.114 (i.e. both venereal disease, and 'bowing' in sexual intercourse).

170 *fits him*: 'punishes him suitably'.

Who knocks?
LEANTIO. Who's there now? Withdraw you, Bianca;
Thou art a gem no stranger's eye must see,
Howev'r thou please now to look dull on me.
Exit [BIANCA].

Enter MESSENGER.

Y'are welcome, sir; to whom your business, pray?
MESSENGER. To one I see not here now.
LEANTIO. Who should that be, sir?
MESSENGER. A young gentlewoman I was sent to.
LEANTIO. A young gentlewoman?
MESSENGER. Ay, sir, about sixteen. Why look you wildly, sir?
LEANTIO. At your strange error. Y'have mistook the house, sir;
There's none such here, I assure you.
MESSENGER. I assure you too:
The man that sent me cannot be mistook.
LEANTIO. Why, who is't sent you, sir?
MESSENGER. The duke.
LEANTIO. The duke!
MESSENGER. Yes, he entreats her company at a banquet
At Lady Livia's house.
LEANTIO. Troth, shall I tell you, sir,
It is the most erroneous business
That e'er your honest pains was abus'd with.
I pray forgive me if I smile a little
(I cannot choose, i'faith, sir) at an error
So comical as this (I mean no harm, though).
His grace has been most wondrous ill-inform'd;
Pray so return it, sir. What should her name be?
MESSENGER. That I shall tell you straight too: Bianca Capella.
LEANTIO. How, sir? Bianca? What do you call th'other?
MESSENGER. Capella. Sir, it seems you know no such, then?
LEANTIO. Who should this be? I never heard o'th'name.

---

176 See Textual note, p. 406.
186 *banquet*: here, 'a repast of sweetmeats, fruit and wine'.
194 *so return it*: 'Take that message back.'

MESSENGER. Then 'tis a sure mistake.
LEANTIO. What if you enquir'd
In the next street, sir? I saw gallants there
In the new houses that are built of late.
Ten to one, there you find her.
MESSENGER. Nay, no matter,
I will return the mistake and seek no further.
LEANTIO. Use your own will and pleasure, sir; y'are welcome.

Exit MESSENGER.

What shall I think of first? Come forth, Bianca.
Thou art betray'd, I fear me.

Enter BIANCA.

BIANCA. Betray'd? How, sir?
LEANTIO. The duke knows thee.
BIANCA. Knows me! How know you that, sir?
LEANTIO. H'as got thy name.
BIANCA. [*aside*] Ay, and my good name too,
That's worse o'th'twain.
LEANTIO. How comes this work about?
BIANCA. How should the duke know me? Can you guess, mother?
MOTHER. Not I with all my wits; sure, we kept house close.
LEANTIO. Kept close! Not all the locks in Italy
Can keep you women so. You have been gadding,
And ventur'd out at twilight to th'court-green yonder,
And met the gallant bowlers coming home;
Without your masks too, both of you, I'll be hang'd else!
Thou hast been seen, Bianca, by some stranger;
Never excuse it.
BIANCA. I'll not seek the way, sir.
Do you think y'have married me to mew me up
Not to be seen? What would you make of me?

---

207 *Knows me*: 'is acquainted/has had carnal knowledge of me'.
216 *masks*: Italian women wore masks or veils out of doors; masks had become the fashion in England by this time.
219 *mew*: immure, shut up (from the practice of putting hawks in a 'mew' or cage when 'mewing' or moulting).

LEANTIO. A good wife, nothing else.
BIANCA. Why, so are some
That are seen ev'ry day, else the devil take 'em.
LEANTIO. No more then: I believe all virtuous in thee
Without an argument. 'Twas but thy hard chance
To be seen somewhere; there lies all the mischief.
But I have devis'd a riddance.
MOTHER. Now I can tell you, son,
The time and place.
LEANTIO. When? Where?
MOTHER. What wits have I!
When you last took your leave, if you remember,
You left us both at window.
LEANTIO. Right, I know that.
MOTHER. And not the third part of an hour after,
The duke pass'd by in a great solemnity
To St Mark's temple; and to my apprehension
He look'd up twice to th'window.
LEANTIO. Oh, there quick'ned
The mischief of this hour.
BIANCA. [*aside*] If you call't mischief,
It is a thing I fear I am conceiv'd with.
LEANTIO. Look'd he up twice, and could you take no warning!
MOTHER. Why, once may do as much harm, son, as a thousand:
Do not you know one spark has fir'd an house,
As well as a whole furnace?
LEANTIO. My heart flames for't!
Yet let's be wise and keep all smother'd closely;
I have bethought a means. Is the door fast?
MOTHER. I lock'd it myself after him.
LEANTIO. You know, mother,
At the end of the dark parlour there's a place
So artificially contriv'd for a conveyance
No search could ever find it. When my father
Kept in for manslaughter, it was his sanctuary;
There will I lock my life's best treasure up.
Bianca!

---

233 *quick'ned*: took origin, life. The word is used of an embryo showing signs of life in the womb, hence Bianca's aside.
244 *artificially*: skilfully, cunningly; *conveyance*: secret passage.

BIANCA. Would you keep me closer yet?
Have you the conscience? Y'are best ev'n choke me up, sir!
You make me fearful of your health and wits,
You cleave to such wild courses. What's the matter?
LEANTIO. Why, are you so insensible of your danger
To ask that now? The duke himself has sent for you
To Lady Livia's, to a banquet, forsooth.
BIANCA. Now I beshrew you heartily, has he so!
And you the man would never yet vouchsafe
To tell me on't till now! You show your loyalty
And honesty at once; and so farewell, sir.
LEANTIO. Bianca, whither now?
BIANCA. Why, to the duke, sir.
You say he sent for me.
LEANTIO. But thou dost not mean
To go, I hope!
BIANCA. No? I shall prove unmannerly,
Rude and uncivil, mad, and imitate you.
Come, mother, come; follow his humour no longer.
We shall be all executed for treason shortly.
MOTHER. Not I, i'faith; I'll first obey the duke,
And taste of a good banquet; I'm of thy mind.
I'll step but up and fetch two handkerchiefs
To pocket up some sweetmeats, and o'ertake thee.
Exit.
BIANCA. [*aside*] Why, here's an old wench would trot into a bawd now
For some dry sucket or a colt in marchpane. *Exit.*
LEANTIO. O thou, the ripe time of man's misery, wedlock,
When all his thoughts, like over-laden trees,
Crack with the fruits they bear, in cares, in jealousies!
Oh that's a fruit that ripens hastily
After 'tis knit to marriage: it begins
As soon as the sun shines upon the bride
A little to show colour. Blessed powers,
Whence comes this alteration? The distractions,

---

270 *dry sucket*: candied fruit; *colt in marchpane*: a young horse made out of marzipan (such edible ornaments were common at 'banquets').

277 *a little to show colour*: i.e. 'Jealousy shows signs of ripening immediately after marriage'.

The fears and doubts it brings are numberless;
And yet the cause I know not. What a peace
Has he that never marries! If he knew
The benefit he enjoy'd, or had the fortune
To come and speak with me, he should know then
The infinite wealth he had, and discern rightly
The greatness of his treasure by my loss.
Nay, what a quietness has he 'bove mine
That wears his youth out in a strumpet's arms,
And never spends more care upon a woman
Than at the time of lust; but walks away,
And if he finds her dead at his return,
His pity is soon done: he breaks a sigh
In many parts, and gives her but a piece on't!
But all the fears, shames, jealousies, costs and troubles,
And still renew'd cares of a marriage bed
Live in the issue when the wife is dead.

Enter MESSENGER.

MESSENGER. A good perfection to your thoughts.
LEANTIO. The news, sir?
MESSENGER. Though you were pleas'd of late to pin an error on me,
You must not shift another in your stead too:
The duke has sent me for you.
LEANTIO. How, for me, sir?
[*Aside*] I see then 'tis my theft; w'are both betray'd.
Well, I'm not the first has stol'n away a maid:
My countrymen have us'd it. – I'll along with you, sir.
Exeunt.

SCENE II

A banquet prepared.
Enter GUARDIANO *and* WARD.

GUARDIANO. Take you especial note of such a gentlewoman,

---

295 *the issue*: the children.
296 *A good perfection*: a successful conclusion, or result.
298 *shift another in your stead too*: 'slip another trick across in your own case'/'substitute another person in your place'.
302 An allusion to the common Italian practice of abducting a girl and legalising the rape by marriage.

She's here on purpose; I have invited her,
Her father and her uncle, to this banquet.
Mark her behaviour well, it does concern you;
And what her good parts are, as far as time
And place can modestly require a knowledge of,
Shall be laid open to your understanding.
You know I'm both your guardian and your uncle:
My care of you is double, ward and nephew,
And I'll express it here.

WARD. 'Faith, I should know her
Now, by her mark, among a thousand women:
A little, pretty, deft and tidy thing, you say?

GUARDIANO. Right.

WARD. With a lusty sprouting sprig in her hair?

GUARDIANO. Thou goest the right way still; take one mark more:
Thou shalt nev'r find her hand out of her uncle's,
Or else his out of hers, if she be near him.
The love of kin'red never yet stuck closer
Than their's to one another; he that weds her
Marries her uncle's heart too.

Cornets.

WARD. Say you so, sir;
Then I'll be ask'd i'th'church to both of 'em.

GUARDIANO. Fall back, here comes the duke.

WARD. He brings a gentlewoman;
I should fall forward rather.

Enter DUKE, BIANCA, FABRITIO, HIPPOLITO, LIVIA, MOTHER, ISABELLA, *and* ATTENDANTS.

DUKE. Come, Bianca,
Of purpose sent into the world to show
Perfection once in woman; I'll believe

---

11 *mark*: description, distinctive characteristic.
12 *deft*: dainty and petite.
14 *a lusty sprouting sprig*: a large ornament in the form of a sprig or spray. Though diamond sprays were common, this is probably a spray of fresh flowers.

Henceforward they have ev'ry one a soul too,
'Gainst all the uncourteous opinions
That man's uncivil rudeness ever held of 'em.
Glory of Florence, light into mine arms!

Enter LEANTIO.

BIANCA. Yon comes a grudging man will chide you, sir.
The storm is now in's heart, and would get nearer
And fall here if it durst; it pours down yonder.
DUKE. If that be he, the weather shall soon clear;
List, and I'll tell thee how. [*Whispers to* BIANCA.]
LEANTIO. [*aside*] A-kissing too?
I see 'tis plain lust now, adultery bold'ned.
What will it prove anon, when 'tis stuff'd full
Of wine and sweetmeats, being so impudent fasting?
DUKE. We have heard of your good parts, sir, which we honour
With our embrace and love. – Is not the captainship
Of Rouans' citadel, since the late deceas'd,
Supplied by any yet?
GENTLEMAN. By none, my lord.
DUKE. [*to* LEANTIO] Take it, the place is yours, then; [LEANTIO *kneels.*]
and as faithfulness
And desert grows, our favour shall grow with't:
Rise now the captain of our fort at Rouans.
LEANTIO. The service of whole life give your grace thanks.
DUKE. Come, sit, Bianca.
LEANTIO. [*aside*] This is some good yet,
And more than ev'r I look'd for; a fine bit

---

28 *ev'ry one a soul too*: In Genesis 2.7 God breathed 'the breath of life' into Adam's nostrils, 'and man became a living soul'. Since there is no mention of God doing a similar office for Eve, a medieval debate grew up on whether woman could be said to have a soul, a question which became a stock misogynist insult by the early seventeenth century.

42, 46 *Rouans*: Fynes Moryson's *Itinerary* (1617), I, Book 2, p. 148, describes eight forts on the walls of Florence, the strongest lying to the south, an area where 'there is a place vulgarly called *le Ruinate*, that is, the ruinous . . . ' This may have suggested the name Rouans, 'ruins'. But see Textual note, p. 406.

To stay a cuckold's stomach. All preferment
That springs from sin and lust, it shoots up quickly,
As gardeners' crops do in the rotten'st grounds:
So is all means rais'd from base prostitution,
Ev'n like a sallet growing upon a dunghill.
I'm like a thing that never was yet heard of,
Half merry and half mad: much like a fellow
That eats his meat with a good appetite,
And wears a plague-sore that would fright a country;
Or rather like the barren, hard'ned ass,
That feeds on thistles till he bleeds again;
And such is the condition of my misery.

LIVIA. Is that your son, widow?

MOTHER. Yes, did your ladyship
Never know that till now?

LIVIA. No, trust me, did I.
[*Aside*] Nor ever truly felt the power of love
And pity to a man, till now I knew him.
I have enough to buy me my desires,
And yet to spare, that's one good comfort. – Hark you,
Pray let me speak with you, sir, before you go.

LEANTIO. With me, lady? You shall; I am at your service.
[*Aside*] What will she say now, trow? More goodness yet?

WARD. I see her now, I'm sure; the ape's so little, I shall scarce feel her. I have seen almost as tall as she sold in the fair for tenpence. See how she simpers it, as if marmalade would not melt in her mouth! She might have the kindness, i'faith, to send me a gilded bull from her own trencher, a ram, a goat, or somewhat to be nibbling; these women, when they come to sweet

---

54 *sallet*: green vegetable or herb used in salads.

59 *barren*: dull-witted.

70 *trow*: 'do you think?'

72–3 *sold in the fair for tenpence*: This is probably a reference to the 'Bartholomew babies' or dolls sold at the fair of that name. 'Sold for tenpence' is an equivalent of the modern 'not worth tuppence'; *marmalade*: preserve made by boiling down any fruit.

75 *a gilded bull*: a marzipan animal, coloured golden. The Ward would find such an emblem of lechery appropriate; but see Additional note, p. 411.

things once, they forget all their friends, they grow so greedy – nay, oftentimes their husbands.

DUKE. Here's a health now, gallants,
To the best beauty at this day in Florence.

BIANCA. Whoe'er she be, she shall not go unpledg'd, sir.

DUKE. Nay, you're excus'd for this.

BIANCA. Who, I, my lord?

DUKE. Yes, by the law of Bacchus; plead your benefit:
You are not bound to pledge your own health, lady.

BIANCA. That's a good way, my lord, to keep me dry.

DUKE. Nay then, I will not offend Venus so much;
Let Bacchus seek his 'mends in another court.
Here's to thyself, Bianca.

[*He drinks, then proffers the cup to* BIANCA.]

BIANCA. Nothing comes
More welcome to that name than your grace.

[*She drinks.*]

LEANTIO. [*aside*] So, so!
Here stands the poor thief now that stole the treasure,
And he's not thought on. Ours is near kin now
To a twin misery born into the world:
First the hard-conscienc'd worldling, he hoards wealth up;
Then comes the next, and he feasts all upon't;
One's damn'd for getting, th'other for spending on't.
O equal justice, thou hast met my sin
With a full weight! I'm rightly now oppress'd:
All her friends' heavy hearts lie in my breast.

DUKE. Methinks there is no spirit amongst us, gallants,
But what divinely sparkles from the eyes
Of bright Bianca: we sat all in darkness
But for that splendour. Who was't told us lately
Of a match-making rite, a marriage-tender?

GUARDIANO. 'Twas I, my lord.

---

84 *plead your benefit*: 'claim your exemption' (an allusion to 'benefit of clergy', by which the literate could claim exemption from the rigours of secular law by pleading that they were under ecclesiastical jurisdiction).

86 *dry*: sober, thirsty/frigid, lacking in emotion/lacking Venerean moisture.

88 *'mends*: legal remedy.

104 *a marriage-tender*: an offer of marriage.

DUKE. 'Twas you indeed. Where
is she?
GUARDIANO. This is the gentlewoman.
FABRITIO. My lord, my daughter.
DUKE. Why, here's some stirring yet.
FABRITIO. She's a dear child to me.
DUKE. That must needs be, you say she is your daughter.
FABRITIO. Nay, my good lord, dear to my purse, I mean,
Beside my person; I nev'r reckon'd that.
She has the full qualities of a gentlewoman:
I have brought her up to music, dancing, what not,
That may commend her sex and stir her husband.
DUKE. And which is he now?
GUARDIANO. This young heir, my lord.
DUKE. What is he brought up to?
HIPPOLITO. [*aside*] To cat and trap.
GUARDIANO. My lord, he's a great ward, wealthy but
simple;
His parts consist in acres.
DUKE. Oh, wise-acres!
GUARDIANO. Y'have spoke him in a word, sir.
BIANCA. 'Las, poor gentlewoman,
She's ill bestead, unless sh'as dealt the wiselier
And laid in more provision for her youth:
Fools will not keep in summer.
LEANTIO. [*aside*] No, nor such wives
From whores in winter.
DUKE. Yea, the voice too, sir?
FABRITIO. Ay, and a sweet breast too, my lord, I hope,

---

107 *some stirring yet*: i.e. 'Here's some life', in contrast to the complaint of line 100; but with the further implication: 'Here is something sexually stimulating.'

115 *cat and trap*: For details of these games, see Additional note, p. 411.

117 *parts*: qualities, accomplishments.

119 *ill bestead*: ill-situated.

121 *Fools will not keep in summer*: 'Keep' also means 'stay within doors', and the allusion is to the bands of idiots who roamed England in the summer months. There is, in addition, a pun on 'fool', the fruit and cream dish.

122 *whores*: There is a probable pun on the homophone 'hoars' = hoar-frosts.

123 *breast*: singing voice; but an old-fashioned expression, witness lines 159–62.

Or I have cast away my money wisely;
She took her pricksong earlier, my lord,
Than any of her kin'red ever did.
A rare child, though I say't, but I'd not have
The baggage hear so much; 'twould make her swell
straight;
And maids of all things must not be puff'd up.

DUKE. Let's turn us to a better banquet, then;
For music bids the soul of a man to a feast,
And that's indeed a noble entertainment
Worthy Bianca's self. You shall perceive, beauty,
Our Florentine damsels are not brought up idlely.

BIANCA. They are wiser of themselves, it seems, my lord,
And can take gifts, when goodness offers 'em.

Music.

LEANTIO. [*aside*] True; and damnation has taught you
that wisdom,
You can take gifts too. Oh that music mocks me!

LIVIA. [*aside*] I am as dumb to any language now
But love's, as one that never learn'd to speak.
I am not yet so old but he may think of me.
My own fault, I have been idle a long time;
But I'll begin the week and paint tomorrow,
So follow my true labour day by day;
I never thriv'd so well as when I used it.

[ISABELLA.]

Song

What harder chance can fall to woman,
Who was born to cleave to some man,
Than to bestow her time, youth, beauty,
Life's observance, honour, duty,
On a thing for no use good,
But to make physic work, or blood
Force fresh in an old lady's cheek?

125–9 *pricksong*: written music, 'pricked' into the paper: Bianca learned sight-reading early. A run of sexual innuendoes (on 'prick' = penis, 'swell', 'be puff'd up' = to be pregnant) is apparent only to the audience.

146–59 See Textual note, p. 406.

151 *physic*: laxative. Mild excitement was held to increase its efficacy. Isabella credits the Ward with the ability only to stir this amount of interest, or to make an old woman blush: he is incapable of provoking real erotic excitement.

She that would be
Mother of fools, let her compound with me.
WARD. [*speaking whilst she sings*] Here's a tune indeed!
Pish! I had rather hear one ballad sung i'th'nose now, of the lamentable drowning of fat sheep and oxen, than all these simpering tunes play'd upon cats' guts and sung by little kitlings.
FABRITIO. How like you her breast now, my lord?
BIANCA. [*to the* DUKE] Her breast!
He talks as if his daughter had given suck
Before she were married, as her betters have;
The next he praises sure will be her nipples.
DUKE. [*to* BIANCA] Methinks now, such a voice to such a husband
Is like a jewel of unvalued worth
Hung at a fool's ear.
FABRITIO. May it please your grace
To give her leave to show another quality?
DUKE. Marry, as many good ones as you will, sir;
The more the better welcome.
LEANTIO. [*aside*] But the less
The better practis'd. That soul's black indeed
That cannot commend virtue. But who keeps it?
The extortioner will say to a sick beggar
'Heaven comfort thee', though he give none himself.
This good is common.
FABRITIO. Will it please you now, sir,
To entreat your ward to take her by the hand
And lead her in a dance before the duke?
GUARDIANO. That will I, sir; 'tis needful. – Hark you, nephew.
FABRITIO. Nay, you shall see, young heir, what y'have for your money,
Without fraud or imposture.

---

154 *compound*: 'come to an agreement (to take my place)'.

159 *little kitlings*: little cats, i.e. little whores, but with an allusion to the piercing tone of 'kits', miniature violins.

169–70 *But the less/The better practis'd*: Good qualities would be less welcome to the Duke if actually exercised. Leantio comments that few 'keep', observe virtue, though all but the most depraved can pay lip-service: '*this* good is common'.

WARD. Dance with her!
Not I, sweet guardiner, do not urge my heart to't,
'Tis clean against my blood. Dance with a stranger!
Let whos' will do't, I'll not begin first with her.
HIPPOLITO. [*aside*] No, fear't not, fool; sh'as took a better order.
GUARDIANO. Why, who shall take her, then?
WARD. Some other gentleman.
Look, there's her uncle, a fine-timber'd reveller;
Perhaps he knows the manner of her dancing too;
I'll have him do't before me. I have sworn, guardiner;
Then may I learn the better.
GUARDIANO. Thou'lt be an ass still.
WARD. Ay, all that, uncle, shall not fool me out:
Pish, I stick closer to myself than so.
GUARDIANO. [*to* HIPPOLITO] I must entreat you, sir, to take your niece
And dance with her. My ward's a little wilful;
He would have you show him the way.
HIPPOLITO. Me, sir?
He shall command it at all hours; pray tell him so.
GUARDIANO. I thank you for him; he has not wit himself, sir.
HIPPOLITO. [*aside to* ISABELLA] Come, my life's peace; I have a strange office on't here.
'Tis some man's luck to keep the joys he likes
Conceal'd for his own bosom, but my fortune
To set 'em out now for another's liking:
Like the mad misery of necessitous man,
That parts from his good horse with many praises,
And goes on foot himself. Need must be obey'd
In ev'ry action, it mars man and maid.

---

181 *blood*: disposition, temper; see Additional note, p. 410.
183 *sh'as took a better order*: she has made better arrangements, by 'dancing' with Hippolito first.
184 *take*: lead in the dance//enjoy sexually.
185 *fine-timber'd*: well-built.
186–7 See Additional note, p. 411.
189–90 'All your insults, uncle, will not fool me into changing my mind: I hold more firmly to my resolutions than that.' See also Textual note, p. 406.
202 *Need*: necessity. The axiom is strongly deterministic.

Music. A dance [*by* HIPPOLITO *and* ISABELLA], *making honours to the* DUKE *and cur'sey to themselves, both before and after.*

DUKE. Signor Fabritio, y'are a happy father,
Your cares and pains are fortunate; you see
Your cost bears noble fruits. Hippolito, thanks.
FABRITIO. Here's some amends for all my charges yet:
She wins both prick and praise where'er she comes.
DUKE. How lik'st, Bianca?
BIANCA. All things well, my lord,
But this poor gentlewoman's fortune; that's the worst.
DUKE. There is no doubt, Bianca, she'll find leisure
To make that good enough; he's rich and simple.
BIANCA. She has the better hope o'th'upper hand, indeed,
Which women strive for most.
GUARDIANO. [*to* WARD] Do't when I bid you, sir.
WARD. I'll venture but a hornpipe with her, guardiner,
Or some such married man's dance.
GUARDIANO. Well, venture something, sir.
WARD. I have rhyme for what I do.
GUARDIANO. But little reason, I think.
WARD. Plain men dance the measures, the cinquepace the gay;
Cuckolds dance the hornpipe; and farmers dance the hay;
Your soldiers dance the round, and maidens that grow big;

---

s.d. *honours*: bows.

208 *prick and praise*: 'Prick' is the centre of an archery butt, so the phrase comes to mean 'success and its acknowledgement'. There is also an obscene innuendo unrecognised by Fabritio.

218 *the measures*: a stately dance in five movements, old-fashioned, suitable for the staid; *the cinquepace*: a primitive galliard, with four hops and a jump, in fast time.

219 *the hornpipe*: a vigorous dance, usually solo, and because of its name, suitable for lonely cuckolds; *the hay*: a rustic dance with a winding, serpentine movement.

220 *the round*: a circling dance; also, a military patrol inspecting sentinels.

You[r] drunkards, the canaries; you[r] whore and bawd, the jig.
Here's your eight kind of dancers, he that finds the ninth,
Let him pay the minstrels.

DUKE. Oh, here he appears once in his own person!
I thought he would have married her by attorney,
And lain with her so too.

BIANCA. Nay, my kind lord,
There's very seldom any found so foolish
To give away his part there.

LEANTIO. [*aside*] Bitter scoff!
Yet I must do't. With what a cruel pride
The glory of her sin strikes by my afflictions!

Music. WARD *and* ISABELLA *dance; he ridiculously imitates* HIPPOLITO.

DUKE. This thing will make shift, sirs, to make a husband,
For aught I see in him. How think'st, Bianca?

BIANCA. 'Faith, an ill-favoured shift, my lord. Methinks
If he would take some voyage when he's married,
Dangerous, or long enough, and scarce be seen
Once in nine year together, a wife then
Might make indifferent shift to be content with him.

DUKE. A kiss! [*Kisses* BIANCA] That wit deserves to be made much on.
Come, our caroche!

GUARDIANO. Stands ready for your grace.

DUKE. My thanks to all your loves. Come, fair Bianca;
We have took special care of you, and provided
Your lodging near us now.

BIANCA. Your love is great, my lord.

DUKE. Once more, our thanks to all.

---

221 *the canaries*: a quick dance thought to come from the Canaries/light, sweet wines from the Canary Islands; *the jig*: a lively dance, rapid and jerky, often associated with lewdness. See also Textual note, p. 406.

225 *by attorney*: by proxy.

230 *glory*: boastfulness; *strikes by*: passes by without regard (cf. *Mad World*, IV.i.85).

231 *shift*: a poor attempt.

233 *ill-favoured shift*: an objectionable attempt/an ugly, offensive substitute/an objectionable change of clothes.

239 *caroche*: a stately kind of coach.

OMNES. All blest honours guard you.

Cornets flourish.

Exeunt all but LEANTIO *and* LIVIA.

LEANTIO. [*to himself*] Oh, hast thou left me then, Bianca, utterly!
Bianca! Now I miss thee. Oh return,
And save the faith of woman! I nev'r felt
The loss of thee till now; 'tis an affliction
Of greater weight than youth was made to bear;
As if a punishment of after-life
Were fall'n upon man here, so new it is
To flesh and blood, so strange, so insupportable;
A torment ev'n mistook, as if a body
Whose death were drowning, must needs therefore suffer it
In scalding oil.

LIVIA. Sweet sir!

LEANTIO. [*to himself*] As long as mine eye saw thee,
I half enjoy'd thee.

LIVIA. Sir?

LEANTIO. [*to himself*] Canst thou forget
The dear pains my love took, how it has watch'd
Whole nights together, in all weathers, for thee,
Yet stood in heart more merry than the tempests
That sung about mine ears (like dangerous flatterers
That can set all their mischief to sweet tunes);
And then receiv'd thee from thy father's window
Into these arms at midnight, when we embrac'd
As if we had been statues only made for't,
To show art's life, so silent were our comforts;
And kiss'd as if our lips had grown together?

LIVIA. [*aside*] This makes me madder to enjoy him now.

---

252 *a torment ev'n mistook*: a mistaken torment. It was often believed that the mode of a man's death was written in his features; this suffering is as mistaken as if a man whose destiny was to drown should undergo it in boiling oil (a fate more appropriate to the 'after-life', the pains of Hell).

259–60 I.e. the tempests, though 'merry' and 'singing about his ears', were (like flatterers) doing damage under the cover of pleasing sound. Leantio's courtship is associated with superficial pleasure concealing destruction.

264 *To show art's life*: to demonstrate how lifelike the artist could make his creation.

LEANTIO. [*to himself*] Canst thou forget all this? And better joys
That we met after this, which then new kisses
Took pride to praise?
LIVIA. [*aside*] I shall grow madder yet. – Sir!
LEANTIO. [*to himself*] This cannot be but of some close bawd's working.
– Cry mercy, lady. What would you say to me?
My sorrow makes me so unmannerly,
So comfort bless me, I had quite forgot you.
LIVIA. Nothing but, ev'n in pity to that passion,
Would give your grief good counsel.
LEANTIO. Marry, and welcome, lady;
It never could come better.
LIVIA. Then first, sir,
To make away all your good thoughts at once of her,
Know most assuredly she is a strumpet.
LEANTIO. Ha! 'most assuredly'! Speak not a thing
So vild so certainly; leave it more doubtful.
LIVIA. Then I must leave all truth, and spare my knowledge
A sin which I too lately found and wept for.
LEANTIO. Found you it?
LIVIA. Ay, with wet eyes.
LEANTIO. O perjurious friendship!
LIVIA. You miss'd your fortunes when you met with her, sir:
Young gentlemen that only love for beauty,
They love not wisely; such a marriage rather
Proves the destruction of affection:
It brings on want, and want's the key of whoredom.
I think y'had small means with her?
LEANTIO. Oh, not any, lady.
LIVIA. Alas, poor gentleman! What meant'st thou, sir,
Quite to undo thyself with thine own kind heart?
Thou art too good and pitiful to woman.
Marry, sir, thank thy stars for this blest fortune
That rids the summer of thy youth so well

270 *close*: secret, furtive.
280 *vild*: vile.

From many beggars, that had lain a-sunning
In thy beams only else, till thou hadst wasted
The whole days of thy life in heat and labour.
What would you say now to a creature found
As pitiful to you, and as it were
Ev'n sent on purpose from the whole sex general
To requite all that kindness you have shown to't?

LEANTIO. What's that, madam?

LIVIA. Nay, a gentlewoman,
And one able to reward good things; ay,
And bears a conscience to't. Couldst thou love such a one
That, blow all fortunes, would never see thee want?
Nay more, maintain thee to thine enemy's envy?
And shalt not spend a care for't, stir a thought,
Nor break a sleep, unless love's music waked thee;
No storm of fortune should. Look upon me,
And know that woman.

LEANTIO. Oh! My life's wealth, Bianca!

LIVIA. Still with her name? Will nothing wear it out?
That deep sigh went but for a strumpet, sir.

LEANTIO. It can go for no other that loves me.

LIVIA. [*aside*] He's vex'd in mind; I came too soon to him.
Where's my discretion now, my skill, my judgement?
I'm cunning in all arts but my own love.
'Tis as unseasonable to tempt him now,
So soon, as a widow to be courted
Following her husband's corse, or to make bargain
By the grave-side, and take a young man there:
Her strange departure stands like a hearse yet

---

295 *beggars*: i.e. impoverished relatives: Bianca and her offspring.
296 *wasted*: squandered/emaciated.
297 *The whole days*: all the days/the healthy days; the 'heat and labour' of commercial and sexual toil would consume him.
304 *bears a conscience to't*: would see it as a duty.
305 *blow all fortunes*: 'come what may', 'let the wind whistle'.
321 *strange*: like a stranger/as yet unfamiliar to him/peculiar. ('Strange' is frequent in these senses in the play).
hearse: a wooden structure erected over the coffin of eminent people, often covered with verses and epitaphs, and allowed to stand for a while in the dead person's parish church before being 'taken down'.

Before his eyes, which time will take down shortly.
Exit.
LEANTIO. Is she my wife till death, yet no more mine?
That's a hard measure. Then what's marriage good for?
Methinks by right I should not now be living,
And then 'twere all well. What a happiness
Had I been made of, had I never seen her;
For nothing makes man's loss grievous to him
But knowledge of the worth of what he loses:
For what he never had, he never misses.
She's gone for ever, utterly; there is
As much redemption of a soul from hell
As a fair woman's body from his palace.
Why should my love last longer than her truth?
What is there good in woman to be lov'd
When only that which makes her so has left her?
I cannot love her now, but I must like
Her sin and my own shame too, and be guilty
Of law's breach with her, and mine own abusing;
All which were monstrous. Then my safest course,
For health of mind and body, is to turn
My heart and hate her, most extremely hate her;
I have no other way. Those virtuous powers
Which were chaste witnesses of both our troths
Can witness she breaks first. And I'm rewarded
With captainship o'th'fort! A place of credit,
I must confess, but poor; my factorship
Shall not exchange means with't; he that died last in't,
He was no drunkard, yet he died a beggar
For all his thrift. Besides, the place not fits me:
It suits my resolution, not my breeding.

325–6 See Additional note, p. 411.

332 An allusion to the proverb: 'There's no redemption from hell' (Tilley, R 60).

335–6 A reference to Neo-Platonic doctrine, which sees physical beauty as the expression of human virtue.

337 *but*: unless.

338–9 *be guilty/Of law's breach with her*: i.e. by condoning adultery.

346–8 *A place of credit,/ . . . my factorship/Shall not exchange means with 't*: a position of honour, but not one to be compared with the post of merchant's agent in terms of financial reward.

351 *It suits my resolution . . . breeding*: 'It fits my courage, but not my low birth.'

Enter LIVIA.

LIVIA. [*aside*] I have tried all ways I can, and have not power
To keep from sight of him. – How are you now, sir?
LEANTIO. I feel a better ease, madam.
LIVIA. Thanks to blessedness!
You will do well, I warrant you, fear it not, sir.
Join but your own good will to't. He's not wise
That loves his pain or sickness, or grows fond
Of a disease whose property is to vex him
And spitefully drink his blood up. Out upon't, sir,
Youth knows no greater loss. I pray let's walk, sir.
You never saw the beauty of my house yet,
Nor how abundantly fortune has bless'd me
In worldly treasure; trust me, I have enough, sir,
To make my friend a rich man in my life,
A great man at my death; yourself will say so.
If you want anything, and spare to speak,
Troth, I'll condemn you for a wilful man, sir.
LEANTIO. Why sure, this can be but the flattery of some dream.
LIVIA. Now by this kiss, my love, my soul and riches,
'Tis all true substance. [*Kisses him.*]
Come, you shall see my wealth, take what you list;
The gallanter you go, the more you please me.
I will allow you, too, your page and footman,
Your race-horses, or any various pleasure
Exercis'd youth delights in. But to me
Only, sir, wear your heart of constant stuff;
Do but you love enough, I'll give enough.
LEANTIO. Troth then, I'll love enough and take enough.
LIVIA. Then we are both pleas'd enough.

Exeunt.

359–60 *spitefully drink his blood up . . . knows no greater loss*: In Renaissance physiology, frustrated passion was held to dry up the life-blood.

364 *friend*: lover.

376 *wear your heart of constant stuff*: i.e. of one colour, as opposed to cloths of 'changeable stuff' like 'changeable taffeta', a silk which, because it changes colour according to the light, is used as an emblem of infidelity. The metaphor may derive ultimately from the practice of wearing liveries to denote allegiance.

SCENE III

Enter GUARDIANO *and* ISABELLA *at one door, and the* WARD *and* SORDIDO *at another.*

GUARDIANO. Now, nephew, here's the gentlewoman again.
WARD. Mass, here she's come again. Mark her now, Sordido.
GUARDIANO. This is the maid my love and care has chose
Out for your wife, and so I tender her to you;
Yourself has been eye-witness of some qualities
That speak a courtly breeding, and are costly.
I bring you both to talk together now;
'Tis time you grew familiar in your tongues:
Tomorrow you join hands, and one ring ties you,
And one bed holds you (if you like the choice).
Her father and her friends are i'th'next room,
And stay to see the contract ere they part;
Therefore dispatch, good ward, be sweet and short.
Like her or like her not, there's but two ways;
And one your body, th'other your purse pays.
WARD. I warrant you, guardiner, I'll not stand all day thrumming,
But quickly shoot my bolt at your next coming.
GUARDIANO. Well said! Good fortune to your birding then. [*Exit*.]
WARD. I never miss'd mark yet.
SORDIDO. Troth, I think, master, if the truth were known, you never shot at any but the kitchen-wench,

---

16 *one your body, th'other your purse pays*: The Ward either marries the bride offered to him, or pays his guardian a fine. See note to I.ii.3–10.

17 *thrumming*: time-wasting (the nap or thrum of a felt hat was raised by rubbing; consequently 'thrumming of hats', the turning of a hat in the hands, became proverbial for indecision).

18 *shoot my bolt*: clinch the deal/fire my cross-bow shot/ejaculate. The 'bird-bolt' was a blunt-headed arrow used for fowling, and was traditionally part of Cupid's armoury. Hence Guardiano's reply, where 'birding' also means 'wenching'. There is also ironic allusion to the proverb: 'A fool's bolt is soon shot' (Tilley, F 515).

20 *mark*: target/the female pudendum.

and that was a she-woodcock, a mere innocent, that was oft lost and cried at eight and twenty.

WARD. No more of that meat, Sordido, here's eggs o'th' spit now; we must turn gingerly. Draw out the catalogue of all the faults of women.

SORDIDO. How, all the faults! Have you so little reason to think so much paper will lie in my breeches? Why, ten carts will not carry it, if you set down but the bawds. All the faults! Pray let's be content with a few of 'em; and if they were less, you would find 'em enough, I warrant you. Look you, sir.

ISABELLA. [*aside*] But that I have th'advantage of the fool
As much as woman's heart can wish and joy at,
What an infernal torment 'twere to be
Thus bought and sold and turn'd and pried into; when, alas,
The worst bit is too good for him! And the comfort is,
H'as but a cater's place on't, and provides
All for another's table; yet how curious
The ass is, like some nice professor on't,
That buys up all the daintiest food i'th'markets
And seldom licks his lips after a taste on't.

SORDIDO. Now to her, now y'have scann'd all her parts over.

WARD. But at [what] end shall I begin now, Sordido?

SORDIDO. Oh, ever at a woman's lip, while you live, sir; do you ask that question?

WARD. Methinks, Sordido, sh'as but a crabbed face to begin with.

SORDIDO. A crabbed face? That will save money.

WARD. How, save money, Sordido?

23–4 *a she-woodcock . . . cried at eight-and-twenty*: a simpleton (the bird being proverbially easy to snare) whose loss was announced by the town-crier (the practice when small children strayed). *Innocent* has here the sense of 'half-wit'.

25–6 *eggs o'th'spit*: Proverbial (Tilley, E.86), meaning 'to have delicate business in hand'.

39 *cater's place*: the position of one who bought provisions for a large household.

40 *curious*: pernickety.

41 *nice professor*: fastidious expert.

SORDIDO. Ay, sir; for having a crabbed face of her own, she'll eat the less verjuice with her mutton: 'twill save verjuice at year's end, sir.

WARD. Nay, and your jests begin to be saucy once, I'll make you eat your meat without mustard.

SORDIDO. And that in some kind is a punishment.

WARD. Gentlewoman, they say 'tis your pleasure to be my wife; and you shall know shortly whether it be mine or no to be your husband. And thereupon thus I first enter upon you. [*Kisses her*] Oh most delicious scent! Methinks it tasted as if a man had stepped into a comfit-maker's shop to let a cart go by, all the while I kiss'd her. It is reported, gentlewoman, you'll run mad for me, if you have me not.

ISABELLA. I should be in great danger of my wits, sir,
For being so forward. [*Aside*] Should this ass kick
backward now!

WARD. Alas, poor soul. And is that hair your own?

ISABELLA. Mine own? Yes, sure, sir; I owe nothing for't.

WARD. 'Tis a good hearing; I shall have the less to pay when I have married you. [*To* SORDIDO] Look, does her eyes stand well?

SORDIDO. They cannot stand better than in her head, I think; where would you have them? And for her nose, 'tis of a very good last.

WARD. I have known as good as that has not lasted a year, though.

---

54 *verjuice*: the acid juice of sour fruit, here crab-apples (hence Sordido's joke), and used as a sauce to meat (hence the Ward's reply).

64 *comfit-maker*: a confectioner, comfits being fruit preserved in sugar.

67–8 'I should be likely to go out of my mind as a result of being so eager/I should be crazy to be so presumptuous.' The aside adds a further ambiguity: 'I would be in danger of being knocked unconscious by this ass's hoofs should I come too close.'

70 *I owe nothing for't*: I.e. 'I don't owe anything to a wig maker.' The Ward's question is offensive, for loss of hair was one symptom of venereal disease.

71 *hearing*: punning on 'hairing', which in some pronunciations was a homophone.

72–3 *does her eyes stand well*: 'Are her eyes well-positioned?' 'Eye' = also, female pudendum.

76 *last*: pattern (alluding to the shoemaker's last).

SORDIDO. That's in the using of a thing; will not any strong bridge fall down in time, if we do nothing but beat at the bottom? A nose of buff would not last always, sir, especially if it came into th'camp once.

WARD. But Sordido, how shall we do to make her laugh, that I may see what teeth she has? For I'll not bate her a tooth, nor take a black one into th'bargain.

SORDIDO. Why, do but you fall in talk with her; you cannot choose but one time or other make her laugh, sir.

WARD. It shall go hard, but I will. – Pray what qualities have you beside singing and dancing? Can you play at shittlecock, forsooth?

ISABELLA. Ay, and at stool-ball too, sir; I have great luck at it.

WARD. Why, can you catch a ball well?

ISABELLA. I have catch'd two in my lap at one game.

WARD. What, have you, woman? I must have you learn to play at trap too, then y'are full and whole.

ISABELLA. Anything that you please to bring me up to I shall take pains to practise.

WARD. [*aside to* SORDIDO] 'Twill not do, Sordido; we shall never get her mouth open'd wide enough.

SORDIDO. No, sir? That's strange! Then here's a trick for your learning.

He yawns [ISABELLA *yawns too, but covers her mouth*].

Look now, look now! quick, quick there.

WARD. Pox of that scurvy, mannerly trick with handkerchief; it hind'red me a little, but I am satisfied. When a fair woman gapes and stops her mouth so, it shows like a cloth stopple in a cream-pot. I have fair hope of her teeth now, Sordido.

79–82 The bridge of the nose was especially vulnerable to syphilis, a disease rife among camp-followers. *Buff* is a stout leather made from ox-hide and used for military uniforms.

84 *bate*: 'allow her to be deficient in'.

90–4 *shittlecock . . . stool-ball . . . two in my lap at one game*: The last exchange makes the allusions to sexual intercourse obvious. For *shittlecock* see the note at II.ii.84–5; *stool-ball* was a country game played chiefly by women and resembled cricket: one player defends a stool, and is out if the ball hits it or is caught from her hand.

96 *trap*: See Additional note, p. 411.

106 *stopple*: stopper.

SORDIDO. Why, then y'have all well, sir, for aught I see.
She's right and straight enough now, as she stands.
They'll commonly lie crooked, that's no matter; wise
gamesters never find fault with that, let 'em lie still so.
WARD. I'd fain mark how she goes, and then I have all;
for of all creatures I cannot abide a splay-footed
woman: she's an unlucky thing to meet in a morning;
her heels keep together so, as if she were beginning an
Irish dance still, and the wriggling of her bum playing
the tune to't. But I have bethought a cleanly shift to
find it: dab down as you see me, and peep of one side
when her back's toward you; I'll show you the way.
SORDIDO. And you shall find me apt enough to peeping;
I have been one of them has seen mad sights
Under your scaffolds.
WARD. [*to* ISABELLA] Will it please you walk, forsooth,
A turn or two by yourself? You are so pleasing to me,
I take delight to view you on both sides.
ISABELLA. I shall be glad to fetch a walk to your love, sir;
'Twill get affection a good stomach, sir.
[*Aside*] Which I had need have, to fall to such coarse victuals.

[*She walks about, whilst they bob down to look at her legs.*]

WARD. Now go thy ways for a clean-treading wench,
As ever man in modesty peep'd under!
SORDIDO. I see the sweetest sight to please my master:
Never went Frenchman righter upon ropes
Than she on Florentine rushes.
WARD. [*to* ISABELLA] 'Tis enough, forsooth,

---

111 *gamesters*: sexual sportsmen.
113 *splay-footed*: Feet which turned out when walking were believed to be one mark of a witch.
116 *Irish dance*: the position described, with the right heel tucked into the left instep, commences the traditional dances from Ireland which were much in vogue in the last years of Elizabeth's reign.
117 *cleanly shift*: neat trick.
118 *dab*: bob.
122 *scaffolds*: raised platforms or stands for holding spectators.
131 *Frenchman . . . upon ropes*: Walking or dancing upon the tightrope, especially by visiting French performers, was a popular Court and City entertainment.
132 *rushes*: used as floor-covering in houses, and also on stage.

ISABELLA. And how do you like me now, sir?
WARD. 'Faith, so well
I never mean to part with thee, sweetheart,
Under some sixteen children, and all boys.
ISABELLA. You'll be at simple pains, if you prove kind,
And breed 'em all in your teeth.
WARD. Nay, by my faith,
What serves your belly for? 'Twould make my cheeks
Look like blown bagpipes.

Enter GUARDIANO.

GUARDIANO. How now, ward and nephew,
Gentlewoman and niece! Speak, is it so or not?
WARD. 'Tis so; we are both agreed, sir.
GUARDIANO. In to your kin'red, then;
There's friends, and wine and music, waits to welcome
you.
WARD. Then I'll be drunk for joy.
SORDIDO. And I for company;
I cannot break my nose in a better action.
Exeunt.

ACT IV

SCENE I

Enter BIANCA *attended by two* LADIES.

BIANCA. How goes your watches, ladies; what's a'clock
now?

136 *at simple pains, if you prove kind*: 'in extreme pain if you are affectionate'/'in the pain appropriate to an idiot, if you run true to type'. Isabella alludes to the belief that a fond husband had toothache when his wife was pregnant.

144 *break my nose in a better action*: 'suffer in a better cause', alluding to the blood-red nose resulting from too many confrontations with the bottle.

1–18 *watches*: These stand also for women, as do 'clocks' for men (both being notoriously unreliable); 'to set one's watch' by men means to sleep with them. Bianca claims a greater moral rectitude, since she 'sets' by the sun (the Duke – who is apparently undemanding).

1 LADY. By mine, full nine.
2 LADY. By mine, a quarter past.
1 LADY. I set mine by St Mark's.
2 LADY. St Antony's,
They say, goes truer.
1 LADY. That's but your opinion, madam,
Because you love a gentleman o'th'name.
2 LADY. He's a true gentleman, then.
1 LADY. So may he be
That comes to me tonight, for aught you know.
BIANCA. I'll end this strife straight. I set mine by the sun;
I love to set by th' best, one shall not then
Be troubled to set often.
2 LADY. You do wisely in't.
BIANCA. If I should set my watch as some girls do
By ev'ry clock i'th'town, 'twould nev'r go true;
And too much turning of the dial's point,
Or tamp'ring with the spring, might in small time
Spoil the whole work too. Here it wants of nine now.
1 LADY. It does indeed, forsooth; mine's nearest truth yet.
2 LADY. Yet I have found her lying with an advocate, which show'd
Like two false clocks together in one parish.
BIANCA. So now, I thank you, ladies. I desire
A while to be alone.
1 LADY. And I am nobody,
Methinks, unless I have one or other with me;
'Faith, my desire and hers will nev'r be sisters.
Ex[*eunt*] LADIES.
BIANCA. How strangely woman's fortune comes about!
This was the farthest way to come to me,
All would have judg'd that knew me born in Venice;
And there with many jealous eyes brought up,
That never thought they had me sure enough
But when they were upon me; yet my hap
To meet it here, so far off from my birthplace,
My friends or kin'red. 'Tis not good, in sadness,
To keep a maid so strict in her young days;

13–14 *dial's point . . . spring*: the male and female genitals.
30 *in sadness*: seriously.

Restraint breeds wand'ring thoughts, as many fasting
days
A great desire to see flesh stirring again.
I'll nev'r use any girl of mine so strictly;
Howev'r they're kept, their fortunes find 'em out;
I see't in me. If they be got in court,
I'll never forbid 'em the country; nor the court,
Though they be born i'th'country. They will come to't,
And fetch their falls a thousand mile about,
Where one would little think on't.

Enter LEANTIO *[richly dressed]*.

LEANTIO. I long to see how my despiser looks,
Now she's come here to court. These are her lodgings.
She's simply now advanc'd; I took her out
Of no such window, I remember, first:
That was a great deal lower, and less carv'd.
BIANCA. How now? What silkworm's this, i'th'name of
pride?
What, is it he?
LEANTIO. A bow i'th'ham to your greatness;
You must have now three legs, I take it, must you not?
BIANCA. Then I must take another, I shall want else
The service I should have; you have but two there.
LEANTIO. Y'are richly placed.
BIANCA. Methinks y'are wondrous
brave, sir.
LEANTIO. A sumptuous lodging!
BIANCA. Y'ave an excellent suit there.
LEANTIO. A chair of velvet!

32–3 *fasting days . . . see flesh stirring*: From 1608 onwards Acts forbidding the killing and eating of meat in Lent were more strictly enforced. See *A Chaste Maid*, II.ii. There is also a bawdy allusion to tumescence in 'stirring'.

39 *fetch their falls a thousand mile about*: i.e. make a thousand mile detour to achieve the loss of their virtue.

43 *simply*: absolutely.

46 *silkworm*: used contemptuously of a dandy who dressed in silk.

48–50 *three legs*: three bows, but obscenely interpreted by Bianca as 'two legs and the penis': the third leg she will have to seek elsewhere, if she wants the 'service' (= deference/ sexual satisfaction) she should have.

51 *brave*: finely dressed.

BIANCA. Is your cloak lin'd through, sir?
LEANTIO. Y'are very stately here.
BIANCA. 'Faith, something proud, sir.
LEANTIO. Stay, stay; let's see your cloth-of-silver slippers.
BIANCA. Who's your shoemaker? H'as made you a neat boot.
LEANTIO. Will you have a pair? The duke will lend you spurs.
BIANCA. Yes, when I ride.
LEANTIO. 'Tis a brave life you lead.
BIANCA. I could nev'r see you in such good clothes
In my time.
LEANTIO. In your time?
BIANCA. Sure, I think, sir,
We both thrive best asunder.
LEANTIO. Y'are a whore!
BIANCA. Fear nothing, sir.
LEANTIO. An impudent, spiteful strumpet!
BIANCA. O sir, you give me thanks for your captainship;
I thought you had forgot all your good manners.
LEANTIO. And to spite thee as much, look there, there read! [*Gives letter.*]
Vex! Gnaw! Thou shalt find there I am not love-starv'd.
The world was never yet so cold or pitiless
But there was ever still more charity found out
Than at one proud fool's door; and 'twere hard, 'faith,
If I could not pass that. Read to thy shame, there:
A cheerful and a beauteous benefactor too,
As ev'r erected the good works of love.
BIANCA. Lady Livia!
[*Aside*] Is't possible? Her worship was my pand'ress.

---

55 *cloth-of-silver*: tissue made of silver threads interwoven with silk or wool.

57 *spurs*: spur-royals, worth two thirds of £1. Bianca interprets 'lend you spurs' to mean 'give you assistance' or 'goad you on', and applies it to her sexual 'riding'. *Spurs* may also mean 'testicles'; cf. *A Mad World*, III.ii.90.

70 *pass that*: pass by the proud fool's door/surpass, get more than the charity there offered.

72 *as ever erected the good works of love*: Ostensibly, a reference to the foundation of charitable institutions as a metaphor of Livia's generosity to her lover; but with an allusion to tumescence.

She dote and send and give, and all to him?
Why, here's a bawd plagu'd home! – Y'are simply
happy, sir,
Yet I'll not envy you.
LEANTIO. No, court-saint, not thou!
You keep some friend of a new fashion.
There's no harm in your devil, he's a suckling;
But he will breed teeth shortly, will he not?
BIANCA. Take heed you play not then too long with him.
LEANTIO. Yes, and the great one too. I shall find time
To play a hot religious bout with some of you,
And perhaps drive you and your course of sins
To their eternal kennels. I speak softly now
('Tis manners in a noblewoman's lodgings,
And I well know all my degrees of duty);
But come I to your everlasting parting once,
Thunder shall seem soft music to that tempest.
BIANCA. 'Twas said last week there would be change of
weather,
When the moon hung so; and belike you heard it.
LEANTIO. Why, here's sin made, and nev'r a conscience
put to't;
A monster with all forehead and no eyes!
Why do I talk to thee of sense or virtue,
That art as dark as death? And as much madness
To set light before thee, as to lead blind folks
To see the monuments, which they may smell as soon

---

75 *plagu'd home*: thoroughly (and fittingly) punished with the same lustful disease she has inflicted on others.

76 *court-saint*: i.e. 'that which the Court holds holy'; probably a mistaken translation of courtesan.

79 *breed teeth*: cut teeth. The image is suggested by the superstitition of the time that witches nursed familiars (here, corrupt lovers) at supernumerary teats.

81 *and the great one too*: the Duke; Leantio implies she also keeps a young gigolo, a 'suckling'.

83 *course*: pack of dogs/flow/on-rush.

90 *hung so*: Probably Bianca makes horns at Leantio, indicating the crescent moon, and mocking him as a cuckold.

91 *put to't*: troubled.

92 *all forehead and no eyes*: 'all effrontery and no moral perception'.

95–6 *to lead blind folks/To see the monuments*: See Additional note, p. 411.

As they behold; marry, oft-times their heads,
For want of light, may feel the hardness of 'em:
So shall thy blind pride my revenge and anger,
That canst not see it now; and it may fall
At such an hour when thou least see'st of all.
So to an ignorance darker than thy womb
I leave thy perjur'd soul. A plague will come! *Exit.*

BIANCA. Get you gone first, and then I fear no greater!
Nor thee will I fear long; I'll have this sauciness
Soon banish'd from these lodgings, and the rooms
Perfum'd well after the corrupt air it leaves.
His breath has made me almost sick, in troth.
A poor, base start-up! Life! Because h'as got
Fair clothes by foul means, comes to rail, and show 'em.

Enter the DUKE.

DUKE. Who's that?

BIANCA. Cry you mercy, sir.

DUKE. Prithee, who's that?

BIANCA. The former thing, my lord, to whom you gave
The captainship; he eats his meat with grudging still.

DUKE. Still!

BIANCA. He comes vaunting here of his new love,
And the new clothes she gave him: Lady Livia;
Who but she now his mistress?

DUKE. Lady Livia?
Be sure of what you say.

BIANCA. He showed me her name, sir,
In perfum'd paper, her vows, her letter,
With an intent to spite me; so his heart said,
And his threats made it good; they were as spiteful
As ever malice utter'd; and as dangerous,
Should his hand follow the copy.

DUKE. But that must not.
Do not you vex your mind; prithee to bed, go.
All shall be well and quiet.

---

101 *when thou least see'st of all*: i.e. in the darkness of sexual pleasure.

114 *vaunting*: boasting.

122 *Should his hand follow the copy*: 'if his actions follow his threats', the metaphor deriving from handwriting exercises after a copybook example.

BIANCA. I love peace, sir.
DUKE. And so do all that love; take you no care for't,
It shall be still provided to your hand.
Exit [BIANCA].
Who's near us there?

Enter MESSENGER.

MESSENGER. My lord?
DUKE. Seek out Hippolito,
Brother to Lady Livia, with all speed.
MESSENGER. He was the last man I saw, my lord. *Exit.*
DUKE. Make haste.
He is a blood soon stirr'd; and as he's quick
To apprehend a wrong, he's bold and sudden
In bringing forth a ruin. I know likewise
The reputation of his sister's honour's
As dear to him as life-blood to his heart;
Beside, I'll flatter him with a goodness to her
Which I now thought on, but nev'r meant to practise
(Because I know her base); and that wind drives him.
The ulcerous reputation feels the poise
Of lightest wrongs, as sores are vex'd with flies.

Enter HIPPOLITO.

He comes; Hippolito, welcome.
HIPPOLITO. My lov'd lord.
DUKE. How does that lusty widow, thy kind sister?
Is she not sped yet of a second husband?
A bed-fellow she has, I ask not that;
I know she's sped of him.
HIPPOLITO. Of him, my lord?
DUKE. Yes, of a bed-fellow. Is the news so strange to
you?

---

130 *a blood soon stirr'd*: a young gallant easily roused/a passionate disposition soon angered: see Additional note, p. 410.

131 *sudden*: swift, impetuous.

132 *ruin*: desperate action, catastrophe.

135–6 The Duke will flatter Hippolito with the intimation that he had thought to bestow a benefit on Livia (a course he had in fact contemplated, but rejected because of her character).

138 *poise*: weight.

142 *sped yet of*: yet equipped with.

HIPPOLITO. I hope 'tis so to all.
DUKE. I wish it were, sir,
But 'tis confess'd too fast. Her ignorant pleasures,
Only by lust instructed, have receiv'd
Into their services an impudent boaster,
One that does raise his glory from her shame,
And tells the midday sun what's done in darkness;
Yet blinded with her appetite, wastes her wealth,
Buys her disgraces at a dearer rate
Than bounteous housekeepers purchase their honour.
Nothing sads me so much as that, in love
To thee and to thy blood, I had pick'd out
A worthy match for her, the great Vincentio,
High in our favour and in all men's thoughts.
HIPPOLITO. O thou destruction of all happy fortunes,
Unsated blood! – Know you the name, my lord,
Of her abuser?
DUKE. One Leantio.
HIPPOLITO. He's a factor!
DUKE. He nev'r made so brave a voyage
By his own talk.
HIPPOLITO. The poor old widow's son!
I humbly take my leave.
DUKE. [*aside*] I see 'tis done.
– Give her good counsel, make her see her error;
I know she'll hearken to you.
HIPPOLITO. Yes, my lord,
I make no doubt, as I shall take the course
Which she shall never know till it be acted;
And when she wakes to honour, then she'll thank me for't.
I'll imitate the pities of old surgeons
To this lost limb, who, ere they show their art,
Cast one asleep, then cut the diseas'd part:

---

152 *wastes*: i.e. *she* wastes.

154 *Than bounteous housekeepers purchase their honour*: i.e. at greater cost than those who achieve reputation by keeping open house with lavish entertainment.

160 *Unsated blood*: insatiate sexual appetite.

170 *old surgeons*: Theodoric of Lucca, a Dominican friar, recommended as early as the thirteenth century the use of sponges soaked in opium or mandragora as an anaesthetic during surgery.

So out of love to her I pity most,
She shall not feel him going till he's lost;
Then she'll commend the cure. *Exit.*

DUKE. The great cure's past.
I count this done already; his wrath's sure,
And speaks an injury deep. Farewell, Leantio;
This place will never hear thee murmur more.

Enter LORD CARDINAL, *attended* [*by* SERVANTS *with lighted candlesticks*].

Our noble brother, welcome!

CARDINAL. Set those lights down.
Depart till you be called.
[*Exeunt* ATTENDANTS.]

DUKE. [*aside*] There's serious business
Fixed in his look; nay, it inclines a little
To the dark colour of a discontentment.
– Brother, what is't commands your eye so powerfully?
Speak, you seem lost.

CARDINAL. The thing I look on seems so
To my eyes, lost for ever.

DUKE. You look on me.

CARDINAL. What a grief 'tis to a religious feeling
To think a man should have a friend so goodly,
So wise, so noble, nay, a duke, a brother;
And all this certainly damn'd!

DUKE. How!

CARDINAL. 'Tis no wonder,
If your great sin can do't. Dare you look up,
For thinking of a vengeance? Dare you sleep,
For fear of never waking, but to death?
And dedicate unto a strumpet's love
The strength of your affections, zeal and health?
Here you stand now. Can you assure your pleasures
You shall once more enjoy her, but once more?

---

175 *cure*: also, care.

s.d. LORD CARDINAL: historically, Ferdinand de'Medici, Francesco's brother and later his successor as Grand Duke of Tuscany.

183 *commands your eye so powerfully*: 'so completely dominates your expression'.

Alas, you cannot! What a misery 'tis, then,
To be more certain of eternal death
Than of a next embrace. Nay, shall I show you
How more unfortunate you stand in sin
Than the low private man? All his offences,
Like enclos'd grounds, keep but about himself,
And seldom stretch beyond his own soul's bounds;
And when a man grows miserable, 'tis some comfort
When he's no further charg'd than with himself:
'Tis a sweet ease to wretchedness. But, great man,
Ev'ry sin thou commit'st shows like a flame
Upon a mountain: 'tis seen far about,
And with a big wind made of popular breath
The sparkles fly through cities; here one takes,
Another catches there, and in short time
Waste all to cinders. But remember still,
What burnt the valleys, first came from the hill.
Ev'ry offence draws his particular pain,
But 'tis example proves the great man's bane.
The sins of mean men lie like scatter'd parcels
Of an unperfect bill; but when such fall,
Then comes example, and that sums up all.
And this your reason grants: if men of good lives,
Who by their virtuous actions stir up others
To noble and religious imitation,
Receive the greater glory after death
(As sin must needs confess), what may they feel
In height of torments and in weight of vengeance,
Not only they themselves not doing well,
But sets a light up to show men to Hell?

DUKE. If you have done, I have. No more, sweet brother.

CARDINAL. I know time spent in goodness is too tedious;
This had not been a moment's space in lust, now.

---

201 See Textual note, p. 406.

202 *enclosed grounds*: fenced-off land.

205 *charg'd*: held responsible/burdened/accused.

209 *with a big wind made of popular breath*: i.e. transmitted on the tide of vulgar gossip.

214 *draws*: brings as a consequence.

216–18 'The sins of inferior men are like the isolated items of an incomplete bill; but when great men die these items are gathered up under the heading "bad example", and laid to the account of the great.'

How dare you venture on eternal pain,
That cannot bear a minute's reprehension?
Methinks you should endure to hear that talk'd of
Which you so strive to suffer. Oh my brother!
What were you, if you were taken now?
My heart weeps blood to think on't; 'tis a work
Of infinite mercy you can never merit,
That yet you are not death-struck, no, not yet.
I dare not stay you long, for fear you should not
Have time enough allow'd you to repent in.
There's but this wall betwixt you and destruction
When y'are at strongest; and but poor thin clay.
Think upon't, brother. Can you come so near it
For a fair strumpet's love, and fall into
A torment that knows neither end nor bottom
For beauty but the deepness of a skin,
And that not of their own neither? Is she a thing
Whom sickness dare not visit, or age look on,
Or death resist? Does the worm shun her grave?
If not (as your soul knows it), why should lust
Bring man to lasting pain, for rotten dust?

DUKE. Brother of spotless honour, let me weep
The first of my repentance in thy bosom,
And show the blest fruits of a thankful spirit;
And if I e'er keep woman more, unlawfully,
May I want penitence at my greatest need;
And wise men know there is no barren place
Threatens more famine, than a dearth in grace.

CARDINAL. Why, here's a conversion is at this time, brother,
Sung for a hymn in Heaven; and at this instant,
The powers of darkness groan, makes all Hell sorry.
First, I praise Heaven; then in my work I glory.
– Who's there attends without?

Enter SERVANTS.

SERVANT. My lord?

CARDINAL. Take up those lights; there was a thicker darkness

---

231 *reprehension*: rebuke.
240 *wall*: i.e. his body.
258–9 Cf. Luke 15.10.

When they came first. The peace of a fair soul
Keep with my noble brother.
Exit CARDINAL, *etc.*
DUKE. Joys be with you, sir!
– She lies alone tonight for't; and must still,
Though it be hard to conquer. But I have vow'd
Never to know her as a strumpet more,
And I must save my oath. If fury fail not,
Her husband dies tonight, or at the most
Lives not to see the morning spent tomorrow;
Then will I make her lawfully mine own,
Without this sin and horror. Now I'm chidden
For what I shall enjoy then unforbidden;
And I'll not freeze in stoves; 'tis but a while
Live like a hopeful bridegroom, chaste from flesh,
And pleasure then will seem new, fair and fresh. *Exit.*

SCENE II

Enter HIPPOLITO.

HIPPOLITO. The morning so far wasted, yet his baseness
So impudent? See if the very sun do not blush at him!
Dare he do thus much, and know me alive!
Put case one must be vicious (as I know myself
Monstrously guilty), there's a blind time made for't;
He might use only that, 'twere conscionable:
Art, silence, closeness, subtlety and darkness
Are fit for such a business. But there's no pity
To be bestow'd on an apparent sinner,
An impudent, daylight lecher. The great zeal
I bear to her advancement in this match
With Lord Vincentio, as the duke has wrought it,
To the perpetual honour of our house,
Puts fire into my blood, to purge the air
Of this corruption, fear it spread too far
And poison the whole hopes of this fair fortune.

---

275 *And I'll not freeze in stoves*: 'Stoves' are rooms heated by hot air from a furnace; 'I'm not a one for being cold in a hot situation.'

4 *Put case*: allowing for argument's sake.

6 *conscionable*: scrupulous, showing a proper regard for the decencies.

9 *apparent*: evident.

I love her good so dearly, that no brother
Shall venture farther for a sister's glory
Than I for her preferment.

Enter LEANTIO *and a* PAGE.

LEANTIO. Once again
I'll see that glist'ring whore shines like a serpent,
Now the court sun's upon her. Page!

PAGE. Anon, sir!

LEANTIO. I'll go in state too; see the coach be ready.
[*Exit* PAGE.]
I'll hurry away presently.

HIPPOLITO. Yes, you shall hurry,
And the devil after you; take that at setting forth!
[*Strikes him from behind with his sword*.]
Now, and you'll draw, we are upon equal terms, sir:
Thou took'st advantage of my name in honour
Upon my sister; I nev'r saw the stroke
Come, till I found my reputation bleeding;
And therefore count it I no sin to valour
To serve thy lust so. Now we are of even hand,
Take your best course against me. You must die.

LEANTIO. [*drawing*] How close sticks envy to man's happiness!
When I was poor, and little car'd for life,
I had no such means offer'd me to die,
No man's wrath minded me. Slave, I turn this to thee,
To call thee to account for a wound lately
Of a base stamp upon me.

HIPPOLITO. 'Twas most fit
For a base metal. Come and fetch one now
More noble, then; for I will use thee fairer
Than thou hast done thine [own] soul or our honour.
[*They fight and* LEANTIO *falls*.]
And there, I think, 'tis for thee.

[VOICES] *within*. Help! help! Oh part 'em!

---

20 *that glist'ring whore shines like a serpent*: The painted courtesan is associated with the serpent of Eden, which was commonly depicted with a woman's head, and which attracted Eve by its beauty, according to tradition.

30 *of even hand*: 'all square'.

37 *base stamp*: base nature/a false imprint on the face of a coin.

38 *base metal*: base metal/base disposition, 'mettle'.

LEANTIO. False wife, I feel now th'hast pray'd heartily for me.
Rise, strumpet, by my fall, thy lust may reign now;
My heart-string and the marriage-knot that tied thee
Breaks both together. [*He dies.*]
HIPPOLITO. There I heard the sound on't,
And never lik'd string better.

Enter GUARDIANO, LIVIA, ISABELLA, WARD, *and* SORDIDO.

LIVIA. 'Tis my brother!
Are you hurt, sir?
HIPPOLITO. Not anything.
LIVIA. Blessed fortune!
Shift for thyself. What is he thou hast kill'd?
HIPPOLITO. Our honour's enemy.
GUARDIANO. Know you this man, lady?
LIVIA. Leantio! My love's joy! [*To* HIPPOLITO] Wounds stick upon thee
As deadly as thy sins! Art thou not hurt?
The devil take that fortune. And he dead!
Drop plagues into thy bowels without voice,
Secret and fearful. – Run for officers!
Let him be apprehended with all speed,
For fear he 'scape away; lay hands on him,
We cannot be too sure; 'tis wilful murder.
You do Heaven's vengeance and the law just service;
You know him not as I do: he's a villain,
As monstrous as a prodigy, and as dreadful.
HIPPOLITO. Will you but entertain a noble patience
Till you but hear the reason, worthy sister!
LIVIA. The reason! That's a jest Hell falls a-laughing at!
Is there a reason found for the destruction
Of our more lawful loves? And was there none
To kill the black lust 'twixt thy niece and thee

---

44 *heart-string*: a tendon or nerve supposed to brace and sustain the heart.
46 *string*: i.e. the string of a musical instrument.
48 *Shift for thyself*: 'Make your escape.'
53 *without voice*: noiselessly.
60 *prodigy*: omen, portent. Grossly misshapen or unnatural births were widely reported in Jacobean England and interpreted as signs.

That has kept close so long?

GUARDIANO. How's that, good madam?

LIVIA. Too true, sir! There she stands, let her deny't;
The deed cries shortly in the midwife's arms,
Unless the parents' sins strike it still-born;
And if you be not deaf and ignorant,
You'll hear strange notes ere long. [*To* ISABELLA]
Look upon me, wench!
'Twas I betray'd thy honour subtilly to him
Under a false tale; it lights upon me now;
His arm has paid me home upon thy breast,
My sweet, belov'd Leantio!

GUARDIANO. Was my judgement
And care in choice so dev'lishly abus'd,
So beyond-shamefully? All the world will grin at me!

WARD. Oh Sordido, Sordido, I'm damn'd, I'm damn'd!

SORDIDO. Damn'd! Why, sir?

WARD. One of the wicked; dost not see't?
A cuckold, a plain reprobate cuckold!

SORDIDO. Nay, and you be damn'd for that, be of good cheer, sir; y'have gallant company of all professions; I'll have a wife next Sunday too, because I'll along with you myself.

WARD. That will be some comfort yet.

LIVIA. [*to* GUARDIANO] You, sir, that bear your load of injuries
As I of sorrows, lend me your griev'd strength
To this sad burthen who, in life, wore actions
Flames were not nimbler. We will talk of things
May have the luck to break our hearts together.

---

67 *close*: hidden.

71 *ignorant*: wilfully disregarding.

74–5 *it lights upon me now;/His arm has paid me home*: 'my treachery returns upon myself; his arm has thoroughly requited me'.

84 *next Sunday*: perhaps with allusion to the proverb (Tilley, W 378): 'Who will have a handsome wife let him choose her upon Saturday and not upon Sunday', when women are dressed to appear beautiful and virtuous. Sunday church was also the traditional place for furthering liaisons.

89–90 *wore actions/Flames were not nimbler*: 'was characterised by behaviour more spirited than fire'.

GUARDIANO. I'll list to nothing but revenge and anger,
Whose counsels I will follow.

Exeunt LIVIA *and* GUARDIANO [*carrying* LEANTIO*'s body*].

SORDIDO. A wife, quoth'a! Here's a sweet plum-tree of your guardiner's graffing!

WARD. Nay, there's a worse name belongs to this fruit yet, and you could hit on't, a more open one: for he that marries a whore looks like a fellow bound all his lifetime to a medlar-tree; and that's good stuff, 'tis no sooner ripe but it looks rotten; and so do some queans at nineteen. A pox on't, I thought there was some knavery abroach, for something stirr'd in her belly the first night I lay with her.

SORDIDO. What, what, sir!

WARD. This is she brought up so courtly! Can sing and dance – and tumble too, methinks. I'll never marry wife again that has so many qualities.

SORDIDO. Indeed, they are seldom good, master. For likely when they are taught so many, they will have one trick more of their own finding out. Well, give me a wench but with one good quality, to lie with none but her husband, and that's bringing-up enough for any woman breathing.

WARD. This was the fault when she was tend'red to me; you never look'd to this.

SORDIDO. Alas, how would you have me see through a great farthingale, sir! I cannot peep through a millstone, or in the going, to see what's done i'th'bottom.

---

94 *plum-tree*: used of the female pudenda, or of a woman considered as a sexual object.

95 *guardiner's graffing*: guardian's/gardener's grafting, i.e. 'splicing', marrying.

96–7 *a worse name . . . a more open one*: i.e. 'open-arse' or medlar, eaten when decayed to a brown pulp, and associated because of its appearance with the female pudenda, and with 'queans', whores.

106 *tumble*: do acrobatics/copulate.

107 *qualities*: skills, accomplishments. Sordido voices a common Jacobean unease at the tendency to educate women in social arts.

117–18 *peep through a millstone*: Proverbial (Tilley, M 965), meaning 'to have a deep understanding of a situation'; *in the going*: in the mill-mechanism/into the woman as she walks.

WARD. Her father prais'd her breast, sh'ad the voice, forsooth! I marvell'd she sung so small, indeed, being no maid; now I perceive there's a young querister in her belly. This breeds a singing in my head, I'm sure.

SORDIDO. 'Tis but the tune of your wive's cinquepace, danc'd in a featherbed. 'Faith, go lie down, master; but take heed your horns do not make holes in the pillowberes! [*Aside*] I would not batter brows with him for a hogshead of angels; he would prick my skull as full of holes as a scrivener's sandbox.

Exeunt WARD *and* SORDIDO.

ISABELLA. [*aside*] Was ever maid so cruelly beguil'd
To the confusion of life, soul and honour,
All of one woman's murd'ring! I'd fain bring
Her name no nearer to my blood than woman,
And 'tis too much of that. Oh shame and horror!
In that small distance from yon man to me
Lies sin enough to make a whole world perish.
– 'Tis time we parted, sir, and left the sight
Of one another; nothing can be worse
To hurt repentance, for our very eyes
Are far more poisonous to religion
Than basilisks to them. If any goodness
Rest in you, hope of comforts, fear of judgements,
My request is, I nev'r may see you more;
And so I turn me from you everlastingly,

120–1 *being no maid*: The Ward seems to use 'maid' in a dialect sense to mean 'a young girl'. He was surprised at her treble voice since she was no 'chicken' and he expected a contralto; now he realises the voice came from the baby, the 'young chorister'.

122 *a singing in my head*: an alleged symptom of cuckoldry.

126 *pillowberes*: pillowcases.

127 *hogshead of angels*: barrel of gold coins, the 'angel' having St Michael on one side.

128 *scrivener's sandbox*: perforated box filled with sand, used for blotting.

130 *confusion*: ruin, destruction.

131–3 *I'd fain . . . much of that*: 'I'd prefer to admit to no closer relation but that of our common sex – and that's too close.'

140 *basilisks*: fabulous reptiles, part cock, part serpent, able to kill by a look.

So is my hope to miss you. But for her,
That durst so dally with a sin so dangerous,
And lay a snare so spitefully for my youth,
If the least means but favour my revenge,
That I may practise the like cruel cunning
Upon her life as she has on mine honour,
I'll act it without pity.

HIPPOLITO. Here's a care
Of reputation and a sister's fortune
Sweetly rewarded by her! Would a silence,
As great as that which keeps among the graves,
Had everlastingly chain'd up her tongue.
My love to her has made mine miserable.

Enter GUARDIANO *and* LIVIA [*and talk apart*].

GUARDIANO. If you can but dissemble your heart's griefs now,
Be but a woman so far.

LIVIA. Peace! I'll strive, sir.

GUARDIANO. As I can wear my injuries in a smile;
Here's an occasion offer'd, that gives anger
Both liberty and safety to perform
Things worth the fire it holds, without the fear
Of danger, or of law; for mischiefs acted
Under the privilege of a marriage-triumph
At the duke's hasty nuptials will be thought
Things merely accidental: all's by chance,
Not got of their own natures.

LIVIA. I conceive you, sir,
Even to a longing for performance on't;
And here behold some fruits.
[*She kneels before* ISABELLA *and* HIPPOLITO.]
Forgive me both.

---

144 *So is my hope to miss you*: i.e. she hopes to avoid meeting Hippolito 'everlastingly' in Hell, by refusing to commit *conscious* incest.

163 *marriage-triumph*: marriage masque. A final masque by disguised revengers had been a dramatic cliché from Kyd's *Spanish Tragedy* onwards.

166 *Not got of their own natures*: 'not conceived out of malicious intention'.

166 *I conceive you, sir*: 'I understand you', but with a series of innuendoes on pregnancy, desire and birth.

What I am now, return'd to sense and judgement,
Is not the same rage and distraction
Presented lately to you; that rude form
Is gone for ever. I am now myself,
That speaks all peace and friendship; and these tears
Are the true springs of hearty, penitent sorrow
For those foul wrongs which my forgetful fury
Sland'red your virtues with. This gentleman
Is well resolv'd now.

GUARDIANO. I was never otherways.
I knew, alas, 'twas but your anger spake it,
And I nev'r thought on't more.

HIPPOLITO. Pray rise, good sister.

ISABELLA. [*aside*] Here's ev'n as sweet amends made for a wrong now
As one that gives a wound, and pays the surgeon:
All the smart's nothing, the great loss of blood,
Or time of hind'rance! Well, I had a mother,
I can dissemble too. – What wrongs have slipp'd
Through anger's ignorance, aunt, my heart forgives.

GUARDIANO. Why, this is tuneful now.

HIPPOLITO. And what I did, sister,
Was all for honour's cause, which time to come
Will approve to you.

LIVIA. Being awak'd to goodness,
I understand so much, sir, and praise now
The fortune of your arm, and of your safety;
For by his death y'have rid me of a sin
As costly as ev'r woman doted on.
'T has pleased the duke so well too that (behold, sir)
H'as sent you here your pardon, which I kiss'd
With most affectionate comfort; when 'twas brought,
Then was my fit just past; it came so well, methought,
To glad my heart. [*She gives him the pardon.*]

HIPPOLITO. I see his grace thinks on me.

LIVIA. There's no talk now but of the preparation
For the great marriage.

HIPPOLITO. Does he marry her, then?

---

177 *well resolv'd*: well satisfied/(ironically) resolute.
183 *hind'rance*: incapacitation.
186 *Why, this is tuneful now*: See Textual note, p. 406.
188 *approve*: demonstrate.

LIVIA. With all speed, suddenly, as fast as cost
Can be laid on with many thousand hands.
This gentleman and I had once a purpose
To have honoured the first marriage of the duke
With an invention of his own. 'Twas ready,
The pains well past, most of the charge bestow'd on't;
Then came the death of your good mother, niece,
And turn'd the glory of it all to black.
'Tis a device would fit these times so well, too,
Art's treasury not better. If you'll join,
It shall be done; the cost shall all be mine.
HIPPOLITO. Y'have my voice first; 'twill well approve my thankfulness
For the duke's love and favour.
LIVIA. What say you, niece?
ISABELLA. I am content to make one.
GUARDIANO. The plot's full, then;
Your pages, madam, will make shift for Cupids.
LIVIA. That will they, sir.
GUARDIANO. You'll play your old part still?
LIVIA. What, is't good? Troth, I have ev'n forgot it!
GUARDIANO. Why, Juno Pronuba, the marriage-goddess.
LIVIA. 'Tis right, indeed.
GUARDIANO. [*to* ISABELLA] And you shall play the nymph
That offers sacrifice to appease her wrath.
ISABELLA. Sacrifice, good sir?
LIVIA. Must I be appeased, then?
GUARDIANO. That's as you list yourself, as you see cause.
LIVIA. Methinks 'twould show the more state in her deity
To be incens'd.
ISABELLA. 'Twould – [*Aside*] but my sacrifice

---

204 *invention*: literary creation, probably by Guardiano, perhaps by the Duke.

205 *charge bestow'd*: cost expended.

213 *The plot's full*: the play is fully cast/the stratagem is perfected.

216 *What, is't good? Troth*: See Textual note, p. 406.

217 *Juno Pronuba*: Queen of the Roman pantheon, and in this aspect the fosterer of marriage contracts (an ironic role for the bawd and marriage breaker).

222–3 *more state in her deity/To be incens'd*: 'more dignity in the goddess if she were angry//censed with incense.'

Shall take a course to appease you, or I'll fail in't,
And teach a sinful bawd to play a goddess. [*Exit.*]

GUARDIANO. For our parts we'll not be ambitious, sir;
Please you walk in and see the project drawn,
Then take your choice.

HIPPOLITO. I weigh not, so I have one.

Exit.

LIVIA. How much ado have I to restrain fury
From breaking into curses! Oh how painful 'tis
To keep great sorrow smother'd! Sure, I think
'Tis harder to dissemble grief than love.
Leantio, here the weight of thy loss lies,
Which nothing but destruction can suffice.

Exeunt [LIVIA *and* GUARDIANO].

SCENE III

Hoboys.
Enter in great state the DUKE *and* BIANCA, *richly attir'd, with* LORDS, CARDINALS, LADIES, *and other* ATTENDANTS. *They pass solemnly over. Enter* LORD CARDINAL *in a rage, seeming to break off the ceremony.*

CARDINAL. Cease, cease! Religious honours done to sin
Disparage virtue's reverence, and will pull
Heaven's thunder upon Florence; holy ceremonies
Were made for sacred uses, not for sinful.
Are these the fruits of your repentance, brother?
Better it had been you had never sorrow'd
Than to abuse the benefit, and return
To worse than where sin left you.
Vow'd you then never to keep strumpet more,
And are you now so swift in your desires
To knit your honours and your life fast to her?
Is not sin sure enough to wretched man
But he must bind himself in chains to't? Worse,
Must marriage, that immaculate robe of honour

---

224 *appease*: propitiate/bring to peace (i.e. the peace of death).
227 *project drawn*: the plan of the masque written out.
228 *weigh*: care.
s.d. *Hoboys*: oboes; *pass over*: ascend and cross the stage, entering and exiting *via* the playhouse yard.

That renders virtue glorious, fair, and fruitful
To her great Master, be now made the garment
Of leprosy and foulness? Is this penitence,
To sanctify hot lust? What is it otherways
Than worship done to devils? Is this the best
Amends that sin can make after her riots?
As if a drunkard, to appease Heaven's wrath,
Should offer up his surfeit for a sacrifice:
If that be comely, then lust's offerings are,
On wedlock's sacred altar.

DUKE. Here y'are bitter
Without cause, brother: what I vow'd, I keep
As safe as you your conscience; and this needs not.
I taste more wrath in't than I do religion,
And envy more than goodness. The path now
I tread is honest, leads to lawful love,
Which virtue in her strictness would not check.
I vow'd no more to keep a sensual woman:
'Tis done; I mean to make a lawful wife of her.

CARDINAL. He that taught you that craft,
Call him not Master long, he will undo you.
Grow not too cunning for your soul, good brother.
Is it enough to use adulterous thefts,
And then take sanctuary in marriage?
I grant, so long as an offender keeps
Close in a privileged temple, his life's safe;
But if he ever venture to come out,
And so be taken, then he surely dies for't:
So now y'are safe; but when you leave this body,
Man's only privileg'd temple upon earth,
In which the guilty soul takes sanctuary,
Then you'll perceive what wrongs chaste vows endure
When lust usurps the bed that should be pure.

---

17 *leprosy*: commonly identified with syphilis.
22 *surfeit*: excess; also, the matter vomited after over-indulgence.
23 *comely*: decent.
26 *this needs not*: this reproof is unnecessary.
31 *a sensual woman*: i.e. a woman kept only for sensual pleasure.
33 *He*: i.e. the Devil.
43 *temple*: an ironic allusion to 1 Corinthians 3.16, where the body is the temple of the Holy Spirit, and not a refuge from God.

BIANCA. Sir, I have read you over all this while
In silence, and I find great knowledge in you,
And severe learning; yet 'mongst all your virtues
I see not charity written, which some call
The first-born of religion; and I wonder
I cannot see't in yours. Believe it, sir,
There is no virtue can be sooner miss'd
Or later welcom'd; it begins the rest,
And sets 'em all in order. Heaven and angels
Take great delight in a converted sinner:
Why should you, then, a servant and professor,
Differ so much from them? If ev'ry woman
That commits evil should be therefore kept
Back in desires of goodness, how should virtue
Be known and honour'd? From a man that's blind
To take a burning taper 'tis no wrong,
He never misses it; but to take light
From one that sees, that's injury and spite.
Pray, whether is religion better serv'd,
When lives that are licentious are made honest,
Than when they still run through a sinful blood?
'Tis nothing virtue's temple to deface;
But build the ruins, there's a work of grace.
DUKE. I kiss thee for that spirit; thou hast prais'd thy wit
A modest way. On, on there!

Hoboys.

CARDINAL. Lust is bold,
And will have vengeance speak, ere't be controll'd.

Exeunt [DUKE, BIANCA *and* ATTENDANTS, CARDINAL].

---

51 *the first-born of religion*: alluding to I Corinthians 13.13ff.

55–6 See note at IV.i.258–9.

57 *professor*: one who 'professes' himself a Christian; also, a member of a religious order.

68–9 i.e. 'It is easy enough to debauch a woman's body (the temple of her virtue) but to restore its virtue (as the Duke will do by marrying Bianca) is an act divinely inspired (and only to be expected from 'Grace', the Duke).

72 *controll'd*: brought to book, put down.

ACT V

SCENE I

Enter GUARDIANO *and* WARD.

GUARDIANO. Speak, hast thou any sense of thy abuse? Dost thou know what wrong's done thee?

WARD. I were an ass else; I cannot wash my face but I am feeling on't.

GUARDIANO. Here, take this galtrop, then; convey it secretly into the place I show'd you. Look you, sir, this is the trap-door to't.

WARD. I know't of old, uncle, since the last triumph; here rose up a devil with one eye, I remember, with a company of fireworks at's tail.

GUARDIANO. Prithee leave squibbing now; mark me and fail not. But when thou hear'st me give a stamp, down with't: the villain's caught then.

WARD. If I miss you, hang me; I love to catch a villain, and your stamp shall go current, I warrant you. But how shall I rise up and let him down too, all at one hole? That will be a horrible puzzle. You know I have a part in't, I play Slander.

GUARDIANO. True, but never make you ready for't.

WARD. No? My clothes are bought and all, and a foul fiend's head with a long contumelious tongue i'th' chaps on't, a very fit shape for Slander i'th'out-parishes.

---

4 *I am feeling on't*: i.e. feeling the cuckold's horns.

5 *galtrop*: the caltrop, used against cavalry, an instrument made with four spikes so that, however it lands, one spike always stands upright.

7 *triumph*: pageant.

11 *squibbing*: punning on 'to squib' = to use smart, sarcastic talk.

15 *stamp shall go current*: be acknowledged as valid (punning on 'stamp' = the imprint on a coin).

22 *chaps*: cheeks.

22–3 *out-parishes*: nine areas exempt from City jurisdiction and not covered by the plague bills, and the site of popular dramatic entertainment of an old-fashioned kind, in which Morality characters such as Slander might appear.

GUARDIANO. It shall not come so far; thou understand'st it not.
WARD. Oh, oh!
GUARDIANO. He shall lie deep enough ere that time, and stick first upon those.
WARD. Now I conceive you, guardiner.
GUARDIANO. Away; list to the privy stamp, that's all thy part.
WARD. Stamp my horns in a mortar if I miss you, and give the powder in white wine to sick cuckolds: a very present remedy for the headache. *Exit* WARD.
GUARDIANO. If this should any way miscarry now,
(As, if the fool be nimble enough, 'tis certain),
The pages that present the swift-wing'd Cupids
Are taught to hit him with their shafts of love
(Fitting his part), which I have cunningly poison'd.
He cannot 'scape my fury; and those ills
Will be laid all on fortune, not our wills.
That's all the sport on't! For who will imagine
That at the celebration of this night
Any mischance that haps can flow from spite? *Exit.*

SCENE II

Flourish. Enter above DUKE, BIANCA, LORD CARDINAL, FABRITIO, *and other* CARDINALS, LORDS *and* LADIES *in state.*

DUKE. Now our fair duchess, your delight shall witness
How y'are belov'd and honour'd: all the glories
Bestow'd upon the gladness of this night
Are done for your bright sake.
BIANCA. I am the more
In debt, my lord, to loves and courtesies
That offer up themselves so bounteously

---

30 *privy*: secret; probably with a pun on 'privy seal'.
32–4 *Stamp my horns in a mortar . . . a very present remedy*: 'Pound my cuckold's horns with a pestle and mortar . . . an immediate cure'. White wine was often a base for medicines and horn an antidote to poison; the Ward suggests a homeopathic remedy for cuckoldom.
36 *certain*: sure not to fail.
37 *present*: act.

To do me honour'd grace, without my merit.
DUKE. A goodness set in greatness! How it sparkles
Afar off, like pure diamonds set in gold.
How perfect my desires were, might I witness
But a fair noble peace 'twixt your two spirits!
The reconcilement would be more sweet to me
Than longer life to him that fears to die.
[*To the* CARDINAL] Good sir!
CARDINAL. I profess peace, and am content.
DUKE. I'll see the seal upon't, and then 'tis firm.
CARDINAL. You shall have all you wish.
[*Kisses* BIANCA.]
DUKE. I have all indeed now.
BIANCA. [*aside*] But I have made surer work; this shall not blind me.
He that begins so early to reprove,
Quickly rid him, or look for little love.
Beware a brother's envy; he's next heir too.
Cardinal, you die this night; the plot's laid surely:
In time of sports death may steal in securely.
Then 'tis least thought on:
For he that's most religious, holy friend,
Does not at all hours think upon his end;
He has his times of frailty, and his thoughts
Their transportations too through flesh and blood,
For all his zeal, his learning, and his light,
As well as we, poor soul, that sin by night.
DUKE. What's this, Fabritio?
FABRITIO. Marry, my lord, the model
Of what's presented.
DUKE. Oh, we thank their loves.
Sweet duchess, take your seat; list to the Argument.
(*Reads*):
There is a nymph that haunts the woods and springs,
In love with two at once, and they with her.
Equal it runs; but to decide these things,

7 *grace . . . merit*: one of Bianca's typically irreverent allusions to Christian and, especially, Protestant doctrine, as derived from Romans 3.20–4.
10 *perfect*: fully satisfied.
29 *soul*: See Textual note, p. 406.
30 *model*: outline, synopsis.

The cause to mighty Juno they refer,
She being the marriage-goddess. The two lovers,
They offer sighs; the nymph, a sacrifice;
All to please Juno, who by signs discovers
How the event shall be. So that strife dies.
Then springs a second; for the man refus'd
Grows discontent, and out of love abus'd
He raises Slander up, like a black fiend,
To disgrace th'other, which pays him i'th'end.

BIANCA. In troth, my lord, a pretty, pleasing Argument,
And fits th'occasion well: envy and slander
Are things soon rais'd against two faithful lovers;
But comfort is, they are not long unrewarded.

Music.

DUKE. This music shows they're upon entrance now.

BIANCA. [*aside*] Then enter all my wishes!

Enter HYMEN *in yellow,* GANYMEDE *in a blue robe powdered with stars, and* HEBE *in a white robe with golden stars, with covered cups in their hands. They dance a short dance, then bowing to the* DUKE *etc.,* HYMEN *speaks.*

HYMEN. [*giving* BIANCA *a cup*] To thee, fair bride, Hymen offers up
Of nuptial joys this the celestial cup;
Taste it, and thou shalt ever find
Love in thy bed, peace in thy mind.

BIANCA. We'll taste you, sure; 'twere pity to disgrace
So pretty a beginning.

DUKE. 'Twas spoke nobly.

GANYMEDE. Two cups of nectar have we begg'd from Jove:
Hebe, give that to Innocence; I this to Love.

---

39 *discovers*: reveals.

44 *pays him*: brings retribution on him.

s.d. HYMEN: the god of marriage, traditionally represented in saffron robes, a detail derived from Ovid, *Metamorphoses*, X.i.
GANYMEDE: a beautiful youth abducted by Zeus to be his cupbearer; his robe shows that Zeus eventually made him into the constellation Aquarius.
HEBE: cupbearer to Zeus (Jupiter or Jove), displaced by Ganymede; her garment represents the Milky Way.
covered cups: cups with attached lids.

[HEBE *gives a cup to the* CARDINAL, GANYMEDE *one to the* DUKE; *both drink*.]

Take heed of stumbling more, look to your way;
Remember still the Via Lactea.

HEBE. Well, Ganymede, you have more faults, though not so known;
I spill'd one cup, but you have filch'd many a one.

HYMEN. No more, forbear for Hymen's sake;
In love we met, and so let's part[ing take]. *Exeunt.*

DUKE. But soft! Here's no such persons in the Argument
As these three, Hymen, Hebe, Ganymede;
The actors that this model here discovers
Are only four: Juno, a nymph, two lovers.

BIANCA. This is some antemasque belike, my lord,
To entertain time; [*Aside*] now my peace is perfect.
– Let sports come on apace; now is their time, my lord.

Music.

Hark you, you hear from 'em.

DUKE. The nymph indeed!

Enter two dress'd like nymphs, bearing two tapers lighted; then ISABELLA *dress'd with flowers and garlands, bearing a censer with fire in it. They set the censer and tapers on Juno's altar with much reverence, this ditty being sung in parts.*

DITTY.

Juno, nuptial-goddess,
Thou that rul'st o'er coupled bodies,
Ti'st man to woman, never to forsake her;
Thou only powerful marriage-maker,
Pity this amaz'd affection,
I love both and both love me;
Nor know I where to give rejection,

---

60 *Via Lactea*: the Milky Way. Hebe lost the post of cupbearer through tripping and exposing herself in an indelicate position, whilst the contents of the cup she was carrying spilled into the heavens to form the Milky Way.

64 *part[ing take]*: See Textual note, p. 406.

69 *antemasque*: a short, often comic, interlude before the masque proper (in this case devised by Bianca).

77 *amaz'd affection*: perplexed feelings.

My heart likes so equally,
Till thou set'st right my peace of life,
And with thy power conclude this strife.

ISABELLA. *Now with my thanks depart you to the springs,*
I to these wells of love.

[*Exeunt the two* NYMPHS.]

Thou sacred goddess
And queen of nuptials, daughter to great Saturn,
Sister and wife to Jove, imperial Juno,
Pity this passionate conflict in my breast,
This tedious war 'twixt two affections;
Crown one with victory, and my heart's at peace.

Enter HIPPOLITO *and* GUARDIANO, *like shepherds.*

HIPPOLITO. *Make me that happy man, thou mighty goddess.*

GUARDIANO. *But I live most in hope, if truest love*
Merit the greatest comfort.

ISABELLA. *I love both*
With such an even and fair affection,
I know not which to speak for, which to wish for,
Till thou, great arbitress 'twixt lovers' hearts,
By thy auspicious grace, design the man:
Which pity I implore.

BOTH [HIPPOLITO *and* GUARDIANO]. *We all implore it.*

ISABELLA. *And after sighs, contrition's truest odours,*

LIVIA *descends like Juno* [*attended by* PAGES *as Cupids*].

I offer to thy powerful deity
This precious incense; may it ascend peacefully.
[*Aside*] And if it keep true touch, my good aunt Juno,
'Twill try your immortality ere't be long;
I fear you'll never get so nigh Heaven again,
When you're once down.

LIVIA. *Though you and your affections*

---

89 *one*: See Textual note, p. 406.

96 *design*: indicate.

99 s.d. *descends*: Livia is lowered from the 'heavens' by a device which keeps her suspended somewhere above the altar from which the poisoned fumes rise.

101 *keep true touch*: prove trustworthy, behave as it should (a metaphor from the testing of gold with a touchstone).

Seem all as dark to our illustrious brightness
As night's inheritance, Hell, we pity you,
And your requests are granted. You ask signs:
They shall be given you; we'll be gracious to you.
He of those twain which we determine for you
Love's arrows shall wound twice; the later wound
Betokens love in age: for so are all
Whose love continues firmly all their lifetime
Twice wounded at their marriage, else affection
Dies when youth ends. [*Aside*] This savour overcomes me!
– *Now for a sign of wealth and golden days,*
Bright-ey'd prosperity which all couples love,
Ay, and makes love, take that!
[*Throws flaming gold upon* ISABELLA *who falls dead.*]
Our brother Jove
Never denies us of his burning treasure
T'express bounty.

DUKE. She falls down upon't;
What's the conceit of that?

FABRITIO. As over-joy'd, belike:
Too much prosperity overjoys us all,
And she has her lapful, it seems, my lord.

DUKE. This swerves a little from the Argument, though.
– Look you, my lords.

GUARDIANO. [*aside*] All's fast; now comes my part to toll him hither;
Then, with a stamp given, he's dispatch'd as cunningly.
[GUARDIANO *stamps on the floor; the trapdoor opens*

---

114 *savour*: See Textual note, p. 407.

117 *makes love*: probably elliptic: 'prosperity causes love'.

117 s.d. *flaming gold*: See Textual note, p. 407 and Additional note, p. 412.

118 *burning treasure*: See Additional note, p. 412.

120 *conceit*: significance.

122 *lapful*: an allusion to Jove's visitation of Danae in a shower of gold, as a result of which Danae (like Isabella) became pregnant; Isabella has 'a belly-full'.

125 *toll him hither*: entice him to the trapdoor. Guardiano presumably motions Hippolito towards him, perhaps with elaborate bowing; a trip as he moves backward over the trap would create enough noise to be mistaken as the signal.

and he himself falls through it. HIPPOLITO *bends over* ISABELLA*'s body.*]

HIPPOLITO. Stark dead! Oh treachery! Cruelly made
away! – How's that?

FABRITIO. Look, there's one of the lovers dropp'd away
too.

DUKE. Why sure, this plot's drawn false; here's no such
thing.

LIVIA. Oh, I am sick to th'death! Let me down quickly.
[*She is lowered to the ground.*]
This fume is deadly. Oh, 't has poison'd me!
My subtlety is sped; her art has quitted me.
My own ambition pulls me down to ruin. [*Dies.*]

HIPPOLITO. Nay, then I kiss thy cold lips, and applaud
This thy revenge in death.
[*He kisses the dead* ISABELLA.]
Cupids shoot [*at* HIPPOLITO].

FABRITIO. Look, Juno's down too!
What makes she there? Her pride should keep aloft.
She was wont to scorn the earth in other shows.
Methinks her peacocks' feathers are much pull'd.

HIPPOLITO. Oh, death runs through my blood, in a wild
flame too!
Plague of those Cupids! Some lay hold on 'em.
Let 'em not 'scape, they have spoil'd me; the shaft's
deadly.

DUKE. I have lost myself in this quite.

HIPPOLITO. My great lords, we are all confounded.

DUKE. How!

HIPPOLITO. Dead: and, ay, worse.

FABRITIO. Dead? My girl dead? I hope
My sister Juno has not serv'd me so.

HIPPOLITO. Lust and forgetfulness has been amongst us,
And we are brought to nothing. Some blest charity
Lend me the speeding pity of his sword
To quench this fire in blood. Leantio's death

---

132 *quitted*: requited/removed (from life).

138 *peacocks' feathers*: Juno's chariot was drawn by peacocks.

144 *Dead; and, ay, worse*: i.e. dead and damned. O may just be right in printing 'and I worse', in which case Hippolito is saying that he is damned (as opposed to Isabella) for committing conscious incest.

Has brought all this upon us (now I taste it)
And made us lay plots to confound each other.
The event so proves it; and man's understanding
Is riper at his fall than all his lifetime.
She, in a madness for her lover's death,
Reveal'd a fearful lust in our near bloods,
For which I am punish'd dreadfully and unlook'd for;
Prov'd her own ruin too; vengeance met vengeance
Like a set match, as if the plague[s] of sin
Had been agreed to meet here altogether.
But how her fawning partner fell, I reach not,
Unless caught by some springe of his own setting,
For on my pain, he never dream'd of dying:
The plot was all his own, and he had cunning
Enough to save himself; but 'tis the property
Of guilty deeds to draw your wise men downward.
Therefore the wonder ceases. Oh this torment!

DUKE. Our guard below there!

Enter a LORD *with a* GUARD.

LORD. My lord?

HIPPOLITO. Run and meet death then,
And cut off time and pain.

[*Runs on the* GUARD*'s halberd, and dies*.]

LORD. Behold, my lord,
H'as run his breast upon a weapon's point.

DUKE. Upon the first night of our nuptial honours
Destruction play her triumph, and great mischiefs
Mask in expected pleasures! 'Tis prodigious!
They're things most fearfully ominous: I like 'em not.
– Remove these ruin'd bodies from our eyes.

[*The bodies are taken away.*]

BIANCA. [*aside*] Not yet? No change? When falls he to the earth?

LORD. Please but your excellence to peruse that paper,
Which is a brief confession from the heart

---

158 *Like a set match*: as if by agreement or conspiracy.
160 *reach*: understand.
161 *springe*: snare.
165 *draw your wise men downward*: i.e. to humiliate them/drag them down to Hell (with an allusion to Guardiano's accident).
172 *prodigious*: ill-omened.

Of him that fell first, ere his soul departed;
And there the darkness of these deeds speaks plainly:
'Tis the full scope, the manner and intent.
His ward, that ignorantly let him down,
Fear put to present flight at the voice of him.

BIANCA. [*aside*] Nor yet?

DUKE. Read, read; for I am lost in sight and strength.

CARDINAL. My noble brother!

BIANCA. Oh the curse of wretchedness!
My deadly hand is fal'n upon my lord.
Destruction take me to thee, give me way;
The pains and plagues of a lost soul upon him
That hinders me a moment!

DUKE. My heart swells bigger yet; help here, break't ope!
My breast flies open next. [*Dies.*]

BIANCA. Oh, with the poison
That was prepar'd for thee, thee, Cardinal!
'Twas meant for thee.

CARDINAL. Poor prince!

BIANCA. Accursed error!
Give me thy last breath, thou infected bosom,
And wrap two spirits in one poison'd vapour.
[*Kisses the* DUKE*'s lips.*]
Thus, thus, reward thy murderer, and turn death
Into a parting kiss. My soul stands ready at my lips,
Ev'n vex'd to stay one minute after thee.

CARDINAL. The greatest sorrow and astonishment
That ever struck the general peace of Florence
Dwells in this hour.

BIANCA. So; my desires are satisfied,
I feel death's power within me!
Thou hast prevail'd in something, cursed poison,
Though thy chief force was spent in my lord's bosom.
But my deformity in spirit's more foul:
A blemish'd face best fits a leprous soul.

---

181 *ignorantly*: unwittingly.

182 *present*: immediate.

189–90 At the moment of death the body's blood supply was supposed to rush to the heart, causing it to swell.

205 *blemish'd face*: It appears that the poison from the Duke's lips eats into Bianca's face, so that her appearance matches her corrupted nature, as Neo-Platonic doctrine expected (see II.ii.426–7).

What make I here? These are all strangers to me,
Not known but by their malice, now th'art gone,
Nor do I seek their pities.
CARDINAL. Oh restrain
Her ignorant, wilful hand!
[BIANCA *seizes the poisoned cup and drinks from it.*]
BIANCA. Now do; 'tis done.
Leantio, now I feel the breach of marriage
At my heart-breaking! Oh the deadly snares
That women set for women, without pity
Either to soul or honour! Learn by me
To know your foes. In this belief I die:
Like our own sex, we have no enemy . . . no enemy.
LORD. See, my lord,
What shift sh'as made to be her own destruction.
BIANCA. Pride, greatness, honours, beauty, youth, ambition,
You must all down together; there's no help for't.
Yet this my gladness is, that I remove,
Tasting the same death in a cup of love. [*Dies.*]
CARDINAL. Sin, what thou art these ruins show too piteously.
Two kings on one throne cannot sit together,
But one must needs down, for his title's wrong;
So where lust reigns, that prince cannot reign long.
Exeunt.

Finis

---

209 *ignorant*: reckless, deliberately blind to moral considerations.
215 *no enemy . . . no enemy*: See Textual note, p. 407.
220 *remove*: depart, die.

THE

CHANGELING:

As it was Acted (with great Applause) at the Privat house in DRURY-LANE, and *Salisbury Court*.

Written by { *THOMAS MIDLETON*, and *WILLIAM ROWLEY*. } Gent'.

Never Printed before.

LONDON,
Printed in the Year, 1653.

Title-page of the 1653 Quarto of *The Changeling*, reproduced by permission of the Master and Fellows, Trinity College, Cambridge.

INTRODUCTORY NOTE

The Trinity College, Cambridge copy of the quarto of *The Changeling* printed for Humphrey Moseley in 1653 has served as copy-text of this edition. It has few important misprints, and was probably set up from a scribal transcript, perhaps of prompt copy, perhaps of foul papers. The play has been frequently reprinted in collections, and there have been four single volume editions. Far and away the best is N.W. Bawcutt's edition for the Revels (1958, revised 1963), which has extensive introduction and notes, and is based on the Huntington Library copy of Q collated with copies in the British Museum and Bodleian Library. P. Thomson produced a poor edition for the New Mermaid (1964), using the British Museum copy collated with modern editions: introduction and notes are thin, and there are substantial textual errors. G.W. Williams's edition for Regents Renaissance (University of Nebraska, 1966; Edward Arnold, London, 1967) offers a good text but adds little to Bawcutt's interpretations. M.W. Black's edition (University of Pennsylvania, Philadelphia, 1966) contributes further suggestions on text and annotation. N.W. Bawcutt has edited a facsimile of the 1653 text (Scolar Press, 1973).

The principal source of *The Changeling* is the fourth of five histories in volume one of John Reynolds's *The Triumphs of God's Revenge against the Crying and Execrable Sin of Murder* (London, 1621). 'The Murdered Substitute Tale' occurs widely in legend and folk-tale, but it is likely that the immediate source for the episode with Diaphanta was *Gerardo, the Unfortunate Spaniard*, either in Leonard Digges's translation (1622) or in the Spanish of G. de Cespedes y Meneses. There are no obvious literary sources for the sub-plot.

Sir Henry Herbert licensed the play on 7 May 1622 for performance by the Lady Elizabeth's Servants at the Phoenix, and the company performed the play at Court, at Whitehall on Sunday 4 January 1623/4. The play was undoubtedly popular, and there are contemporary allusions to it. John Greene's Diary records seeing a performance in March 1634/5, and on 10 August 1639 the Lord Chamberlain protected the play for Beeston's Boys, the King and Queen's Young Company at the Cockpit. The 1653 title-page of the quarto asserts that it has been 'acted with great applause at the private house in Drury Lane (i.e. the Phoenix) and Salisbury Court' (in Whitefriars). In 1659/60 the play was in the repertoire of Rhodes's newly formed company at the Phoenix, and John Downes records that Betterton was particularly applauded for his De Flores and Sheppy 'above all' for his Changeling. This company became the Duke of York's Company and played for a few months at the Salisbury Court Theatre before transferring to the new Duke of York's Theatre in Lincoln's Inn Fields, where according to the title-page of the 1668 re-issue of Q *The Changeling* was performed. Pepys went 'by water to Whitefriars to the Playhouse and there saw *The Changeling*, the first time it hath been acted these twenty years, and it takes exceedingly'. Edward Browne records seeing *The Changeling* around 1662 at the Cardinal's Cap, a Cambridge inn near Pembroke Hall. Three short drolls from *The Changeling* are found in *The Mirror of Complements* (1655), though they cannot be taken as evidence that bits of the action were surreptitiously performed under the Puritans.

In the eighteenth century the play suffered crude and unacknowledged adaptation as *Marcella* by W. Hayley, a main-piece for Drury Lane performed 7 November 1789 with Kemble in the De Flores role as 'Hernandez'. It was not well-received, but did better with a different cast at Covent Garden on Tuesday 10 November and Friday 13 November 1789. A modern adaptation by S.A. Eliot, called *The Loathed Lover*, was published in *Little Theatre Classics*, vol. ii (1920).

The distinction for a first modern revival seems to go to the First Folio Theatre Club at the Interval Theatre Club on 3 May 1950. The BBC broadcast a version omitting the sub-plot on 20 November 1950. On 16 May 1954 a single performance was given by the Pegasus Society at Wyndham's Theatre, and in November 1956 the play was produced at Oxford by the Experimental Theatre Club. A production at the Royal Court Theatre with Mary Ure as Beatrice and Robert Shaw as De Flores ran from 21 February to 18 March 1961. Richard Dunn produced an uncut version for the Lady Margaret Players in the Hall of St John's College, Cambridge, 21–3 January 1964. The Lyceum Company performed *The Changeling* at the Edinburgh Festival in September 1970, and a production opened at the Gardner Centre on 30 September 1971. BBC Television broadcast an outstanding version on 20 January 1974, with Stanley Baker as De Flores and Helen Mirren as Beatrice-Joanna.

DRAMATIS PERSONAE

VERMANDERO, father to BEATRICE.
TOMAZO DE PIRACQUO, a noble lord.
ALONZO DE PIRACQUO, his brother, suitor to BEATRICE.
ALSEMERO, a nobleman, afterwards married to BEATRICE.
JASPERINO, his friend.
ALIBIUS, a jealous doctor.
LOLLIO, his man.
PEDRO, friend to ANTONIO.
ANTONIO, the Changeling.
FRANCISCUS, the counterfeit madman.
DE FLORES, servant to VERMANDERO.
MADMEN.
SERVANTS.

BEATRICE [-JOANNA], daughter to VERMANDERO.
DIAPHANTA, her waiting-woman.
ISABELLA, wife to ALIBIUS.

The Scene: *Alligant.*

---

9 *Changeling*: idiot. But see Additional note, p. 413.
11 DE FLORES: from Latin, meaning 'deflowers'.
17 *Alligant*: Alicante, a seaport on the east coast of Spain, about 75 miles due south of Valencia.

THE CHANGELING

ACT I

SCENE I

Enter ALSEMERO.

ALSEMERO. 'Twas in the temple where I first beheld her,
And now again the same; what omen yet
Follows of that? None but imaginary.
Why should my hopes or fate be timorous?
The place is holy, so is my intent:
I love her beauties to the holy purpose,
And that, methinks, admits comparison
With man's first creation, the place blest,
And is his right home back, if he achieve it.
The church hath first begun our interview,
And that's the place must join us into one;
So there's beginning and perfection too.

Enter JASPERINO.

JASPERINO. Oh, sir, are you here? Come, the wind's fair
with you,
Y'are like to have a swift and pleasant passage.
ALSEMERO. Sure, y'are deceived, friend; 'tis contrary
In my best judgement.
JASPERINO. What, for Malta?
If you could buy a gale amongst the witches,
They could not serve you such a lucky pennyworth
As comes a' God's name.
ALSEMERO. Even now I observ'd
The temple's vane to turn full in my face;
I know 'tis against me.
JASPERINO. Against you?
Then you know not where you are.
ALSEMERO. Not well, indeed.
JASPERINO. Are you not well, sir?

The Changeling: See Additional note, p. 413.
6 *holy purpose*: marriage.
8 *the place blest*: Paradise. See Additional note, p. 413.
19 *a'God's name*: as God's gift, as opposed to forbidden bargains with the occult.
20 *temple's vane*: the windvane on the top of the church.

ALSEMERO. Yes, Jasperino;
Unless there be some hidden malady
Within me, that I understand not.
JASPERINO. And that
I begin to doubt, sir. I never knew
Your inclinations to travels at a pause
With any cause to hinder it, till now.
Ashore you were wont to call your servants up,
And help to trap your horses for the speed;
At sea I have seen you weigh the anchor with 'em,
Hoist sails for fear to lose the foremost breath,
Be in continual prayers for fair winds,
And have you chang'd your orisons?
ALSEMERO. No, friend,
I keep the same church, same devotion.
JASPERINO. Lover I'm sure y'are none, the stoic
Was found in you long ago; your mother
Nor best friends, who have set snares of beauty,
Ay, and choice ones too, could never trap you that way.
What might be the cause?
ALSEMERO. Lord, how violent
Thou art! I was but meditating of
Somewhat I heard within the temple.
JASPERINO. Is this violence? 'Tis but idleness
Compar'd with your haste yesterday.
ALSEMERO. I'm all this while a-going, man.

Enter SERVANTS.

JASPERINO. Backwards, I think sir. Look, your servants.
1 SERVANT. The seamen call; shall we board your trunks?
ALSEMERO. No, not today.
JASPERINO. 'Tis the critical day, it seems, and the sign in
Aquarius.
2 SERVANT. [*aside*] We must not to sea today; this
smoke will bring forth fire!

---

26 *doubt*: fear.
30 *trap your horses for the speed*: 'harness your horses to hasten departure'.
49 *critical*: astrologically crucial.
49 *sign in Aquarius*: Aquarius, the 'Water-carrier', is the eleventh sign of the Zodiac; hence, it is a favourable time for a sea-voyage.
51 Proverbial, alluding to the saying 'there's no smoke without fire' (Tilley, S 569).

ALSEMERO. Keep all on shore; I do not know the end
(Which needs I must do) of an affair in hand
Ere I can go to sea.

1 SERVANT. Well, your pleasure.

2 SERVANT. [*aside*] Let him e'en take his leisure too, we are safer on land.

Exeunt SERVANTS.

Enter BEATRICE, DIAPHANTA, *and* SERVANTS.
[ALSEMERO *greets* BEATRICE *and kisses her.*]

JASPERINO. [*aside*] How now! The laws of the Medes are chang'd, sure! Salute a woman? He kisses too; wonderful! Where learnt he this? And does it perfectly too; in my conscience, he ne'er rehears'd it before. Nay, go on, this will be stranger and better news at Valencia than if he had ransom'd half Greece from the Turk.

BEATRICE. You are a scholar, sir?

ALSEMERO. A weak one, lady.

BEATRICE. Which of the sciences is this love you speak of?

ALSEMERO. From your tongue, I take it to be music.

BEATRICE. You are skilful in't, can sing at first sight.

ALSEMERO. And I have show'd you all my skill at once.
I want more words to express me further,
And must be forc'd to repetition:
I love you dearly.

BEATRICE. Be better advis'd, sir:
Our eyes are sentinels unto our judgements,
And should give certain judgement what they see;
But they are rash sometimes and tell us wonders
Of common things, which, when our judgements find,
They then can check the eyes and call them blind.

ALSEMERO. But I am further, lady; yesterday
Was mine eyes' employment, and hither now
They brought my judgement, where are both agreed.

---

57 *laws of the Medes*: unchangeable laws (Daniel 6.8).

60 *in my conscience*: on my word.

62–3 *Greece from the Turk*: Greece was part of the Ottoman Empire from 1460 to 1830.

67 *sing at first sight*: i.e. 'you can sight-read music'//'make love at a first introduction' (See *Troilus and Cressida*, V.ii.9).

Both Houses then consenting, 'tis agreed;
Only there wants the confirmation
By the hand royal – that's your part, lady.

BEATRICE. Oh, there's one above me, sir. [*Aside*] For five days past
To be recall'd! Sure, mine eyes were mistaken,
This was the man was meant me. That he should come
So near his time, and miss it!

JASPERINO. [*aside*] We might have come by the carriers from Valencia, I see, and sav'd all our sea provision; we are at farthest, sure. Methinks I should do something too: I meant to be a venturer in this voyage. Yonder's another vessel, I'll board her; if she be lawful prize, down goes her topsail!

[*Approaches* DIAPHANTA.]

Enter DE FLORES.

DE FLORES. Lady, your father –

BEATRICE. Is in health, I hope.

DE FLORES. Your eye shall instantly instruct you, lady.
He's coming hitherward.

BEATRICE. What needed then
Your duteous preface? I had rather
He had come unexpected; you must stall
A good presence with unnecessary blabbing;
And how welcome for your part you are,
I'm sure you know.

DE FLORES. [*aside*] Will't never mend, this scorn,
One side nor other? Must I be enjoin'd
To follow still whilst she flies from me? Well,

---

80 *Both Houses then consenting*: both Houses of Parliament, Commons and Lords, senses and judgement, having given their approval.
82 *hand royal*: the royal assent, as to a Parliamentary bill.
83 *one above me*: above the 'royal' Beatrice is the ultimate, God-like authority of her father.
87 *carriers*: land transport.
89 *at farthest*: at the limits of our journey.
91 *lawful prize*: i.e. a vessel which no regulations prohibit him from capturing.
92 *down goes her topsail*: the sign of a ship's surrender.
97 *stall*: forestall/make stale (as in Massinger, *The Bashful Lover*, IV.iii.42). See Textual note, p. 407.
98 *a good presence*: i.e. the impressive bearing of her father.

Fates do your worst, I'll please myself with sight
Of her, at all opportunities,
If but to spite her anger; I know she had
Rather see me dead than living, and yet
She knows no cause for't but a peevish will.
ALSEMERO. You seem'd displeas'd, lady, on the sudden.
BEATRICE. Your pardon, sir, 'tis my infirmity;
Nor can I other reason render you
Than his or hers, of some particular thing
They must abandon as a deadly poison,
Which to a thousand other tastes were wholesome;
Such to mine eyes is that same fellow there,
The same that report speaks of the basilisk.
ALSEMERO. This is a frequent frailty in our nature;
There's scarce a man among a thousand sound,
But hath his imperfection: one distastes
The scent of roses, which to infinites
Most pleasing is, and odoriferous;
One oil, the enemy of poison;
Another wine, the cheerer of the heart,
And lively refresher of the countenance.
Indeed, this fault, if so it be, is general;
There's scarce a thing but is both lov'd and loath'd;
Myself, I must confess, have the same frailty.
BEATRICE. And what may be your poison, sir? I am bold
with you.
ALSEMERO. What might be your desire, perhaps, a cherry.
BEATRICE. I am no enemy to any creature
My memory has, but yon gentleman.
ALSEMERO. He does ill to tempt your sight, if he knew it.
BEATRICE. He cannot be ignorant of that, sir,
I have not spar'd to tell him so; and I want
To help myself, since he's a gentleman
In good respect with my father, and follows him.

---

115 *basilisk*: a mythical beast able to kill by a glance.
117 *thousand sound*: a thousand healthy people. But see Textual note, p. 407.
119 *infinites*: an infinite number of people.
121–3 A reminiscence of Psalm 104.15.
128 See Textual note, p. 407.
133–4 *I want/To help myself*: I lack the means to help myself.
135 *In good respect*: held in esteem.

ALSEMERO. He's out of his place then now.
[*They talk apart.*]

JASPERINO. I am a mad wag, wench.

DIAPHANTA. So methinks; but for your comfort I can tell you, we have a doctor in the city that undertakes the cure of such.

JASPERINO. Tush, I know what physic is best for the state of mine own body.

DIAPHANTA. 'Tis scarce a well govern'd state, I believe.

JASPERINO. I could show thee such a thing with an ingredience that we two would compound together, and if it did not tame the maddest blood i' th' town for two hours after, I'll ne'er profess physic again.

DIAPHANTA. A little poppy, sir, were good to cause you sleep.

JASPERINO. Poppy? I'll give thee a pop i' th' lips for that first, and begin there; [*Kisses her*] poppy is one simple indeed, and cuckoo (what you call't) another. I'll discover no more now, another time I'll show thee all.

BEATRICE. My father, sir.

Enter VERMANDERO *and* SERVANTS.

VERMANDERO. Oh, Joanna, I came to meet thee;
Your devotion's ended?

BEATRICE. For this time, sir.
[*Aside*] I shall change my saint, I fear me; I find
A giddy turning in me. – Sir, this while
I am beholding to this gentleman,
Who left his own way to keep me company,
And in discourse I find him much desirous
To see your castle: he hath deserv'd it, sir,
If ye please to grant it.

VERMANDERO. With all my heart, sir.
Yet there's an article between, I must know

---

139 *doctor*: i.e. Alibius.
145 *ingredience*: See Textual note, p. 407.
151 *simple*: medicine from a single herb or plant; hence, a medicinal herb.
151 *cuckoo (what you call't)*: cuckoo-pint or wild arum, of phallic appearance.
156 *change my saint*: change the object of my religious adoration (to an earthly one).
163 *article between*: a stipulation to be satisfied beforehand.

Your country; we use not to give survey
Of our chief strengths to strangers; our citadels
Are plac'd conspicuous to outward view,
On promonts' tops; but within are secrets.

ALSEMERO. A Valencian, sir.

VERMANDERO. A Valencian?
That's native, sir; of what name, I beseech you?

ALSEMERO. Alsemero, sir.

VERMANDERO. Alsemero? Not the son
Of John de Alsemero?

ALSEMERO. The same, sir.

VERMANDERO. My best love bids you welcome.

BEATRICE. [*aside*] He was wont
To call me so, and then he speaks a most
Unfeigned truth.

VERMANDERO. Oh, sir, I knew your father;
We two were in acquaintance long ago,
Before our chins were worth Iulan down,
And so continued till the stamp of time
Had coin'd us into silver. Well, he's gone;
A good soldier went with him.

ALSEMERO. You went together in that, sir.

VERMANDERO. No, by Saint Jacques, I came behind him;
Yet I have done somewhat too. An unhappy day
Swallowed him at last at Gibraltar
In fight with those rebellious Hollanders,
Was it not so?

ALSEMERO. Whose death I had reveng'd,
Or follow'd him in fate, had not the late league
Prevented me.

VERMANDERO. Ay, ay, 'twas time to breathe.
– Oh, Joanna, I should ha' told thee news,
I saw Piracquo lately.

---

173 *To call me so*: i.e. ' "my best love" is his customary endearment to me, and he is most right in saying I bid Alsemero welcome'.

176 *Iulan down*: the first growth of the beard, the epithet being derived from commentaries on the name of Iulus Ascanius in *Aeneid*, I.267.

181 *Saint Jacques*: St James the Greater, patron saint of Spain.

183 *Gibraltar*: a Dutch victory over the Spanish fleet, 25 April 1607.

186 *late league*: the Treaty of the Hague, 9 April 1609, which provided for a twelve year truce.

BEATRICE. [*aside*] That's ill news.
VERMANDERO. He's hot preparing for his day of triumph;
Thou must be a bride within this sevennight.
ALSEMERO. [*aside*] Ha!
BEATRICE. Nay, good sir, be not so violent; with speed
I cannot render satisfaction
Unto the dear companion of my soul,
Virginity, whom I thus long have liv'd with,
And part with it so rude and suddenly;
Can such friends divide, never to meet again,
Without a solemn farewell?
VERMANDERO. Tush, tush, there's a toy.
ALSEMERO. [*aside*] I must now part, and never meet again
With any joy on earth. – Sir, your pardon,
My affairs call on me.
VERMANDERO. How, sir? By no means;
Not chang'd so soon, I hope. You must see my castle,
And her best entertainment, ere we part;
I shall think myself unkindly us'd else.
Come, come, let's on; I had good hope your stay
Had been a while with us in Alligant;
I might have bid you to my daughter's wedding.
ALSEMERO. [*aside*] He means to feast me, and poisons me beforehand.
– I should be dearly glad to be there, sir,
Did my occasions suit as I could wish.
BEATRICE. I shall be sorry if you be not there
When it is done, sir; – but not so suddenly.
VERMANDERO. I tell you, sir, the gentleman's complete,
A courtier and a gallant, enrich'd
With many fair and noble ornaments;
I would not change him for a son-in-law
For any he in Spain, the proudest he,
And we have great ones, that you know.
ALSEMERO. He's much
Bound to you, sir.

---

190 *his*: See Textual note, p. 407.
198 *toy*: either 'a whim', or, referring to her virginity, 'a thing of no worth'.
206 *Alligant*: Alicante, a seaport south of Valencia.

VERMANDERO. He shall be bound to me,
As fast as this tie can hold him; I'll want
My will else.

BEATRICE. [*aside*] I shall want mine if you do it.

VERMANDERO. But come, by the way I'll tell you more of him.

ALSEMERO. [*aside*] How shall I dare to venture in his castle,
When he discharges murderers at the gate?
But I must on, for back I cannot go.

BEATRICE. [*aside*] Not this serpent gone yet?

[*She drops her glove.*]

VERMANDERO. Look, girl, thy glove's fall'n.
Stay, stay; – De Flores, help a little.

[*Exeunt* VERMANDERO, ALSEMERO, JASPERINO *and* SERVANTS.]

DE FLORES. Here, lady.

(*Offers the glove.*)

BEATRICE. Mischief on your officious forwardness!
Who bade you stoop? They touch my hand no more.
There! For t'other's sake I part with this;

[*Takes off the other glove and throws it down.*]

Take 'em and draw thine own skin off with 'em.

Exeunt [BEATRICE *and* DIAPHANTA .]

DE FLORES. Here's a favour come, with a mischief! Now I know
She had rather wear my pelt tann'd in a pair
Of dancing pumps than I should thrust my fingers
Into her sockets here; I know she hates me,
Yet cannot choose but love her;
No matter; if but to vex her, I'll haunt her still;
Though I get nothing else, I'll have my will. *Exit.*

---

224 *murderers*: small cannon, charged with grapeshot. The phrase relates ironically to future events.

226 *serpent*: See Additional note, p. 413.

226 s.d. Presumably the glove is dropped as a love-token for Alsemero, but (with proleptic symbolism) it is retrieved by De Flores.

232 *Here's a favour come, with a mischief*: 'here's a kindness/love-token come with an accompanying ill-wish'. See also Textual note, p. 407.

SCENE II

Enter ALIBIUS *and* LOLLIO.

ALIBIUS. Lollio, I must trust thee with a secret,
But thou must keep it.
LOLLIO. I was ever close to a secret, sir.
ALIBIUS. The diligence that I have found in thee,
The care and industry already past,
Assures me of thy good continuance.
Lollio, I have a wife.
LOLLIO. Fie, sir, 'tis too late to keep her secret, she's known to be married all the town and country over.
ALIBIUS. Thou goest too fast, my Lollio; that knowledge
I allow no man can be barr'd it;
But there is a knowledge which is nearer,
Deeper, and sweeter, Lollio.
LOLLIO. Well, sir, let us handle that between you and I.
ALIBIUS. 'Tis that I go about, man. Lollio,
My wife is young.
LOLLIO. So much the worse to be kept secret, sir.
ALIBIUS. Why, now thou meet'st the substance of the point;
I am old, Lollio.
LOLLIO. No, sir, 'tis I am old Lollio.
ALIBIUS. Yet why may not this concord and sympathize?
Old trees and young plants often grow together,
Well enough agreeing.
LOLLIO. Ay, sir, but the old trees raise themselves higher and broader than the young plants.
ALIBIUS. Shrewd application! There's the fear man;
I would wear my ring on my own finger;
Whilst it is borrowed it is none of mine,
But his that useth it.
LOLLIO. You must keep it on still then; if it but lie by,
One or other will be thrusting into't.
ALIBIUS. Thou conceiv'st me, Lollio; here thy watchful eye

---

3 *close to a secret*: discreet about/good at searching out secrets.
24–5 i.e. the old become 'higher and broader' by the addition of a cuckold's horns.
27 *ring*: with an allusion to the female *pudendum*, continued in the following lines; *finger* = penis.

Must have employment; I cannot always be
At home.

LOLLIO. I dare swear you cannot.

ALIBIUS. I must look out.

LOLLIO. I know't; you must look out, 'tis every man's case.

ALIBIUS. Here, I do say, must thy employment be:
To watch her treadings, and in my absence
Supply my place.

LOLLIO. I'll do my best, sir; yet surely I cannot see who you should have cause to be jealous of.

ALIBIUS. Thy reason for that, Lollio? 'Tis a comfortable question.

LOLLIO. We have but two sorts of people in the house, and both under the whip, that's fools and madmen; the one has not wit enough to be knaves, and the other not knavery enough to be fools.

ALIBIUS. Ay, those are all my patients, Lollio.
I do profess the cure of either sort;
My trade, my living 'tis, I thrive by it;
But here's the care that mixes with my thrift:
The daily visitants, that come to see
My brainsick patients, I would not have
To see my wife: gallants I do observe
Of quick enticing eyes, rich in habits,
Of stature and proportion very comely:
These are most shrewd temptations, Lollio.

LOLLIO. They may be easily answered, sir; if they come to see the fools and madmen, you and I may serve the turn, and let my mistress alone, she's of neither sort.

ALIBIUS. 'Tis a good ward; indeed, come they to see
Our madmen or our fools, let 'em see no more
Than what they come for; by that consequent
They must not see her, I'm sure she's no fool.

LOLLIO. And I'm sure she's no madman.

ALIBIUS. Hold that buckler fast, Lollio; my trust

---

36 *look out*: travel away from home//beware.
44 *comfortable*: comforting.
53 *daily visitants*: Bethlehem Hospital and other madhouses were resorted to as places of entertainment.
62 *ward*: fencing guard, defensive position.
64 *consequent*: logical sequence.

Is on thee, and I account it firm and strong.
What hour is't, Lollio?

LOLLIO. Towards belly-hour, sir.

ALIBIUS. Dinner time? Thou mean'st twelve o'clock?

LOLLIO. Yes, sir, for every part has his hour: we wake at six and look about us, that's eye-hour; at seven we should pray, that's knee-hour; at eight walk, that's leg-hour; at nine gather flowers and pluck a rose, that's nose-hour; at ten we drink, that's mouth-hour; at eleven lay about us for victuals, that's hand-hour; at twelve go to dinner, that's belly-hour.

ALIBIUS. Profoundly, Lollio! It will be long
Ere all thy scholars learn this lesson, and
I did look to have a new one ent'red; – stay,
I think my expectation is come home.

Enter PEDRO, *and* ANTONIO *like an idiot.*

PEDRO. Save you, sir; my business speaks itself,
This sight takes off the labour of my tongue.

ALIBIUS. Ay, ay, sir, 'tis plain enough; you mean him for my patient.

PEDRO. And if your pains prove but commodious, to give but some little strength to his sick and weak part of nature in him, these are but patterns [*Gives him money*] to show you of the whole pieces that will follow to you, beside the charge of diet, washing and other necessaries fully defrayed.

ALIBIUS. Believe it, sir, there shall no care be wanting.

LOLLIO. Sir, an officer in this place may deserve something; the trouble will pass through my hands.

PEDRO. 'Tis fit something should come to your hands then, sir. [*Gives him money.*]

LOLLIO. Yes, sir, 'tis I must keep him sweet, and read to him. What is his name?

PEDRO. His name is Antonio; marry, we use but half to him, only Tony.

---

75 *pluck a rose*: urinate.
87 *commodious*: effective.
89 *patterns*: samples; i.e. small change as earnest of the high value coins to come.
98 *sweet*: clean and sweet-smelling.
101 *Tony*: The name became a synonym for 'fool' during the seventeenth century.

LOLLIO. Tony, Tony; 'tis enough, and a very good name for a fool. – What's your name, Tony?

ANTONIO. He, he, he! Well, I thank you, cousin; he, he, he!

LOLLIO. Good boy! Hold up your head. He can laugh; I perceive by that he is no beast.

PEDRO. Well, sir,
If you can raise him but to any height,
Any degree of wit, might he attain,
(As I might say) to creep but on all four
Towards the chair of wit, or walk on crutches,
'Twould add an honour to your worthy pains,
And a great family might pray for you,
To which he should be heir, had he discretion
To claim and guide his own; assure you, sir,
He is a gentleman.

LOLLIO. Nay, there's nobody doubted that; at first sight I knew him for a gentleman, he looks no other yet.

PEDRO. Let him have good attendance and sweet lodging.

LOLLIO. As good as my mistress lies in, sir; and as you allow us time and means, we can raise him to the higher degree of discretion.

PEDRO. Nay, there shall no cost want, sir.

LOLLIO. He will hardly be stretch'd up to the wit of a magnifico.

PEDRO. Oh no, that's not to be expected, far shorter will be enough.

LOLLIO. I'll warrant you [I] make him fit to bear office in five weeks; I'll undertake to wind him up to the wit of constable.

PEDRO. If it be lower than that it might serve turn.

LOLLIO. No, fie, to level him with a headborough, beadle, or watchman were but little better than he is; con-

---

106 *laugh*: The capacity for laughter was one Aristotelian distinction between man and beast.

126 *magnifico*: a magistrate of Venice and, by transference, a person of high authority.

131 *constable*: Constables were proverbially stupid, and frequent butts in the drama.

133 *headborough*: a petty constable.

133 *beadle*: a minor parish official charged with keeping order in church, making announcements etc.; *or* a minor legal official acting as court crier and messenger.

stable I'll able him; if he do come to be a justice afterwards, let him thank the keeper. Or I'll go further with you; say I do bring him up to my own pitch, say I make him as wise as myself.

PEDRO. Why, there I would have it.

LOLLIO. Well, go to; either I'll be as arrant a fool as he, or he shall be as wise as I, and then I think 'twill serve his turn.

PEDRO. Nay, I do like thy wit passing well.

LOLLIO. Yes, you may; yet if I had not been a fool, I had had more wit than I have too; remember what state you find me in.

PEDRO. I will, and so leave you; your best cares, I beseech you. *Exit* PEDRO.

ALIBIUS. Take you none with you; leave 'em all with us.

ANTONIO. Oh, my cousin's gone! Cousin, cousin, oh!

LOLLIO. Peace, peace, Tony; you must not cry, child, you must be whipp'd if you do. Your cousin is here still; I am your cousin, Tony.

ANTONIO. He, he! Then I'll not cry, if thou be'st my cousin; he, he, he!

LOLLIO. I were best try his wit a little, that I may know what form to place him in.

ALIBIUS. Ay, do, Lollio, do.

LOLLIO. I must ask him easy questions at first. – Tony, how many true fingers has a tailor on his right hand?

ANTONIO. As many as on his left, cousin.

LOLLIO. Good; and how many on both?

ANTONIO. Two less than a deuce, cousin.

LOLLIO. Very well answered. I come to you again, cousin Tony: how many fools goes to a wise man?

ANTONIO. Forty in a day sometimes, cousin.

LOLLIO. Forty in a day? How prove you that?

ANTONIO. All that fall out amongst themselves, and go to a lawyer to be made friends.

---

135 *able him*: make him fit for.
140 *arrant*: See Textual note, p. 407.
146 *state*: professional position.
163 *two less than a deuce*: i.e none, since tailors were proverbially dishonest.
165–9 *goes to*: make up//visit.

LOLLIO. A parlous fool! He must sit in the fourth form at least, I perceive that. I come again, Tony: how many knaves make an honest man?

ANTONIO. I know not that, cousin.

LOLLIO. No, the question is too hard for you. I'll tell you, cousin, there's three knaves may make an honest man: a sergeant, a jailer, and a beadle; the sergeant catches him, the jailer holds him and the beadle lashes him; and if he be not honest then, the hangman must cure him.

ANTONIO. Ha, ha, ha! That's fine sport, cousin.

ALIBIUS. This was too deep a question for the fool, Lollio.

LOLLIO. Yes, this might have serv'd yourself, though I say't. Once more, and you shall go play, Tony.

ANTONIO. Ay, play at push-pin, cousin; ha, he!

LOLLIO. So thou shalt. Say how many fools are here –

ANTONIO. Two, cousin, thou and I.

LOLLIO. Nay, y'are too forward there, Tony. Mark my question: how many fools and knaves are here? A fool before a knave, a fool behind a knave, between every two fools a knave; how many fools, how many knaves?

ANTONIO. I never learnt so far, cousin.

ALIBIUS. Thou putt'st too hard questions to him, Lollio.

LOLLIO. I'll make him understand it easily. Cousin, stand there.

ANTONIO. Ay, cousin.

LOLLIO. Master, stand you next the fool.

ALIBIUS. Well, Lollio.

LOLLIO. Here's my place. Mark now, Tony, there a fool before a knave.

ANTONIO. That's I, cousin.

LOLLIO. Here's a fool behind a knave, that's I; and between us two fools there is a knave, that's my master; 'tis but we three, that's all.

---

170 *parlous*: contracted from 'perilous'; so, dangerously cunning.

185 *push-pin*: a child's game in which each player attempts to push his pin across that of another player; frequently a euphemism for sexual intercourse.

204 *We three*: probably an allusion to a sign showing two idiots' heads with the inscription 'we three, loggerheads be', the third being the spectator.

ANTONIO. We three, we three, cousin.

Madmen within.

1 WITHIN. Put's head i' th' pillory, the bread's too little.

2 WITHIN. Fly, fly, and he catches the swallow.

3 WITHIN. Give her more onion, or the devil put the rope about her crag.

LOLLIO. You may hear what time of day it is, the chimes of Bedlam goes.

ALIBIUS. Peace, peace, or the wire comes!

3 WITHIN. Cat whore, cat whore, her permasant, her permasant!

ALIBIUS. Peace, I say! – Their hour's come, they must be fed, Lollio.

LOLLIO. There's no hope of recovery of that Welsh madman, was undone by a mouse that spoil'd him a permasant; lost his wits for't.

ALIBIUS. Go to your charge, Lollio, I'll to mine.

LOLLIO. Go to your madmen's ward, let me alone with your fools.

ALIBIUS. And remember my last charge, Lollio. *Exit.*

LOLLIO. Of which your patients do you think I am? Come, Tony, you must amongst your school-fellows now; there's pretty scholars amongst 'em, I can tell you, there's some of 'em at *stultus, stulta, stultum.*

ANTONIO. I would see the madmen, cousin, if they would not bite me.

LOLLIO. No, they shall not bite thee, Tony.

---

206 *bread's too little*: probably a complaint against the keepers for under-supplying the inmates.

207 *Fly, fly, and he catches the swallow*: The Madman imagines he has seen fulfilled the ironic proverb 'Fly and you will catch the swallow' (Tilley, S 1024).

209 *crag*: neck. The rope is both a rope of onions and the hangman's rope.

210–11 *chimes of Bedlam*: i.e. the noise of the insane, crying at feeding-time. 'Bedlam' is a corruption of Bethlehem Hospital, but used of any madhouse.

212 *wire*: a whip of wire.

213 *cat whore, her permasant*: 'her' is stage-Welsh for 'my'; the Welshman reviles his worthless she-cat for failing to protect the cheese of which he was proverbially fond.

221–2 *madmen . . . fools*: the insane and the congenital idiots.

227 *stultus, stulta, stultum*: i.e. there are some who have attained to the three genders of the Latin for 'fool': masculine, feminine – and neuter.

ANTONIO. They bite when they are at dinner, do they not, cuz?

LOLLIO. They bite at dinner, indeed, Tony. Well, I hope to get credit by thee; I like thee the best of all the scholars that ever I brought up, and thou shalt prove a wise man, or I'll prove a fool myself.

Exeunt.

ACT II

SCENE I

Enter BEATRICE *and* JASPERINO *severally.*

BEATRICE. Oh sir, I'm ready now for that fair service
Which makes the name of friend sit glorious on you.
Good angels and this conduct be your guide;
[*She gives a paper.*]
Fitness of time and place is there set down, sir.
JASPERINO. The joy I shall return rewards my service.
Exit.
BEATRICE. How wise is Alsemero in his friend!
It is a sign he makes his choice with judgement.
Then I appear in nothing more approv'd
Than making choice of him;
For 'tis a principle, he that can choose
That bosom well, who of his thoughts partakes,
Proves most discreet in every choice he makes.
Methinks I love now with the eyes of judgement,
And see the way to merit, clearly see it.
A true deserver like a diamond sparkles,
In darkness you may see him, that's in absence,
Which is the greatest darkness falls on love;
Yet he is best discern'd then
With intellectual eyesight. What's Piracquo
My father spends his breath for? And his blessing

---

s.d. *severally*: from different directions.
3 *conduct*: a pass, a paper with directions.

Is only mine as I regard his name,
Else it goes from me, and turns head against me,
Transform'd into a curse. Some speedy way
Must be rememb'red; he's so forward too,
So urgent that way, scarce allows me breath
To speak to my new comforts.

Enter DE FLORES.

DE FLORES. [*aside*] Yonder's she.
Whatever ails me? Now a'late especially,
I can as well be hang'd as refrain seeing her;
Some twenty times a day, nay, not so little,
Do I force errands, frame ways and excuses
To come into her sight, and I have small reason for't,
And less encouragement; for she baits me still
Every time worse than other, does profess herself
The cruellest enemy to my face in town,
At no hand can abide the sight of me,
As if danger or ill-luck hung in my looks.
I must confess my face is bad enough,
But I know far worse has better fortune,
And not endur'd alone, but doted on:
And yet such pick-hair'd faces, chins like witches',
Here and there five hairs, whispering in a corner,
As if they grew in fear one of another,
Wrinkles like troughs, where swine-deformity swills
The tears of perjury that lie there like wash
Fallen from the slimy and dishonest eye;
Yet such a one pluck'd sweets without restraint,

---

21 *as I regard his name*: *either* 'my father's blessing is mine only in so far as I respect my father's authority (name)' *or* 'in so far as I respect the family name (by marrying well)' *or* 'in so far as I heed the name of Piracquo alone'.

22 *turns head*: directs its power. Her father's blessing depends on her marrying the man he has chosen; otherwise it will turn into a curse.

35 *at no hand*: on no account.

40 *pick-hair'd*: perhaps 'sparsely bearded', *or* 'black-haired' *or* 'with bristly hair and beard'.

44 *wash*: watery discharge. The perjured tears lie like a discharge in the crevasses of a swinishly deformed face, as hog-wash on a pig's snout, and fall like swill into the mouth.

And has the grace of beauty to his sweet.
Though my hard fate has thrust me out to servitude,
I tumbled into th' world a gentleman.
She turns her blessed eye upon me now,
And I'll endure all storms before I part with't.

BEATRICE. [*aside*] Again!
– This ominous ill-fac'd fellow more disturbs me
Than all my other passions.

DE FLORES. [*aside*] Now't begins again;
I'll stand this storm of hail though the stones pelt me.

BEATRICE. Thy business? What's thy business?

DE FLORES. [*aside*] Soft and fair,
I cannot part so soon now.

BEATRICE. [*aside*] The villain's fix'd!
– Thou standing toad-pool!

DE FLORES. [*aside*] The shower falls amain now.

BEATRICE. Who sent thee? What's thy errand? Leave my sight.

DE FLORES. My lord your father charg'd me to deliver
A message to you.

BEATRICE. What, another since?
Do't and be hang'd then, let me be rid of thee.

DE FLORES. True service merits mercy.

BEATRICE. What's thy message?

DE FLORES. Let beauty settle but in patience,
You shall hear all.

BEATRICE. A dallying, trifling torment!

DE FLORES. Signior Alonzo de Piracquo, lady,
Sole brother to Tomazo de Piracquo –

BEATRICE. Slave, when wilt make an end?

DE FLORES. Too soon I shall.

BEATRICE. What all this while of him?

47 *to his sweet*: perhaps 'as his sweetheart'. If 'sweet' is used this early as a synonym for 'dessert', the metaphor may be from dining: he has the post-prandial *grace* of Beauty as an accompaniment to his final indulgence.

58 *standing toad-pool*: stagnant and foul water from which toads and other reptiles were held to be bred by the operation of the sun. Presumably De Flores suffers from a repulsive skin disease.

58 *amain*: with full force.

61 *another since*: i.e. in addition to the last, at I.i.93ff.

DE FLORES. The said Alonzo,
With the foresaid Tomazo –
BEATRICE. Yet again?
DE FLORES. Is new alighted.
BEATRICE. Vengeance strike the news!
Thou thing most loath'd, what cause was there in this
To bring thee to my sight?
DE FLORES. My lord your father
Charg'd me to seek you out.
BEATRICE. Is there no other
To send his errand by?
DE FLORES. It seems 'tis my luck
To be i' th' way still.
BEATRICE. Get thee from me.
DE FLORES. So!
[*Aside*] Why, am not I an ass to devise ways
Thus to be rail'd at? I must see her still!
I shall have a mad qualm within this hour again,
I know't, and, like a common Garden-bull,
I do but take breath to be lugg'd again.
What this may bode I know not; I'll despair the less,
Because there's daily precedents of bad faces
Belov'd beyond all reason; these foul chops
May come into favour one day 'mongst his fellows;
Wrangling has prov'd the mistress of good pastime:
As children cry themselves asleep, I ha' seen
Women have chid themselves abed to men.
Exit DE FLORES.
BEATRICE. I never see this fellow, but I think
Of some harm towards me, danger's in my mind still;
I scarce leave trembling of an hour after.
The next good mood I find my father in,
I'll get him quite discarded. Oh, I was
Lost in this small disturbance, and forgot
Affliction's fiercer torrent that now comes
To bear down all my comforts.

---

79 *qualm*: sudden attack of illness or faintness; here, a pang of lust.

80 *common Garden-bull*: an ordinary bull at the Paris Garden, Southwark, where bull-baiting took place.

81 *lugg'd*: teased, worried, baited.

Enter VERMANDERO, ALONZO, TOMAZO.

VERMANDERO. Y'are both welcome,
But an especial one belongs to you, sir,
To whose most noble name our love presents
The addition of a son, our son Alonzo.
ALONZO. The treasury of honour cannot bring forth
A title I should more rejoice in, sir.
VERMANDERO. You have improv'd it well. – Daughter, prepare,
The day will steal upon thee suddenly.
BEATRICE. [*aside*] Howe'er, I will be sure to keep the night,
If it should come so near me.
[BEATRICE *and* VERMANDERO *talk apart*.]
TOMAZO. Alonzo.
ALONZO. Brother?
TOMAZO. In troth I see small welcome in her eye.
ALONZO. Fie, you are too severe a censurer
Of love in all points, there's no bringing on you;
If lovers should mark everything a fault,
Affection would be like an ill-set book,
Whose faults might prove as big as half the volume.
BEATRICE. That's all I do entreat.
VERMANDERO. It is but reasonable;
I'll see what my son says to't. –Son Alonzo,
Here's a motion made but to reprieve
A maidenhead three days longer; the request
Is not far out of reason, for indeed
The former time is pinching.
ALONZO. Though my joys
Be set back so much time as I could wish
They had been forward, yet since she desires it,

---

99 *addition*: the additional title.

100 *treasury of honour*: the whole compendium of honorific titles.

104 *keep the night*: 'stay on watch during the night/keep the night to myself' (denying Alonzo the consummation of his marriage). See also Additional note, p. 415.

108 *there's no bringing on you*: perhaps 'there's no way of making you take a more reasonable view'. However, 'to bring on' = 'to excite sexually', so the phrase may mean 'there's no persuading you to love'. See also Textual note, p. 407.

111 *faults*: printing errors.

The time is set as pleasing as before;
I find no gladness wanting.
VERMANDERO. May I ever
Meet it in that point still. Y'are nobly welcome, sirs.
Exeunt VERMANDERO *and* BEATRICE.
TOMAZO. So: did you mark the dulness of her parting now?
ALONZO. What dulness? Thou art so exceptious still!
TOMAZO. Why, let it go then, I am but a fool
To mark your harms so heedfully.
ALONZO. Where's the oversight?
TOMAZO. Come, your faith's cozened in her, strongly cozened;
Unsettle your affection with all speed
Wisdom can bring it to, your peace is ruin'd else.
Think what a torment 'tis to marry one
Whose heart is leap'd into another's bosom:
If ever pleasure she receive from thee,
It comes not in thy name, or of thy gift;
She lies but with another in thine arms,
He the half-father unto all thy children
In the conception; if he get 'em not,
She helps to get 'em for him, in[s] his passions;
And how dangerous
And shameful her restraint may go in time to,
It is not to be thought on without sufferings.
ALONZO. You speak as if she lov'd some other, then.
TOMAZO. Do you apprehend so slowly?
ALONZO. Nay, and that
Be your fear only, I am safe enough.
Preserve your friendship and your counsel, brother,
For times of more distress; I should depart
An enemy, a dangerous, deadly one,
To any but thyself, that should but think
She knew the meaning of inconstancy,
Much less the use and practice; yet w'are friends.

---

124 *exceptious*: given to making objections.
127 *cozened*: cheated.
137 *in[s] his passions*: takes in his passions (in her imagination). See Textual note, p. 407.
138–9 *And how dangerous . . . go in time to*: 'And what dangerous and shameful consequences will eventually result from restraining her . . . '

Pray, let no more be urg'd; I can endure
Much, till I meet an injury to her,
Then I am not myself. Farewell, sweet brother;
How much w'are bound to heaven to depart lovingly.
Exit.

TOMAZO. Why, here is love's tame madness; thus a man
Quickly steals into his vexation. *Exit.*

SCENE II

Enter DIAPHANTA *and* ALSEMERO.

DIAPHANTA. The place is my charge, you have kept your hour,
And the reward of a just meeting bless you.
I hear my lady coming; complete gentleman,
I dare not be too busy with my praises,
Th'are dangerous things to deal with. *Exit.*

ALSEMERO. This goes well;
These women are the ladies' cabinets,
Things of most precious trust are lock['d] into 'em.

Enter BEATRICE.

BEATRICE. I have within mine eye all my desires;
Requests that holy prayers ascend heaven for,
And brings 'em down to furnish our defects,
Come not more sweet to our necessities
Than thou unto my wishes.

ALSEMERO. W'are so like
In our expressions, lady, that unless I borrow
The same words, I shall never find their equals.
[*Kisses her.*]

BEATRICE. How happy were this meeting, this embrace,
If it were free from envy! This poor kiss,
It has an enemy, a hateful one,
That wishes poison to't; how well were I now
If there were none such name known as Piracquo,

4–5 Diaphanta is fearful of Beatrice-Joanna's jealousy, though indicating her own interest in Alsemero.

10 *And brings 'em down to furnish our defects*: 'and brings down from heaven providential gifts (the answer to 'requests') to supply our deficiencies and human limitations'. See Additional note, p. 414.

Nor no such tie as the command of parents!
I should be but too much blessed.
ALSEMERO. One good service
Would strike off both your fears, and I'll go near it too,
Since you are so distress'd; remove the cause,
The command ceases; so there's two fears blown out
With one and the same blast.
BEATRICE. Pray, let me find you, sir.
What might that service be, so strangely happy?
ALSEMERO. The honourablest piece 'bout man, valour.
I'll send a challenge to Piracquo instantly.
BEATRICE. How? Call you that extinguishing of fear,
When 'tis the only way to keep it flaming?
Are not you ventured in the action,
That's all my joys and comforts? Pray, no more, sir.
Say you prevail'd, you're danger's and not mine then;
The law would claim you from me, or obscurity
Be made the grave to bury you alive.
I'm glad these thoughts come forth; oh, keep not one
Of this condition, sir; here was a course
Found to bring sorrow on her way to death;
The tears would ne'er 'a' dried till dust had chok'd 'em.
Blood-guiltiness becomes a fouler visage,
[*Aside*] And now I think on one. I was to blame,
I ha' marr'd so good a market with my scorn;
'T had been done questionless. The ugliest creature
Creation fram'd for some use, yet to see
I could not mark so much where it should be!
ALSEMERO. Lady –
BEATRICE. [*aside*] Why, men of art make much of poison,
Keep one to expel another; where was my art?
ALSEMERO. Lady, you hear not me.

---

22 *strike off*: The metaphor is of the removal of fetters.

23–4 *remove . . . ceases*: an allusion to a scholastic tag, *ablata causa, tollitur effectus*, 'remove the cause and the effect ceases'.

25 *let me find you*: let me understand your meaning.

36–7 *one/Of this condition*: one thought of this type.

42 *marr'd so good a market*: Proverbial (*Oxford Dictionary of English Proverbs*, 3rd edition, 1970, p. 512); by her insults, she has spoiled a good opportunity.

44 *for some use*: This draws on the traditional doctrine that everything in nature has some use or purpose, even the apparently dangerous. A common source was Montaigne, *Essais*, III. chap. 1, 'De L'Utile et de L'Honneste'.

BEATRICE. I do especially, sir;
The present times are not so sure of our side
As those hereafter may be; we must use 'em then
As thrifty fools their wealth, sparingly now,
Till the time opens.
ALSEMERO. You teach wisdom, lady.
BEATRICE. Within there! Diaphanta!

Enter DIAPHANTA.

DIAPHANTA. Do you call, madam?
BEATRICE. Perfect your service, and conduct this gentleman
The private way you brought him.
DIAPHANTA. I shall, madam.
ALSEMERO. My love's as firm as love e'er built upon.
Exeunt DIAPHANTA *and* ALSEMERO.

Enter DE FLORES.

DE FLORES. [*aside*] I have watch'd this meeting, and do wonder much
What shall become of t'other; I'm sure both
Cannot be serv'd unless she transgress; happily
Then I'll put in for one: for if a woman
Fly from one point, from him she makes a husband,
She spreads and mounts then like arithmetic,
One, ten, a hundred, a thousand, ten thousand,
Proves in time sutler to an army royal.
Now do I look to be most richly rail'd at,
Yet I must see her.
BEATRICE. [*aside*] Why, put case I loath'd him
As much as youth and beauty hates a sepulchre,
Must I needs show it? Cannot I keep that secret
And serve my turn upon him? – See, he's here.
– De Flores!

---

52 *opens*: proves more favourable.
59 *happily*: in that case.
60 *put in for one*: As with 'serv'd' in the previous line, the expression has a sexual innuendo beyond the usual meaning of 'apply for a share'.
64 *sutler*: supplier to an army.
69 *serve my turn upon him*: use him for my own purposes. Beatrice accidentally and ironically picks up De Flores's expression in line 59.

DE FLORES. [*aside*] Ha, I shall run mad with joy!
She call'd me fairly by my name, De Flores,
And neither rogue nor rascal.
BEATRICE. What ha' you done
To your face a'late? Y'have met with some good physician;
Y'have prun'd yourself, methinks; you were not wont
To look so amorously.
DE FLORES. [*aside*] Not I;
'Tis the same physnomy, to a hair and pimple,
Which she call'd scurvy scarce an hour ago;
How is this?
BEATRICE. Come hither; nearer, man.
DE FLORES. [*aside*] I'm up to the chin in heaven!
BEATRICE. Turn, let me see.
Faugh, 'tis but the heat of the liver, I perceiv't;
I thought it had been worse.
DE FLORES. [*aside*] Her fingers touch'd me!
She smells all amber.
BEATRICE. I'll make a water for you shall cleanse this
Within a fortnight.
DE FLORES. With your own hands, lady?
BEATRICE. Yes, mine own, sir; in a work of cure
I'll trust no other.
DE FLORES. [*aside*] 'Tis half an act of pleasure
To hear her talk thus to me.
BEATRICE. When w'are us'd
To a hard face, 'tis not so unpleasing;
It mends still in opinion, hourly mends,
I see it by experience.
DE FLORES. [*aside*] I was bless'd
To light upon this minute; I'll make use on't.
BEATRICE. Hardness becomes the visage of a man well,
It argues service, resolution, manhood,
If cause were of employment.

---

74 *prun'd*: preened (as does a bird)/cut away deformities.
75 *amorously*: fit to be loved.
80 *heat of the liver*: The liver was traditionally the seat of violent passions; the diagnosis is ironically appropriate.
82 *all amber*: i.e. of ambergris, perfumed.
83 *water*: medicinal wash.

DE FLORES. 'Twould be soon seen,
If e'er your ladyship had cause to use it.
I would but wish the honour of a service
So happy as that mounts to.
BEATRICE. We shall try you.
– Oh, my De Flores!
DE FLORES. [*aside*] How's that? She calls me hers already,
'my De Flores'!
– You were about to sigh out somewhat, madam?
BEATRICE. No, was I? I forgot. – Oh!
DE FLORES. There 'tis again,
The very fellow on't.
BEATRICE. You are too quick, sir.
DE FLORES. There's no excuse for't now; I heard it twice,
madam;
That sigh would fain have utterance, take pity on't,
And lend it a free word; 'las, how it labours
For liberty! I hear the murmur yet
Beat at your bosom.
BEATRICE. Would creation –
DE FLORES. Ay, well said, that's it.
BEATRICE. Had form'd me man!
DE FLORES. Nay, that's not it.
BEATRICE. Oh, 'tis the soul of freedom!
I should not then be forc'd to marry one
I hate beyond all depths; I should have power
Then to oppose my loathings, nay, remove 'em
For ever from my sight.
DE FLORES. [*aside*] O blest occasion!
– Without change to your sex, you have your wishes.
Claim so much man in me.
BEATRICE. In thee, De Flores?
There's small cause for that.
DE FLORES. Put it not from me;
It's a service that I kneel for to you. [*Kneels.*]
BEATRICE. You are too violent to mean faithfully;
There's horror in my service, blood and danger;
Can those be things to sue for?

---

113 *occasion*: opportunity.
118 *to mean faithfully*: to intend honest service.

DE FLORES. If you knew
How sweet it were to me to be employed
In any act of yours, you would say then
I fail'd, and us'd not reverence enough
When I receive the charge on't.
BEATRICE. [*aside*] This is much, methinks;
Belike his wants are greedy, and to such
Gold tastes like angels' food. – Rise.
DE FLORES. I'll have the work first.
BEATRICE. [*aside*] Possible his need
Is strong upon him. – There's to encourage thee;
[*Gives him money.*]
As thou art forward and thy service dangerous,
Thy reward shall be precious.
DE FLORES. That I have thought on;
I have assur'd myself of that beforehand.
And know it will be precious; the thought ravishes.
BEATRICE. Then take him to thy fury!
DE FLORES. I thirst for him.
BEATRICE. Alonzo de Piracquo!
DE FLORES. His end's upon him; he shall be seen no more.
BEATRICE. How lovely now dost thou appear to me!
Never was man dearlier rewarded.
DE FLORES. I do think of that.
BEATRICE. Be wondrous careful in the execution.
DE FLORES. Why, are not both our lives upon the cast?
BEATRICE. Then I throw all my fears upon thy service.
DE FLORES. They ne'er shall rise to hurt you.
BEATRICE. When the deed's done,
I'll furnish thee with all things for thy flight;
Thou may'st live bravely in another country.
DE FLORES. Ay, ay, we'll talk of that hereafter.

---

126 *angels' food*: the bread of heaven, '*panis angelorum*', given as manna to the Jews in the wilderness, and in the New Testament associated with the Body of Christ, the true 'heavenly manna', distributed in the eucharist.

129 *As thou art forward*: 'to the degree that you are courageous and energetic'.

132 *ravishes*: The choice of verb indicates De Flores's expectation of subsequent events.

140 *cast*: throw of the dice.

BEATRICE. [*aside*] I shall rid
myself
Of two inveterate loathings at one time,
Piracquo, and his dog-face. *Exit.*
DE FLORES. Oh my blood!
Methinks I feel her in mine arms already,
Her wanton fingers combing out this beard,
And, being pleased, praising this bad face.
Hunger and pleasure, they'll commend sometimes
Slovenly dishes, and feed heartily on 'em,
Nay, which is stranger, refuse daintier for 'em.
Some women are odd feeders. – I'm too loud.
Here comes the man goes supperless to bed,
Yet shall not rise tomorrow to his dinner.

Enter ALONZO.

ALONZO. De Flores.
DE FLORES. My kind, honourable lord.
ALONZO. I am glad I ha' met with thee.
DE FLORES. Sir?
ALONZO. Thou canst
show me
The full strength of the castle?
DE FLORES. That I can, sir.
ALONZO. I much desire it.
DE FLORES. And if the ways and straits
Of some of the passages be not too tedious for you,
I will assure you, worth your time and sight, my lord.
ALONZO. Puh, that shall be no hindrance.
DE FLORES. I'm your servant
then.
'Tis now near dinner time; 'gainst your lordship's
rising
I'll have the keys about me.
ALONZO. Thanks, kind De Flores.

---

147 *his dog-face*: an insulting epithet applied to De Flores.
147 *blood*: lust, sensual desire; presumably, De Flores's pulses are racing. The blood was taken to be both the vital fluid and also the seat of violent animal passion. See Additional note, p. 410.
160 *straits*: narrow passages.
164 *rising*: i.e. leaving the table.

DE FLORES. [*aside*] He's safely thrust upon me beyond hopes.

Exeunt.

ACT III

SCENE I

Enter ALONZO *and* DE FLORES.
(*In the act-time* DE FLORES *hides a naked rapier.*)

DE FLORES. Yes, here are all the keys. I was afraid, my lord,
I'd wanted for the postern, this is it.
I've all, I've all, my lord: this for the sconce.
ALONZO. 'Tis a most spacious and impregnable fort.
DE FLORES. You'll tell me more, my lord. This descent
Is somewhat narrow, we shall never pass
Well with our weapons, they'll but trouble us.
ALONZO. Thou say'st true.
DE FLORES. Pray let me help your lordship.
ALONZO. 'Tis done. Thanks, kind De Flores.
DE FLORES. Here are hooks, my lord,
To hang such things on purpose.

He hangs up the swords.

ALONZO. Lead, I'll follow thee.

Exeunt at one door and enter at the other.

SCENE II

DE FLORES. All this is nothing; you shall see anon
A place you little dream on.

---

s.d. *act-time*: the interval between Acts.
2 *postern*: a side- or back-door.
3 *sconce*: a small fort or earth-work.
2 *A place you little dream on*: the grave; but as so often with Middleton, there is the further implication that Hell also waits.

ALONZO. I am glad
I have this leisure; all your master's house
Imagine I ha' taken a gondola.
DE FLORES. All but myself, sir [*Aside*] which makes up my safety.
My lord, I'll place you at a casement here
Will show you the full strength of all the castle.
Look, spend your eye awhile upon that object.
ALONZO. Here's rich variety, De Flores.
DE FLORES. Yes, sir.
ALONZO. Goodly munition.
DE FLORES. Ay, there's ordnance, sir,
No bastard metal, will ring you a peal like bells
At great men's funerals. Keep your eye straight, my lord;
Take special notice of that sconce before you,
There you may dwell awhile. [*Takes up the rapier.*]
ALONZO. I am upon't.
DE FLORES. And so am I. [*Stabs him.*]
ALONZO. De Flores! Oh, De Flores!
Whose malice hast thou put on?
DE FLORES. Do you question
A work of secrecy? I must silence you. [*Stabs him.*]
ALONZO. Oh, oh, oh!
DE FLORES. I must silence you. [*Stabs him.*]
So here's an undertaking well accomplish'd.
This vault serves to good use now. – Ha, what's that
Threw sparkles in my eye? – Oh, 'tis a diamond
He wears upon his finger; it was well found,
This will approve the work. What, so fast on?
Not part in death? I'll take a speedy course then,
Finger and all shall off. [*Cuts off the finger*] So now I'll clear
The passages from all suspect or fear. *Exit with body.*

---

11 *bastard metal*: i.e. metal with impurities, or with another metal mixed with it.
14 *dwell*: rest the eye on/remain in (after the murder).
23 *approve*: give proof of.
25 This emblematic detail was added by Middleton. The cleaving of ring to finger attests the binding nature of the betrothal contract, which only unnatural murder can cut through; even then, the contract cannot be annulled.
26 *suspect*: suspicion.

SCENE III

Enter ISABELLA *and* LOLLIO.

ISABELLA. Why, sirrah? Whence have you commission
To fetter the doors against me? If you
Keep me in a cage, pray whistle to me,
Let me be doing something.

LOLLIO. You shall be doing, if it please you; I'll whistle to you if you'll pipe after.

ISABELLA. Is it your master's pleasure or your own,
To keep me in this pinfold?

LOLLIO. 'Tis for my master's pleasure, lest being taken in another man's corn, you might be pounded in another place.

ISABELLA. 'Tis very well, and he'll prove very wise.

LOLLIO. He says you have company enough in the house, if you please to be sociable, of all sorts of people.

ISABELLA. Of all sorts? Why, here's none but fools and
madmen.

LOLLIO. Very well; and where will you find any other, if you should go abroad? There's my master and I to boot too.

ISABELLA. Of either sort one, a madman and a fool.

LOLLIO. I would ev'n participate of both then, if I were as you; I know y'are half mad already, be half foolish too.

ISABELLA. Y'are a brave, saucy rascal! Come on, sir,
Afford me then the pleasure of your bedlam;
You were commending once today to me
Your last-come lunatic: what a proper
Body there was without brains to guide it,
And what a pitiful delight appear'd
In that defect, as if your wisdom had found
A mirth in madness; pray, sir, let me partake,
If there be such a pleasure.

5–6 *whistle . . . if you'll pipe after*: he will whistle if the caged bird will agree to sing. *Doing* is probably used with obscene innuendo; so also *whistle* and *pipe*: Lollio is making a covert advance.

8 *pinfold*: pen, pound.

10 *pounded*: impounded/sexually pressed.

20 *participate*: 'share in the nature of', 'take part in'; another sly advance.

LOLLIO. If I do not show you the handsomest, discreetest madman, one that I may call the understanding madman, then say I am a fool.

ISABELLA. Well, a match, I will say so.

LOLLIO. When you have a taste of the madman, you shall, if you please, see Fools' College, o' th' side; I seldom lock there, 'tis but shooting a bolt or two, and you are amongst 'em. *Exit. Enter presently.* – Come on, sir, let me see how handsomely you'll behave yourself now.

Enter FRANCISCUS.

FRANCISCUS. How sweetly she looks! Oh, but there's a wrinkle in her brow as deep as philosophy. Anacreon, drink to my mistress' health, I'll pledge it; stay, stay, there's a spider in the cup! No, 'tis but a grape-stone; swallow it, fear nothing, poet; so, so, lift higher.

ISABELLA. Alack, alack, 'tis too full of pity
To be laugh'd at. How fell he mad? Canst thou tell?

LOLLIO. For love, mistress; he was a pretty poet too, and that set him forwards first; the Muses then forsook him; he ran mad for a chambermaid, yet she was but a dwarf neither.

FRANCISCUS. Hail, bright Titania!
Why stand'st thou idle on these flow'ry banks?
Oberon is dancing with his Dryades;
I'll gather daisies, primrose, violets,
And bind them in a verse of poesy.

---

35 *a match*: a bargain.

38 *shooting a bolt or two*: pulling back a bolt, probably with a punning reference to the proverb 'A fool's bolt is soon shot', and thus a covert insult to Isabella.

43 *Anacreon*: Pliny, *Natural History* VIII.7 (trans. P. Holland, 1601, I.159) and others recount that Anacreon choked to death on a grape-stone whilst drinking a cup of wine.

45 *there's a spider in the cup*: This alludes to the folk belief that spiders were poisonous and that to knowingly drink one meant death.

53–5 *Titania . . . Oberon*: King and Queen of Faery; Franciscus insinuates that Alibius is enjoying himself with other 'nymphs', and invites Isabella to solace herself with him. The names perhaps derive from *A Midsummer Night's Dream.*

LOLLIO. Not too near; you see your danger.
[*Shows the whip.*]

FRANCISCUS. Oh, hold thy hand, great Diomed!
Thou feed'st thy horses well, they shall obey thee;
Get up, Bucephalus kneels. [*Kneels.*]

LOLLIO. You see how I awe my flock; a shepherd has not his dog at more obedience.

ISABELLA. His conscience is unquiet; sure that was
The cause of this. A proper gentleman.

FRANCISCUS. Come hither, Esculapius; hide the poison.

LOLLIO. Well, 'tis hid.
[*Hides the whip.* FRANCISCUS *rises.*]

FRANCISCUS. Didst thou never hear of one Tiresias, a famous poet?

LOLLIO. Yes, that kept tame wild-geese.

FRANCISCUS. That's he; I am the man.

LOLLIO. No!

FRANCISCUS. Yes, but make no words on't; I was a man seven years ago.

LOLLIO. A stripling I think you might.

FRANCISCUS. Now I'm a woman, all feminine.

LOLLIO. I would I might see that.

FRANCISCUS. Juno struck me blind.

LOLLIO. I'll ne'er believe that; for a woman, they say, has an eye more than a man.

FRANCISCUS. I say she struck me blind.

LOLLIO. And Luna made you mad; you have two trades to beg with.

FRANCISCUS. Luna is now big-bellied, and there's room

---

59 *Diomed*: King of the Bistonians in Thrace, who fed his horses on human flesh.

61 *Bucephalus*: the monstrous horse of Alexander, which only he could ride; Lollio is invited to 'mount'.

66 *Esculapius*: the Greek god of medicine; hence an ironic epithet for the keeper of a mad-house.

68 *Tiresias*: Theban prophet who changed from a man to a woman and reverted seven years later. Juno struck him blind for revealing that women enjoyed sexual intercourse more than men.

70 *tame wild-geese*: a cant term for prostitutes.

80 *eye*: i.e. the pudendum.

82 *Luna*: the moon, which makes mad the lunatic. Madness and blindness are two qualifications for begging.

84 *big-bellied*: full moon/pregnant.

For both of us to ride with Hecate;
I'll drag thee up into her silver sphere,
And there we'll kick the dog, and beat the bush,
That barks against the witches of the night;
The swift lycanthropi that walks the round,
We'll tear their wolvish skins and save the sheep.
[*He tries to seize* LOLLIO.]

LOLLIO. Is't come to this? Nay then, my poison comes forth again [*Shows the whip*] Mad slave, indeed, abuse your keeper!

ISABELLA. I prithee, hence with him, now he grows dangerous.

FRANCISCUS. (*sings*) *Sweet love, pity me.*
Give me leave to lie with thee.

LOLLIO. No, I'll see you wiser first; to your own kennel.

FRANCISCUS. No noise, she sleeps, draw all the curtains round;
Let no soft sound molest the pretty soul
But love, and love creeps in at a mouse-hole.

LOLLIO. I would you would get into your hole!
Exit FRANCISCUS.
Now, mistress, I will bring you another sort, you shall be fool'd another while; Tony, come hither, Tony; look who's yonder, Tony.

Enter ANTONIO.

ANTONIO. Cousin, is it not my aunt?

LOLLIO. Yes, 'tis one of 'em, Tony.

ANTONIO. He, he! How do you, uncle?

LOLLIO. Fear him not, mistress, 'tis a gentle nidget; you

---

85 *Hecate*: Greek goddess of witchcraft and magic, regarded as an underworld manifestation of Diana/Artemis, goddess of the moon.

87 *kick the dog and beat the bush*: The dog and the bush belong to the man in the moon.

89 *lycanthropi*: suffers from lycanthropia, a delusion in which the victim believes he is a wolf and acts accordingly.

96 *lie*: have sexual intercourse.

100 *mouse-hole*: also, the female pudendum.

105 *aunt*: There is the usual pun on the meaning 'prostitute', 'bawd'.

108 *nidget*: contracted from 'an idiot', hence, fool.

may play with him, as safely with him as with his bauble.
ISABELLA. How long has thou been a fool?
ANTONIO. Ever since I came hither, cousin.
ISABELLA. Cousin? I'm none of thy cousins, fool.
LOLLIO. O mistress, fools have always so much wit as to claim their kindred.
MADMAN. (*within*) Bounce, bounce, he falls, he falls!
ISABELLA. Hark you, your scholars in the upper room are out of order.
LOLLIO. Must I come amongst you there? Keep you the fool, mistress; I'll go up and play left-handed Orlando amongst the madmen. *Exit.*
ISABELLA. Well, sir.
ANTONIO. 'Tis opportuneful now, sweet lady! Nay,
Cast no amazing eye upon this change.
ISABELLA. Ha!
ANTONIO. This shape of folly shrouds your dearest love,
The truest servant to your powerful beauties,
Whose magic had this force thus to transform me.
ISABELLA. You are a fine fool indeed.
ANTONIO. Oh, 'tis not strange:
Love has an intellect that runs through all
The scrutinous sciences, and, like
A cunning poet, catches a quantity
Of every knowledge, yet brings all home
Into one mystery, into one secret
That he proceeds in.
ISABELLA. Y'are a parlous fool.
ANTONIO. No danger in me: I bring naught but love
And his soft-wounding shafts to strike you with.
Try but one arrow; if it hurt you,

---

110 *bauble*: fool's stick surmounted by a carved head with asses' ears/penis.

113 *cousin*: besides indicating a wide range of blood relationships, the word also covers those liaisons implied by the modern term 'just good friends'; hence Isabella's indignant repudiation.

120–1 *left-handed*: i.e. a cack-handed version of Ariosto's hero in *Orlando Furioso*.

124 *amazing*: amazed.

131 *scrutinous*: accurately examining, searching.

I'll stand you twenty back in recompense.
[*Kisses her.*]

ISABELLA. A forward fool too!

ANTONIO. This was love's teaching:
A thousand ways he fashion'd out my way,
And this I found the safest and [the] nearest
To tread the Galaxia to my star.

ISABELLA. Profound, withal! Certain, you dream'd of this;
Love never taught it waking.

ANTONIO. Take no acquaintance
Of these outward follies; there is within
A gentleman that loves you.

ISABELLA. When I see him,
I'll speak with him; so in the meantime keep
Your habit, it becomes you well enough.
As you are a gentleman, I'll not discover you;
That's all the favour that you must expect;
When you are weary, you may leave the school,
For all this while you have but play'd the fool.

Enter LOLLIO.

ANTONIO. And must again. – He, he! I thank you, cousin;
I'll be your valentine tomorrow morning.

LOLLIO. How do you like the fool, mistress?

ISABELLA. Passing well, sir.

LOLLIO. Is he not witty, pretty well for a fool?

ISABELLA. If he hold on as he begins, he is like to come to something.

LOLLIO. Ay, thank a good tutor; you may put him to't; he begins to answer pretty hard questions. Tony, how many is five times six?

ANTONIO. Five times six is six times five.

LOLLIO. What arithmetician could have answer'd better? How many is one hundred and seven?

---

141 See Textual note, p. 408. Love suggested a thousand schemes to achieve his desire.

143 *Galaxia*: the Milky Way.

159 *to come to something*: not an indication that Antonio may hope, but an ironic comment: the 'something' to which he may attain is probably the gallows.

160 *put him to't*: test him.

ANTONIO. One hundred and seven is seven hundred and one, cousin.

LOLLIO. This is no wit to speak on; will you be rid of the fool now?

ISABELLA. By no means, let him stay a little.

MADMAN. (*within*) Catch there, catch the last couple in hell!

LOLLIO. Again! Must I come amongst you? Would my master were come home! I am not able to govern both these wards together. *Exit.*

ANTONIO. Why should a minute of love's hour be lost?

ISABELLA. Fie, out again! I had rather you kept
Your other posture; you become not your tongue
When you speak from your clothes.

ANTONIO. How can he freeze
Lives near so sweet a warmth? Shall I alone
Walk through the orchard of the Hesperides,
And cowardly not dare to pull an apple?
This with the red cheeks I must venter for.
[*Tries to kiss her.*]

Enter LOLLIO *above.*

ISABELLA. Take heed, there's giants keep 'em.

LOLLIO. [*aside*] How now, fool, are you good at that?
Have you read Lipsius? He's past *Ars Amandi*; I believe
I must put harder questions to him, I perceive that –

ISABELLA. You are bold without fear too.

---

171 *catch the last couple in hell*: an allusion to 'barley-brake', a game in which one couple occupies the middle ground ('hell') and attempts to catch other couples as they run through. Caught couples assist the original pair until the last couple has been drawn in. See Additional note, p. 414.

179 *speak from your clothes*: speak out of the part suggested by your fool's garb.

181 *orchard of the Hesperides*: a mythical orchard beyond the rim of the western world, which bore golden apples.

183 *venter*: venture.

184 *giants*: The orchard of the Hesperides was guarded by the Hesperides, daughters of Atlas and Hesperus, and by a hundred-headed dragon, Ladon, offspring of the Giant Tython.

186 *Justus Lipsius*: (1547–1606), a Neo-Stoic scholar and jurist, whose name is here introduced solely for the pun.

186 *Ars Amandi*: Ovid's *Art of Love*, which Antonio appears to have mastered.

ANTONIO. What should I fear,
Having all joys about me? Do you smile,
And love shall play the wanton on your lip,
Meet and retire, retire and meet again;
Look you but cheerfully, and in your eyes
I shall behold mine own deformity,
And dress myself up fairer; I know this shape
Becomes me not, but in those bright mirrors
I shall array me handsomely.

LOLLIO. Cuckoo, cuckoo! *Exit.*

[Enter] MADMEN *above, some as birds, other as beasts.*

ANTONIO. What are these?

ISABELLA. Of fear enough to part us;
Yet they are but our schools of lunatics,
That act their fantasies in any shapes
Suiting their present thoughts; if sad, they cry;
If mirth be their conceit, they laugh again.
Sometimes they imitate the beasts and birds,
Singing, or howling, braying, barking; all
As their wild fancies prompt 'em.

[Exeunt MADMEN.*]*

Enter LOLLIO.

ANTONIO. These are no fears.

ISABELLA. But here's a large one, my man.

ANTONIO. Ha, he! That's fine sport indeed, cousin.

LOLLIO. I would my master were come home, 'tis too much for one shepherd to govern two of these flocks; nor can I believe that one churchman can instruct two benefices at once; there will be some incurable mad of the one side, and very fools on the other. Come, Tony.

ANTONIO. Prithee, cousin, let me stay here still.

LOLLIO. No, you must to your book now, you have play'd sufficiently.

---

196 *cuckoo*: Lollio's cry implies that Alibius is being cuckolded.

209–10 *instruct two benefices*: an allusion to the common and much-resented practice of augmenting clerical stipends by holding benefices in plurality.

ISABELLA. Your fool is grown wondrous witty.
LOLLIO. Well, I'll say nothing; but I do not think but he will put you down one of these days.
Exeunt LOLLIO *and* ANTONIO.
ISABELLA. Here the restrained current might make breach,
Spite of the watchful bankers; would a woman stray,
She need not gad abroad to seek her sin,
It would be brought home one ways or other.
The needle's point will to the fixed north:
Such drawing arctics women's beauties are.

Enter LOLLIO.

LOLLIO. How dost thou, sweet rogue?
ISABELLA. How now?
LOLLIO. Come, there are degrees, one fool may be better than another.
ISABELLA. What's the matter?
LOLLIO. Nay, if thou giv'st thy mind to fool's-flesh, have at thee! [*He tries to kiss her.*]
ISABELLA. You bold slave, you!
LOLLIO. I could follow now as t'other fool did:
'What should I fear,
Having all joys about me? Do you but smile,
And love shall play the wanton on your lip,
Meet and retire, retire and meet again;
Look you but cheerfully, and in your eyes
I shall behold my own deformity,
And dress myself up fairer; I know this shape
Becomes me not'
– and so as it follows; but is not this the more foolish way?
Come, sweet rogue; kiss me, my little Lacedemonian.
Let me feel how thy pulses beat; thou hast a thing about thee would do a man pleasure, I'll lay my hand on't.

---

218 *put you down*: 'overcome you by his intelligence'/'surmount you sexually'.
220 *bankers*: dyke-builders.
224 *drawing arctics*: magnetic poles that attract the compass needle.
243 *Lacedemonian*: literally, a Spartan; a reference to the faithless Helen of Sparta.

ISABELLA. Sirrah, no more! I see you have discovered
This love's knight-errant, who hath made adventure
For purchase of my love; be silent, mute,
Mute as a statue, or his injunction
For me enjoying, shall be to cut thy throat:
I'll do it, though for no other purpose,
And be sure he'll not refuse it.
LOLLIO. My share, that's all: I'll have my fool's part with you.
ISABELLA. No more! Your master.

Enter ALIBIUS.

ALIBIUS. Sweet, how dost thou?
ISABELLA. Your bounden servant, sir.
ALIBIUS. Fie, fie, sweetheart,
No more of that.
ISABELLA. You were best lock me up.
ALIBIUS. In my arms and bosom, my sweet Isabella,
I'll lock thee up most nearly. Lollio,
We have employment, we have task in hand;
At noble Vermandero's, our castle-captain,
There is a nuptial to be solemniz'd
(Beatrice-Joanna, his fair daughter, bride)
For which the gentleman hath bespoke our pains:
A mixture of our madmen and our fools,
To finish (as it were) and make the fag
Of all the revels, the third night from the first;
Only an unexpected passage over,
To make a frightful pleasure, that is all,
But not the all I aim at; could we so act it,
To teach it in a wild, distracted measure,
Though out of form and figure, breaking time's head,

---

249 *purchase*: achieving.
257 *bounden*: duty-bound/imprisoned.
267 *fag*: the conclusion.
269 *unexpected passage over*: a sudden, brief irruption into the festivities.
273 *breaking time's head*: probably a musical variation on the proverbial 'breaking Priscian's head'. Priscian was a celebrated Latin grammarian, and the expression was widely used of committing a grammatical solecism; here the offence is against musical time, for the 'measure' is to be unrhythmic, irregular.

It were no matter; 'twould be heal'd again
In one age or other, if not in this.
This, this, Lollio, there's a good reward begun,
And will beget a bounty, be it known.

LOLLIO. This is easy, sir, I'll warrant you: you have about you fools and madmen that can dance very well; and 'tis no wonder your best dancers are not the wisest men; the reason is, with often jumping they jolt their brains down into their feet, that their wits lie more in their heels than in their heads.

ALIBIUS. Honest Lollio, thou giv'st me a good reason,
And a comfort in it.

ISABELLA. Y'ave a fine trade on't,
Madmen and fools are a staple commodity.

ALIBIUS. Oh, wife, we must eat, wear clothes, and live;
Just at the lawyer's haven we arrive:
By madmen and by fools we both do thrive.

Exeunt.

SCENE IV

Enter VERMANDERO, ALSEMERO, JASPERINO, *and* BEATRICE.

VERMANDERO. Valencia speaks so nobly of you, sir,
I wish I had a daughter now for you.

ALSEMERO. The fellow of this creature were a partner
For a king's love.

VERMANDERO. I had her fellow once, sir,
But Heaven has married her to joys eternal;
'Twere sin to wish her in this vale again.
Come, sir, your friend and you shall see the pleasures
Which my health chiefly joys in.

ALSEMERO. I hear the beauty of this seat largely.

VERMANDERO. It falls much short of that.

Exeunt. Manet BEATRICE.

BEATRICE. So, here's one
step

---

286 *staple*: basic.
288 *lawyer's haven*: i.e. the port of wealth, which lawyers achieve by exploiting the mad and the foolish.
6 *vale*: i.e. the world as the 'Valley of Tribulation', 'vale of tears'.
9 *largely*: extensively expressed/everywhere I go.

Into my father's favour; time will fix him.
I have got him now the liberty of the house;
So wisdom by degrees works out her freedom;
And if that eye be dark'ned that offends me,
(I wait but that eclipse) this gentleman
Shall soon shine glorious in my father's liking,
Through the refulgent virtue of my love.

Enter DE FLORES.

DE FLORES. [*aside*] My thoughts are at a banquet; for the deed,
I feel no weight in't, 'tis but light and cheap
For the sweet recompense that I set down for't.
BEATRICE. De Flores.
DE FLORES. Lady?
BEATRICE. Thy looks promise cheerfully.
DE FLORES. All things are answerable: time, circumstance,
Your wishes, and my service.
BEATRICE. Is it done then?
DE FLORES. Piracquo is no more.
BEATRICE. My joys start at mine eyes; our sweet'st delights
Are evermore born weeping.
DE FLORES. I've a token for you.
BEATRICE. For me?
DE FLORES. But it was sent somewhat unwillingly;
I could not get the ring without the finger.
[*He shows the finger.*]
BEATRICE. Bless me! What hast thou done?
DE FLORES. Why, is that more
Than killing the whole man? I cut his heart-strings.
A greedy hand thrust in a dish at court
In a mistake hath had as much as this.

---

14 *eye be dark'ned*: See Additional note, p. 415.
18 See Textual note, p. 408.
28 *I could not get the ring without the finger*: As at lines 37–8 of this scene, and earlier at III.ii.24, this emblem signifies the indissolubility of the bond made between Alonzo and Beatrice. Betrothal was regarded by many as the binding contract.
32 *as much as this*: i.e. fingers have been lost in the rush of knives into a dish to secure a portion.

BEATRICE. 'Tis the first token my father made me send him.
DE FLORES. And I made him send it back again
For his last token; I was loath to leave it,
And I'm sure dead men have no use of jewels.
He was as loath to part with't, for it stuck
As if the flesh and it were both one substance.
BEATRICE. At the stag's fall the keeper has his fees;
'Tis soon applied: all dead men's fees are yours, sir.
I pray, bury the finger, but the stone
You may make use on shortly; the true value,
Take't of my truth, is near three hundred ducats.
DE FLORES. 'Twill hardly buy a capcase for one's conscience, though,
To keep it from the worm, as fine as 'tis.
Well, being my fees, I'll take it;
Great men have taught me that, or else my merit
Would scorn the way on't.
BEATRICE. It might justly, sir;
Why, thou mistak'st, De Flores, 'tis not given
In state of recompense.
DE FLORES. No, I hope so, lady;
You should soon witness my contempt to't then!
BEATRICE. Prithee, thou look'st as if thou wert offended.
DE FLORES. That were strange, lady; 'tis not possible
My service should draw such a cause from you.
Offended? Could you think so? That were much
For one of my performance, and so warm
Yet in my service.
BEATRICE. 'Twere misery in me to give you cause, sir.
DE FLORES. I know so much, it were so, misery
In her most sharp condition.
BEATRICE. 'Tis resolv'd then;

---

38 *flesh . . . substance*: The language alludes to the Biblical doctrine that husband and wife become one flesh, a union symbolised here by the indivisibility of finger and betrothal ring.

39 *keeper*: The warden of a game park had a right to the skin, head and other parts of a deer, when killed.

44 *capcase*: a wallet, protective cover, travelling bag.

45 *worm*: i.e. the gnawings of remorse, with a probable further allusion to the sufferings of Hell, 'where their worm dieth not, and the fire is never quenched' (Mark 9.48).

Look you, sir, here's three thousand golden florins:
I have not meanly thought upon thy merit.

DE FLORES. What, salary? Now you move me!

BEATRICE. How, De Flores?

DE FLORES. Do you place me in the rank of verminous fellows,
To destroy things for wages? Offer gold?
The life blood of man! Is anything
Valued too precious for my recompense?

BEATRICE. I understand thee not.

DE FLORES. I could ha' hir'd
A journeyman in murder at this rate,
And mine own conscience might have [slept at ease]
And have had the work brought home.

BEATRICE. [*aside*] I'm in a labyrinth;
What will content him? I would fain be rid of him.
– I'll double the sum, sir.

DE FLORES. You take a course
To double my vexation, that's the good you do.

BEATRICE. [*aside*] Bless me! I am now in worse plight than I was;
I know not what will please him. – For my fear's sake,
I prithee make away with all speed possible.
And if thou be'st so modest not to name
The sum that will content thee, paper blushes not;
Send thy demand in writing, it shall follow thee.
But prithee take thy flight.

DE FLORES. You must fly too then.

BEATRICE. I?

DE FLORES. I'll not stir a foot else.

BEATRICE. What's your meaning?

DE FLORES. Why, are not you as guilty, in, I'm sure,
As deep as I? And we should stick together.
Come, your fears counsel you but ill; my absence
Would draw suspect upon you instantly;
There were no rescue for you.

BEATRICE. [*aside*] He speaks home.

---

69 *journeyman*: a day labourer, a professional.
70 *[slept at ease]*: See Textual note, p. 408.
86 *suspect*: suspicion.

DE FLORES. Nor is it fit we two, engag'd so jointly,
Should part and live asunder. [*Tries to kiss her.*]
BEATRICE. How now, sir?
This shows not well.
DE FLORES. What makes your lip so strange?
This must not be betwixt us.
BEATRICE. [*aside*] The man talks wildly.
DE FLORES. Come, kiss me with a zeal now.
BEATRICE. [*aside*] Heaven, I doubt him!
DE FLORES. I will not stand so long to beg 'em shortly.
BEATRICE. Take heed, De Flores, of forgetfulness,
'Twill soon betray us.
DE FLORES. Take you heed first;
Faith, y'are grown much forgetful, y'are to blame in't.
BEATRICE. [*aside*] He's bold, and I am blam'd for't!
DE FLORES. I have eas'd
You of your trouble, think on't; I'm in pain,
And must be eas'd of you; 'tis a charity;
Justice invites your blood to understand me.
BEATRICE. I dare not.
DE FLORES. Quickly!
BEATRICE. Oh, I never shall!
Speak it yet further off that I may lose
What has been spoken, and no sound remain on't.
I would not hear so much offence again
For such another deed.
DE FLORES. Soft, lady, soft;
The last is not yet paid for. Oh, this act
Has put me into spirit; I was as greedy on't
As the parch'd earth of moisture, when the clouds weep.
Did you not mark, I wrought myself into't,
Nay, sued and kneel'd for't? Why was all that pains took?
You see I have thrown contempt upon your gold;
Not that I want it [not] for I do piteously:

90 *strange*: unfriendly.
92 *doubt*: fear, suspect.
107 *spirit*: courage/sexual desire; see Additional note, p. 410.
109 *wrought myself into't*: i.e. worked to have the job given me.

In order I will come unto't, and make use on't.
But 'twas not held so precious to begin with,
For I place wealth after the heels of pleasure;
And were I not resolv'd in my belief
That thy virginity were perfect in thee,
I should but take my recompense with grudging,
As if I had but half my hopes I agreed for.
BEATRICE. Why, 'tis impossible thou canst be so wicked,
Or shelter such a cunning cruelty,
To make his death the murderer of my honour!
Thy language is so bold and vicious,
I cannot see which way I can forgive it
With any modesty.
DE FLORES. Push, you forget yourself!
A woman dipp'd in blood, and talk of modesty!
BEATRICE. Oh misery of sin! Would I had been bound
Perpetually unto my living hate
In that Piracquo, than to hear these words.
Think but upon the distance that creation
Set 'twixt thy blood and mine, and keep thee there.
DE FLORES. Look but into your conscience, read me there,
'Tis a true book, you'll find me there your equal.
Push! Fly not to your birth, but settle you
In what the act has made you, y'are no more now;
You must forget your parentage to me:
Y'are the deed's creature; by that name
You lost your first condition, and I challenge you,
As peace and innocency has turn'd you out,
And made you one with me.
BEATRICE. With thee, foul villain?
DE FLORES. Yes, my fair murd'ress! Do you urge me?
Though thou writ'st maid, thou whore in thy affection!
'Twas chang'd from thy first love, and that's a kind
Of whoredom in thy heart; and he's chang'd now,

---

113 *In order*: in due time.
116 *resolv'd*: certain.
136 *parentage to me*: i.e. 'You must forget your origins in dealing with me' *or* 'You must forget your parents in favour of me.'
138 *first condition*: original innocence. See Additional note, p. 413.
141 *urge*: provoke.
144 *chang'd*: i.e. from life to death.

To bring thy second on, thy Alsemero,
Whom (by all sweets that ever darkness tasted)
If I enjoy thee not, thou ne'er enjoy'st;
I'll blast the hopes and joys of marriage,
I'll confess all; my life I rate at nothing.
BEATRICE. De Flores!
DE FLORES. I shall rest from all lovers' plagues then;
I live in pain now: that shooting eye
Will burn my heart to cinders.
BEATRICE. Oh, sir, hear me.
DE FLORES. She that in life and love refuses me,
In death and shame my partner she shall be.
BEATRICE. [*kneels*] Stay, hear me once for all; I make thee master
Of all the wealth I have in gold and jewels;
Let me go poor unto my bed with honour,
And I am rich in all things.
DE FLORES. Let this silence thee:
The wealth of all Valencia shall not buy
My pleasure from me;
Can you weep Fate from its determin'd purpose?
So soon may [you] weep me.
BEATRICE. Vengeance begins;
Murder, I see, is followed by more sins.
Was my creation in the womb so curs'd,
It must engender with a viper first?
DE FLORES. Come, rise, and shroud your blushes in my bosom; [*Raises her.*]
Silence is one of pleasure's best receipts;
Thy peace is wrought for ever in this yielding.
'Las, how the turtle pants! Thou'lt love anon
What thou so fear'st and faint'st to venture on.
Exeunt.

---

146 *by all sweets that ever darkness tasted*: See Additional note, p. 413.

165–6 See Additional note, p. 413. 'Was a curse laid on me in my mother's womb, condemning me to make love with a hideous, unnatural being before I could do so with a normal man?'

168 *receipts*: recipes.

169 *peace . . . for ever*: See Additional note, p. 413.

170–1 *turtle*: turtle-dove; The lines echo Jonson's *Hymenaei*, lines 453–4.

ACT IV

SCENE I

[*Dumb show.*]

Enter GENTLEMEN, VERMANDERO *meeting them with action of wonderment at the flight of* PIRACQUO. *Enter* ALSEMERO, *with* JASPERINO *and* GALLANTS; VERMANDERO *points to him, the* GENTLEMEN *seeming to applaud the choice.* [*Exeunt in procession* VERMANDERO] ALSEMERO, JASPERINO, *and* GENTLEMEN; BEATRICE *the bride following in great state, accompanied with* DIAPHANTA, ISABELLA, *and other* GENTLEWOMEN; DE FLORES *after all, smiling at the accident;* ALONZO'S *ghost appears to* DE FLORES *in the midst of his smile, startles him, showing him the hand whose finger he had cut off. They pass over in great solemnity.*

Enter BEATRICE.

BEATRICE. This fellow has undone me endlessly;
Never was bride so fearfully distress'd.
The more I think upon th' ensuing night,
And whom I am to cope with in embraces,
One who's ennobled both in blood and mind,
So clear in understanding (that's my plague now),
Before whose judgement will my fault appear
Like malefactors' crimes before tribunals;
There is no hiding on't – the more I dive
Into my own distress. How a wise man
Stands for a great calamity! There's no venturing
Into his bed (what course soe'er I light upon)
Without my shame, which may grow up to danger;
He cannot but in justice strangle me
As I lie by him, as a cheater use me.

---

s.d. *accident*: event.

1 *undone me endlessly*: seduced me without remission/destroyed me eternally. See Additional note, p. 413.

5 *who's*: See Textual note, p. 408.

11 *Stands for*: represents.

'Tis a precious craft to play with a false die
Before a cunning gamester. Here's his closet,
The key left in't, and he abroad i'th' park;
Sure 'twas forgot; I'll be so bold as look in't.
[*She opens the closet.*]
Bless me! A right physician's closet 'tis,
Set round with vials; every one her mark too.
Sure he does practise physic for his own use,
Which may be safely call'd your great man's wisdom.
What manuscript lies here? 'The Book of Experiment,
Call'd *Secrets in Nature*'. So 'tis, 'tis so;
'How to know whether a woman be with child or no'.
I hope I am not yet. If he should try though!
Let me see, folio forty-five. Here 'tis;
The leaf tuck'd down upon't, the place suspicious.
'If you would know whether a woman be with child
or not,
Give her two spoonfuls of the white water in glass C.
– Where's that glass C? Oh, yonder, I see't now.
– 'And if she be with child she sleeps full twelve hours
after; if not, not.'
None of that water comes into my belly;
I'll know you from a hundred. I could break you now,
Or turn you into milk, and so beguile
The master of the mystery, but I'll look to you.
Ha! That which is next is ten times worse:
'How to know whether a woman be a maid or not'.
If that should be applied, what would become of me?
Belike he has a strong faith of my purity,
That never yet made proof; but this he calls
'A merry sleight, but true experiment, the author
Antonius Mizaldus. Give the party you suspect the
quantity of a spoonful of the water in the glass M,

16 *precious craft*: difficult and refined art; *die* = dice.
23 *your great man's wisdom*: because it protects the great from poisoning.
25 *Secrets in Nature*: extracts from *De Arcanis Naturae* by Antonius Mizaldus (1520–78). The work does not contain these tests, but similar ones are found in Mizaldus's *Centuriae IX. Memorabilium.*
38 *I'll look to you*: 'I'll watch out for you.'
43 *made proof*: put to the test.

which, upon her that is a maid, makes three several
effects: 'twill make her incontinently gape, then fall
into a sudden sneezing, last into a violent laughing;
else dull, heavy, and lumpish.'
Where had I been?
I fear it, yet 'tis seven hours to bedtime.

Enter DIAPHANTA.

DIAPHANTA. Cuds, madam, are you here?
BEATRICE. [*aside*] Seeing that wench now,
A trick comes in my mind; 'tis a nice piece
Gold cannot purchase. – I come hither, wench,
To look my lord.
DIAPHANTA. [*aside*] Would I had such a cause
To look him too! – Why, he's i' th' park, madam.
BEATRICE. There let him be.
DIAPHANTA. Ay, madam, let him compass
Whole parks and forests, as great rangers do;
At roosting time a little lodge can hold 'em.
Earth-conquering Alexander, that thought the world
Too narrow for him, in the end had but his pit-hole.
BEATRICE. I fear thou art not modest, Diaphanta.
DIAPHANTA. Your thoughts are so unwilling to be known, madam;
'Tis ever the bride's fashion towards bedtime
To set light by her joys, as if she ow'd 'em not.
BEATRICE. Her joys? Her fears, thou would'st say.
DIAPHANTA. Fear of what?
BEATRICE. Art thou a maid, and talk'st so to a maid?
You leave a blushing business behind,
Beshrew your heart for't!

---

47 *several*: different, clearly distinguished.
48 *incontinently*: immediately and unrestrainedly.
51 *Where had I been*: 'What would have happened to me (if I had not discovered this)?'
53 *Cuds*: a mild oath, contracted from 'God save me.'
54 *nice piece*: scrupulous woman.
62 *pit-hole*: the grave/the female pudendum. Cf. Juvenal, *Satire* X, 168–72.
66 *ow'd*: owned.
69 *blushing business*: i.e. she must already have fallen to a man.

DIAPHANTA. Do you mean good sooth,
madam?
BEATRICE. Well, if I'd thought upon the fear at first,
Man should have been unknown.
DIAPHANTA. Is't possible?
BEATRICE. I will give a thousand ducats to that woman
Would try what my fear were, and tell me true
Tomorrow, when she gets from't; as she likes,
I might perhaps be drawn to't.
DIAPHANTA. Are you in earnest?
BEATRICE. Do you get the woman, then challenge me,
And see if I'll fly from't; but I must tell you
This by the way, she must be a true maid,
Else there's no trial, my fears are not hers else.
DIAPHANTA. Nay, she that I would put into your hands,
madam,
Shall be a maid.
BEATRICE. You know I should be sham'd else,
Because she lies for me.
DIAPHANTA. 'Tis a strange humour;
But are you serious still? Would you resign
Your first night's pleasure, and give money too?
BEATRICE. As willingly as live; [*Aside*] alas, the gold
Is but a by-bet to wedge in the honour.
DIAPHANTA. I do not know how the world goes abroad
For faith or honesty; there's both requir'd in this.
Madam, what say you to me, and stray no further?
I've a good mind, in troth, to earn your money.
BEATRICE. Y'are too quick, I fear, to be a maid.
DIAPHANTA. How? Not a maid? Nay, then you urge me,
madam;
Your honourable self is not a truer
With all your fears upon you –
BEATRICE. [*aside*] Bad enough then.
DIAPHANTA. Than I with all my lightsome joys about me.
BEATRICE. I'm glad to hear't; then you dare put your
honesty

---

70 *Do you mean good sooth*: 'Are you in earnest?'
83 *lies*: copulates//deceives. *Humour* = whim.
87 *by-bet*: a side-bet, an added inducement to get her to stake her honour.
92 *quick*: eager, lively/pregnant.
93 *urge*: provoke.

Upon an easy trial?
DIAPHANTA. Easy? Anything.
BEATRICE. I'll come to you straight.
[*Goes to the closet.*]
DIAPHANTA. [*aside*] She will not search me, will she,
Like the forewoman of a female jury?
BEATRICE. Glass M; ay, this is it. – Look, Diaphanta,
You take no worse than I do. [*Drinks.*]
DIAPHANTA. And in so doing,
I will not question what 'tis, but take it. [*Drinks.*]
BEATRICE. [*aside*] Now if the experiment be true, 'twill praise itself,
And give me noble ease: – begins already;
[DIAPHANTA *gapes.*]
There's the first symptom; and what haste it makes
To fall into the second, there by this time!
[DIAPHANTA *sneezes.*]
Most admirable secret! On the contrary,
It stirs me not a whit, which most concerns it.
DIAPHANTA. Ha, ha, ha!
BEATRICE. [*aside*] Just in all things and in order,
As if 'twere circumscrib'd; one accident
Gives way unto another.
DIAPHANTA. Ha, ha, ha!
BEATRICE. How now, wench?
DIAPHANTA. Ha, ha, ha! I am so-so light
At heart – ha, ha, ha! – so pleasurable.
But one swig more, sweet madam.
BEATRICE. Ay, tomorrow;
We shall have time to sit by't.
DIAPHANTA. Now I'm sad again.
BEATRICE. [*aside*] It lays itself so gently, too! – Come, wench,

---

100 *forewoman of a female jury*: This is probably a reference to the notorious divorce action involving the Countess of Essex in 1613, during which she was examined by a panel of matrons.
108 *admirable*: wonderful.
109 *which most concerns it*: 'whose lack of virginity it is its function to detect'.
112 *circumscrib'd*: with its specific effects laid down for it.
112 *accident*: symptom.
118 *lays itself*: subsides, disperses its own effects.

Most honest Diaphanta I dare call thee now.
DIAPHANTA. Pray tell me, madam, what trick call you this?
BEATRICE. I'll tell thee all hereafter; we must study
The carriage of this business.
DIAPHANTA. I shall carry't well,
Because I love the burthen.
BEATRICE. About midnight
You must not fail to steal forth gently,
That I may use the place.
DIAPHANTA. Oh, fear not, madam,
I shall be cool by that time. – The bride's place,
And with a thousand ducats! I'm for a justice now,
I bring a portion with me; I scorn small fools.
Exeunt.

SCENE II

Enter VERMANDERO *and* SERVANT.

VERMANDERO. I tell you, knave, mine honour is in question,
A thing till now free from suspicion,
Nor ever was there cause. Who of my gentlemen
Are absent? Tell me and truly how many and who.
SERVANT. Antonio, sir, and Franciscus.
VERMANDERO. When did they leave the castle?
SERVANT. Some ten days since, sir, the one intending to
Briamata, th' other for Valencia.
VERMANDERO. The time accuses 'em. A charge of murder
Is brought within my castle gate, Piracquo's murder;
I dare not answer faithfully their absence.
A strict command of apprehension
Shall pursue 'em suddenly, and either wipe
The stain off clear, or openly discover it.
Provide me winged warrants for the purpose.

121–2 *carry*: perform/support in intercourse.
128 *portion*: a dowry, which will recommend her now to a *big* fool, a justice.
8 *Briamata*: In Middleton's source, Vermandero's country house ten leagues away.
11 *answer faithfully*: account for them confidently.

See, I am set on again.

Exit SERVANT.

Enter TOMAZO.

TOMAZO. I claim a brother of you.

VERMANDERO. Y'are too hot,
Seek him not here.

TOMAZO. Yes, 'mongst your dearest bloods,
If my peace find no fairer satisfaction;
This is the place must yield account for him,
For here I left him, and the hasty tie
Of this snatch'd marriage gives strong testimony
Of his most certain ruin.

VERMANDERO. Certain falsehood!
This is the place indeed; his breach of faith
Has too much marr'd both my abused love,
The honourable love I reserv'd for him,
And mock'd my daughter's joy; the prepar'd morning
Blush'd at his infidelity; he left
Contempt and scorn to throw upon those friends
Whose belief hurt 'em. Oh 'twas most ignoble
To take his flight so unexpectedly,
And throw such public wrongs on those that lov'd him.

TOMAZO. Then this is all your answer?

VERMANDERO. 'Tis too fair
For one of his alliance; and I warn you
That this place no more see you. *Exit.*

Enter DE FLORES.

TOMAZO. The best is,
There is more ground to meet a man's revenge on.
– Honest De Flores?

DE FLORES. That's my name indeed.
Saw you the bride? Good sweet sir, which way took she?

TOMAZO. I have bless'd mine eyes from seeing such a false one.

---

16 *set on*: badgered, harassed.
30 *Whose belief hurt 'em*: 'whose trust in him caused them to be injured'.
34 *alliance*: family.

DE FLORES. [*aside*] I'd fain get off, this man's not for my company;
I smell his brother's blood when I come near him.
TOMAZO. Come hither, kind and true one; I remember
My brother lov'd thee well.
DE FLORES. Oh purely, dear sir!
[*Aside*] Methinks I am now again a-killing on him,
He brings it so fresh to me.
TOMAZO. Thou canst guess, sirrah
(One honest friend has an instinct of jealousy),
At some foul guilty person?
DE FLORES. 'Las, sir,
I am so charitable I think none
Worse than myself. – You did not see the bride then?
TOMAZO. I prithee name her not. Is she not wicked?
DE FLORES. No, no, a pretty, easy, round-pack'd sinner,
As your most ladies are, else you might think
I flatter'd her; but, sir, at no hand wicked,
Till th' are so old their chins and noses meet,
And they salute witches. I am call'd, I think, sir.
[*Aside*] His company ev'n o'erlays my conscience.
Exit.
TOMAZO. That De Flores has a wondrous honest heart;
He'll bring it out in time, I'm assur'd on't.
Oh, here's the glorious master of the day's joy;
'Twill not be long till he and I do reckon.

Enter ALSEMERO.

Sir!
ALSEMERO. You are most welcome.
TOMAZO. You may call that word back;
I do not think I am, nor wish to be.
ALSEMERO. 'Tis strange you found the way to this house then.
TOMAZO. Would I'd ne'er known the cause! I'm none of those, sir,

---

46 *jealousy*: suspicion.
51 *round-pack'd sinner*: i.e. 'firm in her curves, and solid with sin'.
53–5 'They are not really evil until they lose their looks in old age, and consort with witches.' But see Textual note, p. 408.
56 *o'erlays my conscience*: 'oppresses my heart and mind'.

That come to give you joy and swill your wine;
'Tis a more precious liquor that must lay
The fiery thirst I bring.
ALSEMERO. Your words and you
Appear to me great strangers.
TOMAZO. Time and our swords
May make us more acquainted. This the business:
I should have a brother in your place;
How treachery and malice have dispos'd of him,
I'm bound to inquire of him which holds his right,
Which never could come fairly.
ALSEMERO. You must look
To answer for that word, sir.
TOMAZO. Fear you not,
I'll have it ready drawn at our next meeting.
Keep your day solemn. Farewell, I disturb it not;
I'll bear the smart with patience for a time. *Exit.*
ALSEMERO. 'Tis somewhat ominous this, a quarrel ent'red
Upon this day. My innocence relieves me,

Enter JASPERINO.

I should be wondrous sad else. – Jasperino,
I have news to tell thee, strange news.
JASPERINO. I ha' some too,
I think as strange as yours; would I might keep
Mine, so my faith and friendship might be kept in't!
Faith, sir, dispense a little with my zeal,
And let it cool in this.
ALSEMERO. This puts me on,
And blames thee for thy slowness.
JASPERINO. All may prove nothing;
Only a friendly fear that leapt from me, sir.
ALSEMERO. No question it may prove nothing; let's partake it, though.

---

66 *lay*: allay.
75 *it*: i.e. his sword, which will be 'drawn up' as a formal answer.
76 *keep your day solemn*: 'Celebrate your wedding with due solemnity.'
84–5 *dispense . . . this*: 'Free me from the obligations of warm friendship in this instance.'
85 *puts me on*: 'excites my curiosity'.

JASPERINO. 'Twas Diaphanta's chance (for to that wench
I pretend honest love, and she deserves it)
To leave me in a back part of the house,
A place we chose for private conference;
She was no sooner gone, but instantly
I heard your bride's voice in the next room to me;
And, lending more attention, found De Flores
Louder than she.
ALSEMERO. De Flores? Thou art out now.
JASPERINO. You'll tell me more anon.
ALSEMERO. Still I'll prevent thee:
The very sight of him is poison to her.
JASPERINO. That made me stagger too, but Diaphanta
At her return confirm'd it.
ALSEMERO. Diaphanta!
JASPERINO. Then fell we both to listen, and words pass'd
Like those that challenge interest in a woman.
ALSEMERO. Peace! quench thy zeal; 'tis dangerous to thy bosom.
JASPERINO. Then truth is full of peril.
ALSEMERO. Such truths are.
– Oh, were she the sole glory of the earth,
Had eyes that could shoot fire into kings' breasts,
And touch'd, she sleeps not here! Yet I have time,
Though night be near, to be resolv'd hereof;
And prithee, do not weigh me by my passions.
JASPERINO. I never weigh'd friend so.
ALSEMERO. Done charitably.
That key will lead thee to a pretty secret [*Gives key.*]
By a Chaldean taught me, and I've [made]
My study upon some. Bring from my closet
A glass inscrib'd there with the letter M,

---

90 *pretend*: offer.
96 *out*: mistaken.
97 *Still I'll prevent thee*: i.e. 'I'll forestall further slanders by pointing out their inherent implausibility.'
102 *challenge interest*: claim rights.
107 *touch'd*: tainted, corrupted.
112 *Chaldean*: a soothsayer or astrologer, not necessarily a native of Chaldea, though the term derives from descriptions of Chaldean practices in the Book of Daniel.

And question not my purpose.
JASPERINO. It shall be done, sir.
Exit.
ALSEMERO. How can this hang together? Not an hour since,
Her woman came pleading her lady's fears,
Deliver'd her for the most timorous virgin
That ever shrunk at man's name, and so modest,
She charg'd her weep out her request to me
That she might come obscurely to my bosom.

Enter BEATRICE.

BEATRICE. [*aside*] All things go well. My woman's preparing yonder
For her sweet voyage, which grieves me to lose;
Necessity compels it, I lose all else.
ALSEMERO. [*aside*] Push! Modesty's shrine is set in yonder forehead.
I cannot be too sure though. – My Joanna!
BEATRICE. Sir, I was bold to weep a message to you;
Pardon my modest fears.
ALSEMERO. [*aside*] The dove's not meeker;
She's abus'd, questionless.

Enter JASPERINO [*with glass*].

– Oh, are you come, sir?
BEATRICE. [*aside*] The glass, upon my life! I see the letter.
JASPERINO. Sir, this is M.
ALSEMERO. 'Tis it.
BEATRICE. [*aside*] I am suspected.
ALSEMERO. How fitly our bride comes to partake with us!
BEATRICE. What is't, my lord?
ALSEMERO. No hurt.
BEATRICE. Sir, pardon me,
I seldom taste of any composition.
ALSEMERO. But this, upon my warrant, you shall venture on.
BEATRICE. I fear 'twill make me ill.

---

121 *obscurely*: in darkness.
134 *composition*: a made-up drink.

ALSEMERO. Heaven forbid that!
BEATRICE. [*aside*] I'm put now to my cunning; th' effects I know,
If I can now but feign 'em handsomely. [*She drinks.*]
ALSEMERO. [*to* JASPERINO] It has that secret virtue, it ne'er miss'd, sir,
Upon a virgin.
JASPERINO. Treble qualitied?
[BEATRICE *gapes, then sneezes.*]
ALSEMERO. By all that's virtuous, it takes there, proceeds!
JASPERINO. This is the strangest trick to know a maid by.
BEATRICE. Ha, ha, ha!
You have given me joy of heart to drink, my lord.
ALSEMERO. No, thou hast given me such joy of heart
That never can be blasted.
BEATRICE. What's the matter, sir?
ALSEMERO. [*to* JASPERINO] See, now 'tis settled in a melancholy,
Keep[s] both the time and method. – My Joanna,
Chaste as the breath of Heaven, or morning's womb
That brings the day forth, thus my love encloses thee.
[*Embraces her.*]
Exeunt.

SCENE III

Enter ISABELLA *and* LOLLIO.

ISABELLA. Oh heaven! Is this the waiting moon?
Does love turn fool, run mad, and all [at] once?
Sirrah, here's a madman, akin to the fool too,
A lunatic lover.
LOLLIO. No, no, not he I brought the letter from?
ISABELLA. Compare his inside with his out, and tell me.
[*Gives him the letter.*]
LOLLIO. The out's mad, I'm sure of that; I had a taste

---

1 *waiting*: (?) attendant, lying-in-wait, ominous. See Textual note, p. 408.

6 *inside with his out*: i.e. the contents of the letter with the cover/his actual nature with his disguise.

on't. 'To the bright Andromeda, chief chambermaid to the Knight of the Sun, at the sign of Scorpio, in the middle region, sent by the bellows-mender of Aeolus. Pay the post.' This is stark madness.

ISABELLA. Now mark the inside. [*Takes the letter*] 'Sweet lady, having now cast off this counterfeit cover of a madman, I appear to your best judgement a true and faithful lover of your beauty.'

LOLLIO. He is mad still.

ISABELLA. 'If any fault you find, chide those perfections in you which have made me imperfect; 'tis the same sun that causeth to grow and enforceth to wither, –'

LOLLIO. Oh rogue!

ISABELLA. '– Shapes and transhapes, destroys and builds again; I come in winter to you dismantled of my proper ornaments; by the sweet splendour of your cheerful smiles, I spring and live a lover.'

LOLLIO. Mad rascal still!

ISABELLA. 'Tread him not under foot, that shall appear an honour to your bounties. I remain – mad till I speak with you, from whom I expect my cure – Yours all, or one beside himself, Franciscus.'

LOLLIO. You are like to have a fine time on't; my master and I may give over our professions. I do not think but you can cure fools and madmen faster than we, with little pains too.

ISABELLA. Very likely.

LOLLIO. One thing I must tell you, mistress: you perceive that I am privy to your skill; if I find you minister

---

8–10 *Andromeda . . . Aeolus*: Presumably Franciscus calls Isabella Andromeda because he intends to act as Perseus, rescuing her from the dragon Alibius; *chambermaid* is an obvious pun, the *Knight of the Sun* appears in Diego Ortunez de Calahorra, *The Mirror of Princely Deeds and Knighthood*, translated from the Spanish in nine parts (1578–1601); in astrology, *Scorpio* governs the *middle region*, the privy parts; *Aeolus* is god of the winds; bellows-makers are elsewhere in Middleton associated with bawds.

36–7 *minister once and set up in the trade*: commit adultery and become a whore.

once and set up the trade, I put in for my thirds, I shall be mad or fool else.

ISABELLA. The first place is thine, believe it, Lollio,
If I do fall –

LOLLIO. I fall upon you.

ISABELLA. So.

LOLLIO. Well, I stand to my venture.

ISABELLA. But thy counsel now, how shall I deal with 'em?

LOLLIO. Why, do you mean to deal with 'em?

ISABELLA. Nay, the fair understanding, how to use 'em.

LOLLIO. Abuse 'em! That's the way to mad the fool, and make a fool of the madman, and then you use 'em kindly.

ISABELLA. 'Tis easy, I'll practise; do thou observe it.
The key of thy wardrobe.

LOLLIO. There; fit yourself for 'em, and I'll fit 'em both for you. *[Gives her the key.]*

ISABELLA. Take thou no further notice than the outside. *Exit.*

LOLLIO. Not an inch; I'll put you to the inside.

Enter ALIBIUS.

ALIBIUS. Lollio, art there? Will all be perfect, think'st thou?
Tomorrow night, as if to close up the solemnity,
Vermandero expects us.

LOLLIO. I mistrust the madmen most; the fools will do well enough, I have taken pains with them.

ALIBIUS. Tush, they cannot miss; the more absurdity
The more commends it, so no rough behaviours

---

37 *thirds*: third share, Isabella being divided between him, Alibius and Franciscus. 'Thirds' was the legal share of captures and certain fines (the remainder being due to the crown), and the traditional portion of a deceased husband's estate which was due to the wife.

43 *I stand to my venture*: 'I will abide by my fortune'; a 'venturer' took a share in a commercial voyage's risks and expenses, receiving a commensurate portion of any profits.

44–5 *deal*: cope//have intercourse with.

46 *the fair understanding*: 'interpret my words in a decent sense'.

49 *kindly*: kindly/according to their natures.

50 *practise*: execute a plot or intrigue, involving deceit.

55 *I'll put you to the inside*: Obscene; 'put to' = swive (cf. *Love's Labour's Lost*, IV.ii.74–5).

Affright the ladies; they are nice things, thou know'st.

LOLLIO. You need not fear, sir; so long as we are there with our commanding pizzles, they'll be as tame as the ladies themselves.

ALIBIUS. I will see them once more rehearse before they go.

LOLLIO. I was about it, sir; look you to the madmen's morris, and let me alone with the other. There is one or two that I mistrust their fooling; I'll instruct them, and then they shall rehearse the whole measure.

ALIBIUS. Do so; I'll see the music prepar'd. But Lollio,
By the way, how does my wife brook her restraint?
Does she not grudge at it?

LOLLIO. So, so; she takes some pleasure in the house, she would abroad else. You must allow her a little more length, she's kept too short.

ALIBIUS. She shall go along to Vermandero's with us;
That will serve her for a month's liberty.

LOLLIO. What's that on your face, sir?

ALIBIUS. Where, Lollio? I see nothing.

LOLLIO. Cry you mercy, sir, 'tis your nose; it show'd like the trunk of a young elephant.

ALIBIUS. Away, rascal! I'll prepare the music, Lollio.

Exit ALIBIUS.

LOLLIO. Do, sir, and I'll dance the whilst. Tony, where art thou, Tony?

Enter ANTONIO.

ANTONIO. Here, cousin; where art thou?

LOLLIO. Come, Tony, the footmanship I taught you.

ANTONIO. I had rather ride, cousin.

LOLLIO. Ay, a whip take you; but I'll keep you out. Vault in; look you, Tony: fa, la, la, la, la. [*Dances.*]

ANTONIO. Fa, la, la, la, la. [*Dances.*]

LOLLIO. There, an honour.

ANTONIO. Is this an honour, cuz? [*Bows.*]

LOLLIO. Yes, and it please your worship.

---

65 *pizzles*: whips made from the dried penises of bulls.
70 *fooling*: See Textual note, p. 409.
83 *elephant*: perhaps a sign of a cuckold; more probably Lollio suggests Alibius is being led by the nose.
89 *ride*: also, 'mount sexually'.
93 *honour*: a bow.

ANTONIO. Does honour bend in the hams, cuz?

LOLLIO. Marry, does it, as low as worship, squireship, nay, yeomandry itself sometimes, from whence it first stiffened. There, rise, a caper.

ANTONIO. Caper after an honour, cuz?

LOLLIO. Very proper; for honour is but a caper, rise[s] as fast and high, has a knee or two, and falls to th' ground again. You can remember your figure, Tony?

Exit.

ANTONIO. Yes, cousin; when I see thy figure, I can remember mine.

Enter ISABELLA, [*like a madwoman*].

ISABELLA. Hey, how he treads the air! Shough, shough,
t'other way!
He burns his wings else. Here's wax enough below,
Icarus, more than will be cancelled these eighteen
moons. [ANTONIO *falls*.]
He's down, he's down! What a terrible fall he had!
Stand up, thou son of Cretan Dedalus,
And let us tread the lower labyrinth;
I'll bring thee to the clue. [ANTONIO *rises*.]

---

96 *Does honour bend in the hams*: This is ostensibly an enquiry about the right execution of the bow, but with the punning query 'Do those of high rank abase themselves so?' Lollio answers that those of high rank will demean themselves to officials, squires, even yeomen; but since there appears to be a pun on 'bow in the hams' = 'to copulate', Lollio may be suggesting that those of rank will stoop to low liaisons.

101 *caper*: leap/brief frolic.

104 *figure*: set of movements in dancing/appearance.

108 *Icarus*: son of Daedalus, who made him wings to fly with; but Icarus flew too near the sun and melted the wax that attached them to his shoulders. *cancelled*: used up (as sealing-wax on deeds).

111 *the lower labyrinth*: According to one version of the legend, Daedalus and Icarus were imprisoned in the labyrinth which Daedalus had constructed to hold the Minotaur, as a punishment for conniving at Ariadne's assistance to Theseus in killing the man-bull. Ariadne gave Theseus a ball of thread to mark his way into the maze and be the 'clue' to guide him out. It has been suggested that the maze is a *lower* labyrinth as opposed to that of the sky; but it is more probable that Isabella makes a mock advance, inviting Antonio to 'tread' with her the labyrinth of sexual love.

ANTONIO. Prithee, cuz, let me alone.
ISABELLA. Art thou now drown'd?
About thy head I saw a heap of clouds,
Wrapp'd like a Turkish turbant; on thy back
A crook'd chameleon-colour'd rainbow hung
Like a tiara down unto thy hams.
Let me suck out those billows in thy belly;
Hark how they roar and rumble in the straits!
Bless thee from the pirates.
ANTONIO. Pox upon you; let me alone!
ISABELLA. Why shouldst thou mount so high as Mercury,
Unless thou hadst reversion of his place?
Stay in the moon with me, Endymion,
And we will rule these wild, rebellious waves,
That would have drown'd my love.
ANTONIO. I'll kick thee if again thou touch me,
Thou wild unshapen antic; I am no fool,
You bedlam!
ISABELLA. But you are, as sure as I am, mad.
Have I put on this habit of a frantic,
With love as full of fury, to beguile
The nimble eye of watchful jealousy,
And am I thus rewarded? [*She reveals herself.*]
ANTONIO. Ha, dearest beauty!
ISABELLA. No, I have no beauty now,
Nor never had, but what was in my garments.
You, a quick-sighted lover? Come not near me!
Keep your caparisons, y'are aptly clad;

114–26 There is a continuing reference to the Icarian Sea, in which Icarus drowned.

118 *tiara*: a high head-dress, sometimes a turban, which here has a tail hanging down the back.

119 *suck out those billows in your belly*: Probably again this is an indecent advance under the guise of insane allusion to the legend.

120 *straits*: narrows/intestines; but see also Textual note, p. 409.

124 *reversion of his place*: the right of succeeding Mercury as winged messenger of the gods.

125 *Endymion*: a beautiful youth loved by Luna (the moon); Isabella imagines herself the moon goddess controlling tides.

129 *antic*: clown, grotesque figure.

138 *caparisons*: the coverings of a horse, and (by transference) clothes on a human beast.

I came a feigner to return stark mad. *Exit.*

Enter LOLLIO.

ANTONIO. Stay, or I shall change condition,
And become as you are.

LOLLIO. Why, Tony, whither now? Why, fool?

ANTONIO. Whose fool, usher of idiots? You coxcomb!
I have fool'd too much.

LOLLIO. You were best be mad another while then.

ANTONIO. So I am, stark mad; I have cause enough;
And I could throw the full effects on thee,
And beat thee like a fury!

LOLLIO. Do not, do not; I shall not forbear the gentleman under the fool, if you do; alas, I saw through your fox-skin before now. Come, I can give you comfort; my mistress loves you, and there is as arrant a madman i' th' house as you are a fool, your rival, whom she loves not; if after the masque we can rid her of him, you earn her love, she says, and the fool shall ride her.

ANTONIO. May I believe thee?

LOLLIO. Yes, or you may choose whether you will or no.

ANTONIO. She's eas'd of him; I have a good quarrel on't.

LOLLIO. Well, keep your old station yet, and be quiet.

ANTONIO. Tell her I will deserve her love. [*Exit.*]

LOLLIO. And you are like to have your desire.

Enter FRANCISCUS.

FRANCISCUS. (*sings*) 'Down, down, down a-down a-down'
and then with a horse-trick,
To kick Latona's forehead, and break her bowstring.

---

143 *usher*: door-keeper, subordinate teacher.

149 *forbear*: spare.

156 *ride*: mount sexually.

159 *eas'd*: There is a verbal parallel to the main plot, III.iv.97–9, which points both similarity and contrast between the two actions.

162 *desire*: See Textual note, p. 409.

164 *horse-trick*: horse-play, prancing in imitation of a performing horse.

165 *Latona*: the mother of Artemis/Diana, here confused with Artemis herself, commonly depicted as a huntress with a bow. Rowley may have written 'Latonia' = daughter of Latona.

LOLLIO. This is t'other counterfeit; I'll put him out of his humour. [*Takes out letter and reads*] 'Sweet lady, having now cast off this counterfeit cover of a madman, I appear to your best judgement a true and faithful lover of your heauty.' – This is pretty well for a madman.

FRANCISCUS. Ha! What's that?

LOLLIO. 'Chide those perfections in you which [have] made me imperfect.'

FRANCISCUS. I am discover'd to the fool.

LOLLIO. I hope to discover the fool in you, ere I have done with you. 'Yours all, or one beside himself, Franciscus.' – This madman will mend sure.

FRANCISCUS. What do you read, sirrah?

LOLLIO. Your destiny, sir; you'll be hang'd for this trick, and another that I know.

FRANCISCUS. Art thou of counsel with thy mistress?

LOLLIO. Next her apron strings.

FRANCISCUS. Give me thy hand.

LOLLIO. Stay, let me put yours in my pocket first. [*Puts away the letter*] Your hand is true, is it not? It will not pick? I partly fear it, because I think it does lie.

FRANCISCUS. Not in a syllable.

LOLLIO. So; if you love my mistress so well as you have handled the matter here, you are like to be cur'd of your madness.

FRANCISCUS. And none but she can cure it.

LOLLIO. Well, I'll give you over then, and she shall cast your water next.

FRANCISCUS. Take for thy pains past. [*Gives him money*]

LOLLIO. I shall deserve more, sir, I hope; my mistress loves you, but must have some proof of your love to her.

FRANCISCUS. There I meet my wishes.

LOLLIO. That will not serve, you must meet her enemy and yours.

180–1 *this trick, and another that I know*: fraud, and the act of adultery.

185 *yours*: i.e. 'your hand(writing)'. Lollio pretends a fear that the 'hand' will pick his pocket if he places it there, since the 'hand' appears to express dishonest sentiments.

193–4 *cast your water*: 'diagnose your ailment by analysing your urine'.

FRANCISCUS. He's dead already!

LOLLIO. Will you tell me that, and I parted but now with him?

FRANCISCUS. Show me the man.

LOLLIO. Ay, that's a right course now, see him before you kill him in any case; and yet it needs not go so far neither, 'tis but a fool that haunts the house and my mistress in the shape of an idiot. Bang but his fool's coat well-favouredly, and 'tis well.

FRANCISCUS. Soundly, soundly!

LOLLIO. Only reserve him till the masque be past; and if you find him not now in the dance yourself, I'll show you. In, in! My master!

FRANCISCUS. He handles him like a feather. Hey!
[*Exit dancing.*]

Enter ALIBIUS.

ALIBIUS. Well said. In a readiness, Lollio?

LOLLIO. Yes, sir.

ALIBIUS. Away then, and guide them in, Lollio;
Entreat your mistress to see this sight.
Hark, is there not one incurable fool
That might be begg'd? I have friends.

LOLLIO. I have him for you, one that shall deserve it too.
[*Exit.*]

ALIBIUS. Good boy, Lollio.

[*Enter* ISABELLA, *then* LOLLIO *with* MADMEN *and* FOOLS.]
The MADMEN *and* FOOLS *dance.*

ALIBIUS. 'Tis perfect; well, fit but once these strains,
We shall have coin and credit for our pains.
Exeunt.

---

208 *well-favouredly*: soundly, severely.
214 *Well said*: a stock commendation, meaning 'well done'.
219 *That might be begg'd*: that might be sought as a ward, so as to enjoy as guardian the profits of his estate. In his reply Lollio may be thinking of Alibius himself or of the disguised lovers.
222 *fit but once these strains*: 'make the strains of the music fit the mad antics of the dance', or 'only get the music ready'.

ACT V

SCENE I

Enter BEATRICE. *A clock strikes one.*

BEATRICE. One struck, and yet she lies by't! Oh my fears!
This strumpet serves her own ends, 'tis apparent now,
Devours the pleasure with a greedy appetite,
And never minds my honour or my peace,
Makes havoc of my right. But she pays dearly for't:
No trusting of her life with such a secret,
That cannot rule her blood to keep her promise.
Beside, I have some suspicion of her faith to me,
Because I was suspected of my lord,
And it must come from her. Hark! By my horrors,
Another clock strikes two. *Strikes two.*

Enter DE FLORES.

DE FLORES. Pist! Where are you?
BEATRICE. De Flores?
DE FLORES. Ay. Is she not come from him yet?
BEATRICE. As I am a living soul, not.
DE FLORES. Sure the devil
Hath sow'd his itch within her. Who'd trust
A waiting-woman?
BEATRICE. I must trust somebody.
DE FLORES. Push, they are termagants,
Especially when they fall upon their masters
And have their ladies' first-fruits; th'are mad whelps,
You cannot stave 'em off from game royal. Then
You are so harsh and hardy, ask no counsel;
And I could have help'd you to a[n] apothecary's daughter,
Would have fall'n off before eleven, and thank['d] you too.

---

16 *termagant*: a savage deity, supposedly worshipped by Mohammedans, and, by transference, a fierce, shrewish woman.

19 *stave 'em off from game royal*: divert them from hunting game which are a royal preserve.

20 *harsh*: See Textual note, p. 409.

BEATRICE. Oh me, not yet? This whore forgets herself.
DE FLORES. The rascal fares so well. Look, y'are undone,
The day-star, by this hand! See Phosphorus plain
yonder.
BEATRICE. Advise me now to fall upon some ruin,
There is no counsel safe else.
DE FLORES. Peace, I ha't now;
For we must force a rising, there's no remedy.
BEATRICE. How? Take heed of that.
DE FLORES. Tush, be you quiet,
Or else give over all.
BEATRICE. Prithee, I ha' done then.
DE FLORES. This is my reach: I'll set some part a-fire
Of Diaphanta's chamber.
BEATRICE. How? Fire, sir?
That may endanger the whole house.
DE FLORES. You talk of danger when your fame's on
fire?
BEATRICE. That's true; do what thou wilt now.
DE FLORES. Push! I aim
At a most rich success, strikes all dead sure:
The chimney being a-fire, and some light parcels
Of the least danger in her chamber only,
If Diaphanta should be met by chance then,
Far from her lodging (which is now suspicious),
It would be thought her fears and affrights then
Drove her to seek for succour; if not seen
Or met at all, as that's the likeliest,
For her own shame she'll hasten towards her lodging;
I will be ready with a piece high-charg'd,
As 'twere to cleanse the chimney. There, 'tis proper
now,
But she shall be the mark.
BEATRICE. I'm forc'd to love thee now,

---

25 *day star. Phosphorus*: Gk. the morning star; in Latin, Lucifer. See Additional note, p. 415, and Textual note, p. 409.

26 *to fall upon some ruin*: to happen upon some desperate action or catastrophe.

31 *reach*: plan.

37 *light parcels*: small items of insufficient body to cause a serious fire.

45 *piece*: fowling-piece, gun.

46 *There, 'tis proper now*: 'the plan is now fit for execution'.

'Cause thou provid'st so carefully for my honour.
DE FLORES. 'Slid, it concerns the safety of us both,
Our pleasure and continuance.
BEATRICE. One word now, prithee:
How for the servants?
DE FLORES. I'll despatch them,
Some one way, some another in the hurry,
For buckets, hooks, ladders. Fear not you;
The deed shall find its time; and I've thought since
Upon a safe conveyance for the body too.
How this fire purifies wit! Watch you your minute.
BEATRICE. Fear keeps my soul upon't, I cannot stray
from't.

Enter ALONZO'S GHOST.

DE FLORES. Ha! What art thou that tak'st away the light
'Twixt that star and me? I dread thee not.
'Twas but a mist of conscience – all's clear again.
Exit.
BEATRICE. Who's that, De Flores? Bless me! It slides by!
[*Exit* GHOST.]
Some ill thing haunts the house; 't has left behind it
A shivering sweat upon me. I'm afraid now.
This night hath been so tedious. Oh, this strumpet!
Had she a thousand lives, he should not leave her
Till he had destroy'd the last. – List! Oh my terrors!
Struck three o'clock.
Three struck by Saint Sebastian's!
[*Voice*] *within.* Fire, fire, fire!
BEATRICE. Already? How rare is that man's speed!
How heartily he serves me! His face loathes one,
But look upon his care, who would not love him?
The east is not more beauteous than his service.
[*Voice*] *within.* Fire, fire, fire!

Enter DE FLORES; *Servants pass over, ring a bell.*

DE FLORES. Away, despatch! Hooks, buckets, ladders! –
that's well said;
The fire-bell rings, the chimney works; my charge;

---

58 *light*: See Additional note, p. 415.
70 *loathes*: disgusts.
75 *charge*: powder and shot for the gun.

The piece is ready. *Exit.*
BEATRICE. Here's a man worth loving –

Enter DIAPHANTA.

Oh, y'are a jewel.
DIAPHANTA. Pardon frailty, madam;
In troth I was so well, I ev'n forgot myself.
BEATRICE. Y'have made trim work.
DIAPHANTA. What?
BEATRICE. Hie quickly to your chamber;
Your reward follows you.
DIAPHANTA. I never made
So sweet a bargain. *Exit.*

Enter ALSEMERO.

ALSEMERO. O my dear Joanna
Alas, art thou risen too? I was coming,
My absolute treasure.
BEATRICE. When I miss'd you,
I could not choose but follow.
ALSEMERO. Th'art all sweetness!
The fire is not so dangerous.
BEATRICE. Think you so, sir?
ALSEMERO. I prithee tremble not; believe me, 'tis not.

Enter VERMANDERO *and* JASPERINO.

VERMANDERO. Oh bless my house and me!
ALSEMERO. My lord your father.

Enter DE FLORES *with a piece.*

VERMANDERO. Knave, whither goes that piece?
DE FLORES. To scour the chimney. *Exit.*
VERMANDERO. Oh, well said, well said;
That fellow's good on all occasions.
BEATRICE. A wondrous necessary man, my lord.
VERMANDERO. He hath a ready wit, he's worth 'em all, sir;
Dog at a house of fire; I ha' seen him sing'd ere now.
The piece goes off.

---

93 *Dog at*: skilled at.

– Ha, there he goes.
BEATRICE. 'Tis done.
ALSEMERO. Come, sweet, to bed now;
Alas, thou wilt get cold.
BEATRICE. Alas, the fear keeps that out;
My heart will find no quiet till I hear
How Diaphanta, my poor woman, fares;
It is her chamber, sir, her lodging chamber.
VERMANDERO. How should the fire come there?
BEATRICE. As good a soul as ever lady countenanc'd,
But in her chamber negligent and heavy;
She 'scap'd a mine twice.
VERMANDERO. Twice?
BEATRICE. Strangely twice, sir.
VERMANDERO. Those sleepy sluts are dangerous in a house,
And they be ne'er so good.

Enter DE FLORES.

DE FLORES. O poor virginity,
Thou hast paid dearly for't!
VERMANDERO. Bless us! What's that?
DE FLORES. A thing you all knew once – Diaphanta's burnt.
BEATRICE. My woman, oh my woman!
DE FLORES. Now the flames
Are greedy of her; burnt, burnt, burnt to death, sir!
BEATRICE. Oh, my presaging soul!
ALSEMERO. Not a tear more;
I charge you by the last embrace I gave you
In bed before this rais'd us.
BEATRICE. Now you tie me;
Were it my sister, now she gets no more.

Enter SERVANT.

---

100 *countenanc'd*: patronised, employed.
101 *heavy*: sluggish, slovenly.
102 *mine*: catastrophe, violent conflagration.
102 *strangely*: surprisingly, miraculously.
105 *What's that*: Probably De Flores carried not Diaphanta's body (V.i.55 makes that unlikely) but the charred remains of some still recognisable outer garment, one worn earlier by Diaphanta on stage.

VERMANDERO. How now?
SERVANT. All danger's past; you may now take your rests, my lords, the fire is throughly quench'd. – Ah, poor gentlewoman, how soon was she stifled!
BEATRICE. De Flores, what is left of her inter,
And we as mourners all will follow her;
I will entreat that honour to my servant,
Ev'n of my lord himself.
ALSEMERO. Command it, sweetness.
BEATRICE. Which of you spied the fire first?
DE FLORES. 'Twas I, madam.
BEATRICE. And took such pains in't too? A double goodness!
'Twere well he were rewarded.
VERMANDERO. He shall be;
De Flores, call upon me.
ALSEMERO. And upon me, sir.
Exeunt [all except DE FLORES.]
DE FLORES. Rewarded? Precious! Here's a trick beyond me;
I see in all bouts both of sport and wit,
Always a woman strives for the last hit. *Exit.*

SCENE II

Enter TOMAZO.

TOMAZO. I cannot taste the benefits of life
With the same relish I was wont to do.
Man I grow weary of, and hold his fellowship
A treacherous, bloody friendship; and because
I am ignorant in whom my wrath should settle,
I must think all men villains, and the next
I meet, whoe'er he be, the murderer
Of my most worthy brother. – Ha! What's he?

Enter DE FLORES, *passes over the stage.*

Oh, the fellow that some call honest De Flores;
But methinks honesty was hard bested
To come there for a lodging – as if a queen

126 *sport*: physical amusement/sexual pleasure.
10 *hard bested*: hard put to it.

Should make her palace of a pest-house.
I find a contrariety in nature
Betwixt that face and me: the least occasion
Would give me game upon him. Yet he's so foul
One would scarce touch [him] with a sword he loved
And made account of; so most deadly venomous,
He would go near to poison any weapon
That should draw blood on him; one must resolve
Never to use that sword again in fight,
In way of honest manhood, that strikes him;
Some river must devour't, 'twere not fit
That any man should find it. – What, again?

Enter DE FLORES.

He walks a' purpose by, sure, to choke me up,
To infect my blood.
DE FLORES. My worthy noble lord.
TOMAZO. Dost offer to come near and breathe upon me?
[*Strikes him.*]
DE FLORES. A blow! [*Draws his sword.*]
TOMAZO. Yea, are you so prepar'd?
I'll rather, like a soldier, die by th' sword. [*Draws.*]
Than like a politician by thy poison.
DE FLORES. Hold, my lord, as you are honourable.
TOMAZO. All slaves that kill by poison are still cowards.
DE FLORES. [*aside*] I cannot strike; I see his brother's wounds
Fresh bleeding in his eye, as in a crystal.
– I will not question this; I know y'are noble;
I take my injury with thanks given, sir,
Like a wise lawyer; and as a favour
Will wear it for the worthy hand that gave it.
[*Aside*] Why this from him that yesterday appear'd
So strangely loving to me?
Oh, but instinct is of a subtler strain;
Guilt must not walk so near his lodge again;

---

12 *pest-house*: hospital for those suffering from infectious diseases, especially plague.
15 *give me game*: 'give me occasion for quarrelling'; 'to be in game' = to be engaged in hunting.
17 *made account of*: valued.
33 *crystal*: crystal ball.

He came near me now. *Exit.*
TOMAZO. All league with mankind I renounce for ever,
Till I find this murderer; not so much
As common courtesy, but I'll lock up;
For in the state of ignorance I live in,
A brother may salute his brother's murderer,
And wish good speed to th' villain in a greeting.

Enter VERMANDERO, ALIBIUS *and* ISABELLA.

VERMANDERO. Noble Piracquo!
TOMAZO. Pray keep on your way, sir,
I've nothing to say to you.
VERMANDERO. Comforts bless you, sir.
TOMAZO. I have forsworn compliment, in troth I have, sir;
As you are merely man, I have not left
A good wish for you, nor any here.
VERMANDERO. Unless you be so far in love with grief
You will not part from't upon any terms,
We bring that news will make a welcome for us.
TOMAZO. What news can that be?
VERMANDERO. Throw no scornful smile
Upon the zeal I bring you, 'tis worth more, sir.
Two of the chiefest men I kept about me
I hide not from the law or your just vengeance.
TOMAZO. Ha!
VERMANDERO. To give your peace more ample satisfaction,
Thank these discoverers.
TOMAZO. If you bring that calm,
Name but the manner I shall ask forgiveness in
For that contemptuous smile upon you;
I'll perfect it with reverence that belongs
Unto a sacred altar. [*Kneels.*]
VERMANDERO. Good sir, rise;
Why, now you overdo as much a' this hand
As you fell short a' t'other. Speak, Alibius.
ALIBIUS. 'Twas my wife's fortune, as she is most lucky
At a discovery, to find out lately
Within our hospital of fools and madmen
Two counterfeits slipp'd into these disguises:
Their names, Franciscus and Antonio.

VERMANDERO. Both mine, sir, and I ask no favour for
'em.
ALIBIUS. Now that which draws suspicion to their habits,
The time of their disguisings agrees justly
With the day of the murder.
TOMAZO. O blest revelation!
VERMANDERO. Nay more, nay more, sir (I'll not spare
mine own
In way of justice), they both feign'd a journey
To Briamata, and so wrought out their leaves.
My love was so abus'd in't.
TOMAZO. Time's too precious
To run in waste now; you have brought a peace
The riches of five kingdoms could not purchase.
Be my most happy conduct; I thirst for 'em;
Like subtle lightning will I wind about 'em,
And melt their marrow in 'em.

Exeunt.

SCENE III

Enter ALSEMERO *and* JASPERINO.

JASPERINO. Your confidence, I'm sure, is now of proof;
The prospect from the garden has show'd
Enough for deep suspicion.
ALSEMERO. The black mask
That so continually was worn upon't
Condemns the face for ugly ere't be seen:
Her despite to him, and so seeming bottomless.

---

76 *habits*: clothes.

81 *wrought out their leaves*: cunningly obtained permission to go.

85 *conduct*: guide.

86–7 Lightning was held capable of melting marrow without damaging the skin, and so became an image for sudden, undetectable murder.

1 *of proof*: impenetrable, like armour. However, from the context it is possible that the phrase here means 'capable of being put to the test', 'on trial'.

3 *The black mask*: i.e. Beatrice's treacherous pretence of hatred for De Flores; the obvious superficial deceit suggests an underlying viciousness.

JASPERINO. Touch it home then; 'tis not a shallow probe
Can search this ulcer soundly; I fear you'll find it
Full of corruption. 'Tis fit I leave you;
She meets you opportunely from that walk;
She took the back door at his parting with her.
Exit JASPERINO.
ALSEMERO. Did my fate wait for this unhappy stroke
At my first sight of woman? – She's here.

Enter BEATRICE.

BEATRICE. Alsemero!
ALSEMERO. How do you?
BEATRICE. How do I?
Alas! How do you? You look not well.
ALSEMERO. You read me well enough, I am not well.
BEATRICE. Not well, sir? Is't in my power to better you?
ALSEMERO. Yes.
BEATRICE. Nay, then y'are cur'd again.
ALSEMERO. Pray resolve me one question, lady.
BEATRICE. If I can.
ALSEMERO. None can so sure. Are you honest?
BEATRICE. Ha, ha, ha! That's a broad question, my lord.
ALSEMERO. But that's not a modest answer, my lady.
Do you laugh? My doubts are strong upon me.
BEATRICE. 'Tis innocence that smiles, and no rough brow
Can take away the dimple in her cheek.
Say I should strain a tear to fill the vault,
Which would you give the better faith to?
ALSEMERO. 'Twere but hypocrisy of a sadder colour,
But the same stuff. Neither your smiles nor tears
Shall move or flatter me from my belief:
You are a whore!
BEATRICE. What a horrid sound it hath!
It blasts a beauty to deformity;

---

7 *Touch it home*: get to the root of the matter, the quick of the ulcer.
12–13 See Additional note, p. 414.
20 *honest*: chaste.
21 *broad*: wide/coarse.
26 *strain a tear to fill the vault*: 'produce enough water to fill the heavens'.

Upon what face soever that breath falls,
It strikes it ugly: oh, you have ruin'd
What you can ne'er repair again.

ALSEMERO. I'll all demolish, and seek out truth within
you,
If there be any left. Let your sweet tongue
Prevent your heart's rifling; there I'll ransack
And tear out my suspicion.

BEATRICE. You may, sir,
'Tis an easy passage. Yet, if you please,
Show me the ground whereon you lost your love;
My spotless virtue may but tread on that
Before I perish.

ALSEMERO. Unanswerable!
A ground you cannot stand on; you fall down
Beneath all grace and goodness when you set
Your ticklish heel on't; there was a visor
O'er that cunning face, and that became you;
Now impudence in triumph rides upon't;
How comes this tender reconcilement else
'Twixt you and your despite, your rancorous loathing,
De Flores? He that your eye was sore at sight of,
He's now become your arm's supporter, your lip's
saint!

BEATRICE. Is there the cause?

ALSEMERO. Worse; your lust's devil,
Your adultery!

BEATRICE. Would any but yourself say that,
'Twould turn him to a villain.

ALSEMERO. 'Twas witness'd
By the counsel of your bosom, Diaphanta.

BEATRICE. Is your witness dead then?

---

41 *ground*: foundation, basic reason.

46 *ticklish*: wanton, lascivious; *visor*: mask.

52 *arm's supporter*: physical prop; but it is probable that there is an allusion to the grotesque figures who served as 'supporters' to a coat of arms.

52 *lip's saint*: i.e. 'that adored person to whom your lips pay devotion'. The phrase ironically echoes Beatrice's proleptic comment on first meeting Alsemero, 'I shall change my saint, I fear me' (I.i.56).

53 *lust's devil*: See Additional note, p. 413.

ALSEMERO. 'Tis to be fear'd
It was the wages of her knowledge, poor soul;
She liv'd not long after the discovery.
BEATRICE. Then hear a story of not much less horror
Than this your false suspicion is beguil'd with;
To your bed's scandal I stand up innocence,
Which even the guilt of one black other deed
Will stand for proof of: your love has made me
A cruel murd'ress.
ALSEMERO. Ha!
BEATRICE. A bloody one;
I have kiss'd poison for't, strok'd a serpent:
That thing of hate, worthy in my esteem
Of no better employment, and him most worthy
To be so employ'd, I caus'd to murder
That innocent Piracquo, having no
Better means than that worst, to assure
Yourself to me.
ALSEMERO. Oh, the place itself e'er since
Has crying been for vengeance, the temple
Where blood and beauty first unlawfully
Fir'd their devotion, and quench'd the right one;
'Twas in my fears at first, 'twill have it now.
Oh, thou art all deform'd!
BEATRICE. Forget not, sir,
It for your sake was done; shall greater dangers
Make the less welcome?
ALSEMERO. Oh, thou shouldst have gone
A thousand leagues about to have avoided
This dangerous bridge of blood; here we are lost.
BEATRICE. Remember I am true unto your bed.
ALSEMERO. The bed itself's a charnel, the sheets shrouds
For murdered carcasses. It must ask pause
What I must do in this; meantime you shall

---

62 *stand up innocence*: See Textual note, p. 409. Probably a legal metaphor: 'Against the scandalous charge that your bed is dishonoured I maintain my innocence.' Cf. *Antony and Cleopatra*, I.i.40, for the same idiom.
66 *serpent*: See Additional note, p. 413.
74 *blood*: sexual desire.
75 *the right one*: i.e. religious zeal.
76 *'twill have it now*: the temple will have vengeance.
80 *about*: around. She should have made a detour.

Be my prisoner only. Enter my closet;
Exit BEATRICE.
I'll be your keeper yet. Oh, in what part
Of this sad story shall I first begin? – Ha!

Enter DE FLORES.

This same fellow has put me in. – De Flores!
DE FLORES. Noble Alsemero?
ALSEMERO. I can tell you
News, sir; my wife has her commended to you.
DE FLORES. That's news indeed, my lord; I think she would
Commend me to the gallows if she could,
She ever lov'd me so well. I thank her.
ALSEMERO. What's this blood upon your band, De Flores?
DE FLORES. Blood? No, sure, 'twas wash'd since.
ALSEMERO. Since when, man?
DE FLORES. Since t'other day I got a knock
In a sword-and-dagger school. I think 'tis out.
ALSEMERO. Yes, 'tis almost out, but 'tis perceiv'd though.
I had forgot my message; this it is:
What price goes murder?
DE FLORES. How sir?
ALSEMERO. I ask you, sir;
My wife's behindhand with you, she tells me,
For a brave bloody blow you gave for her sake
Upon Piracquo.
DE FLORES. Upon? 'Twas quite through him, sure.
Has she confess'd it?
ALSEMERO. As sure as death to both of you,
And much more than that.
DE FLORES. It could not be much more;
'Twas but one thing, and that – she's a whore.
ALSEMERO. It could not choose but follow. Oh cunning devils!
How should blind men know you from fair-fac'd saints?

89 *put me in*: given me the cue.
95 *band*: collar.
102 *behindhand with*: indebted to.

BEATRICE. (*within*) He lies, the villain does belie me!
DE FLORES. Let me go to her, sir.
ALSEMERO. Nay, you shall to her.
– Peace, crying crocodile, your sounds are heard!
– Take your prey to you, get you in to her, sir.
Exit DE FLORES.
I'll be your pander now; rehearse again
Your scene of lust, that you may be perfect
When you shall come to act it to the black audience
Where howls and gnashings shall be music to you.
Clip your adult'ress freely, 'tis the pilot
Will guide you to the Mare Mortuum,
Where you shall sink to fadoms bottomless.

Enter VERMANDERO, ALIBIUS, ISABELLA, TOMAZO, FRANCISCUS *and* ANTONIO.

VERMANDERO. Oh, Alsemero, I have a wonder for you.
ALSEMERO. No, sir, 'tis I, I have a wonder for you.
VERMANDERO. I have suspicion near as proof itself
For Piracquo's murder.
ALSEMERO. Sir, I have proof
Beyond suspicion for Piracquo's murder.
VERMANDERO. Beseech you, hear me; these two have been disguis'd
E'er since the deed was done.
ALSEMERO. I have two other
That were more close disguis'd than your two could be
E'er since the deed was done.
VERMANDERO. You'll hear me: these mine own servants –
ALSEMERO. Hear me: those nearer than your servants,
That shall acquit them and prove them guiltless.
FRANCISCUS. That may be done with easy truth, sir.
TOMAZO. How is my cause bandied through your delays!

---

112 *crying crocodile*: The crocodile was thought to shed hypocritical tears as it killed its victims.
116–17 See Additional note, p. 413.
118 *clip*: embrace.
119 *Mare Mortuum*: Latin for the Dead Sea, which was thought to be bottomless; this, however, has suggested also the bottomless pit of Hell, to which Beatrice will pilot De Flores, as did Charon over the Styx.
134 *bandied*: tossed aside.

Purgatory -

'Tis urgent in blood and calls for haste.
Give me a brother alive or dead:
Alive, a wife with him; if dead, for both
A recompense for murder and adultery.
BEATRICE. (*within*) Oh, oh, oh!
ALSEMERO. Hark, 'tis coming to you.
DE FLORES. (*within*) Nay, I'll along for company.
BEATRICE. (*within*) Oh, oh!
VERMANDERO. What horrid sounds are these?
ALSEMERO. Come forth, you twins of mischief.

Enter DE FLORES, *bringing in* BEATRICE [*wounded*].

DE FLORES. Here we are; if you have any more
To say to us, speak quickly, I shall not
Give you the hearing else; I am so stout yet,
And so, I think, that broken rib of mankind.
VERMANDERO. An host of enemies ent'red my citadel
Could not amaze like this: Joanna! Beatrice-Joanna!
BEATRICE. Oh, come not near me, sir, I shall defile you;
I am that of your blood was taken from you
For your better health; look no more upon't,
But cast it to the ground regardlessly;
Let the common shewer take it from distinction.
Beneath the stars, upon yon meteor
Ever hung my fate, 'mongst things corruptible;
I ne'er could pluck it from him; my loathing
Was prophet to the rest, but ne'er believ'd;

---

138 *adultery*: Rowley may carelessly have made Tomazo refer to Beatrice's liaison with De Flores, which he cannot know. But according to much Jacobean opinion, the formal contract with Alonzo was a binding marriage, as is symbolised in III.iv.28, 37–8; Tomazo may regard the marriage to Alsemero as a form of adultery.

146 *broken rib of mankind*: Beatrice, a daughter of the primal Eve who was made from the rib of Adam (Man) in Genesis 2.21–3. See Additional note, p. 413.

150–1 An allusion to the practice of blood-letting.

153 *common shewer*: main drain.

154 *yon meteor*: i.e. De Flores. As opposed to the pure, fixed stars, meteors belonged to the sub-lunary world of corruption and decay; the influence of stars might be beneficent, but meteors were provoked by, or resulted in, evil. See Additional note, p. 414.

Mine honour fell with him, and now my life.
Alsemero, I am a stranger to your bed.
Your bed was coz'ned on the nuptial night,
For which your false bride died.

ALSEMERO. Diaphanta!

DE FLORES. Yes, and the while I coupled with your mate
At barley-brake; now we are left in Hell.

VERMANDERO. We are all there, it circumscribes here.

DE FLORES. I lov'd this woman in spite of her heart;
Her love I earn'd out of Piracquo's murder.

TOMAZO. Ha! my brother's murtherer?

DE FLORES. Yes, and her honour's prize
Was my reward; I thank life for nothing
But that pleasure; it was so sweet to me
That I have drunk up all, left none behind
For any man to pledge me.

VERMANDERO. Horrid villain!
Keep life in him for further tortures.

DE FLORES. No!
I can prevent you; here's my penknife still;
It is but one thread more. [*Stabs himself*] – And now 'tis cut.
Make haste, Joanna, by that token to thee;
Canst not forget, so lately put in mind,
I would not go to leave thee far behind. *Dies.*

BEATRICE. Forgive me, Alsemero, all forgive;
'Tis time to die when 'tis a shame to live. *Dies.*

VERMANDERO. Oh, my name is ent'red now in that record
Where till this fatal hour 'twas never read.

ALSEMERO. Let it be blotted out; let your heart lose it,
And it can never look you in the face,

---

163 *barley-brake*: See note on III.iii.171.

163–4 *Hell . . . circumscribes here*: See Additional note, p. 414. Vermandero continues the metaphor of 'barley-brake', seeing the whole cast as within the central circle which indicates the limits of 'hell'; there seems to be an incidental reminiscence of Marlowe's *Dr Faustus*, II.i. 510–12.

175 *that token*: i.e. the wound he has just given himself.

180 *record*: the heavenly record which lists criminal actions.

Nor tell a tale behind the back of life
To your dishonour; justice hath so right
The guilty hit that innocence is quit
By proclamation, and may joy again.
– Sir, you are sensible of what truth hath done;
'Tis the best comfort that your grief can find.
TOMAZO. Sir, I am satisfied; my injuries
Lie dead before me. I can exact no more,
Unless my soul were loose, and could o'ertake
Those black fugitives that are fled from thence,
To take a second vengeance; but there are wraths
Deeper than mine, 'tis to be fear'd, about 'em.
ALSEMERO. What an opacous body had that moon
That last chang'd on us! Here's beauty chang'd
To ugly whoredom; here, servant obedience
To a master-sin, imperious murder;
I, a suppos'd husband, chang'd embraces
With wantonness, but that was paid before;
Your change is come too, from an ignorant wrath
To knowing friendship. Are there any more on's?
ANTONIO. Yes, sir, I was chang'd too, from a little ass as
I was to a great fool as I am, and had like to ha' been
chang'd to the gallows, but that you know my
innocence always excuses me.
FRANCISCUS. I was chang'd from a little wit to be stark
mad,
Almost for the same purpose.
ISABELLA. [*to* ALIBIUS] Your change is still behind
But deserve best your transformation;
You are a jealous coxcomb, keep schools of folly,

186–8 'The innocent are acquitted by public proclamation of the truth.'

193 *black fugitives that are fled from thence*: i.e. the damned souls of Beatrice and De Flores which have left the bodies which lie before Tomazo. But see Textual note, p. 409.

196 *opacous*: darkened, obscured, and therefore malevolent or of ill-omen.

197 *chang'd*: See Additional note, p. 413.

201 *wantonness, but that was paid before*: i.e. Diaphanta, whose adultery was paid by her murder.

202 *Your change*: Tomazo's.

207 *innocence*: guiltlessness/idiocy (idiots not being held criminally responsible).

209 *still behind*: yet to come.

And teach your scholars how to break your own head.
ALIBIUS. I see all apparent, wife, and will change now
Into a better husband, and never keep
Scholars that shall be wiser than myself.
ALSEMERO. Sir, you have yet a son's duty living,
Please you accept it. Let that your sorrow,
As it goes from your eye, go from your heart;
Man and his sorrow at the grave must part.

EPILOGUE

ALSEMERO. All we can do to comfort one another,
To stay a brother's sorrow for a brother,
To dry a child from the kind father's eyes,
Is to no purpose, it rather multiplies;
Your only smiles have power to cause relive
The dead again, or in their rooms to give
Brother a new brother, father a child;
If these appear, all griefs are reconcil'd.

Exeunt OMNES.

Finis

---

212 *break your own head*: i.e. with cuckold's horns.
221 *stay*: check, solace.
223 *multiplies*: i.e. increases grief.

NOTES

Beatrice — Greed - whim - naïvety.
De Flores - ~~love~~ (uncontrolled) lust.

Tragic Pity.

exegesis

HAMARTIA

Sexism

ARISTOTLEAN

①

Through catastrophe

Classic

dénouement of time

Bloody end.

(Greed)

severed finger.

Sub-plot

Fools & madmen → goes to great lengths to make distinctions. Obviously Symbolic.

fool - vicious or impious person (BIBLICAL)

madman — one who behaves like a lunatic

Madness - delusion resembling insanity

Deflo e "fire"

TEXTUAL NOTES

Abbreviations

Black	*The Changeling*, ed. M.W. Black (University of Pennsylvania, Philadelphia) 1966.
Brooke	*English Drama 1580–1642*, ed. C.F. Tucker Brooke and N.B. Paradise (London), 1933.
Bullen	*The Works of Thomas Middleton*, ed. A.H. Bullen, 8 vols. (London) 1885–6.
Dilke	*Old English Plays*, ed. C.W. Dilke, 6 vols. (London) 1814–15.
Dyce	*Works of Thomas Middleton*, ed. A. Dyce, 5 vols. (London) 1840.
F	Fountainwell Drama Texts, Oliver & Boyd, Edinburgh.
Gomme	*Jacobean Tragedies*, ed. A.H. Gomme (Oxford) 1969.
NM	The New Mermaid editions, Ernest Benn Ltd., London.
R	The Revels Plays, Methuen & Co. Ltd., London.
RR	Regents Renaissance Drama Series, Edward Arnold, London.
Schelling	*Typical Elizabethan Plays*, ed. F.E. Schelling and M.W. Black (New York) 1948.
Taylor	M.J.H. Taylor, 'A critical old-spelling edition of Thomas Middleton's *A Mad World*', unpublished Ph.D. thesis, University of Birmingham, 1963.
O	Octavo
OED	*Oxford English Dictionary*
Partridge	*A Dictionary of Slang*, ed. E. Partridge, 6th edition (London) 1967.
Q	Quarto
Q1	First Quarto
Q2	Second Quarto
s.d.	Stage direction
s.h.	Speech heading
SOD	*Shorter Oxford English Dictionary*, third edition revised, with addenda and corrections, by C.T. Onions (London) 1965.

A Mad World, My Masters

A second quarto of this play, printed 1640, is a reprint of Q1 which corrects a few obvious mistakes and makes many more. Some directions which indicate details of staging in the Caroline period appear in these notes, but a full collation of Q, Q corrected and Q2 can be found in RR.

DRAMATIS PERSONAE, 4 PENITENT BROTHEL: In s.d.s beginning IV.i and IV.iv this character is called by Q1 and Q2 'Penitent Once-Ill'. Since the change of name commences at Penitent's reformation, Middleton may have intended it to stand in his final text.

DRAMATIS PERSONAE, 11, 21 HAREBRAIN: In Q1 and Q2 this character becomes 'Hargrave' at IV.i.75, 76, at IV.iv.4, 54, in s.d.s at IV.iv.14, 73, and in s.h. at IV.iv.92 (though s.h.s elsewhere in the scene still indicate 'Harebrain'). The name changes again to 'Shortrod' at V.i.10, 15, though s.h.s again read 'Harebrain'. At V.ii.3 s.h. again indicates 'Shortrod', and this is continued to the end in both quartos. Though other variations in the names of characters could be due to compositors' errors, the name 'Shortrod', with its implication that Harebrain is sexually inadequate, is likely to be Middletonian. It is probable that it represents the author's first intention, imperfectly corrected in the copy behind Q1. Compare the character name 'Shortyard' in *Michaelmas Term.*

DRAMATIS PERSONAE, 12 GUNWATER: From s.d. beginning IV.ii until the end of the play this character is called 'Gumwater' by both quartos; Gumwater is a solution of gum-arabic in water, and it is possible that it indicates a character who salivates from toothless gums.

I.i.127 *Skirt*: So Q1 and Q2; but Dyce and later editors emend to 'shirt', presumably reading the title as a jocular allusion to the quality of Brothel's linen (not to his trade, since the Dramatis Personae describes him as a 'country gentleman'). Taylor alone defends Q.

I.i.205 *well-plac'd*: So Dyce; Qs read 'plac'st'.

I.ii.92 *entertain*: So Q1. Q2 substitutes the less archaic 'entertainment'.

II.i.7 *stockings*: Q1 'stockins' characterises Sir Bounteous through his speech: 'stockins' is a vulgar and dialectal pronunciation (Dobson, *English Pronunciation*, II, 950–1).

II.i.87 *lord's*: So Dyce; Q1 and Q2 read 'love's'.

II.ii.19 *chambers*: Q prints 'champers', probably by foul case.

II.vi.137 *guests*: So Q2; Q1 reads 'guesse'.

II.vi.end: Between Acts II and III Q2 prints the direction 'A Song, sung by the musitians, and after the Song, a Country dance, by the Actors in their Vizards to a new footing. Exeunt.' Q2 seems to have been set up from Q1, and the title page indicates that the play was performed by Queen Henrietta's Men at Salisbury Court, which was used by them from 1637 to 1642: the nature of the two s.d.s at the end of Acts II and V suggest that Q2 was not derived from a copy of Q1 which had been used for prompt copy in the theatre, but was printed as an accompaniment to a revival and sold as the 'book of the play'.

III.i.119 *breed*: So Q1; Q2 reads 'bred', which is possibly right.

III.ii.64 *coral*: So Dyce; the spelling variant of the quartos, 'Curall', probably reflects the 'cure-all' properties attributed to it.

III.ii.91 *cost*: So Q1. Q2 emends to 'lost'. As it stands, the remark is best taken as a request for doctor's fees for the ingredients, which Sir Bounteous refers to the Courtesan, to whom he has already given money. Q2 relates the remark clearly to this earlier gift.

III.ii.222 *Hey, hy, hy*: This could also be taken as simulated sobbing, rather than expostulation. Q gives no help in deciding.

III.iii.102 *half-moons*: So Q1. Q2, probably clarifying after the fashion had changed and the term become obscure, reads 'Periwigs'.

IV.i.21 *clock*: So Q2. Uncorrected Q1 reads 'clack', and this was miscorrected to 'cloak' later in the process of printing.

IV.i.29 *bear*: So Dyce. Q1 and Q2 read 'better'.

IV.i.48 *our*: So Dyce. Q1 and Q2 read 'her', which is weaker but accepted by RR.

IV.i.58, 59 *seiz'd . . . Seize*: So Dyce. Q1's 'seard . . . Ceare' and Q2's 'seard . . . Seare' clearly derive from a misreading of the secretary hand *z* as *r*.

IV.i.88 *rustling*: This edition. Q reads 'rufling', which RR renders 'ruffling'. This makes some sense, but it is more likely that by foul case *fl* was printed for *sl* (in the next section of the case).

IV.iv.72 *his*: So Dyce; the quartos read 'her'.

IV.v.22 *By your favour, lady*: So Taylor, treating line 23 as a reply to

Follywit's solicitation, and comparing *More Dissemblers*, I.ii.192. Q1 and Q2 read: '. . . what ere comes ont; by your favour Ladies.// *Enter the Mother*.' RR would accept Q, treating 'by your favour, ladies' as addressed to the audience, presumably as an apology for prosecuting an affair before them.

IV.v.78 *maid*: So Dyce; the quartos read 'man'. The error is curious, and it is just possible that Middleton was using 'man' in the generic sense – 'I never saw perfect humanity before' – and relishing the apparent paradox.

V.i.26 s.d. *SERVANT*: The quartos print 'Semus' here, and in s.h.s to lines 28 and 45. This is almost certainly the result of misreading the Latin 'Servus'.

V.i.104 *Pox*: So Dyce; both quartos read 'Post'. Taylor suggests that a more likely misreading is 'post' for 'soft', which would then introduce an aside.

V.i.120 *face*: So RR. The quartos read 'fact', which gives a plausible meaning: 'The ruby betrays her and blushes for her deed'; but this is likely to be a sensible misreading of the character *e* in secretary hand.

V.i.139 *turn*: After this question Q1 gives a new s.h.: '*Sir Bo.* What else lack you?' Presuming that something has dropped out, Q2 prints a phrase for Follywit between the two queries: 'Excellent well, sir'.

V.i.149 *watch*: So RR. Both quartos print 'watch time', which may be right, since *OED* records 'watch-clock', meaning an alarum clock. Both Qs print 'watch' elsewhere.

V.ii.124 *dizzy constables*: So Q1 in its corrected state. Uncorrected copies of Q1 read 'ditch constables', and it is just possible that this is what Middleton wrote: *Partridge*, p. 225, records 'Ditch' as a Cockney colloquialism for 'Shoreditch' at a later period, and Follywit's men were 'stay'd at town's end' by the constable. Or 'ditch-constable' may be an unrecorded analogue to contemptuous expressions such as 'hedge-priest'.

V.ii.161 s.h. [HAREBRAIN]: Q1 gives the meaningless s.h. 'Nub', which Q2 corrects to 'Gun'. Editors except Taylor have followed this suggestion, even though Gunwater has no other speech and never addresses his master thus.

V.ii.274 *prize . . . prize*: So Dyce, correcting the quartos' 'peece . . . peece'. The two are easily confused in secretary hand.

V.ii. *Finis*: Q2 adds the direction 'The end of the fifth and last Act: marching over the stage hand in hand.' Q2 also adds 'The catch for the Fifth Act, sung by SIR BOUNTEOUS to his guests'; Bullen prints the text, but points out that it also appears (slightly variant) in Blount's 1632 edition of Lyly's *Alexander and Campaspe*, I.ii. Probably the song was not by Middleton or Lyly, but enjoyed a vogue in the late 1630s.

A Chaste Maid in Cheapside

DRAMATIS PERSONAE, 11 *DAHUMMA*: So Q here and at II.ii.46 and s.d. beginning Act V, whilst the less meaningful 'DAHANNA' appears in s.d. after I.i.106, at I.i.17 and I.ii.2: probably different compositors read the copy text differently.

I.i.95 *Maximus*: So Q. F and others 'correct' to '*maxime*'; but this is undergraduate Latin.

I.i.135 s.d. MOLL: Q gives s.d. '*Enter* Mary', but this is only the formal name of which 'Moll' is the diminutive. Her mother calls her 'Mary' at I.i.25.

I.i.143 *wound*: So Q. F and others would read 'are wound', whereas R wishes to emend to 'sound', positing an unlikely misreading of *w* for *s*. It is possible that a word has dropped out, but 'wound' is the past tense of a verb 'to wind' = 'to go, to proceed', which *SOD* records as being in use as an intransitive up till 1608.

I.i.162 *pick a famine*: Substantially Q, 'picke a Famine'; but F and R would follow Dyce in interpreting this as 'peak a' famine' = 'dwindle, waste away, because of starvation'.

I.i.172 *Oh turn, sir, turn*: So Q, 'O turne Sir, turne'. R, following Dyce, emends to 'O Tim, sir, Tim', suggesting that 'turne' was influenced by the beginning of the previous speech. It is more likely, perhaps, that Sir Walter is pretending some reluctance, and Yellowhammer is begging him to 'turn in' and partake of hospitality.

I.i.212 *Just such another gentlewoman that's your daughter sir*: So Q, followed by NM and R (which cites E.A. Abbott, *A Shakesperian Grammar* (1879), para. 108 in support). F, following Dyce, would prefer to punctuate thus: 'Just such another gentlewoman – that's your daughter, sir?'

II.i.52 *sing*: So Q. The verb is perfectly intelligible as a synonym for 'copulate with' (cf. *Troilus and Cressida*, V.ii.9–10, 'She will sing any man at first sight. – And any man may sing her . . . '). However, NM suggests an interesting emendation, 'sting', noting that lust is often emblematised in Middleton as a flesh-fly; this would make excellent sense of the next phrase. F suggests merely emending to 'sin'.

II.i.124 LADY KIX. *Hist!*: So Q, giving the exclamation to '*Lady*.' NM follows, but other editors assign it to Touchwood Junior attracting his brother's attention.

II.i.171 *Master*: Q prints 'Mr', which Dyce expanded to 'Master', R to 'Mistress'. 'Mr' should be expanded to 'Mistress' twice in this quarto, but Q's normal abbreviation for the female is 'Mris', and occurs often. 'Master' would be appropriate to a male speaker!

II.i.201–4 The allocation of speeches is conjectural. Q assigns the whole passage to '*Lady*', but there are obvious signs of disturbance in the text, especially the reversal in Q of lines 203 and 204, which all editors interchange.

II.ii.179 *Now*: Q reads 'Not', which F retains, annotating the line as 'I wager a shoulder of mutton that it is not so'. The bet, however, seems to be on differing opinions as to the contents of the basket, either 'a quarter of lamb' or 'a shoulder of mutton', for 1 Promoter feels he has lost when the contents prove to be 'of more weight' than the lamb would be.

III.ii.25 *Spirit*: This edition. Q reads 'spirit'.

III.ii.92 *Sit you all, merry ladies*: No punctuation in Q. R would place the comma after 'merry'.

III.iii.69–70 Punctuation as Q. R places a semi-colon after 'in spite of censure', and would interpret 'in spite of your mutual recrimination'; but this gives a somewhat unusual meaning to 'censure'.

III.iii.135 *Ay, curse*: Q reads 'I curse', followed by NM.

III.iii.139 The dash appears in Q, and probably replaces an obscenity deleted by the Master of the Revels, the printer, or the author. A less likely possibility is that the actor was intended to *ad lib*.

IV.i.1–26 The Latin is printed as in Q, save that I have followed Dyce in emending '*disputus*' at lines 16 and 24 to *disputas*, the mistake being easy when reading secretary hand. Other corrections made by Dyce, followed by R, are probably unjustified: in line 13 they alter *rationalibus* to '*rationalis*', in line 14 *dicere* to '*dici*', and in lines 20 and 25 *sum* to '*sumus*'. Though such changes serve the cause of pure Latinity, Middleton's Latin may not have been so good, or he may have intended solecisms appropriate to the characters. Printers are likely to have taken more care over setting the Latin, and it is hard to imagine that they mis-read in these instances.

IV.i.66 *as*: Q prints 'Asse' to point the pun on ass/arse.

IV.i.122 *to a heart*: So Q. F would emend to the more common 'to a hair', arguing that this may have appeared in the copy in the form 'to a Heare', which a compositor could easily misread as 'to a Heart'.

IV.i.126–35 Again, the Latin is printed as in Q, on the grounds that its shortcomings are deliberately or accidentally authorial. Dyce and R read '*abundas*' in place of *abundis* in line 127, '*abundas*' for *abundat* in line 132, '*simul et arte*' for *simule arte* in line 134, whilst *parata* in line 135 (perhaps thought to be in agreement with *natura* in Q) is by Dyce emended to '*parato*' and by F and R to '*paratus*'. Q prints '*homauculus*' in line 133, which is probably merely a mis-printing of *homunculus*.

IV.i.183 THE SONG: This was probably inserted at a later date during a revival, when the actors no longer had a boy who could sing in Welsh. The first nine lines (and two additional lines) appear in Middleton's *More Dissemblers Besides Women*, which reads 'thought' in place of *taught* in line 191, as do R and some manuscripts of the song.

IV.i.202ff. This stanza is defective and clearly needs emendation if it is to be sung. F added a second *quickly* in line 204 (on the analogy of line 186). This edition supplies also a complete line – *We always are behind it* – after line 206 to make sense of the stanza, with the minimum disturbance of Q: this suggestion also has the 'advantage' of a typically Middletonian allusion to anal intercourse (cf. *A Mad World*, III.iii.65) which suits the general tone of innuendo.

IV.i.250 A second dash occurs here in Q, again probably the result of censorship by the Master of the Revels, the printer, or the author. It is just possible that it is an indication to an actor to whisper, and this is the best way for a modern actor to cover the lacuna.

IV.i.254 A third dash occurs in the text here. See previous note.

IV.i.291 *in Anno*: There is again a lacuna in Q at this point, but no dash is printed. Dyce's suggestion, followed by some editors, was that the actor was merely left free to concoct a plausible date. R suspects an obscenity, which is more likely. Perhaps the line once read 'in *Anno Domino*' (strictly '*Domini*' would be correct) and rhymed with 'fellow' in line 274 to form a further couplet: *Domino* would then be omitted because of the prohibition against the use of the names of God. 'Domino' may perhaps be cant for the female pudendum, but the domino was a type of loose cloak worn chiefly at masquerades.

IV.i.312 *coral*: Q prints 'Curral'. See note on *A Mad World*, III.ii.64.

IV.iii.53 The line is punctuated substantially as in Q. R would repunctuate: 'Are you content, sir? Till then she shall be watch'd!'

IV.iii.79 *Sir*: So Q. R believes the word has been picked up mistakenly from the previous line, and would emend to 'So'.

V.i.19 *left*: So Q. NM, R and others would emend to 'lost', and a confusion of the two words is likely. However, the text makes sense as it stands.

V.i.25 Q closes this line with a stop rather than a dash, and many editors think something may have dropped from the text. Dyce inserted 'mads thee' at the end of the line.

V.i.73 *he too*: So NM. Various attempts have been made to emend Q's 'ho to': Dyce read 'O too' and Bullen 'O, O', whilst F would emend to 'go to', glossing this as an exclamation of self-reproach. 'He too' seems the most plausible, referring back to God in the previous line ('the sight of Heaven').

V.iv.75–6 R plausibly transposes 'now' to the beginning of the next line.

V.iv.89 *say*: So Q. NM prefers to alter this to the more modern form, 'saw', and there was possibly a slip in the printing.

V.iv.105 *Flectere si nequeo superos Acheronta movebo*: Q's odd Latin, '*Flectere si neguro Superos Acheronta mourbo*' is unlikely to be deliberate, for it derives from two simple errors in reading secretary hand: *e* has been read as *r* (twice) and *q* as *g*.

V.iv.116 *falacis*: So Q. Dyce, followed by R, would emend to '*falleris*' = 'you lie'. F prefers a slighter alteration to '*falacia*' = a false argument, 'a fallacy'. Q, however, has a certain plausibility as it stands, and would presumably translate as a second person singular meaning 'you argue fallaciously'. In the generally obscene context of Tim's speeches, it is possible that his conclusion was accompanied by an obscene dismissive gesture, emphasising a pun: '*ergo, phalluses!*' Compare a similar pun in the Clown's speech in *Antony and Cleopatra*, V.ii.257: 'This is most falliable, the worm's an odd worm'.

V.iv.124 Q prints a dash, probably representing a suppressed obscenity, 'cunts', or an appropriate gesture. Or Yellowhammer may interrupt Tim.

Women Beware Women

DRAMATIS PERSONAE, 11, 15 BIANCA: 'BRANCHA' is the invariable spelling of O, here, in the text, and in s.d.s and s.h.s throughout. Dyce and all later editors save F have emended to 'Bianca', both because the historical character was Bianca Capello and because in more than twelve places the metre seems to demand a tri-syllabic form. I find this last argument compelling. The easy confusion between *e* and *r* in Middleton's secretary hand (see note to *A Chaste Maid*, V.iv.105) suggests that Middleton called his character 'Beancha Capella'. A hard *c* in Latin and Italian is indicated by 'ch' in Middleton's texts.

I.i.104 *perfit*: So O, whose spellings are generally more modern than pre-Commonwealth printings of Jacobean plays; presumably the unusual form was preserved because the meaning was different to 'perfect', the form adopted by most editors.

I.i.127 *send*: So O, followed by modern editors. However, this reads somewhat awkwardly as a petition to heaven to send a future peace in which Bianca may enjoy her love, or as a conditional clause: I would prefer to read a past tense, 'Heaven *sent* a quiet place with this man's love', which seems to fit better Bianca's prior and subsequent statements that she has all she could wish already.

I.ii.56 *Light her now, brother!*: So O. Various suggestions have been made for emendation: Bullen would read 'Like enow' (unnecessarily assigning 'Brother' to Livia) but has to posit an unlikely stage of oral transmission of the text. P. Simpson, *Modern Language Review*, xxxiii (1938), p. 45, suggests 'Plight her now' (again giving 'Brother' to Livia), but this contradicts Guardiano's preference for delaying the marriage, expressed earlier. A more plausible emendation would be 'Flight her now, brother!', since *SOD* records 'flight' as a transitive verb from 1571, meaning 'to put to flight; hence, to frighten'. Perhaps Fabritio is being urged to rout Livia in the 'flyting', the passage of wit.

I.ii.226 *Welcome it?*: O reads 'welcome it:'. R would emend to 'well fare it', i.e. send it on its way, presuming a compositor's faulty memorisation of wordplay on fare/welfare in line 226, and substitution of a play on welcome/come (line 221). The emendation is ingenious and plausible, but O makes sense as it stands, and the occurrence of 'Farewell' in line 228 would then be inelegant.

II.i.17 *sew'd up*: O reads 'sow'd up'; but Dyce's emendation 'summ'd up' is attractive in the context and presumes only that *m* was misread as *w*, or that *w* was accidently substituted in the printing.

II.i.49 *I'd*: O reads 'I'll'.

II.i.60 *Sir, your stars bless. – You simple, lead her in*: Substantially O, which prints only a semi-colon after 'bless'. There are various alternative suggestions. Dyce read 'Sir, your stars bless you. Simple, lead her in.' NM was uneasy at such an address to a servant and preferred to change a letter 'Sir, your stars bless you simply', as did Bullen.

II.ii.22 *strangely*: So editors, emending O's 'strangly', partly because of the number of words in the play from the root 'strange'. Guardiano must be intending the adverb in its weak sense of 'extremely' (so Livia at II.ii.183), for he finds the Duke's passion not 'strange' but perfectly explicable. At II.ii.183 O uses the modern spelling, so we should perhaps emend 'strangly' to 'strongly'.

II.ii.80 *world's end*: So O. NM suggests the emendation 'word's end'.

II.ii.155 *merrily*: So editors; O appears to have misread copy text's 'merilie' as 'merelie', and printed 'meerly' in accordance with its own spelling habits.

II.ii.160 *'Mongst knights' wives or widows*: O reads ' 'Mongst Knights, Wives, or Widows', which NM (after Dyce) interprets by punctuating: 'And 'tis a general observation/'Mongst knights: wives or widows, we account/Ourselves old . . . ' This is possible, but the observation appears to be one made by the women rather than the men; 'Lady Livia' is presumably herself a 'knight's widow'.

II.ii.202 *I'faith*: Uncorrected O groups this with the previous phrase, but corrected copies insert a question-mark after 'request'. Either may be right.

III.i.12 *grudging of a scolding*: So O; Dyce, Bullen and F would substitute 'or' for *of*, implying not that the daughter-in-law jibbed at a scolding but that she resented and scolded her mother-in-law. R unconvincingly glosses *grudging* as 'slight symptom'.

III.i.77 *pewterer*: So O. NM and R presume that dittography had occurred, and shorten to 'pewter', which may be right.

III.i.111 *this as*: O reads 'this? as', which R emends thus.

III.i.176 *thou please*: O reads 'thou pleas'd', but terminal 'd' was probably misread as 'e'. Dyce emended to 'thou'rt pleas'd'; perhaps the line should read 'Howev'r thou *pleas'st* now to look dull on me'.

III.ii.42, 46 *Rouans*: So O. This can hardly be a mis-print for 'Rouens', not least because Leantio is clearly not anticipating that his post will take him far from Florence. F suggests that O should be interpreted 'Rovans', this perhaps being the name given by Middleton's unknown source to the village of Rovezzano, just outside Florence to the east.

III.ii.146–59 O prints the Ward's speech beside Isabella's song, an indication that they take place simultaneously.

III.ii.182 *whos'*: So O. This is presumably a contracted form of 'who so', but it may be a mistake for 'who'.

III.ii.189 *Ay, all that, uncle, shall not fool me out*: So this edition. O prints 'I, all that Uncle, shall not fool me out', and there are a variety of interpretations. NM reads 'Ay, all that "uncle" shall not fool me out', but Gomme prefers 'I? All that uncle shall not fool me out', taking 'uncle' as a reference to Hippolito, so that the line would mean 'Hippolito shall not make a fool of me'. An additional note suggests that O's 'I, all that Uncle' could also mean 'Ay, I am all that, Uncle'.

III.ii.221 *You*[*r*] . . . *you*[*r*] : So editors. O prints 'You . . . you' in this line, and it is possible that the Ward has the traditional intuition of the Fool, and is intended to address 'You drunkards' to the men present, and 'you whore and bawd' to Isabella and Livia.

IV.i.201 *low*: So Dyce, followed by all editors. O prints 'love', which Gomme suggests could make sense: 'the love-private man' is the one who keeps his love to himself or within what is allowed him.

IV.ii.22 O mis-allocates this line to PAGE.

IV.ii.42 *pray'd*: O reads 'praid'. NM would emend this to 'paid', but the irony of O as it stands is probably preferable.

IV.ii.186 *this is*: O prints 'thus', reading 'Why thus tuneful now!' This makes some sense as an exclamation; but Gomme points out that O uses question-marks and exclamation-marks indiscriminately, so that O could be interpreted as a suspicious query at Isabella's change of tune.

IV.ii.216 *What, is't good? Troth*: Substantially as O, which reads 'What, is't good? troth, I have ev'n forgot it.' NM re-punctuates: 'What is't? good troth, I have ev'n forgot it!'; but O makes sense as Livia's query about the quality of her role in the masque.

V.ii.29 *soul*: So O; Bianca has perhaps adopted the princely plural. NM and others emend to 'souls'.

V.ii.64 *part*[*ing take*] : So NM, supplying a rhyme. O prints only 'let's part', which is perhaps right, if some lines immediately previous have dropped from the text.

V.ii.89 *one*: So F and R. O prints 'me', followed by NM; but this makes less good sense.

V.ii.114 *savour*: So most editors. O reads 'favor', which can only be right if 'this favor overcomes me' is assigned to Isabella; probably *f* was accidently substituted for long *s* by foul case.

V.ii.117 s.d. *flaming gold*: The stage direction derives in substance from a manuscript annotation by a seventeenth-century hand, extant in the Yale University copy of O.

V.ii.215 *no enemy . . . no enemy*: So this edition, following O's 'no enemy, no enemy'. Most editors regard this repetition as a ditto-graph.

The Changeling

The collaboration between the two authors of *The Changeling* is generally agreed to have been unusually close. Nevertheless, there is almost no dispute among scholars as to who wrote particular scenes: Rowley is credited with the first and last scenes together with the whole of the sub-plot, and Middleton is agreed to have been responsible for the remainder. There is a tendency to credit Middleton with the whole design, if only because certain relevant features are less well executed in Rowley's part.

I.i.97 *stall*: So Q. Some editors emend to 'stale' = make flat, deprive of zest, but this is unnecessary.

I.i.117 *sound*: So Q, retained by NM and R. NM explains that 'the possession of a slight imperfection is a criterion of normality'. Old editors and RR emend to 'found'. The confusion of long *s* and *f* by foul case is common, and both alternatives are equally plausible.

I.i.128 *What might be your desire, perhaps, a cherry*: So most editors. Q, followed by Gomme, reads 'And what might be your desire perhaps, a cherry'; but 'And' is usually regarded as an accidental repetition of the beginning of the previous line. Brooke keeps Q by printing a question-mark after 'desire', but the device of answering question by question seems somewhat forced.

I.i.145 *ingredience*: So this edition, on the analogy of *A Mad World*, II.v.53. Q reads 'Ingredian', from which a final *s* has perhaps been dropped. Most editors emend to 'ingredient'.

I.i.190 *his*: Conjectured by Dyce. The majority of editors follow Q in printing 'this', probably an anticipation from the next line.

I.i.232 *come, with a mischief! Now I know*: So most editors, Q reading 'Here's a favour come; with a mischief: Now/I know she had rather wear my pelt tan'd/'. RR interprets Q's suspect lineation to mean that 'now' should be taken with the first phrase.

I.ii.140 *arrant*: Q prints 'errant', probably pointing a pun on 'errant' = 'wandering, erring'.

II.i.46 *pluck'd*: So Gomme and R, following Q's 'pluck't'. Dilke, NM and RR emend to 'plucks'.

II.i.107–8 *too severe a censurer/Of love*: So Q. RR prints a semi-colon after 'censurer' and takes the whole of line 108 together.

II.i.108 *there's no bringing on you*: So Dilke, followed by most editors. R suggests that Q, which prints no punctuation after 'you', may be right in linking the phrase with the next line; the meaning would then be 'I cannot make you realise that . . . '

II.i.137 *in*[*s*] *his passions*: So this edition; Q reads 'in his passions'. Because the phrase is extra-metrical and hard to interpret, many editors prefer to omit altogether, though there is widespread unease at so doing, since the phrase survives on a page where seven minor mistakes have been carefully corrected in the printing. It has been suggested that 'in his passions' is a s.d. to the actor playing Tomazo, but Tomazo appears to be controlled and confident throughout this speech. Of those who keep Q, Black takes 'him' to refer to the lover and 'his' to the husband; Gomme comments that 'presumably the lover's passions inspire the woman to beget children (though by her husband)'.

The solution may lie in reading 'in' as a verb from which the third person singular ending has dropped. *OED* records 'in' from Old English as a verb meaning 'to take in', and cites Florio's *Montaigne II* (1632), iv, 201 for the sense 'to take in mentally': 'He hath assuredly understood and inned the very imagination and the true conceit of the author'. The phrase would then echo the sense of line 134, meaning 'she imagines she takes in the passions of her lover'.

II.ii.33 *you're*: So Dyce and RR, interpreting Q's 'your', which other editors emend to 'y'are'.

II.ii.80 *Faugh*: So Dyce and most editors. Q prints 'vaugh'.

II.ii.163 *Puh*: So Q. NM and R emend to the more characteristically Middletonian 'Push'.

III.iii.141 *he*: So most editors, following Dyce. Q and Gomme read 'she', which could refer to Venus; but it follows less well from the previous lines.

III.iv.18 *at a banquet; for the deed,/I feel*: So Dyce, followed by many editors. Q reads 'My thoughts are at a banquet for the deed,/I feel'. In general, Q's punctuation inspires little confidence, though it is here followed by Dilke, R and RR.

III.iv.70 [*slept at ease*]: Inserted first by Dilke to repair a lacuna in Q, this brilliant suggestion has been adopted by all editors except Gomme, who thinks Q intelligible as it stands.

III.iv.112 *want it* [*not*]: The second negative was supplied by Dilke and accepted by most editors.

IV.i.5 *who's*: So Dyce. Q reads 'both', which is probably an anticipation.

IV.i.97 *I'm glad to hear't; then*: So Schelling, NM and RR. Q punctuates 'I'm glad to hear't then, you dare . . . ', which is followed by some editors.

IV.ii.54 *chins and noses*: So Dyce, followed by most editors. Q prints 'sins and vices', which Gomme accepts as making good sense, even if less vivid than Dyce's emendation.

IV.ii.56 *'Twill*: So Dilke and all subsequent editors except Gomme, who follows Q's 'I will'.

IV.ii.112 [*made*]: Supplied by Dyce, but not regarded as a necessary emendation by all editors.

IV.iii.1 *waiting*: So Q, followed by R. Dilke suggested 'waning moon', but this is now rejected, on the grounds that a waning moon might be expected to herald a return to sanity. RR emends to 'waxing moon', arguing that the two minims which form *x* in one version of secretary hand have been mis-read as *it*.

If *m* was at some stage inverted to *w*, perhaps the copy text read 'Is this the maiting moon'; i.e. 'Is this the moon under which all creation seems to feel the urge to mate?'

IV.iii.45 *Why*: So Dilke and all subsequent editors. Q prints 'We'.

IV.iii.70 *fooling*: So Q and modern editors. Bullen suggested the emendation 'footing', which is attractive; but Lollio is probably alluding to Antonio and Franciscus.

IV.iii.106 *he*: Dilke and all editors. Q reads 'she'.

IV.iii.120 *straits*: So Dyce, followed by later editors. Q and Dilke read 'streets'.

IV.iii.162 *desire*: So Q. Dyce conjectured that this should read 'desert', and some editors have found the resultant polyptoton attractive.

IV.iii.179 *What do you read, sirrah?*: So Dilke and all editors. Q prints 'What? Do you read . . . ' but Lollio's answer seems to justify the re-pointing.

V.i.20 *harsh*: So Q. Bullen follows Dyce's conjecture 'rash', which is plausible but not strictly necessary.

V.i.25 *Phosphorus*: So Dilke, followed by all editors. Q prints 'Bosphorus'.

V.i.95 *Alas*: So Q and most editors. Black regards the second, extra-metrical 'Alas' as an accidental repetition and omits it. 'The fear keeps that out' might then be either a simple reply, or an aside.

V.iii.62 *innocence*: So Q and most editors. RR emends to 'innocent', arguing that *t* has been mis-read as *c*, a common error in interpreting secretary hand.

V.iii.193 *thence*: So Q and all editors, who justify the quarto reading on the ground that 'thence' relates to the dead bodies before Tomazo. Rowley may have written 'hence', and an initial stroke may have been read at some later stage as *t*.

ADDITIONAL NOTES

A Mad World, My Masters

I.i.104 *blood*: (also *Chaste Maid*, I.i.162, II.i.14; *Women Beware Women*, I.i.80, I.ii.185, III.ii.75; *Changeling*, II.ii.146, III.iv.107). According to traditional Greek physics, Universal Matter had imposed upon it various 'forms', Hot, Cold, Dry and Moist. These combined in pairs to form the four Elements, Earth, Water, Air and Fire, from which all existent matter was formed. In Chaos the Elements had been in a state of perpetual warfare, until brought into harmony by the Creator.

Renaissance medical theory closely followed the Greeks, and the Galenic system (developed from Hippocrates) was still the basis of medical education. Galen held that the four Elements had their counterpart in four 'fluent' or liquid parts of the body, the four Humours: Blood (hot and moist), Phlegm (cold and moist), Choler or Yellow Bile (hot and dry) and Melancholy or Black Bile (cold and dry). Perfect health in the world of man, as in the greater world, depended upon a balance, and diseases either moral, mental or physical could be caused by a temporary imbalance of humours. A remedy appropriate to the Humour, either a sudorific, a purgative, a diuretic or a blood-letting, was employed to purge any excess.

A more lasting predominance of one humour over the others conditioned a man's disposition, either sanguine, phlegmatic, choleric or melancholy: 'sanguine are merry, melancholy sad, phlegmatic dull, by reason of the abundance of those humours' (Burton, *Anatomy of Melancholy*, Part 1, Sec. 2, Mem. 5). Such predominance might also govern one's choice of career: doctors were held to have a predominance of Yellow Bile, and were by nature irascible.

Blood had particular symbolic importance for the dramatists, for according to Burton it is 'a hot, sweet, temperate, red humour . . . whose office is to nourish the whole body, to give it strength and colour, being dispersed by the veins through every part of it. And from it spirits are first begotten in the heart, which afterwards by the arteries are communicated to the other parts'. These *spirits* were three, natural, vital and animal. 'The natural are begotten in the liver, and thence dispersed through the veins, to perform those natural actions. The vital spirits are made in the heart of the natural, which by the arteries are transported to all the other parts; if the spirits cease, then life ceaseth . . . The animal spirits, formed of the vital, brought up to the brain, and diffused by the nerves to the subordinate members, give sense and motion to them all' (Part 1, Sec. 1, Mem. 2, Sub. 2).

Since the 'spirits' played a vital role in consciousness, life and generation of new life, the *blood* from which they were begotten became a symbol of life, vigour, passion and sexual desire, and a predominance of blood was held to condition passionate and lascivious behaviour. *Blood* also meant 'birth', 'lineage', and since Elements seek their natural level (Fire rising, Water falling from Air but bursting in springs above the Earth), it seems that blood was also thought to seek its own level: those with 'high blood' were suited to eminence, tended to high living, and aspired to it if displaced from their station.

A Chaste Maid in Cheapside

III.ii.98 *countess*: Probably the extravagance of the laying-in is a reference to the childbed of the Countess of Salisbury, reported by John Chamberlain on 4 February 1612/13: 'About this day sevennight the Countess of Salisbury was brought abed of a daughter, and lies in very richly, for the hangings of her chamber, being white satin, embroidered with gold (or silver) pearl, is valued at fourteen thousand pounds' (*Letters*, ed. N.E. McClure (1939), I, 415).

Women Beware Women

I.ii.87 s.d.; III.ii.115; III.iii.96 *cat and trap, trapstick*: J. Strutt, *Sports and Pastimes of the People of England* (1801) p. 86, calls Tip-Cat or Cat 'a rustic pastime': 'its denomination is derived from a piece of wood called a *cat*, with which it is played; the cat is about six inches in length, and an inch and a half or two inches in diameter, and diminished from the middle to both ends, in the shape of a double cone; by this curious contrivance the place of the trap and of the ball are at once supplied, for when the cat is laid upon the ground, the player with his cudgel [or cat-stick] strikes it smartly, it matters not at which end, and it will rise with a rotatory motion, high enough for him to beat it away as it falls, in the same manner as he would a ball.' The more complicated version was Trap or Trap-ball, in which a ball was placed on one end of a wooden pivot (the trap); the other end was struck with the trapstick, causing the ball to fly into the air. It then had to be driven away with the stick.

I.ii.223–5 *Methought . . . hearing*: New Mermaid understands the passage somewhat differently: 'Isabella seems to be saying that trouble is more readily apprehended intuitively ("we understand") than intellectually (by "hearing") and that, having grasped her uncle's meaning from his stammered phrases, she will not wait for a further explanation but will anticipate ("prevent") bad news; in thus meeting it ("welcome it") she will stop him from speaking further.' I prefer to take O's colon after 'welcome it' as indicating an exclamatory question, and interpret 'prevent' in the more modern sense already widespread in the seventeenth century. The 'Than' of line 225 should perhaps be taken as the modern 'then', giving the sense 'we are over-quick to grasp the import of bad news'; but O makes sense as it stands.

I.iii.51–2; II.ii.294; II.ii.418; III.ii.75–6; III.ii.185–7; III.ii.325–6; IV.i.94–8

Predeterminism and subconscious knowledge in 'Women Beware Women'

Beyond the degree of social and economic determinism suggested by the action of the play is a deeper determinism conveyed through persistent dramatic irony. Characters seem to have a subconscious knowledge of the pattern of events, past, present and future, yet they are unable to raise this knowledge to a level at which they might benefit from it. Before the seduction of Bianca, the Mother whose office is to guard the girl comments on the role of the *rook*, otherwise the 'duke', in a chess game which has already become disturbingly proleptic: '*when you spoke there came a paltry rook/Full in my way, and chokes up all my game*' (II.ii.294). When Bianca has fallen, the Mother observes of the rook/duke whose moves have ironically paralleled those of the stage action: '*H'as done me all the mischief in this game*' (II.ii.418). Yet in the next scene she has no conscious apprehension that anything has taken place. Similarly, the Ward appears to have subconscious knowledge of his actual situation when he expects Isabella '*to send me a gilded bull from her own trencher, a ram, a goat, or somewhat to be nibbling*' (III.ii.75–6): these animals are not only emblematic of lechery, but they are all horned – and the Ward is cuckolded even before he is married. His 'knowledge' seems to condition his unwillingness to dance with Isabella and his insistence that her uncle lead off with the Ward's betrothed: '*Look, there's her uncle, a fine-timber'd reveller;/Perhaps he knows the manner of her dancing too;/I'll have him do't before me*' (III.ii.185–7; also 215–16). Leantio has perhaps an intimation of the two 'riders', himself and the Duke, which his wife will bear, an intimation which occasions the irony at I.iii.51–2: '*I have such luck to flesh: I never bought a horse but he bore double.*' Leantio, deserted by Bianca, gives vent to sentiments which ironically anticipate his own elimination as a block to Bianca's 'redeeming' marriage with the Duke: '*Methinks by right I should not now be living,/And then 'twere all well*' (III.ii.325–6). Yet more disturbing is the language of Leantio's reproach to Bianca in the confrontation scene: '*as much madness/To set light before thee, as to lead blind folks/To see the monuments which they may smell as soon/As they behold – Marry, oft-times their heads,/For want of light, may feel the hardness of 'em*' (IV.i.94–8). Bianca was seduced by being led 'blind' to see the 'monument' – she felt his 'hardness', and smelt the 'infectious mists and mildews hang at's eyes'. But Leantio does not know consciously the circumstances of Bianca's seduction, so it seems that some supra-rational recollection of them is here influencing the terms of his denunciation. The total effect of these ironies is to extend the metaphor of the chess game to the whole action, where characters play according to a predetermined pattern and may on occasions have an intimation of their role in it, without being able to influence the progress of the game.

II.ii.422–5 *Now bless me from a blasting . . . doomsday dwells upon him*: Bianca blesses herself as if she had seen a sexually aroused devil: *blasting* was used of a sudden infection attributed to the breath of a malignant power. *Infectious mists and mildews* at the Duke's eyes are probably symptoms of venereal disease, for Bianca expect to catch leprosy/syphilis from him. She associates the Duke with Satan, who in Dante's *Inferno* 'wept/From his six eyes, and down his triple chin/Runnels of tears and bloody slaver dripped' (Canto XXXIV, 51–4, trans. D.L. Sayers). *The weather of a doomsday* is those inflictions of plague, earthquake and tempest which the Book of Revelation sees as preceding Judgement Day, when Satan and his victims will be put down.

V.ii.117 s.d. *flaming gold*: V.ii.118 *burning treasure*: The stage direction derives substantially from a seventeenth-century annotation in the

Yale university copy of the first edition. The appearance of Juno in this masque probably resembled that of Juno in Jonson's *Hymenaei*, lines 212–26: her throne was 'supported by two beautiful peacocks', and 'above her the *region of fire*, with a continual motion, was seen to whirl circularly, and Jupiter standing in the top (figuring the *heaven*) brandishing his thunder'. Probably the 'flaming gold' came from the 'region of fire', and this would fit the reference to Jove's 'burning treasure', and to the Danae-like 'lapful' that Isabella gets (line 122).

The Changeling

DRAMATIS PERSONAE, 9, and Title: *The Changeling*: Though the Dramatis Personae relates this title only to the supposed idiot Antonio, the speeches at V.iii.196–219 clearly indicate that the dramatists intended it to have a wider application. A 'changeling' was an ugly or mentally deficient child substituted by the fairies for a normal child which they had stolen, and the term was also applied to the stolen child. By extension the word comes to mean 'half-wit' or 'idiot', and is thus used of Antonio. But 'changeling' had further meanings: a woman who was inconstant in her affections, an untrustworthy or wavering person, an inferior substitute, someone who has undergone transformations. One or other of these meanings is appropriate to most of the characters in the play.

Beatrice-Joanna is the most obvious 'changeling': her affection, as De Flores reminds her, '*'Twas chang'd from thy first love, and that's a kind/Of whoredom in thy heart*' (III.iv.143–4), and later her love will be transferred from Alsemero to De Flores, a change indicative of her moral decline and of the alteration in her spiritual and social standing (III.iv.133–40). Moreover, her amorality though she is a daughter of the upright Vermandero makes her a spiritual 'changeling', a cuckoo in the nest.

Beatrice's change conditions other changes: the unfortunate Piracquo is 'chang'd' from life to death (III.iv.144); Diaphanta must change from virtue to whoredom and become a 'changeling', an inferior substitute in Alsemero's bed, and then suffer the same change as Piracquo; Alsemero unwittingly '*chang'd embraces with wantonness*' (V.iii.200–1). At the close, the revenger Tomazo is changed '*from an ignorant wrath/To knowing friendship*' (V.iii.203–4). The lovers of the sub-plot are made idiots, 'changelings', by love's madness, but the husband Alibius will '*change now/Into a better husband*' (V.iii.213–14). Finally, the whole cast, 'circumscribed' by Hell, are descendants of the original changelings, Adam and Eve, who lost their 'first condition' and were turned out of Paradise.

I.i.7–9, I.i.226; III.iv.138–9, III.iv.146, III.iv.166, III.iv.169; IV.i.1; V.iii.53, V.iii.66, V.iii.114–17, V.iii.146

'The Changeling' and the myth of the fall of man

The ostensibly naturalistic plot of the play is by persistent allusion related to the Biblical story of the Fall of man in Genesis 3. Alsemero interprets his encounters with Beatrice-Joanna in the temple as indicating that he will by marriage re-establish a pre-lapsarian state: *that methinks, admits comparison/With man's first condition, the place blest,/ And is his right home back, if he achieve it* (I.i.7–9). But Beatrice is another Eve, *that broken rib of mankind* (V.iii.146, alluding to Genesis 2.21–3, Eve's creation from Adam's rib), and she is haunted by a 'fallen' gentleman, De Flores, whose lust and physical repulsiveness (II.i.58, 82–5 *et passim*) associate him with the Devil in stage moralities. De Flores is persistently linked with the Satanic Snake, being called *serpent* (I.i.226, V.iii.66) and *viper* (III.iv.166), and, more explicitly, *lust's devil* (V.iii.53). He swears by the pleasures of Hell, linked with those of sexuality – *by all the sweets that ever darkness tasted* (III.iv. 146) – and he interprets Beatrice's complicity in his murder of Piracquo as a second Fall, initiating another Expulsion from Eden: *You lost your first condition, and I challenge you,/As peace and innocency has turn'd you out* (III.iv.138–9). Beatrice herself accepts her sexual corruption as eternal damnation: *This fellow has undone me endlessly* (IV.i.1). Submission takes her out of moral conflict to the 'peace' of permanent commitment to one side: *Thy peace is wrought for ever in this yielding* the Devil-figure assures her (III.iv.169). Finally, Alsemero invites De Flores to prepare to re-enact his seduction of Beatrice for the amusement of the devils in Hell, who relish the torments of the damned: *rehearse again/Your scene of lust, that you may be perfect/When you shall come to act it to the black audience/Where howls and gnashings shall be music to you* (V.iii.114–17), alluding to the 'weeping and gnashing of teeth' of those cast into 'outer darkness' and 'the furnace of fire', Matthew 8.12, 13.42, 50, 22.13, 24.51, 25.30).

II.ii.9–11; III.iii.171, III.iv.165–6; V.iii.12–13, V.iii.154–7, V.iii.162–4

Calvinist predestination in 'The Changeling'

According to Calvin's teaching the Fall of Adam and Eve not only predestined all their descendents to depravity but was itself predestined. Beatrice/Eve has some understanding of the inevitability of her fate – *Was my creation in the womb so curs'd/It must engender with a viper first?* (III.iv.165–6) – and she finally acknowledges De Flores as her destiny: *Beneath the stars, upon yon meteor/Ever hung my fate, 'mongst things corruptible;/I ne'er could pluck it from him; my loathing/Was prophet to the rest, but ne'er believ'd* (V.iii.154–7). Similarly, Alsemero/Adam, already uneasy in the first scene, turns in Act V to explicit questions about predestination: *Did my fate wait for this unhappy stroke/At my first sight of woman?* (V.iii.12–13).

In the days of her naivety, Beatrice is made to express the position of the execrated Arminians on the question of divine Grace: *Requests that holy prayers ascend heaven for,/And brings 'em down to furnish our defects/Come not more sweet to our necessities* (II.ii.9–11). In effect, Beatrice is shown as regarding prayer as 'turning on the tap' of God's grace, which will then repair the *defects* of human nature: she is in complete opposition to the Calvinist view that no human action can initiate the gift of Grace, which is bestowed by God on his elect, irrespective of human merit, merit which is anyway an illusion, since mankind does not merely have 'defects' but is totally depraved.

Beatrice learns in the course of the play to accept the Calvinist position as an accurate analysis of the human situation; and in this she is representative of the other characters. The Gnostic strain of Calvinism is apparent in the symbolism of the game of barley-brake, played by the fools and madmen of the sub-plot (III.iii.171) and made an image of sexual congress by De Flores at the close; the initial couple draw all the other couples into the central circle, until all are enclosed by 'Hell': *I coupled with your mate/At barley-brake; now we are left in Hell* (V.iii.162–3). Vermandero grimly assents to the Calvinist doctrine of hereditary damnation, transmitted by copulation: *We are all there, it circumscribes here* (V.iii.164).

II.i.103–4 *The day will steal upon thee suddenly . . . I will be sure to keep the night*: An abstruse but disturbing use of Biblical allusion. Vermandero's injunction to 'prepare' associates the marriage with Judgement Day itself: 'For ye yourselves know perfectly, that the day of the Lord shall come, even as a thief in the night . . . But ye, brethren, are not in darkness, that that day should come on you, as it were a thief' (1 Thessalonians 5.2–4 in the Geneva version). Revelation 3.3 takes up the theme: 'If therefore thou wilt not watch, I will come on thee as a thief, and thou shalt not know what hour I will come upon thee'; and in the context of Beatrice-Joanna's intention to 'keep the night', Revelation 16.15 is grimly appropriate: 'Behold, I come as a thief. Blessed is he that watcheth and keepeth his garments, lest he walk naked, and men see his filthiness'.

III.iv.14 *And if that eye be dark'ned that offends me*: A savagely ironic echo of Scripture. Beatrice-Joanna, contemplating murder, recalls Zechariah prophesying against the worthless shepherd of Israel – 'his right eye shall be utterly darkened' (11.17) – and the Psalmist cursing the ungodly: 'Let their eyes be darkened, that they see not . . . Let them be blotted out of the book of life' (Ps. 69.23–8). There is further recall of Matthew 18.9: 'And if thine eye offend thee, pluck it out and cast it from thee' (King James). The nexus of allusions is completed by one more appropriate to Beatrice's own darkened eye: 'But if thine eye be evil, thy whole body shall be full of darkness. If therefore the light that is in thee be darkness, how great is that darkness? (Matthew 6.23).

V.i.25, 59 *The day-star, by this hand! See Phosphorus plain yonder*: The importance of this stage appearance will be clearer when it is realised that Phosphorus is in Latin *Lucifer*, the morning star, identified in Isaiah 14. 12–15 with Satan: 'How art thou fallen from heaven, O day star, son of the morning! . . . And thou saidst in thine heart, I will ascend into heaven, I will exalt my throne above the stars of God . . . I will be like the Most High. Yet thou shalt be brought down to hell, to the uttermost parts of the pit'. Under this star the Devil-figure De Flores conceives his plan for murder amidst a last-act conflagration; but when the shadow of Alonzo's ghost (line 58) interposes between the Vice character and the Satanic *light* under which he acts, De Flores endures a temporary 'mist of conscience'. Probably pyrotechnics were used to represent the star emblematically in the Jacobean theatre, and modern productions should attempt something similar.

Play not written for scrutiny

loose ends - even in Shakespe

Cut off finger → De Flo. + Beat.

only separation bond

a bloody end.

Contiguity - causal relation

Smoke index of fire.

Dumb show Act IV.

Interpret. Icon
Symbol
Index

Camp America
Dept R667
37 Queens Gate
London SW7

Angus Macdonald
837 9560.

'Anti-Petrarchism'

Realization of Sonnet hyperbole.

Cruelty of Beatrice.

unworthiness of De Flo.

Madness of franciscus

juxtaposed with theories of court carnality.

c.f. "12th Night"